WRITING & GRAMMAR

WORKTEXT

Fourth Edition

8

bju press®
Greenville, South Carolina

PLEASE NOTE: At BJU Press we take seriously our responsibility to provide educational materials that are appropriate for students. In doing so, however, we may at times use texts that do not fall within a biblical worldview. Usage of such texts does not constitute an endorsement of their content or theological positions. Such inclusions serve to develop student discernment and comply with accepted academic standards.

Writing and Grammar 8, Student Worktext
Fourth Edition

Coordinating Writer
Joaquim C. Remelgado, MA

Writers
Bethany Harris, MA, MEd
Wendy Huffman, MEd
Lois Oldenburg, MS

Biblical Worldview
Renton Rathbun, PhD
Bryan Smith, PhD

Academic Integrity
Jeff Heath, EdD

Academic Oversight
Rebecca del Toro, MEd
Rachel Santopietro, MEd

Project Editors
Natalie Bonczek
Miguel del Toro, MA

Project Coordinator
Laura Yankelitis

Book and Cover Designer
Drew Fields

Cover Illustrator
Tim Banks

Page Layout
Carrie Walker

Permissions
Ruth Bartholomew
Carrie Hanna

Illustrators
Tim Banks
Serena Malyon
Daniel Limon (Beehive Illustration)
Lynda Slattery

Photo credits appear on pages 541–543.

Acknowledgments appear on pages 544–45.

The text for this book is set in Adobe Minion Pro, Adobe Myriad Pro, Arial MT, Avenir Next by Monotype Typography, Coniferous by OH no Type Co., Duality by Typodermic, Gin by Fort Foundry, Henderson Slab by Sudtipos, Nelson by Laura Worthington Type, Palatino, Times, Times New RomanPS, and Trailmade by Adam Ladd.

ISBN 978-1-62856-908-7

15 14 13 12 11 10 9 8 7 6

CONTENTS

CHAPTERS

TOOLS IN YOUR HANDS

EQUIPPED TO IMITATE THE CREATOR

WHAT'S IN YOUR TOOLBOX?

Verbs, nouns, semicolons, phrases—these grammar terms are probably familiar to you by now. Most students begin learning these concepts in elementary school. Seeing that you are being taught these concepts again this year may naturally lead you to ask, "Why do I keep learning this? When am I going to use this in 'real life?'"

Perhaps you have already asked these questions and been told by your parents or teacher that learning grammar and writing is important for getting a good job and being successful in life. While this answer is true, grammar and writing are important for even more significant reasons.

When God created the world, He used language to speak the world into existence (Genesis 1). When God created humans, He made them like Himself—in His image. Being created in God's image means that we have the privilege and responsibility to imitate our Creator by using language to communicate. Because your communication is part of being an image-bearer, the words you choose to use and the way you choose to use them have a tremendous impact on the lives of others.

Using language is meant to be an image-bearing activity. It was designed to help you fulfill the two greatest commandments in Scripture: to love God and to love others. This textbook's goal is to teach you how to use language to express Christlikeness in your speech and writing.

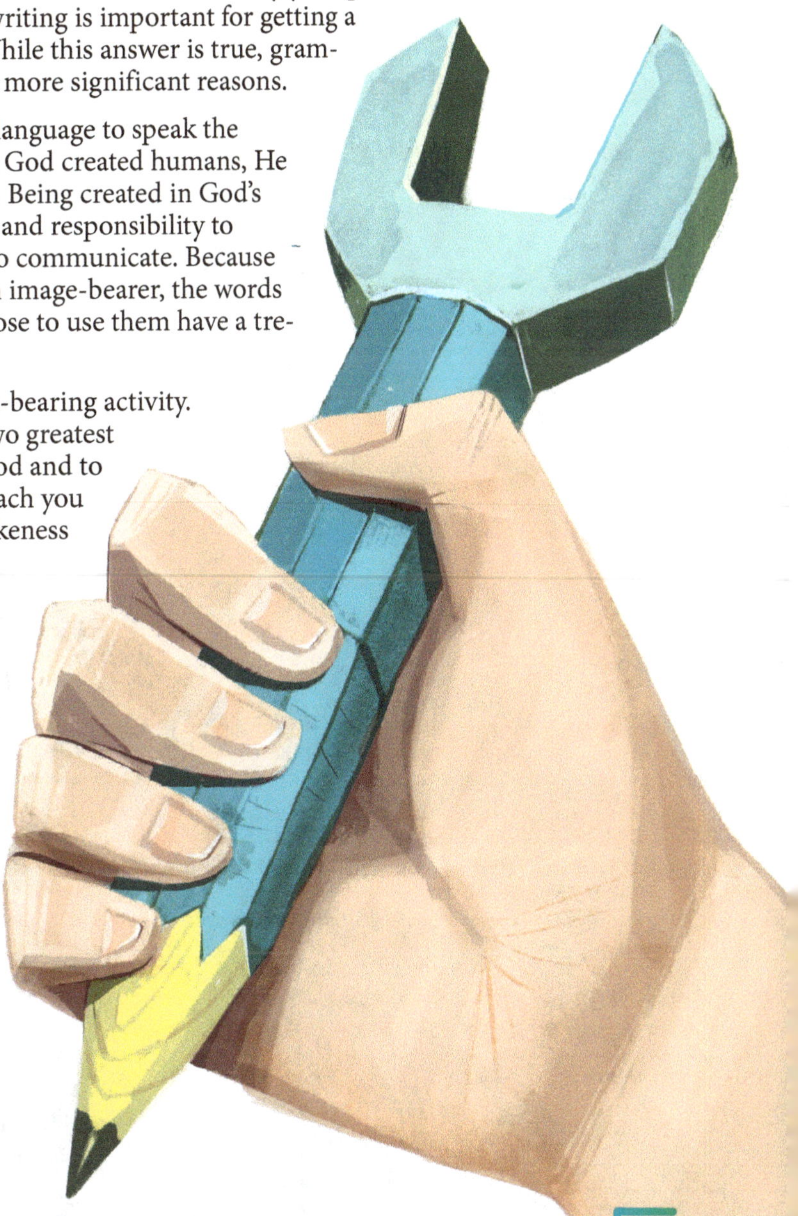

Throughout this year, you will learn about grammar, but you will also learn through the Grammar Toolboxes how to use grammar to improve your writing. Additionally, the Writing Toolboxes and the writing chapters will give you opportunities to practice different types of writing. This practice will help prepare you for your final multigenre project. Most importantly, this process will show how you can use your writing to communicate truth, show love to others, and glorify God.

CHAPTER 1 COMPOSING TEXTS

WHY SHOULD I WRITE?

Take a moment to think about the things you enjoy. Do you enjoy art? Sports? Music? The activities and interests you love are important because they are a way for you to express who you are as an individual.

A popular topic today, self-expression *refers to communicating your thoughts, feelings, ideas, and values. People express themselves in all sorts of ways—through fashion, possessions, music, activities, and even vocational choices. Writing is just one form of self-expression. However, is self-expression good for Christians? Is God pleased when a person focuses on making choices that express his unique personality?*

Self-Expression vs. Christ-Expression

It may surprise you to know that God created humans to express themselves. God was the first one to express Himself when He created the universe (Psalm 19:1–6). He then continued to express Himself through His Son, His Word, and the Holy Spirit's working in our hearts. Since we are made in God's image, we echo this desire to communicate our thoughts and feelings. Because God values everyone He creates (Psalm 139:13–16), each one of us has something valuable to express.

While self-expression is natural to everybody, our fallen world likes to define this term as doing whatever you want, even if it is sinful. Self-expression is often used to promote a self-centered lifestyle. The Bible therefore teaches believers to go beyond self-expression and focus on **Christ-expression:** expressing who they are in Christ. The more believers grow in their relationship with God, the more they will naturally use their talents to express Christ-like thoughts that glorify God and show care for others. Although each Christian is a unique person who will express things differently, the central theme of a Christian's ideas should ultimately focus on the glory of God and on His two greatest commandments: loving God and loving others.

You may think writing is necessary only for practical reasons: writing a report, crafting emails, or delivering a presentation. While it is true that writing is a practical life skill, you may not realize that, for believers, writing is also an opportunity to express true identity in Christ. A Christian can use writing to communicate unique ideas and God's truth to others; and, if it is done well, his writing could change lives and even influence an entire culture. Most importantly, that believer will be expressing ideas that bring glory to God.

Important Worldview Ideas

The writing opportunities and instruction you receive will help you explore what it means to express yourself in a Christlike way through writing. As you work through the assignments, you will visit and revisit the following four themes: empathy, logic, virtue, and discernment.

Exploring these themes will help you formulate and apply a biblical understanding of effective Christ-expression. Take the opportunities for Christ-expression in this book as a challenge and a gift. Use them to refine your ability to communicate with others and shine the light of Christ into a dark world.

EMPATHY

Empathy refers to the ability to put oneself in someone else's shoes and to connect with how another person thinks and feels.

LOGIC

Logic is the ability to reason, to connect various ideas and facts, and to draw rational conclusions from them.

VIRTUE

Virtue refers to something or someone who is morally excellent in quality.

DISCERNMENT

Biblical discernment is the ability to evaluate a thing, idea, or course of action based on the standard of God's Word (Psalm 119:9–12).

Reflection Questions:

- What do you think might be some forms of Christ-expression that the Bible directly requires of all believers?
- How might the four biblical worldview themes relate to these kinds of Christ-expression?

The Craft of Writing

Have you ever felt a sense of dread when your teacher announced a writing assignment? Have you ever worked for hours on a paper only to have it returned with LOTS of corrections and a mediocre grade (or worse)? Have you ever gotten upset during the writing process?

Much of this book will focus on teaching you the specifics of how to write well from a technical standpoint. Foundational to the craft of writing are six traits that are present in any written work. Think of these as big categories that various writing tasks and skills may be filed under. As you learn new skills, you will discover which of the six traits they enhance. Excellence in each trait better achieves a writer's purpose.

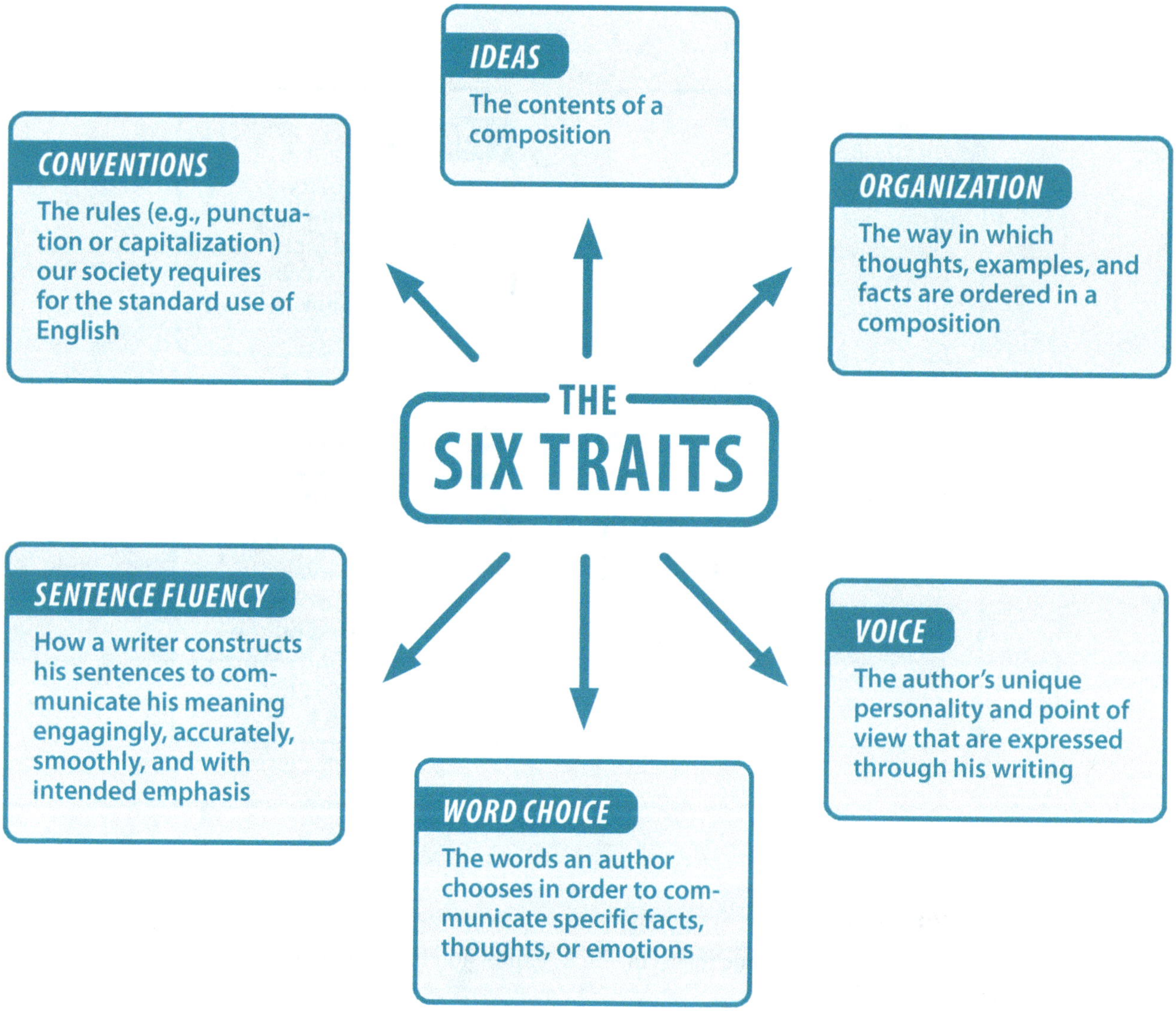

Reflection Question:

- Describe how at least one of the four worldview themes applies to each of the six writing traits.

Practice the Skill

Read the following scenarios and decide which trait each scenario relates to. Some may have more than one answer.

1. Rosie chose to write about her favorite topic, horses and their habitat.

   ____

2. Brian found three spelling errors when he read my paper.

   ____

3. I really want to meet that writer; she sounds like she loves her topic!

   ____

4. Matt must present any IT changes to each department in his company. He usually begins his presentations by giving background information so that no one gets lost during his explanations.

   ____

   ____

5. Nick tells me that my writing confuses him as much as my talking. I rarely finish a full thought before my brain is moving on to another!

   ____

6. The doctor used so many terms I did not know! How am I supposed to know what *pathogenesis* means?

   ____

Building a Paper

When someone wants to build a house, he does not start by digging a foundation or putting up walls. He must first carefully plan his project by creating detailed blueprints. He then executes his plan by following the guidelines in the blueprint.

Similarly, writing a paper involves specific steps. Each of your major writing assignments will follow the five steps of the writing process. When following these steps, remember two principles. First, good writing never "just happens." It is difficult to produce a quality composition without completing the entire writing process. Second, the writing process is often repetitive. You may revisit at least one of the stages more than once in an assignment. Reconsidering and reshaping what you have already planned or written is a natural and necessary part of the process.

Creating a Blueprint

Without a doubt, the planning stage is key to the success of a project. To return to our house-building example, you cannot build a durable house without first creating a well-designed blueprint. By getting only one element wrong, you can sabotage the whole structure's stability. The same is true of your compositions. Good planning cannot be neglected.

Determining Your Purpose

As a writer you must determine your **purpose** or reason for writing. Some common writing purposes include describing, informing, persuading, or entertaining. These purposes often require very different content and methods to make the composition most effective. For instance, when writing a science report on volcanoes (an informational purpose), do not become sidetracked with a suspenseful tale of how you nearly fell into the caldera of Mauna Loa. Knowing your purpose is very important to the success of your composition.

Considering Your Audience

It is also crucial to consider your **audience**, the person or group to whom you are writing. This is an opportunity for you to practice Christ-expression by showing empathy. First, study basic characteristics of your audience that might change how you address them. For example, what stage of life are they in? What are they most concerned about (their jobs, children, friends, possessions)? Do they share similar hobbies? Do they largely share a common worldview? Once you have studied general traits such as these, put yourself in their shoes by asking the following questions:

- What relationship do I have to my audience?
- What information does my audience already know about my topic?
- Is my audience hostile, friendly, or indifferent to my perspective?
- What aspect of my topic is likely to interest them?

Answering these questions can help determine how to approach all six of the writing traits in a composition. For example, writing to your principal or parent would require a more respectful tone and formal word choice than a text to your best friend; addressing an audience of experts on your topic means you should not have to define basic terms; and speaking to a hostile audience might demand that you start by discussing beliefs you share in order to disarm them. As you can see, using empathy to consider the audience will help you craft a caring and effective message.

Choosing a Topic

Choose a topic that you enjoy. If you like your topic, you will be excited to write about it, and you will keep your reader interested in what you have to say. Try the following methods to find a good topic.

Making a List

Make a list of people, places, and events from your experiences. To help remember your past, examine photograph albums, scrapbooks, and diaries. To help examine your present, make a map of your house, school, or neighborhood. Think about your daily routines. Observe the people around you. Your list will be full of possible topic ideas.

Asking Questions

Use the journalist's questions to help you identify details about something that interests you. Ask yourself *who*? *what*? *where*? *when*? *why*? and *how*? The answers to these questions may lead to more questions. Eventually you will have several ideas to explore. Look at this example:

Brainstorming

Brainstorming is a technique you can use on your own or with a group. Start by writing down one topic. Then list everything about the topic that you can remember. When you have finished, you will have many topic possibilities, both general and specific. Below are some of the results of a brainstorming session about a family vacation in England.

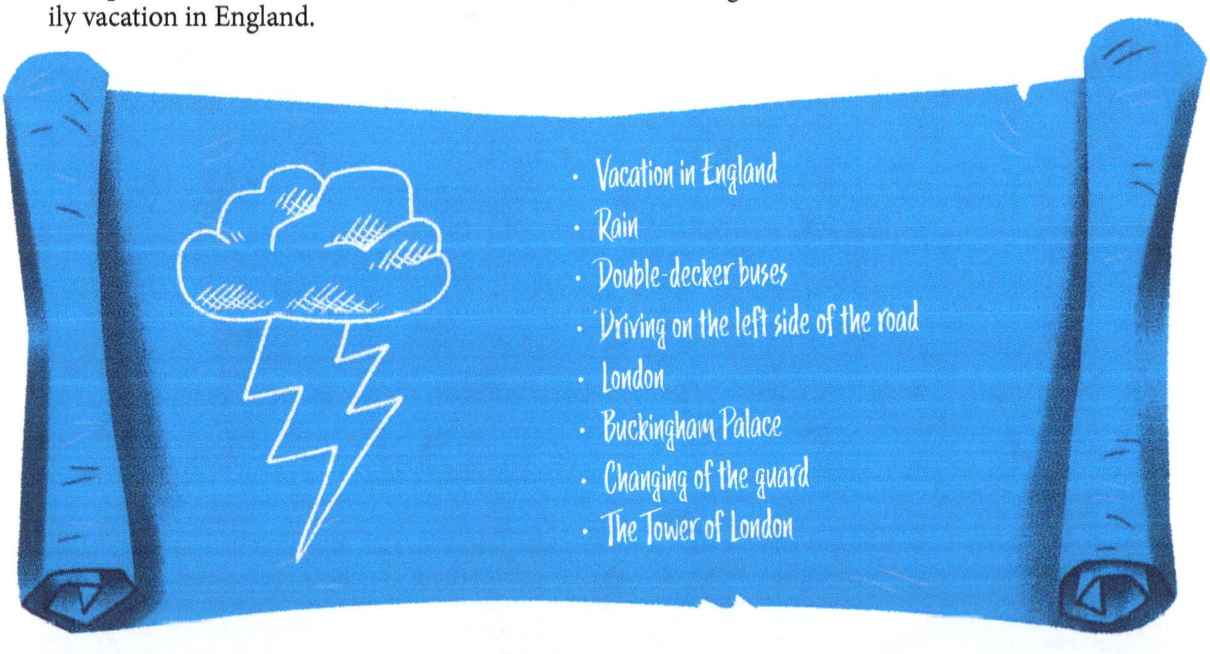

Clustering

Clustering is similar to brainstorming but goes one step further. Instead of brainstorming a simple list, clustering yields an information map that shows relationships between ideas. Clustering will help you generate topic ideas and suggest ways of organizing your information. Write down a general topic and circle it. Then write down any related ideas and circle them. Next, draw lines connecting ideas to one another and to the main topic. Look at this example of a cluster diagram:

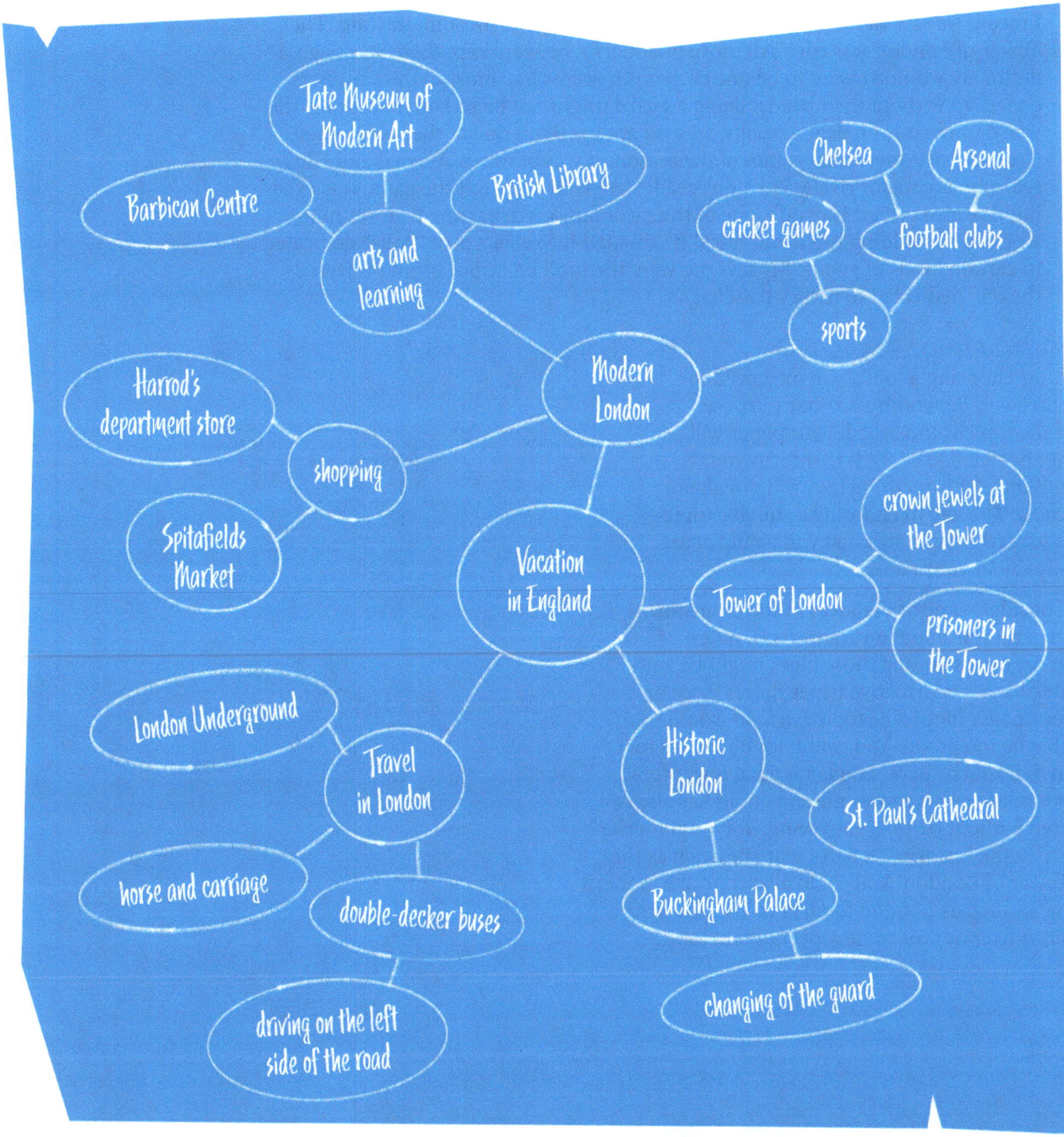

Freewriting

Freewriting can help spark creativity. Choose a general topic. Then set a time limit (five minutes, for example) and determine to write about that topic for the entire time without stopping. Do not stop to change a word or to correct punctuation. When the time is up, read what you have just written and look for ideas to explore further. Freewriting about a vacation in England, for example, might look something like this.

> I guess I'll write about our trip to England last spring. But what about England? I mean, we saw so much stuff. London was probably the most interesting. The Tower of London was cool. All those prisoners who were kept there years ago. I definitely wouldn't want to be one of them! It seems like most of the prisoners ended up without their heads. Being a guard might not be so bad. Except for the weird uniforms, I mean. Actually, we also got to attend one of the last football ("soccer," to Americans) games of the season. It was between Arsenal and Chelsea, who are major rivals. We didn't really care who won, but the game was exciting! We also visited Harrod's, one of the most famous department stores in the world. The building is old and huge! It's divided into all sorts of "halls" dedicated to certain kinds of goods. My favorite were the food halls, but Mom preferred the one dedicated to luxury handbags.

Narrowing a Topic

After choosing a topic, you may need to narrow it, depending on your purpose. If the topic is too broad, your paper will not be detailed enough to inform your audience of something they did not already know. The key to choosing a suitable topic is to start imagining what you would actually say in your paper.

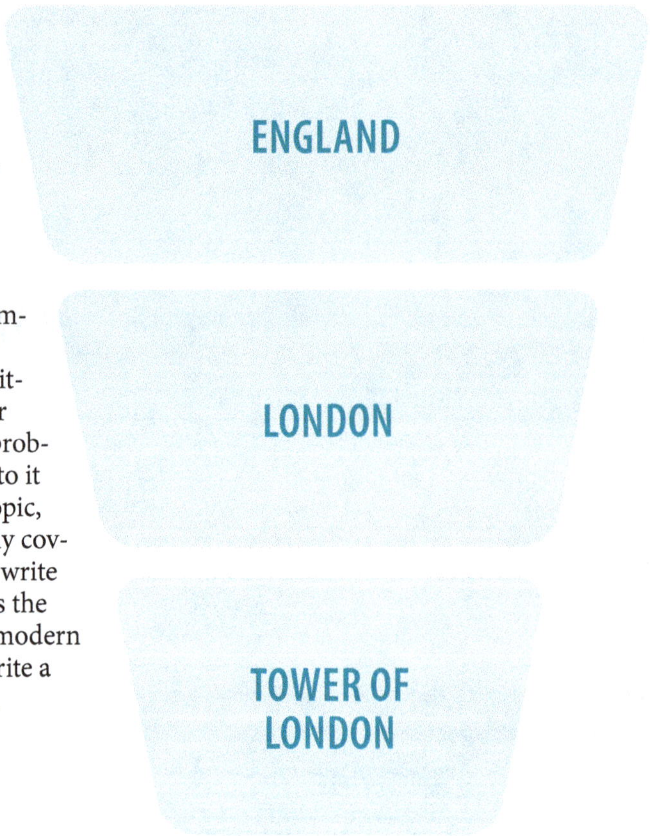

Consider some of the ideas in the brainstorming example about a vacation to London. What topics among those ideas might be suitable for an informative paper that is three or four pages long? The topic *England* would probably be too broad. You could not do justice to it in that much space. *London* is a narrower topic, but neither its past nor present could be fully covered without further narrowing. You might write about the history of a particular site, such as the Tower of London. You could also choose a modern topic, such as London football clubs, and write a short overview of some aspect of that topic.

Gathering Information

Now that you have determined your purpose, identified your audience, and decided on a topic, you need to gather information about your topic. First, list everything you already know about your topic. You can use the same methods for gathering information that you used to choose a topic: listing, asking questions, brainstorming, clustering, or freewriting. When you have finished, look at the information you have gathered. Do you have enough information to interest your audience and achieve your purpose?

If more information is needed, you may want to research your topic. Look for facts in books and periodicals from the library or from credible online sources. You could also interview someone you know who is an expert on your topic. In Chapter 6, you will learn where to find sources, how to evaluate those sources, and how to properly incorporate good research into your paper.

Practice the Skill

Read the following paragraph and answer the questions.

If our castle were attacked, we would easily be conquered. We need to build towers on the walls and dig a moat around the castle. Towers that jut out from the walls would help defending archers who shoot along the walls to push attackers back. A moat would prevent enemies from digging under the walls and coming up inside the castle. Please consider building these additions for the defense of our castle and the safety of our people before the enemy attacks and it is too late.

1. Who might the writer of this paragraph be?

   ____

2. Who is the intended audience for this paragraph?

   ____

3. What is the purpose of this paragraph?

   ____

Review the Skill

Read the following paragraph and answer the questions.

The new drawbridge works very well. It not only looks nice but also keeps away all invaders. Your men had the job completed in less than two weeks. They were responsible and undemanding. They agreed to do the job in exchange for food and lodging. Since my castle is well equipped, I was able to keep the men with no problems. I also wanted to send you a little gift of appreciation for all your organization and hard work.

1. Who might the writer of this paragraph be?

____

2. Who is the intended audience for this paragraph?

____

____

3. What is the purpose of this paragraph?

____

____

Use the Skill

Working with a partner, choose a broad topic to write about. Identify your purpose and audience, brainstorm the topic, and create an organized list or a cluster diagram of the topics you brainstorm. Narrow your topic together, aiming for one that you could write a four-page informative paper on.

Setting a Cornerstone: The Thesis Statement

The cornerstone of a building is the first stone that is set for the foundation. This one stone determines how every other stone is set. The cornerstone of your paper will be your **thesis statement**. The thesis statement states the main idea of your paper in one sentence. The purpose of the rest of your paper is to prove or explain your thesis statement. A good thesis statement tells the audience your topic and what you will say about that topic.

Poor: I would like to talk about stained glass windows.
Good: Although they cannot speak, stained glass windows tell intricate stories.

Outlining Your Ideas

The basic purpose of an outline is to organize a writer's ideas. The most important ideas become main points. Any points or specific details (examples, quotations, analogies, etc.) developing these main points become subpoints that are visually ranked beneath the main points they explain or support.

There are two different types of outlines. A **topic outline** uses only phrases—no sentences or verbs (verbals may be used). Each point in a numbered or lettered series should have the same grammatical form. For example, your main points could all be either prepositional phrases, nouns, or adjectives.

Thesis Statement: The book of Genesis shows that Joseph's three most prominent characteristics are integrity, resourcefulness, and humility.

I. Integrity
  A. As a slave
    1. Caring for all Potiphar's goods
    2. Refusing to sin with Potiphar's wife
  B. As a prisoner
    1. Keeping charge of the other prisoners
    2. Helping the butler and baker in their need
II. Resourcefulness
  A. As a household manager
  B. As a ruler in Egypt
    1. Storing during the good years
    2. Distributing during the bad years
III. Humility
  A. As a dream interpreter
    1. Giving credit to God
    2. Advising Pharaoh
  B. As a brother
    1. Forgiving his brothers
    2. Using his power to help others

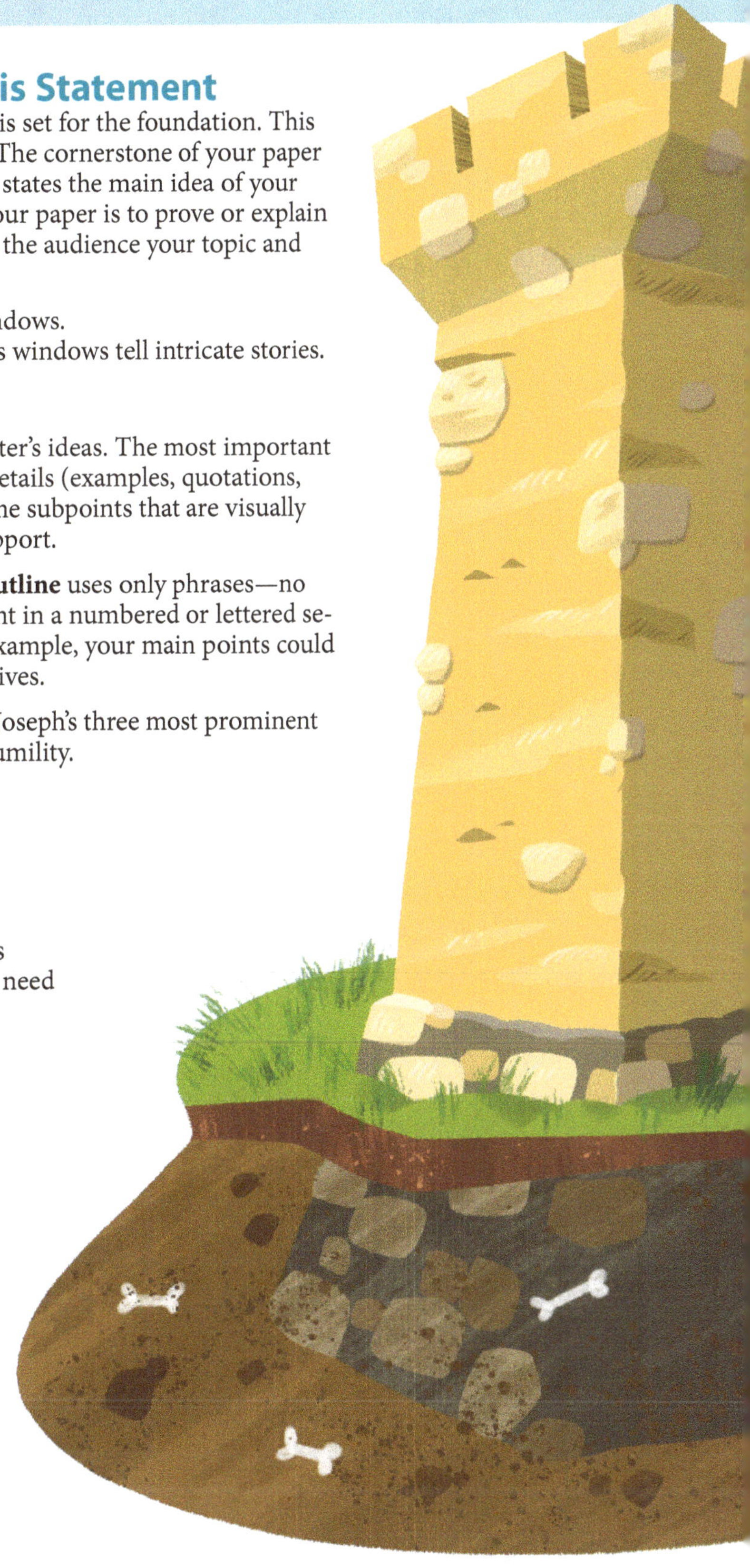

A **sentence outline** includes more information than a topic outline because every point is a complete sentence.

Thesis Statement: The book of Genesis shows that Joseph's three most prominent characteristics are integrity, resourcefulness, and humility.

I. Joseph showed integrity despite his hardships.
  A. He showed integrity after being sold into slavery.
    1. His honesty allowed Potiphar to trust him with all his goods.
    2. He refused to sin with Potiphar's wife.
  B. He showed integrity after being wrongly imprisoned.
    1. His integrity led him to faithfully oversee other prisoners.
    2. He showed kindness to the butler and baker by helping them understand their dreams.
II. Joseph showed resourcefulness by being an efficient manager.
  A. His hard work and God's blessing caused Potiphar to get richer.
  B. His resourcefulness helped him save Egypt from famine.
    1. He stored up extra grain during the good years.
    2. He distributed grain during the bad years.
III. Joseph consistently showed humility despite his hardships and successes.
  A. He showed humility as a dream interpreter.
    1. He gave credit to God for his ability to interpret dreams.
    2. He advised Pharaoh to prepare for the famine but did not promote himself.
  B. He showed humility with his brothers.
    1. He forgave his brothers.
    2. He used his power to help others instead of only helping himself.

Practice the Skill

Create a topic outline using the cluster diagram "Vacation in England" on page 9.

Ordering Ideas

When outlining, organize your paper in a way that helps the reader see how your points relate to and support your main idea. The best way to outline clearly is to follow an organizational method. The following chart identifies some classic types:

Organization Types		
Method	**Definition**	**Types of Writing**
Chronological Order	Presents events in the sequence of their occurrence	Narratives, history, biography, reports, processes, instructions
Spatial Order	Organizes according to how something is physically arranged or encountered	Description of a place or an object
Order of Importance	Moves from least important to most important or vice versa	Argumentative, persuasive, informative, and descriptive writing
Illustration	States a principle and then uses examples, analogies, or other details to illustrate it	Argumentative and informative writing (e.g., for science, theology, history, government, policy)
Cause-Effect	Explains how certain results were caused by events (e.g., actions, choices, other events)	History, science, math, literary analysis
Comparison/Contrast	Takes two or more persons, objects, or ideas and shows how they are similar or different	Science, literary analysis, description, policy, proposal

Writing with Logic

Imagine if God had created a world that was not logical: if every day were a different season, if gravity did not always exist, or if some foods that were good for us one day were poisonous the next. Humans could never live in a world like that. Since we imitate and need the orderliness God has created, we should follow the same principle in our writing. When you draft your paper, focus on communicating your ideas in a way that is organized and logical to your readers, or your paper will fail to accomplish its purpose. Remember that the first draft will by no means be perfect, and that is fine. There will be plenty of opportunities to fine-tune what you say later in the revising stage. For now, focus on getting your thoughts down in a logical manner.

As you draft your paper, follow your outline closely to ensure the paper stays organized and relates to your thesis. However, as you write, you may see a need to change your outline. Just be sure its contents stay well structured and work together to prove your thesis.

Creating Coherence

One important quality to pursue when drafting is **coherence**, how well your ideas relate to one another. We have all had the experience of listening to people whose thoughts seem scattered. Encountering incoherent communicators is a frustrating experience that you do not want to inflict on your audience.

You have already begun working on coherence by following a specific organizational model (chronological order, spatial order, etc.). The following chart lists transitional words that help signal the organizational model to the reader.

Transitional Words by Organizational Method

Organization	Some Transitional Words to Use
Chronological Order	To begin with, first/second/third, next, then, later, after, before, meanwhile, until, finally, last
Spatial Order	Nearby, further on, on the other side, to the right/left, behind, in front of
Order of Importance	Of lesser importance, of equal importance, equally, by the same token, primarily, most importantly, above all, indeed, in fact, notably
Illustration	For example, for instance, in addition, that is, to illustrate, in the same way, furthermore
Cause-Effect	So that, in order to, as a result, therefore, consequently
Comparison/Contrast	Similarly, likewise, also, correspondingly, in the same way, neither . . . nor, in contrast, on the other hand, alternatively, however, instead, on the contrary, nevertheless, but, either . . . or

Practice the Skill

Read the following paragraphs and decide which type of organization each uses. Underline the transitional words and phrases that the writer employed. Some words and phrases will be particular to the paragraph's topic.

Paragraph 1:

As the centuries have passed, armor has become more complex to give soldiers added protection against enemies. At first, knights wore coats of chain mail, which consisted of many small iron rings that were linked together. Then, during the twelfth century, they began wearing more chain mail so that their arms and legs were covered. Later, in the fourteenth century, knights added plates to both their torsos and limbs. These plates were made of either iron or steel and were riveted to a cloth covering. By the early fifteenth century, knights had begun wearing full suits of armor. These suits protected the entire body but still were flexible enough to allow the knight to run, mount his horse, or lie down without the aid of his squire. As guns became more common, full armor fell out of favor. However, armor worn over the torso remained popular as protection against bullets and shrapnel. Today, soldiers' gear includes strong synthetic fibers, such as Kevlar, sometimes reinforced with plates made from other strong materials. Until wars cease, armies will continue to find new and stronger materials to use as armor.

____

____

Paragraph 2:
Medieval castles were fortresses with special defensive features to block attackers from entering. To begin with, there was often a moat (wet or dry) surrounding the castle which prevented enemies from digging under, climbing over, or destroying the walls. Only one point of entry—the gatehouse passage through the castle's thick walls—remained. There, attackers faced several barriers. First, the heavy timber drawbridge which normally spanned the ditch could be moved, often becoming a barrier instead of a passage. Drawbridges were operated from inside the castle and were difficult to overcome. If the enemy managed to do so, a portcullis awaited next inside the entryway. A portcullis was a heavy grilled gate overlaid in iron. Descending from above, a portcullis slid along grooves in the walls to block the passage. Once beyond a portcullis, attackers had to survive "murder holes" placed in the gatehouse ceiling. From above through these holes, defenders poured hazardous materials (e.g., scalding water, rocks, or tar) onto enemies below. Attackers trapped between a dropped portcullis and the barred castle gates became sitting ducks for these weapons. Finally, the castle gates themselves required a battering ram to overcome. All these defensive features made castles formidable fortresses in medieval times.

Paragraph 3:
The lord of the manor employed several different men to help him run his estate. His most important employee was the steward. The steward's job was to keep track of the accounting books, organize workers to accomplish various tasks around the manor, and oversee the manor court whenever the lord was absent. The bailiff was second in rank to the steward. Although the bailiff was normally a peasant, he was generally a little better off than most peasants. His job was to oversee repairs and manage the peasants who worked on the manor. The bailiff's assistant was the reeve. The reeve directly supervised the work done on the manor, making sure that the workers began on time and that nothing was stolen from the lord. Each of these men fulfilled a specific task to ensure the smooth running of the manor.

Writing Strong Paragraphs

Organizing ideas and using good transitions are ways to craft strong, coherent paragraphs. A **paragraph** consists of a group of sentences closely related to one main idea.

The Paragraph's Three Parts

Traditionally, paragraphs require three parts. First, the main idea of the paragraph is usually stated in the **topic sentence**. The topic sentence is usually, but not always, the first sentence in a paragraph. For example, the topic sentence of a paragraph that talks about the duties of a knight could be, "During medieval times, the knight had several important responsibilities." Next come **supporting sentences** which use details, examples, facts, or other methods to develop the idea stated by the topic sentence. Finally, a **concluding sentence** joins all the ideas together by restating the topic sentence so that the paragraph will be complete.

Practice the Skill

Write a good topic sentence for each of the following paragraphs.

Paragraph 1:
Peasant women worked in the fields alongside their husbands in order to provide food and clothing for their families. Wives and daughters of craftsmen helped in the family workshop or operated as tradeswomen themselves. Noblewomen organized and ran their large households and sometimes oversaw the family businesses. Hard work was a part of every woman's life during medieval times.

____

____

Paragraph 2:
Most bards knew hundreds of songs and poems. Some bards wrote their own songs and poems. The most popular bards were the ones who could hold their audience's attention for long periods of time. Traveling bards were called minstrels. Many kings and knights hired minstrels to perform at a meal, but the minstrel was paid only if his work was considered worthy. Bards needed to be expert entertainers in order to make a living.

____

____

Developing Your Paragraph

Every paragraph should have **full development** of its topic with enough meaningful material to share. Avoid including either too little or too much information. The following chart provides examples of ways to develop ideas into complete paragraphs.

Paragraph Development		
Kind	**Definition**	**Example**
Fact	A statement that can be proved	During the Middle Ages, farming was the chief economic activity.
Example	An instance or event	The Middle Ages began with the end of the Roman Empire.
Statistic	A fact expressed in numbers	The danger of fire was great in medieval Europe. Rouen, France, burned six times in twenty-five years.
Incident/Anecdote	Brief personal account that illustrates the point	My visit to Chepstow Castle in Wales helped me understand the primitive nature of medieval life.
Sensory Details	The use of sense words—taste, touch, smell, etc.	Peasants slept on dry, musty, scratchy bags of straw.
Reasons	Explanation of a truth, general principle, or logical conclusion	Because many merchants became peasant farmers during the Middle Ages, the influence of towns diminished.

Practice the Skill

Identify the kind of information used to develop the paragraph's topic.

Paragraph 1:
In Germany, castle design was influenced by the type of land the castle was built on. For example, some castles took advantage of the natural protection of crags, hills, and mountains and did not need as many walls surrounding them. Others were built on the banks of the Rhine River, which formed a natural barrier on at least one side of the castle. The *Wasserburg*, a type of castle protected by water, was common in flatter areas.

____

Paragraph 2:
Many medieval castles still stand today. Last summer when I was in Europe, I was able to see Caerphilly Castle in South Wales. I learned that it is the largest castle in Wales. We also visited Saumur Castle in France. Interestingly, it was at one time used as a prison. I especially enjoyed seeing the Pfalzgrafenstein, which was built on an island in the Rhine by King Ludwig I of Bavaria. Our tour guide told us that it was originally used as a toll station.

Caerphilly Castle in South Wales

____

Revising for the Writing Traits

Have you ever hastily written a paper the night before it was due and turned it in without looking at it? If you did, your teacher probably found some obvious mistakes that hurt your grade and might have even caused you embarrassment. No one writes a perfect paper on the first try. In this writing stage, you will learn to revise your paper by analyzing your use of five of the six writing traits. The sixth trait, conventions, will be the focus of the next stage of writing.

Revising for Ideas

Revision of the first draft should always be re-vision—seeing the material again. Begin the revision process by analyzing your paper for the first of the five writing traits: ideas. Read your rough draft to see whether you have stated clearly and fully what you wanted to say.

Key Questions for Ideas

- Are my ideas fully developed?
- Are my ideas clearly expressed, or have I said anything that could be misleading or confusing?

Revising for Organization

It is not enough to have a paper with good ideas. The ideas must also be organized in a way that is logical to the reader. Be sure to have a clear introduction in which you introduce the topic and state the thesis. The body of the paper should support the thesis and follow one of the organizational methods mentioned in the last lesson. The conclusion should summarize your ideas and restate the thesis using different words.

Key Questions for Organization

- Do I have a clear introduction, thesis statement, body, and conclusion?
- Does my paper have unity? Does my paper have coherence?

Revising for Sentence Fluency

Evaluate the individual sentences in your paragraphs. The words should flow smoothly and engage your reader. Check that you used a variety of sentence types and transitional words and phrases. Your ideas should be concisely stated; avoid being wordy or redundant.

Key Questions for Sentence Fluency

- Is my paper concise?
- Does my draft contain redundancies?
- Do my sentences vary in their type, length, and beginning?
- Do I vary my transitional words and phrases?

Revising for Word Choice

Look at your use of word choice and correct inaccurate or imprecise words. Vague words, such as *thing* or *stuff*, fail to give the reader a clear idea of what you are trying to communicate. Precise words, such as *item* or *parcels*, make your meaning clear.

You also want to use words that focus on showing, not just telling, your ideas. Use **concrete imagery** (words that appeal to the senses) to show the audience what you are describing. For example, instead of saying, "The bread was good," try, "The warm, soft bread melted on my tongue." Do not rely on adjectives and adverbs alone. Try to use precise nouns and verbs too.

Key Questions for Word Choice

- Do I use precise words?
- Do I use a good variety of words?
- Do I use concrete, vivid imagery to show the reader what I am describing?

Revising for Voice

Be sure that the voice you use in your writing is appropriate for your message, audience, and genre. While a formal tone is necessary for a serious composition such as a research paper you wrote for your teacher, it would not work well for a fictitious story that you wrote to entertain your friends. You also need to make sure your voice is consistent. A paper that begins very seriously should not abruptly shift into a paper that is lighthearted and humorous.

Key Questions for Voice

- Is my voice appropriate for my message, audience, and genre?
- Is my voice consistent throughout my composition?

Practice the Skill

Use the key questions to revise the following paragraph.

People ate a variety of foods during medieval times. Beef, mutton (sheep), and venison (deer) served as the basic meats. Most people liked it. Various kinds of wild birds also ended up on the menu. Peacocks and cranes were exotic dishes that were served on special occasions. This is strange because people do not really eat those kinds of birds anymore, at least not in America. However, they might still eat them in some foreign countries. Meat was often eaten with onions, garlic, and herbs from the castle garden. Dried peas and beans were the most common vegetables. Also, fruits, such as apples and pears in the northern areas and figs, grapes, oranges, and lemons in the southern areas, were gathered from the castle orchards and served as delicacies. Puddings made from milk were also favorite dishes. Medieval cooks knew how to make good food. Also, poultry and eggs were common dishes.

PEER REVIEWS

Constructive Criticism

During both the revising and proofreading stages of the writing process, you will participate in **peer reviews** during which you will read and correct a classmate's paper while a classmate does the same with your paper. A peer review consists of both writing corrective notes and talking to your classmate in person about how he can improve his paper. This activity may be difficult for you because you do not want someone to see your mistakes or because the criticism of your paper may seem like a personal attack. These feelings are natural, but the Bible talks about the wisdom of humbling yourself and listening to correction (Proverbs 15:32–33). Keep in mind that this activity will not only make you a stronger writer, but it will also improve the way you listen and speak to others.

Proofreading Symbols

Before beginning a peer review, you will need to first familiarize yourself with the annotation marks below. Some of these symbols refer to grammar rules that you may be unfamiliar with right now, but you will learn these rules as the year progresses.

Ideas		
pr phr Phrase more precisely.	**dev ¶** Develop paragraph more fully.	
Organization		
¶ New paragraph	**no ¶** Do not begin new paragraph here.	 Move
∧∨ Add	 Delete	
Sentence Fluency		
FS Fused sentence	**sent log** Make sentence parts relate to each other more logically.	**MM** Misplaced modifier
var More sentence variety needed	**CS** Comma splice	**DM** Dangling modifier
wdy Wordy	**frag** Fragment	
Word Choice		
awk Awkward phrasing	**pr wd** More precise word needed	**w wd** Wrong word
Voice		
voice Use active voice.		
Conventions		
ital Italicize	**sp** Spelling error	**S/V agr** Verb needs to agree with subject.
pct Correct punctuation needed	**tns** Consistent tense needed	≡ Capital letter
P/A agr Pronoun needs to agree with antecedent.	/ Lowercase	∧∨ Add
 Delete		

Giving Helpful Suggestions

In order to have successful peer reviews, it is important that you follow specific guidelines both when you are speaking to a classmate about his paper and when a classmate is speaking to you about your paper.

Guidelines for responding to your classmate's feedback:

- Show by your verbal responses, facial expressions, and body language that you are sincerely interested in his feedback.
- Do not interrupt.
- Listen for total meaning instead of focusing only on one thing your classmate says.
- Ask questions for clarification.
- Repeat what the speaker says to be sure you correctly understand him.

Remember, there is no need to get defensive. Even if you do not agree with your peer, listen politely and ask questions rather than arguing. Keep in mind that your peer is only providing suggestions for how he thinks you can improve your paper. You are not *required* to follow a suggestion unless it refers to an obvious error.

Guidelines for giving feedback to your classmate:

- Always start by stating what you liked about the paper.
- Make sure your comments refer to particular words, phrases, or sentences that need improvement. A vague comment, such as "Parts of the paper are confusing," is not helpful.
- With each comment, offer a specific solution for how your peer can improve. A comment such as "This sentence does not make sense" would be better if it were changed to "This sentence might be clearer if you said . . ."
- Be sure your comments are kind. This is an opportunity to practice empathy and follow the Golden Rule by not making a comment that you would not want someone to make about your paper (Matthew 7:12). For example, instead of saying, "This paragraph is awful," you can say, "I think this paragraph would be better if . . ."
- Always end your peer review by restating the good things about the paper.

Practice the Skill

Review the paragraph below as if it were written by a peer. Annotate problems and make comments.

In the midle ages, serfs were peasants who farmed on land owned by the feudal lord most serfs could not read. There were not even many lords who could read. Reading was mostly learned by the monks and priests. So back to serfs, they kept a portion of the Crops they grew in the fields, but most of the food went to the lord of the manor. In many cases, the lord owned not only the field but also each family that farmed on his land. Although there are still lords in Europe, there ain't no serfs no more. This system kept the poor poor and the wealthy wealthy. Serfs had to fight for the right to make something of themselves.

PROOFREADING

The Sixth Writing Trait

During the revising stage, you revised for ideas, organization, sentence fluency, word choice, and voice. During the **proofreading** stage, you will revise for conventional errors. You may have already found and corrected some errors in your paper, but now you are looking for any mistakes that have gone unnoticed up to this point.

Key Questions for Conventions

- Do I follow the rules for spelling, grammar, capitalization, and punctuation?

Your first reaction to proofreading for conventions and mechanics may be something like this: "Why do I have to care about this? It just gets in my way!" When it comes to self-expression, writers often resist any perceived interference in their freedom. However, believers who understand Christ-expression recognize that when they write, they are representing Christ to others. Rules or other boundaries help them communicate their messages in logical and respectful ways. This reflects the orderliness of God. Also, fixing conventional errors is a way of showing love for readers. You have demonstrated that you understand their needs and have fixed any potential problems that could cause confusion. Correcting these errors is a way of showing your readers your care for them, the credibility of your message, and the orderly character of God and His creation. Below is a list of common problems and suggested solutions.

Problems	Solutions
Grammar: Do I have any fragments, fused sentences, or comma splices?	Figure out what is missing from a fragment and complete the sentence, or join it to an adjacent sentence. Divide the fused sentence or comma splice and punctuate it correctly.
Usage: Do my subjects and verbs agree, and do my pronouns and antecedents agree?	Put a singular subject with a singular verb and a plural subject with a plural verb. Follow the rules for pronoun-antecedent agreement in Chapter 5.
Punctuation: Have I omitted any punctuation marks or used any marks incorrectly?	Read each sentence carefully. Check the rules in Chapter 17.
Capitalization: Does every sentence begin with a capital letter? Are all proper nouns and proper adjectives capitalized?	Look for specific people, places, events, and objects. Check the rules in Chapter 17.
Spelling: Have I misspelled any words?	Look deliberately at every word. Check uncertain spellings against a good dictionary.

Proofreading Strategies

Good proofreading takes practice. Good proofreaders know they will not find every error in a single reading. Use the following strategies to help you proofread:

- Focus by using a blank sheet of paper to cover the part you have not yet read.
- Read the paper aloud. You may hear an error that you did not see when you read your paper silently.
- Look at the words in reverse order; begin reading at the end of the paper and work towards the beginning. This tactic will force you to look at each word individually for spelling or capitalization errors.
- Read the paper through more quickly a few times, looking each time for some particular problem area that has been difficult for you in the past. For instance, it is fairly easy to spot comma errors when you read looking only for commas.

Practice the Skill

Using the tactics listed above, proofread and rewrite the paragraph below.

During the middle ages European society was composed primarily of three classes of people; the clergy, the nobility, and the pesants. Each played an important part in shaping European life and culture. There roles in society have been described simply: the clergy were called to prey; the nobility, to fight; and the peasants, to work. Accordingly each group represents an institution of medeval Europe—the church, the fudal system, and the manor.

PUBLISHING

Developing a Title

After planning, drafting, revising, and proofreading, it is now time to publish the paper. Publishing a paper simply means sharing it with others. Before publishing, choose a title that captures the reader's attention. For example, "Peasants" is too broad because it does not let the reader know anything about the paper's specific topic. A better title would be "A Medieval Peasant's Daily Life" or "Why Did Peasants Stay Peasants?" Both titles let the audience know the topic of the paper.

The Writing Notebook

What do Mark Twain, Thomas Jefferson, Ludwig van Beethoven, and George Lucas have in common? They kept notebooks and regularly recorded random ideas that sometimes ended up being published in their famous works.

Throughout this year, you will keep a writing notebook containing several sections in which you will record your compositions as well as your ideas and topics. You can go back to them anytime you wish. An idea you write down today might spark an even greater idea when you read it months from now. The notebook will also allow you to see your progress as a writer.

Multimedia Skills

There are many different ways to publish a paper. Below are just a few traditional methods for publishing paragraphs or essays:

- Put together a class literary collection.
- Use the compositions for programs (parent-teacher fellowships, holiday programs, etc.).
- Share them with a classroom audience, such as an English class.
- Read the work aloud to an audience, such as family or friends.

Although these methods are still good ways to publish your paper, advances in technology make it possible to publish using **multimedia**. A writer can now publish or promote his work through a website, blog, video channel, or social media site and possibly reach millions of people.

Although technology can benefit writers, it also has a major drawback. Since people have access to so much information, they might not spend a lot of time reading any one selection. If writing fails to hold their attention, they will quickly move on to something else. It is therefore especially important to capture and hold the audience's attention when using technology to publish. This textbook will teach you multimedia skills that will help you effectively publish your materials.

Speaking and Listening Skills

When an author publishes a book, he does not just send it to a publishing company and hope it sells. He often promotes his book by reading parts of it at libraries, talking to people about it at a book-signing event, or discussing it at various conferences. This year you will have opportunities to communicate your ideas through presentations when you publish some of your compositions. This part of the publishing process requires the use of speaking and listening skills to successfully communicate a message to an audience. Presentations that are logical and easy to follow are appealing. One of the most common fears is the fear of public speaking, and this is one reason presentations are so hard to do. You will learn several techniques to help speakers and listeners become more confident and effective.

Practice the Skill

Answer the questions.

1. What is the impact of each of the following publishing methods?
   - Reading or talking about your paper to an audience
   - Putting your paper on a blog
   - Sharing your paper on social media
2. How should you use discernment to determine the best publishing choice for your paper? How does this choice relate to the idea of Christ-expression?

DEFINITION PARAGRAPHS
Writing Trait: Ideas

Listen Up!
The following paragraph defines and explains cyberbullying. Read the text and answer the following questions about this mentor text.

MENTOR TEXT

Cyberbullying is bullying that takes place over digital devices like cell phones, computers, and tablets. Cyberbullying can occur through SMS, Text, and apps, or online in social media, forums, or gaming where people can view, participate in, or share content. Cyberbullying includes sending, posting, or sharing negative, harmful, false, or mean content about someone else. It can include sharing personal or private information about someone else causing embarrassment or humiliation. Some cyberbullying crosses the line into unlawful or criminal behavior.

—US Department of Health and Human Services, "What Is Cyberbullying"

1. What is the literal definition of cyberbullying?
2. The author expands the literal definition by including what information about cyberbullying?
3. Using the chart on page 21 for reference, write the kind of information the author uses to develop the paragraph.

Take Notes!
Summarize the components of and process for writing a definition paragraph.

Components of a Definition Paragraph
Definition paragraphs are distinguished by the content they develop; they define a term, object, idea, attitude, or emotion. They normally start with the literal definition of the word. After defining the term, the writer then builds upon the definition by using specific examples, famous quotes, analogies, or explanations of what a subject is (or is not). These paragraphs can be formal and serious or informal and funny.

Writing a Definition Paragraph
1. Choose a word you want to define. Try to choose an abstract word that can mean different things to different people (such as *love*, *honor*, or *freedom*).
2. Write a topic sentence in which you introduce and define your word or phrase with the dictionary definition.
3. Think of what tone you want to convey: serious, lighthearted, or humorous.
4. Think of creative material (facts, statistics, anecdotes, sensory details, or reasons) that will explain your definition. Your supporting material should fit the tone you wish to convey.

5. Write your paragraph.
6. Add a visual. Choose an illustration that you think best expresses the definition you are writing. For example, an illustration of the word *sacrifice* could include a soldier standing at the grave of his comrade.

Partner Up!

Gather information for a paragraph defining *laziness*.

1. Record the dictionary definition of the word.
2. Use at least four of the approaches below to expand your definition.
   - Reasons people are lazy
   - Behavior that results from laziness
   - An example from the Bible
   - An example from history
   - An analogy describing an aspect of laziness
   - A quality that opposes or contrasts with laziness
3. Number your supporting points in the order you would place them in a definition paragraph.
4. Suggest a few transitional words or phrases that might help link your points logically to each other.

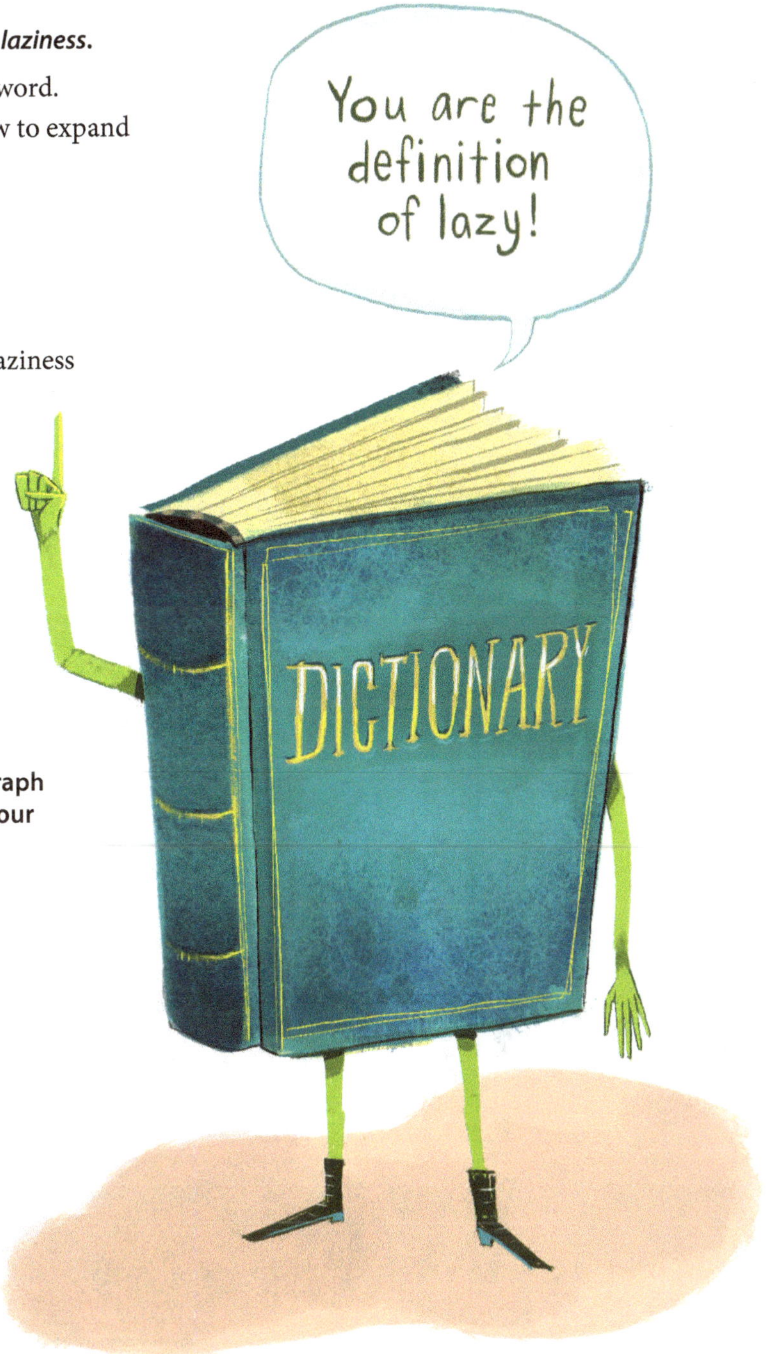

Try It Out!

Using the information you gathered in the Partner Up! section, write a definition paragraph about laziness. Add a visual that illustrates your definition.

CHAPTER 2

SENTENCES

DOES YOUR MESSAGE MAKE SENSE?

Have you ever gotten a message you did not understand? You wished you could ask the author what he meant. Whether you are writing a friend or writing a school report, writing clear, precise, complete sentences will ensure that you communicate effectively.

DISCOVER!

Barry uses a variety of sentence types in the following excerpt. Can you find all four sentence types?

MENTOR TEXT

"Hey, bandits at two o'clock high!" Eddie Pulaski shouted over the intercom. He was manning the twin Browning machine guns in the upper turret.

Instinctively, I swung my gun up to the two o'clock high position. I could see nothing but blue sky and scattered wisps of clouds. Off in the distance, sky and ground blurred together, making it impossible to distinguish the horizon.

How can Eddie do that? He always spots them first.

After repeatedly straining my eyes, I finally made out what Pulaski had seen—a dozen specks, ahead of us to the right, and rapidly closing from a higher altitude.

"Yup! [. . .] Messerschmitts!" came Eddie's voice again.

Because of our combined airspeeds, the fighters closed the distance incredibly fast. In no time, they tilted their wings and began a dive toward our formation.

"Ready, Yoder?" Eddie called over the intercom, his voice rising in pitch.

"You bet!"

"Cut the chatter," Lt. Conover called over the intercom. "Shoot your guns, not your mouths."

—Rick Barry, *Gunner's Run*

SENTENCES

A sentence is a group of words containing a subject and a predicate and expressing a complete thought.

Four Types of Sentences

Sentences have four functions in English: to declare, to question, to command, and to exclaim. These functions give us the names for the four types of sentences. In addition, the function of a sentence will often determine which type of punctuation to place at the end of that sentence.

A **declarative sentence** makes a statement and ends with a period.

Our visit to Hawaii will last five days**.**

An **interrogative sentence** asks a question and ends with a question mark.

Where is your ticket**?**

An **imperative sentence** gives a command or makes a request and ends with a period or, occasionally, an exclamation point.

Please help me with this luggage**.**
Don't drop that suitcase**!**

An **exclamatory sentence** expresses strong emotion and ends with an exclamation point.

I can't wait to arrive in Honolulu**!**

Subjects and Predicates

Every sentence includes two main parts, a **subject** and a **predicate**. The subject names the person, place, thing, or idea that the sentence discusses. The predicate makes a statement about the subject.

The subject usually comes at or near the beginning of the sentence. The **simple subject** is the main noun or pronoun in the sentence. The **complete subject** includes the simple subject and its modifiers.

The most populous ***city*** *in Europe* is London.
The Great Fire *of 1666* almost destroyed London.

The predicate usually follows the subject. The **simple predicate** is the main verb (with any accompanying helping verb) in the sentence. The **complete predicate** includes the simple predicate and its modifiers, objects, or other completers.

London ***has hosted*** *three Summer Olympic Games.*
The London Underground ***is*** *one of the oldest underground railway networks in the world.*

Most **imperative sentences** seem to have only a predicate. Because these sentences are commands or requests, the subject is understood to be *you*. Only an imperative sentence can have understood *you* as its subject.

S **P**
(*You*) Tell me about your trip to London.
S **P**
(*You*) Please find Harrods on this map.

Practice the Skill

Identify each sentence as *declarative, interrogative, imperative*, or *exclamatory*. Place the appropriate punctuation mark at the end of each sentence.

_______________ 1. A matador is a man who fights a bull in a special contest

_______________ 2. Would you want to have a matador's job

_______________ 3. I definitely would not

_______________ 4. A *matador de toros* is a highly skilled matador

_______________ 5. Don't get too close to the bull

Draw a vertical line between the complete subject and the complete predicate. Underline the simple subject(s) once and the simple predicate(s) twice. If the subject is understood *you*, draw a vertical line before the complete predicate.

6. The Alcazar in Segovia, Spain, appears as a lofty and noble bulwark.

7. This castle rests on a rocky cliff.

8. Segovia's Alcazar is a rather long castle.

9. However, many photographs and drawings reveal only part of the castle's length.

Alhambra Palaces in Granada, Andalusia, Spain

10. Look at the beautiful silhouette.

11. Another famous Spanish castle and tourist attraction in Granada, Spain, is the Alhambra.

12. The Alhambra was built by the Moors between 1248 and 1354.

13. Observe and examine the twenty-three towers on the wall.

14. *Alhambra* derives from words meaning "the red" in Arabic.

15. The Alhambra is one of the most important examples of Islamic architecture.

Review the Skill

Identify each sentence as *declarative*, *interrogative*, *imperative*, or *exclamatory*. Place the appropriate punctuation mark at the end of each sentence.

________________________ 16. A piñata is beautiful

________________________ 17. Have you ever broken a piñata

________________________ 18. Mexican children try to break the piñata to get the candy inside

________________________ 19. Move out of the way when the candy falls

________________________ 20. Start picking up the candy, and share with everyone

Draw a vertical line between the complete subject and the complete predicate. Underline the simple subject(s) once and the simple predicate(s) twice. If the subject is understood *you*, draw a vertical line before the complete predicate.

21. Spain consists of fifty provinces.
22. This picturesque country borders France and Portugal.
23. Millions travel to Spain each year.
24. Notice all the historical landmarks.
25. Many tourists visit the castles along the countryside.
26. However, an avid sports fan or other visitor may choose a soccer game instead.
27. Soccer is called football in Spain.
28. Many Spaniards enjoy old folk songs.
29. Their traditional costumes are always bright and colorful.
30. Explore and enjoy this beautiful country.

Use the Skill

Write a paragraph telling a friend about a favorite place you have visited. Use all four sentence types. Effectively incorporate at least one sentence with the subject understood *you*. Underline each subject once and each verb twice.

CONJUNCTIONS AND COMPOUND SUBJECTS AND PREDICATES

Conjunctions

A **conjunction** is a connecting word that joins words or groups of words in a sentence.

Coordinating Conjunctions

A **coordinating conjunction** connects sentence parts that have the same function within the sentence. The parts of the sentence joined by a coordinating conjunction make up a **compound part** of the sentence.

The chart below lists commonly used coordinating conjunctions.

Conjunction	Basic Meaning
and	same or equal
nor	opposite or contrasting (negative items)
but	opposite or contrasting
yet	alternative or contrasting
or	alternative or choice
for	because or since
so	therefore or consequently

A coordinating conjunction can join single **words** that have the same function within a sentence.

Jerrold **and** *Sara* are fishing off the dock. (compound simple subject)
Sara *tried* **but** *failed* to bait her hook. (compound simple predicate)
No fish were caught by *Jerrold* **or** *Sara*. (compound object of the preposition)

A coordinating conjunction can also join **phrases** that have the same function.

A team of soccer players **and** *a bunch of volunteers* cleaned up the abandoned field. (compound complete subject)

The group *collected trash* **and** *mowed the grass*. (compound complete predicate)

It was *after lunchtime* **but** *before suppertime* that they finished the job. (compound adverbial prepositional phrase)

Two of the volunteers were *the junior-high principal* **and** *the high-school dramatics coach*. (compound complete predicate noun)

Since coordinating conjunctions join grammatical parts of equal rank, a comma and one of these conjunctions can also join two **independent clauses**.

Jan and Joanie tried out for cheerleading, **but** *Jan did not make the squad.*

Horace and Marilyn snorkeled in the bay, **and** *they saw many exotic fish.*

The Scripture commands us to love the sinner, **yet** *we are not to love the sin.*

Correlative Conjunctions

Correlative conjunctions are conjunctions that are used in pairs. They also join sentence parts of the same grammatical type. The correlative conjunctions are divided in the sentence, but they work together to relate the two sentence parts. These are the most common pairs of correlative conjunctions.

Correlative Conjunction Pairs
both . . . and
neither . . . nor
either . . . or
not only . . . but also

Neither *Kathy* **nor** *Joe* have finished their research papers. (compound subject)

They need **both** *to search* the library **and** *read* many books. (compound infinitive phrase)

Joe **not only** *found* many books **but also** *began* to read them. (compound verb)

Kathy will search **either** *in the library* **or** *on her computer*. (compound prepositional phrase)

Practice the Skill

Circle each coordinating conjunction. Underline the compound simple subjects once and the compound simple predicates twice.

1. Believers should not disobey or rebel against their Lord.
2. Satan's pride and willfulness led to his desire for glory.
3. Jews and Gentiles have been blessed through Abraham.
4. Moses could see but not enter the Promised Land.
5. Saul's disobedience and selfish desire led to his removal from the throne.
6. David heeded God's command and defeated the Philistines.
7. Solomon succeeded his father David and built the temple at God's command.
8. Ananias and Sapphira answered falsely.
9. With Christ's power, we can defeat and overcome sin.
10. "Repent ye, and believe the gospel" (Mark 1:15).

Circle the correlative conjunctions. Underline the words or phrases that the conjunctions join.

11. Both the oceans and the seas are awe-inspiring parts of creation.
12. At God's command, bodies of water have either dried up or overflowed their boundaries.
13. God not only commanded Jonah but also enabled him.
14. Jonah neither sailed to Ninevah nor preached to the Ninevites.
15. Both Jonah's willfulness and disobedience are lessons we can learn from.
16. Jonah not only tried to run from God but also found it impossible.
17. The sailors both took Jonah and cast him into the sea.
18. Jonah was neither drowned in the ocean nor killed by the big fish.
19. Jonah either complained to God or sheltered under a gourd.
20. Neither man's stubbornness nor his rebellion is pleasing to God.

Review the Skill

Combine the following pairs of sentences using the correlative conjunctions indicated in parentheses to create one sentence with compound parts.

21. Writing practice will help improve your learning skills. Reading practice will help improve your learning skills. (*both . . . and*)

____

22. You must adopt a positive mental attitude to be successful in class. You must put forth a lot of effort to be successful in class. (*both . . . and*)

____

23. Listen carefully to guide your learning during class. Take notes to guide your learning during class. (*either . . . or*)

____

24. To improve your note-taking skills, logically organize your notes. At least make your notes legible. (*either . . . or*)

____

25. Talk to your teacher when class content is unclear. You can also ask your teacher questions. (*both . . . and*)

____

26. A messy study spot will not improve your academic performance. An irregular study schedule will not improve your academic performance. (*neither . . . nor*)

____

27. You may study on your own. You may also study with a friend or two. (*not only . . . but also*)

____

28. Stop procrastinating. Plan ahead. (*both . . . and*)

____

29. Take a short nap to break up your study time. Physical activity can also break up your study time. (*either . . . or*)

____

30. Using your class time wisely will help you become a better student. You also need to use your after-school time wisely. (*not only . . . but also*)

____

____

Combine the following pairs of sentences using the conjunctions indicated in parentheses to create one sentence with compound parts.

31. Notecards are a good tool for studying. Class notes are a good tool for studying. (*and*)

____

32. Ask the questions on your cards to yourself. Move the notecards you find the most troublesome to the front. (*and*)

____

____

33. You can compare notes with your partner. You can also ask questions of your partner. (*both . . . and*)

____

34. Rereading text assignments will help you to retain what you learn. It is also good to memorize key terms. (*both . . . and*)

____

35. Memorizing is one way to learn. Clustering ideas may help you remember them better. (*but*)

____

36. Teach a partner the content you are studying. Take notes as a partner teaches you. (*either . . . or*)

____

37. Do not study overtime on things you already know. Do not multitask to "kill two birds with one stone." (*neither . . . nor*)

____

38. A well-known physicist, Richard Fenyman, recommended identifying what you want to learn. He recommended using analogies to explain it to a five-year-old. (*and*)

____

____

39. Find the study strategy that works best for you. Use a variety of strategies. (*either . . . or*)

____

40. These strategies will help you now. These strategies will put you on the road to a lifetime of learning. (*not only . . . but also*)

____

Use the Skill

Write a sentence for each of the following conjunctions: *nor, but, or, and, neither . . . nor, not only . . . but also,* and *both . . . and.* Underline the words or phrases that the conjunctions join.

SENTENCES IN INVERTED ORDER

In most sentences, the subject comes before the predicate. However, some sentences, such as interrogative sentences, are in **inverted order**. The subject may come after the predicate or between parts of the predicate.

> *Was* the **Spanish Armada** a failure?
> *Did* **Phillip II** *overestimate* the Armada's ability?

Inverted order also often happens when the words *there* or *here* introduce a sentence and come before the verb. Rarely are the words *there* or *here* subjects. More often than not, the words *there* or *here* are adverbs.

> There *were* 130 **ships** in the fleet sent by King Phillip II to invade England.
> Here *was* the first naval **battle** entirely fought with large guns firing iron projectiles.

You can rearrange inverted sentences to make sure you have found the subject and the predicate.

> The **Spanish Armada** *was* a failure.
> **Phillip II** *did overestimate* the Armada's ability.
> One hundred thirty **ships** in the fleet sent by King Phillip II to invade England *were* there.
> The first naval **battle** entirely fought with large guns firing iron projectiles *was* here.

Practice the Skill

Underline the simple subject(s) once and the simple predicate(s) twice.

1. Are chinchillas native to North America?
2. A chinchilla is a small South American rodent.
3. There are chinchilla ranches in Europe, North America, and South Africa today.
4. After whom are they named?
5. The Spanish named them after the Chincha Indians and sold the fur in Europe.
6. The Chincha Indians and Inca Indians ate chinchillas.
7. Chinchillas eat roots and grasses.
8. Here is a book on chinchillas.
9. Do you know their weight at birth?
10. They weigh slightly more than one ounce.

Review the Skill

Underline the simple subject(s) once and the simple predicate(s) twice.

1. Where is the city of Seville?
2. Seville is a city in southern Spain.
3. There are many famous stories about Seville.
4. Do you know any of the stories?
5. Was Don Quixote born in Seville?
6. There is a famous bell tower in Seville.
7. What activities do people in Seville enjoy?
8. There are festivals and bullfights in the city.
9. Bullfighters must be very strong physically.
10. There are few cities as beautiful and attractive as Seville.

Use the Skill

Write one interrogative sentence, one sentence introduced with *there*, and one sentence introduced with *here*.

USING PARALLEL STRUCTURES TO EXPAND OR COMBINE

Writing Trait: Sentence Fluency

Listen Up!

Jim Murphy paints an unforgettable picture of the Great Chicago Fire of 1871 that destroyed miles of the city, killed an estimated 300 people, and left thousands homeless. See if you can find any compound subjects and predicates and their connecting conjunctions.

MENTOR TEXT

While hundreds of fires were still burning on Tuesday, such as at the coal works, most of them were under control. Enough anyway for the rubble to have cooled somewhat, allowing citizens to explore what had been their city.

The burnt district was over four miles long and one mile wide; 17,500 buildings and 73 miles of street had been destroyed. Joseph Medill, the forty-eight-year-old publisher of the *Tribune*, surveyed the scene and recalled "more widespread, soul-sickening desolation than mortal eye ever beheld since the destruction of Jerusalem. The proud and stately city of yesterday . . . had sunk into cellars and basements. What had hours before been the mart of commerce was now an indescribable chaos of broken columns, fallen walls, streets covered with debris, melted metal, charred and blackened trees standing like spectres. Thousands of columns of smoke and enveloping tongues of flame still rose out of the tumbling ruins. . . . Great [grain] elevators had disappeared. The tall spires of churches, the Courthouse dome, the stately blocks that were the pride of the city and the admiration of visitors, the noted landmarks . . . everything had disappeared."

—Jim Murphy, *The Great Fire*

Take Notes!

Draw a T-Chart and label one side *Correct* and the other *Incorrect*. List correct and incorrect ways to combine parallel structures.

To be a skillful writer, you must learn strategies for expanding and combining sentences to create fluency in your writing. The good news is you already have the tools in your toolbox—words, phrases, and clauses. The strategies you learn will allow you to vary sentence structure, change sentence emphasis, avoid choppiness, and say exactly what you wish to say—all to guide the audience's understanding. Yes, a writer has the ability to influence his readers' thinking. What an opportunity! God has created us to think and reason. Our minds need logically ordered ideas to understand what a writer is trying to say. Now is the time to begin mastering the tools God has given you for communication.

GRAMMAR TOOLBOX

One strategy for "playing" with existing sentence patterns is to combine two sentences by compounding identical structures. When these structures are identical and of equal importance, they are said to be **parallel**. Effective speakers and writers depend on parallelism to bring clarity and emphasis, making their messages concise and memorable.

Read the mentor text again. Look at the independent clause that says, "17,500 buildings and 73 miles of street had been destroyed." Suppose instead of compounding the subjects, Murphy had written, "17,500 buildings had been destroyed. 73 miles of street had been destroyed." Note the choppiness resulting from the repetition. Unskillful use of parallel structures can distract the reader or listener from the flow of thought and cause unnecessary wordiness.

Now analyze this version of the second sentence: "Joseph Medill . . . surveyed the scene and was recalling 'more widespread, soul-sickening desolation than mortal eye ever beheld.'" Is this a compound structure? Is there a coordinating conjunction? This is a compound structure with a coordinating conjunction, but note the lack of balance and rhythm. What is the problem? The compound parts joined by the conjunction do not have the same grammatical structure and are not parallel. The past-tense verb, "surveyed," is not parallel with the participle, "recalling." Compound structures that are not parallel are called **faulty parallelism**; they can distract the reader or listener and hinder the intended meaning and emphasis.

Partner Up!

Work with a partner to rewrite the following paragraph. Combine sentences to create parallel structures, and correct compound structures that are not parallel.

Our family ventured to the mountains for what turned out to be a memorable camping trip. Dad tried to set up the tent. My brother and I tried to set up the tent. The wind increased in strength. The wind was pulling the stakes out of the ground. My brother and I could neither hold onto the fabric nor grabbed the stakes. The tent went flying! Dad tried to retrieve the tent. He lost it over a nearby cliff. Mom saved the day! She laid our sleeping bags in the back of the SUV. We settled in for a warm night. We settled in for a windless night.

Try It Out!

Write a paragraph about a memorable trip or vacation. Include at least two compound subjects and two compound predicates. Try to vary the types of conjunctions you use, and be sure the compound structures you create are parallel.

FRAGMENTS AND INTERJECTIONS

Fragments

A **fragment** is a group of words wrongly capitalized and punctuated as though it were a sentence. Unlike a sentence, a fragment fails to express a complete thought.

There are two types of fragments. The first type may have a subject but not a predicate or vice versa. The other type has both a subject and a predicate but also includes a word that makes the fragment unable to stand alone as a sentence.

The famous Alhambra in Granada.
Although the Moors were defeated in 1492.

Correct a fragment by supplying the missing information or by joining it to another fragment or sentence that completes the thought.

The famous Alhambra in Granada is a Moorish palace.
Although the Moors were defeated in 1492, their influence on Spanish architecture survived.

Interjections

Interjections are single words or short phrases closely related to a neighboring sentence. They can stand alone or be joined to the sentence. They can express relief, agreement, disagreement, greeting, politeness, hesitation, distress, or even pain. Many interjections show strong feeling. Notice the location of interjections and their punctuation in these sentences.

Relief: *Whew!* I'm glad that test on Spain is over!
Agreement: *Yes,* I think I did well.
Greeting: *Hi,* Shawn, how did you do on the test?
Hesitation: Derek, *um,* didn't do very well.
Distress: *Ouch!* Just thinking about that test hurts my head!

Practice the Skill

Label each group of words *S* (sentence) or *F* (fragment).

_______ 1. The Rock of Gibraltar is an impressive picture of power and protection.

_______ 2. On a small peninsula in southeastern Spain.

_______ 3. The land area of Gibraltar is only 2.5 square miles.

_______ 4. Because Gibraltar is controlled by Britain.

_______ 5. The people commonly speak both English and Spanish.

_______ 6. Gibraltar is the location of the famous Gorham's Cave.

_______ 7. An exciting cave with stalactites and mysterious passageways.

_______ 8. Because there are historic fortresses and castles.

_______ 9. Millions of tourists visit Gibraltar each year.

_______ 10. To see the breathtaking Rock of Gibraltar.

Underline the interjections.

11. Hey, have you ever heard about the *USS Maine*?
12. No, what happened?
13. Well, the ship was sunk on February 15, 1898, in Havana Harbor.
14. An explosion ripped through the *Maine*'s hull. Bang!
15. Wow! Do you know the cause of the explosion?
16. No one is sure—sorry—but the fate of the *Maine* started the Spanish-American War.
17. Did a mysterious explosion start a whole war? Incredible!
18. Yes, the cause was either a large mine beneath the ship or an accidental fire on the ship.
19. I did not know that. Thanks.
20. Sure, it was no problem.

Review the Skill

Rewrite the fragments from numbers 1–10 to make complete sentences. You may combine groups of words. If a group of words is already a sentence, write *Sentence* in the blank.

21. ______________________________

22. ______________________________

23. ______________________________

24. ______________________________

25. ______________________________

26. ______________________________

27. ______________________________

28. ______________________________

29. ______________________________

30. ______________________________

Underline the interjections.

31. My, the *USS Constitution* is the oldest commissioned naval vessel still afloat.

32. Hmm, it could go about thirteen knots (or about fifteen miles) an hour.

33. Indeed, that does not seem very fast to us.

34. Boy! It had an excellent record.

35. It challenged the mighty British navy and defeated several British ships in the War of 1812. Amazing!

36. Okay, why was its nickname "Old Ironsides"?

37. Because cannonballs bounced off its thick wooden ironlike sides, it earned the nickname "Old Ironsides." Cool.

38. Yes, its design was revolutionary; it combined the best parts of different designs.

39. Man, the *Constitution* even circled the world in the 1840s.

40. This marvel-for-its-time never lost a battle. Whew!

Use the Skill

Rewrite the following paragraph, fixing the four fragments and punctuating the two interjections.

It was a hot, humid day at camp, so Kristi and Abbie wanted to go tubing in the creek. Each girl selected an inner tube. Carried it around her waist to the creek. "Brr the water is freezing," said Kristi as they stepped into the creek. Kristi sat down carefully. In the middle of her tube. Abbie leaped onto hers. Kristi tried to stay in the middle of the current, but Abbie went in the middle. On the sides, and even in the trees. When they were finished. Both Abbie and Kristi were all wet. "Well at least we're not so hot anymore!" said Abbie.

FUSED SENTENCES AND COMMA SPLICES

Fused Sentences

A **fused sentence** consists of two or more sentences incorrectly joined without any punctuation. A fused sentence does not clearly show where one idea ends and another begins.

Incorrect: Many different invaders have settled Spain over the years the Romans were only one group to conquer Spain.

Incorrect: Roman soldiers first invaded Spain more than two hundred years before Christ's birth Rome eventually ruled both Spain and Portugal.

Comma Splices

A **comma splice** consists of two or more sentences incorrectly joined by only a comma. Like a fused sentence, a comma splice does not clearly separate the two sentences.

Incorrect: The Romans built many roads and bridges in Spain, their most impressive structures may be the aqueducts.

Incorrect: The Romans' language was Latin, Spanish developed from Latin over a period of several centuries.

You can correct a fused sentence or a comma splice by separating the sentences or by joining them correctly. If you separate the sentences with an end mark, remember to begin the next sentence with a capital letter. In order to join them correctly, first make sure the ideas are clearly and logically related. Then, join them with either a comma and a coordinating conjunction or a semicolon.

Correct: Many different invaders have settled Spain over the years. The Romans were only one group to conquer Spain.

Correct: Roman soldiers first invaded Spain more than two hundred years before Christ's birth. Rome eventually ruled both Spain and Portugal.

Correct: The Romans built many roads and bridges in Spain, but their most impressive structures may be the aqueducts.

Correct: The Romans' language was Latin; Spanish developed from Latin over a period of several centuries.

Practice the Skill

Label each group of words *S* (sentence), *FS* (fused sentence), or *CS* (comma splice).

_______ 1. Rodrigo Diaz de Vivar, a famous Spanish soldier, is commonly known as El Cid.

_______ 2. Beginning in 1086, several Spanish cities did not want to be conquered by King Alfonso VI they asked the Muslim Almoravids to help them.

_______ 3. The Almoravids conquered much of Spain, Seville fell in 1091.

_______ 4. Many other cities were conquered Valencia did not fall to the Almoravids.

_______ 5. The Valencians rebelled against their ruler, and El Cid decided to take control of the city.

_______ 6. The Valencians did not want El Cid as their ruler, he blockaded the city for twenty months.

_______ 7. The Valencians faced starvation no one could take food into the city.

_______ 8. The city surrendered on June 17, 1094, El Cid allowed the people to own property and to choose their own religions.

_______ 9. El Cid ruled the city until his death in 1099.

_______ 10. El Cid is now considered a national hero, many stories about him are myths, however.

Review the Skill

Rewrite numbers 1–10, changing the fused sentences and comma splices to correct sentences. If a group of words is already a sentence, write *Sentence* in the blank.

11. ______________________________

12. ______________________________

____

13. ______________________________

14. ______________________________

15. ______________________________

16. ______________________________

17. ______________________________

18. ______________________________

____

19. ______________________________

20. ______________________________

Use the Skill

Rewrite the following paragraph to correct each fragment, fused sentence, or comma splice. There are five errors.

A famous Spanish national hero is El Cid his real name was Rodrigo Diaz de Vivar. The name *El Cid* probably comes from an Arabic term. He was born near Burgos, Spain. El Cid served in Sancho II's and Alfonso VI's armies, he was a famous warrior. An accusation of disloyalty in 1081. This accusation caused El Cid's banishment from Alfonso's army the armies suffered without the great warrior. El Cid paid men for his own personal army. His army gave him great power, he also had vast wealth. El Cid captured Valencia and became a great legend. *The Poem of the Cid* commemorates El Cid.

PROCESS PARAGRAPHS
Writing Traits: Ideas, Organization

Listen Up!
Read the mentor text. Can you identify the topic sentence of this passage?

MENTOR TEXT

Every summer, when the cows were giving the most milk, Mrs. Robertson would make enough cheese to carry the family through the winter.

She saved a gallon of milk from each of the morning and evening milkings and let it stand overnight. The next morning she soaked a small piece of rennet in half a cup of water. Rennet, made from the dried stomach of a newborn calf, makes the protein particles in the milk clump together. Soon after she added the rennet water to the milk, whey (watery milk) appeared on top and curds (thick, custardlike clumps of protein) underneath. She cut the curds into small cubes, then stirred the curds and whey over a small fire. When the curds crumbled, she strained off the whey by pouring the mixture into a loosely woven basket lined with cheesecloth. Next, she mixed in some salt. The salted curds were stored in a cool place. Heavy weights (stones or bricks) were placed on top, and over many months the cheese was pressed until it became compact and solid. This was called curing the cheese.

—Barbara Greenwood, *A Pioneer Sampler*

Try outlining the process Mrs. Robertson uses. What words helped to guide you through the cheese-making process?

Take Notes!
In your own words, define a process paragraph and describe how it is organized.

A process paragraph details a series of steps for doing or making something. All the steps should be explained. What if Mrs. Robertson forgot to soak the piece of rennet in water? Would the curds separate from the whey? What if a homeowner forgot to include his street address when giving directions to his house? Or what if internet instructions forgot to include the "install" step? All necessary steps must be included when explaining a process.

Not all process paragraphs need to have the steps in a chronological sequence. For instance, a financial expert could explain how to budget money, or a teacher could explain how to set up a class notebook. A strict *chronological* order might not be necessary in such cases, but the steps should be in a *logical* order the reader or listener can follow. Each step should be clear—avoid wordiness or irrelevant details. Remember, your purpose is to be considerate of your readers. How can you best guide them through the process?

WRITING TOOLBOX

Process Paragraph Outline

I. Topic Sentence (identifies the process to be described; sometimes identifies the purpose of the process)
II. Body (lists the steps of the process)
III. Conclusion (states or restates the purpose of the process)

Transitional Words

Try reading the mentor text without the transitional words. Did it make as much sense? How do the transitional words help the reader or listener? The following are possible transitional words for detailing a process:

first	second	next	last
to begin with	then	eventually	ultimately
before	during	after that/afterward	finally
initially	meanwhile	following that	in the end
in the beginning	once you have	later	the final stage/step

Partner Up!

1. Take turns orally explaining the steps for performing your favorite hobby or skill to your partner (e.g., how to make chocolate chip cookies, how to serve a volleyball, or how to budget your study time).
2. Take turns retelling your process, this time pointing out your thesis statement, the transitional words you use, and your concluding statement.
3. Carefully listen to your partner's process, and give suggestions to improve clarity.

Try It Out!

Now explain that process in writing. Remember your audience's need for logically ordered and clearly connected points to aid understanding.

1. Write an outline for the process you explained to your partner.
2. Write a process paragraph that includes a clear thesis statement, clearly identifiable steps indicated by transition words, and a concluding statement.

CHAPTER REVIEW

Sentence Types and Punctuation

Identify each sentence as *declarative, interrogative, imperative,* or *exclamatory*. Place the appropriate punctuation mark at the end of each sentence.

_______________ 1. What is your favorite month of the year

_______________ 2. My favorite month is May

_______________ 3. Lilies, May's official flowers, are so beautiful

_______________ 4. Tell me which birthstone belongs to the month of May

_______________ 5. If you look in the encyclopedia, you will find the answer

Simple Subjects

Find the simple subject, single or compound, in each sentence. Write in the blank the letter that corresponds to the correct answer.

_____ 6. The lovely month of May has some of the most pleasant weather of the year.
- **A** month
- **B** May
- **C** weather

_____ 7. During May, spring flowers are just beginning to bloom.
- **A** May, spring
- **B** spring, flowers
- **C** flowers

_____ 8. White and pink dogwoods and blue and yellow violets are some of May's flowers.
- **A** dogwoods, violets
- **B** pink dogwoods, yellow violets
- **C** white and pink, blue and yellow

_____ 9. Look at the mother birds waiting for their eggs to hatch.
- **A** birds
- **B** (You)
- **C** Look

_____ 10. The green appearance of the landscape and the new flowers are two exciting occurrences in May.
- **A** appearance, landscape
- **B** landscape, flowers
- **C** appearance, flowers

Simple Predicates

Find the simple predicate, single or compound, in each sentence. Write in the blank the letter that corresponds to the correct answer.

_______ 11. When is Mother's Day officially celebrated?
- **A** officially celebrated
- **B** is celebrated
- **C** is officially

_______ 12. On Mother's Day, give your mother a present and show her your gratefulness.
- **A** give, present
- **B** give, gratefulness
- **C** give, show

_______ 13. Armed Forces Day, the third Saturday of May, recognizes all divisions of the military and honors those in the armed forces.
- **A** recognizes, divisions
- **B** honors, forces
- **C** recognizes, honors

_______ 14. Do you observe Memorial Day on the last Monday of May?
- **A** Do you
- **B** Do observe
- **C** you observe

_______ 15. Here are the flowers placed on the soldiers' graves by family members.
- **A** are placed
- **B** (You)
- **C** flowers

Conjunctions and Interjections

Underline each coordinating or correlative conjunction once and each interjection twice.

16. My friend Wanda is deaf, but she and I still have much in common.
17. When I complete my sign language class, she and I will be able to communicate better.
18. Wow! The class is both interesting and challenging!
19. Sign language is a silent yet expressive form of communication.
20. Well, as a result of taking the class, I hope to begin a deaf ministry in my church or my community.

Brooklyn Bridge

Sentence Structure

Label each group of words *S* (sentence), *F* (fragment), *FS* (fused sentence), or *CS* (comma splice).

_______ 21. On May 8, 1884, Harry S. Truman was born, John F. Kennedy was born on May 29, 1917.

_______ 22. Charles Lindbergh flew solo across the Atlantic on May 21, 1927, and Amelia Earhart was the first woman to fly across the Atlantic on May 20, 1932.

_______ 23. The opening of the Brooklyn Bridge on May 24, 1883, and the Golden Gate Bridge on May 27, 1937.

_______ 24. May 10, 1869, marks the completion of the first continental railroad a golden spike was used at the completion point.

_______ 25. The British abandoned the occupation of Palestine on May 14, 1948, Israel was then an independent nation.

CHAPTER 3

VERBS

HOW CAN VERBS AFFECT MY READER'S FEELINGS?

Think of the different ways you can say "My friend spoke": "My friend yelled." "My friend whispered." "My friend argued." "My friend pleaded." Although the verbs in these sentences all describe vocal communication, they imply very different ideas that may affect the way you feel about the situation.

DISCOVER!

The passage below describes life during Colonial times. Read this selection and see whether you can identify the action verbs.

MENTOR TEXT

Rachel stood in a dark corner of her father's barn. Earthy aromas perfumed the air, and morning light filtered through cracks in the planked walls. The cows were munching, the sheep bleating, the pigs slopping, and the chickens brooding. Two geese pecked at kernels of corn scattered over the dirt floor. The dog lay by a fire beneath the laundry cauldron, where a week's worth of wash simmered in scented water.

—Thomas J. Brodeur, *Regina Silsby's Secret War*

What kind of picture do these action verbs help create in your mind? How do these verbs affect the reader and contribute to the overall mood of the selection? How important is it to use language that will affect the reader?

RECOGNIZING VERBS

A **verb** expresses action (what someone or something does) or state of being (what someone or something is like).

An **action verb** shows either external or internal action.

Morgan *rode* the bike.
Morgan *thought* about the bike.

A **state-of-being verb** describes a state or condition. The most common state-of-being verb is the word *be*, which has eight forms (*am*, *is*, *are*, *was*, *were*, *be*, *being*, *been*).

The bike *was* old.
It *is* too old to repair.

Because a verb acts as the main word in the predicate, it is important to know how to find verbs in sentences. Nearly every verb can have *-s* or *-ing* added to it without changing the verb's root meaning. Any word that fits into the following test frames can be a verb:

Verb Test Frame	
He/It _____s.	He/It is ______ing.
He runs.	He is running.
It floats.	It is floating.

Practice the Skill

Underline the verbs.

1. The Hebrew language is one of the oldest languages in the world.
2. The Hebrew alphabet consists of twenty-two letters.
3. One writes Hebrew from right to left, unlike English with its left-to-right movement.
4. Hebrew is the language of some of the oldest and best works of literature.
5. The Old Testament has the most remaining examples of ancient Hebrew.
6. The Jews revived the language after their reunification in Israel.
7. Many Jewish people around the world speak Hebrew today.
8. Hebrew speakers throughout the world pronounce the Hebrew language differently from each other.
9. Modern Hebrew literature includes novels about important current issues.
10. Mastery of classical Hebrew remains a goal for some modern scholars.

Review the Skill

Underline the verbs. Identify each verb as *action* or *state-of-being*.

_______________ 11. Hannah dedicated her son to God.

_______________ 12. As a child Samuel lived at the temple.

_______________ 13. Eli was the high priest at this time.

_______________ 14. One night a strange voice woke Samuel.

_______________ 15. Samuel ran into Eli's room.

_______________ 16. "Here am I."

_______________ 17. Samuel listened to Eli's advice.

_______________ 18. The Lord called Samuel again.

_______________ 19. This time Samuel was ready.

_______________ 20. Now Samuel is the messenger of God.

Use the Skill

Look at numbers 1–20 and identify the sentences that have only state-of-being verbs. Revise these sentences to include at least one action verb.

TRANSITIVE AND INTRANSITIVE VERBS

A **transitive verb** (TrV) is an action verb that needs another word to complete the idea of the sentence. It is called a transitive verb because it transfers its action to a receiver in the predicate called a direct object.

A **direct object** (DO) is a noun or pronoun in the predicate that receives the action of a verb. To find the direct object, first find the subject and the verb; then ask "whom or what?"

S TrV DO
Luke repaired the car.
Luke repaired *what?* (car)

S TrV DO
I congratulated Nick.
I congratulated *whom?* (Nick)

The direct object is compound if more than one word answers the question "whom or what?"

S TrV DO DO
Luke repaired the car and the boat.
Luke repaired *what?* (car and boat)

S TrV DO DO
I congratulated Nick and Gerald.
I congratulated *whom?* (Nick and Gerald)

An **indirect object** (IO) is a noun or pronoun that tells *to whom* or *for whom* the verb's action is done. If a sentence has an indirect object, it always comes between the transitive verb and the direct object. To find the indirect object, first find the subject, verb, and direct object; then ask "to whom or for whom?"

S TrV IO DO
Annie gave her mother a gift.
Annie gave a gift *to whom?* (mother)

S TrV IO IO DO
Annie gave her mother and father an anniversary gift.
Annie gave an anniversary gift *to whom?* (mother and father)

An **intransitive verb** (InV) is an action verb that does not need a direct or indirect object to complete the idea of the sentence.

S InV
The violets bloomed.

S InV
The violets bloomed in the garden.

Practice the Skill

Label the sentence patterns *S-InV*, *S-TrV-DO*, or *S-TrV-IO-DO*. Write the labels above the appropriate words in each sentence.

1. God created Adam and Eve on the sixth day.
2. God granted Adam and Eve authority over all of the animals.
3. Adam named the animals.
4. Adam and Eve thrived in the garden.
5. God gave Adam a warning about the tree of knowledge of good and evil.
6. Adam and Eve still sinned against God.
7. They forfeited their home in the Garden of Eden.
8. God made them clothes from animal skins.
9. Then He sent them out of the garden.
10. Today, the world suffers because of sin.

Review the Skill

Label the sentence pattern *S-InV*, *S-TrV-DO*, or *S-TrV-IO-DO*. Write the labels above the appropriate words in each sentence.

11. Sin brings separation from God.
12. Old Testament saints needed a priest for representation before God.
13. The priests inherited no land from God.
14. Instead, God called them to ministry.
15. The people brought the priests animals for sacrifice on the altar.
16. Once a year the high priest entered the holy of holies.
17. There he sprinkled blood on the mercy seat.
18. At the cross, the need for an earthly high priest ceased.
19. God sent believers Jesus as their High Priest.
20. Today Jesus Christ intercedes for believers in heaven.

Use the Skill

Write two original sentences using transitive verbs and two original sentences using intransitive verbs.

LINKING VERBS

A **linking verb** (LV) does not show action. Instead, it acts something like an equal sign because it links the subject to a word in the predicate that renames or describes the subject. State-of-being verbs (*am, is, are, was, were, be, being, been*) often act as linking verbs.

S LV
Mrs. Crawford is a teacher.
Mrs. Crawford = teacher

S LV
Brownies are my favorite dessert.
Brownies = dessert

Some words can function as action verbs or linking verbs depending on how they are used in the sentence.

Hannah *smelled* the food. (The verb *smelled* is action because the subject did the action of smelling.)
The food *smells* good. (The verb *smells* is linking because the subject did not do the action of smelling.)
Isaiah *looked* for his glasses. (The verb *looked* is action because the subject did the action of looking.)
Isaiah's glasses *look* good on him. (The verb *look* is linking because the subject did not do the action of looking.)

Verbs Used as Either Action or Linking	
become	sound
stay	feel
grow	taste
seem	look
appear	remain
smell	

A **predicate noun** (PN) is a noun or pronoun in the complete predicate that follows the linking verb and renames the subject.

S LV PN
Elisha is a student.

A **predicate adjective** (PA) is an adjective in the complete predicate that follows the linking verb and describes the subject.

S LV PA
Elisha is smart.

It is possible for sentences to have either compound predicate nouns or compound predicate adjectives.

S LV PN PN
Elisha is a student and an athlete.

S LV PA PA
Elisha is smart and funny.

Practice the Skill

Label the sentence patterns *S-LV-PN* or *S-LV-PA*.
Write the labels above the appropriate words in each sentence.

1. Israel is a fascinating country.
2. The land of Israel is not very large.
3. Its lack of natural harbors was a protection against invaders from the sea.
4. The coastal plain was very open and fertile.
5. The central range was the site of Israel's most important cities.
6. Hazor became Palestine's largest city during the biblical period.
7. The terrain in Judea is very rugged.
8. The Jordan Valley is a small part of a fault from Africa to Asia.
9. The Dead Sea is very salty.
10. Woodlands and pasture were abundant in the territory of Gilead.

Review the Skill

Label the sentence patterns *S-InV*, *S-TrV-DO*, *S-TrV-IO-DO*, *S-LV-PN*, or *S-LV-PA*. Write the labels above the appropriate words in each sentence.

11. On his deathbed, Elisha called King Joash to his side.

12. With great love for Elisha, the king wept over him.

13. Elisha was a wise counselor for Israel.

14. Elisha gave Joash an assignment.

15. The king struck the ground with the arrows.

16. The arrows were symbols of God's deliverance.

17. After only three blows, the king became still.

18. The prophet's response sounded angry.

19. Now King Joash had only three deliverances from the Lord.

20. The victories of Israel were incomplete.

Use the Skill

Use linking verbs to write four original sentences describing somebody you admire.

HELPING VERBS

Helping verbs, also called *auxiliaries*, are words that are added to the main verb in a sentence to give a special meaning or emphasis or to express time.

Together, the helping verb and the main verb form the **complete verb**. A complete verb may be a single verb with no helping verbs, or it could have one or more helping verbs and the main verb.

> Jesus possibly *built* wooden items in Joseph's carpenter shop. (The action verb *built* is the complete verb.)
>
> He probably *had worked* with Joseph many times. (The helping verb *had* and the action verb *worked* make up the complete verb.)

State-of-being verbs are commonly used as helping verbs. Note that state-of-being verbs can be used as either a linking verb (which would be serving as the main verb in the sentence) or a helping verb.

> The secretary *is trying* to reach her boss by phone. (The state-of-being verb *is* is a helping verb because it is helping the main verb *trying*.)
>
> She *is* patient. (*Is* is the complete verb because it is acting as a linking verb.)

Common Helping Verbs

am	have	shall
is	has	should
are	had	can
was	do	could
were	does	may
be	did	might
being	will	must
been	would	

Troublesome Helping Verbs

May/Can

May usually means "to be allowed or permitted to." *Can* generally means "to have the ability to."

> You *may* go to the ball game after dinner.
>
> I am amazed that you *can* do fifty pushups.

Shall/Will

In older styles of English, *shall* and *will* often had different meanings. Today, *will* usually indicates the future.

> I *will* attend the concert tonight.
>
> Jordan *will* accompany me.
>
> You *will* meet us afterwards, right?

Shall is used in two main ways: a question of preference or a formal statement. Both ways include the pronouns *I* and *we*.

> *Shall* I find you a seat?
>
> We *shall* make every effort to serve you.
>
> I *shall* strive to make your stay a pleasant one.

Practice the Skill

Underline the complete verb in each sentence. Write *HV* over any helping verbs.

1. Paul uses a footrace as an example in his first letter to the Corinthians.
2. The Corinthians must have been familiar with this sport.
3. Races probably were held at the Olympic games in Greece.
4. Roman sports were more violent than Greek sports.
5. Men would fight each other to the death.
6. At other times they might place criminals, slaves, and even Christians in an arena with wild animals.
7. Often, the contestants did not have any weapons for protection.
8. The contestants could not survive the brutal attacks.
9. Many people had been killed in the Roman arenas by the end of the era.
10. The Romans did many disgusting things merely for entertainment.

Review the Skill

Underline the correct verb from the choices in parentheses.

11. (May, Can) we attend the performance of *Two Gentlemen of Verona* tonight, Mom?
12. Debora (may, can) give us a ride.
13. Mr. Pierce (will, shall) direct the play.
14. (May, Can) we get the actors' autographs after the play?
15. (Will, Shall) we go to our seats?
16. We (will, shall) sit on the main floor in the fifth row.
17. Soon the curtain (will, shall) rise.
18. The actors (may, can) play their parts well.
19. (Will, Shall) we go home now?
20. (May, Can) we see another play sometime soon?

Use the Skill

Write a five-sentence story in which you tell of a real or fictional conversation you had with your parent about wanting to go to a friend's party. Use *may* or *can* and *will* or *shall* at least one time.

PRINCIPAL PARTS OF VERBS

Verbs have four basic forms: **present**, **present participle**, **past**, and **past participle**. These forms are called the **principal** (or main) **parts** of a verb.

The **present participle** is formed by adding *-ing* to the present form of the verb.

The **past participle** uses a form of the helping verb *have* and the past form of the verb.

Most verbs are considered **regular verbs.** They form the past and past participle by adding *-d* or *-ed* to the present.

Present	Present Participle	Past	Past Participle
climb	climbing	climbed	(have) climbed
hope	hoping	hoped	(have) hoped

Irregular verbs form the past and past participle in various ways.

Present	Present Participle	Past	Past Participle
begin	beginning	began	(have) begun
take	taking	took	(have) taken

Note that the "irregularity" of irregular verbs does not extend to the present participle; it is still formed the same way. Only the past and past participle forms are affected.

The table on pages 76–77 lists the principle parts for some irregular and troublesome verbs. Words marked with an asterisk (*) are regular verbs but are often mistakenly treated as irregular verbs and are therefore considered troublesome. The present participle is not included in this list.

Present	Past	Past Participle
bring	brought	(have) brought
burst	burst	(have) burst
choose	chose	(have) chosen
climb*	climbed*	(have) climbed*
come	came	(have) come
do	did	(have) done
drag*	dragged*	(have) dragged*
draw	drew	(have) drawn
drink	drank	(have) drunk
drive	drove	(have) driven

Present	Past	Past Participle
drown*	drowned*	(have) drowned*
eat	ate	(have) eaten
fall	fell	(have) fallen
feed	fed	(have) fed
get	got	(have) got, gotten
give	gave	(have) given
go	went	(have) gone
grow	grew	(have) grown
hang*	hanged*	(have) hanged*
hang	hung	(have) hung
keep	kept	(have) kept
lay	laid	(have) laid
lead	led	(have) led
lie	lay	(have) lain
ride	rode	(have) ridden
ring	rang	(have) rung
rise	rose	(have) risen
run	ran	(have) run
see	saw	(have) seen
set	set	(have) set
shine	shined*	(have) shined*
shine	shone	(have) shone
shrink	shrank, shrunk	(have) shrunk, shrunken
sing	sang, sung	(have) sung
sit	sat	(have) sat
slay	slew	(have) slain
sneak*	sneaked, snuck*	(have) sneaked, snuck*
speak	spoke	(have) spoken
steal	stole	(have) stolen
swim	swam	(have) swum
take	took	(have) taken
throw	threw	(have) thrown

Practice the Skill

Underline the correct verb from the choices in parentheses. Check for any helping verbs before you choose the verb.

1. After Jesus' death, his friends (took, taken) his body to the tomb.
2. On the first day of the week, several women (went, gone) to the sepulcher.
3. An angel (sit, sat) at the tomb's entrance.
4. In the garden, Mary had (saw, seen) Jesus.
5. Jesus had (spoke, spoken) Mary's name.
6. She (fell, fallen) at Jesus' feet.
7. The two disciples had (ran, run) to the empty tomb.
8. Jesus (slew, slain) death.
9. He had (rose, risen) from the dead.
10. The time had (come, came) for Jesus to return to heaven.

Review the Skill

Write in the blank the correct past or past participle form of the verb in parentheses.

________________ 11. The historian Josephus (*write*) about the destruction of Jerusalem.

________________ 12. In the early first century, tension (*grow*) between the Jews and the Romans.

________________ 13. By AD 66 fighting had (*break*) out.

________________ 14. The High Priest Ananias had (*oppose*) the revolt.

________________ 15. The Jewish rebels quickly (*kill*) him.

________________ 16. In AD 70 the Romans (*destroy*) Jerusalem.

________________ 17. They (*carry*) off the golden candlesticks, the trumpets, and the other valuable pieces from the temple.

________________ 18. A few small groups of Jews (*resist*) for three more years.

________________ 19. Masada (*fall*) to the Roman army in AD 73.

________________ 20. The Romans had (*conquer*) the Jews.

TROUBLESOME VERB PAIRS

There are three verb pairs that give many people trouble either because they do not understand the meaning of each word in the pair or because they mistake a transitive verb for an intransitive verb. Knowing the verbs' meanings and principal parts helps writers use them correctly.

Lie/Lay

The verb *lie* means "to recline." It is an intransitive verb and never has a direct object.

lie: Every afternoon I *lie* on the plush new carpet to rest.
lying: My dog often joins me when I *am lying* there.
lay: Yesterday, I *lay* on the couch instead.
lain: I *had lain* there for only ten minutes before I fell asleep.

The verb *lay* means "to put or place." It is a transitive verb and must have a direct object.

lay: Every afternoon I *lay* my backpack on my bed.
laying: I *have been laying* it on my bed all year.
laid: Yesterday, I *laid* my backpack on the table.
laid: Mom was surprised that I *had laid* my backpack down neatly.

Sit/Set

The verb *sit* means "to be in a seated position." It is an intransitive verb and does not have a direct object.

sit: I *sit* at my desk to do my homework.
sitting: I *had been sitting* at my dad's desk.
sat: Last week I *sat* at a new desk to use the computer.
sat: Because I *had sat* at the same desk for so long, the new one seemed strange.

The verb *set* means "to put or place." It is a transitive verb and requires a direct object.

set: Jordan *sets* his books on the shelf.
setting: He *will be setting* them there tomorrow.
set: He *set* them there yesterday.
set: However, his sister *has set* the books on the floor so she can dust.

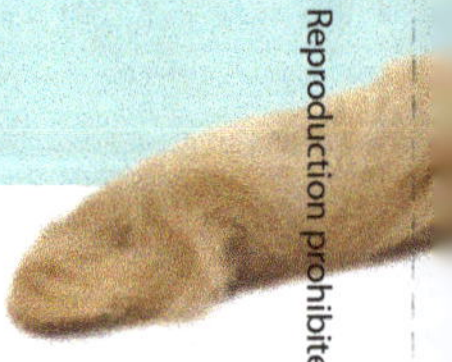

Rise/Raise

The verb *rise* means "to go up." It is an intransitive verb and does not have a direct object.

rise: The muffins *rise* quickly.
rising: They *are rising* right now.
rose: The bread *rose* slowly yesterday.
risen: By now both loaves *have risen* to twice their size.

The verb *raise* means "to make something go up." It is a transitive verb and requires a direct object.

raise: When I need to ask a question in class, I *raise* my hand.
raising: I *was raising* my hand when the teacher called on me.
raised: Alayna *raised* the trophy after her victory in the soccer game.
raised: She *has raised* a trophy in the last three games she has won.

Practice the Skill

Underline the correct verb from the choices in parentheses.

1. Development in printing technology (rose, raised) competition between newspaper publishers.
2. Workers (sit, set) the newspaper type in proper position and prepared the type with the proper ink.
3. This type, which consisted of raised characters carved on separate wood or metal blocks, (sat, set) on a wooden shelf waiting to be used.

4. Newspaper men (rose, raised) very early in the morning.
5. These men had to be sure they (sit, set) everything in order and had the type arranged and ready to use.
6. The job was tedious, and if these men had (lain, laid) down, they would probably have fallen asleep.
7. The men (sat, set) each letter down carefully next to the others.
8. When they (rose, raised) the letter board, every letter had to remain in place.
9. To protect their backs from hurting, some printers (sat, set) in high-backed chairs while they arranged the letters.
10. After everything was finished, the men (lay, laid) down in complete exhaustion.

Review the Skill

Write in the blank the correct form of *lie/lay*, *sit/set*, or *rise/raise*. Some sentences may have more than one correct answer.

______________________ 11. Dad _?_ from his chair to get the Bible.

______________________ 12. He often _?_ in his chair when he reads the Bible.

______________________ 13. Dad _?_ his Bible on the shelf near the door.

______________________ 14. I usually _?_ on the sofa while I read the Bible.

______________________ 15. I _?_ early in the morning to spend at least an hour in God's Word.

______________________ 16. When I'm finished, I usually _?_ my Bible on the end table by my bed.

______________________ 17. Last year, my dad and I decided to _?_ money to send Bibles to people in poor countries.

______________________ 18. Since we were able to send over so many Bibles with the money we received, we _?_ a goal to do this every year.

______________________ 19. It makes us happy to think of people in other countries who can now _?_ at their tables and read God's Word to their families.

______________________ 20. Recently, many publishers have _?_ the price for new Bibles.

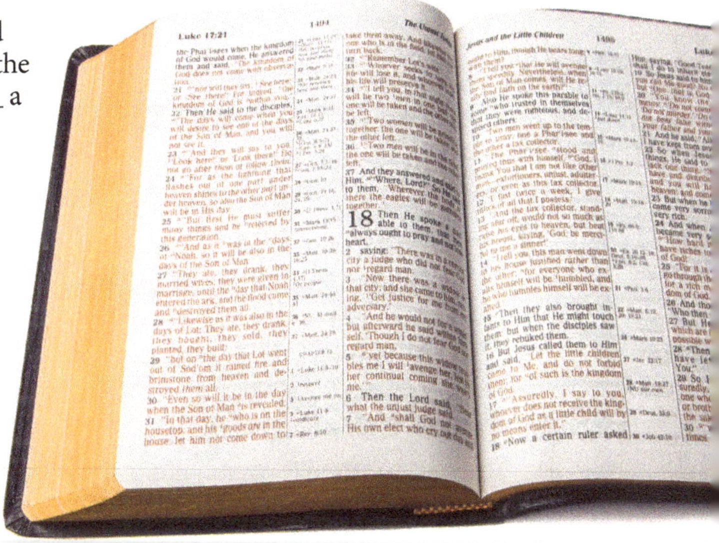

Use the Skill

Write six sentences about what has happened to you so far this school year. In your sentences, write a correct form for each troublesome verb.

THE SIMPLE TENSES

Most verbs change their form to indicate time: present, past, or future. **Tense** helps differentiate what happened yesterday from what is happening today and what will happen tomorrow. All tenses are made from the four principal parts.

There are three **simple tenses**: **present**, **past**, and **future**.

Present Tense

The present tense sometimes makes a statement about something that is true right now. The present tense form of a verb is the same as the verb's present principal part.

God *loves* us.
He *sees* all our actions.

With action verbs, the present tense tells what is usually or habitually done.

We *use* math skills every day.

When a singular noun or the pronoun *he*, *she*, or *it* is the subject of the sentence, *-s* or *-es* is added to the present tense.

The runner *sprints* to the finish line.
He *wishes* he can go.

When a plural noun, a pronoun, or *I* or *you* is the subject of the sentence, the present tense verb does not change.

The fans *cheer* the sprinters on.
We *cheer* for some of the same people.
I *cheer* for my favorite athletes.
You *cheer* for your friends too.

Past Tense

The past tense tells what has already occurred. The past principal part is used for the past tense.

Collin *moved* the equipment out of the way.
Gerald almost *tripped* over a loose cord.

Future Tense

The future tense makes a statement about something that will happen in the future. The future tense form of the verb uses the present principal part plus the helping verbs *will* or *shall*.

Holli's friends *will arrive* shortly for the party.
She *will know* about the surprise soon enough.

Practice the Skill

Underline the verbs. Identify each verb as *past*, *present*, or *future* tense.

____________________ 1. Philippi gets its name from Philip of Macedon, Alexander the Great's father.

____________________ 2. Philip conquered the city shortly after 360 BC.

____________________ 3. Paul first introduced the gospel to Philippi about four hundred years later.

____________________ 4. At Philippi, Paul saw his first European converts.

____________________ 5. These converts included Lydia and a jailer.

____________________ 6. The Philippian Christians remained loyal to Paul even during his imprisonment.

____________________ 7. Paul wrote the book of Philippians while a Roman prisoner.

____________________ 8. In it he warns the Philippians of the danger of disunity and pride.

____________________ 9. He instructs them in the importance of servanthood.

____________________ 10. This book will encourage readers in times of trial.

Review the Skill

Complete each sentence with the given verb in the tense indicated.

__________________ 11. Jerusalem _?_ a very old city with a rich history. (*state-of-being*, present)

__________________ 12. In ancient times it _?_ near important trade routes. (*lie*, past)

__________________ 13. It also _?_ a strategic military stronghold for the nation who controlled it. (*provide*, past)

__________________ 14. The Bible possibly _?_ its first mention of Jerusalem in Genesis 14:18. (*make*, present)

__________________ 15. In this passage, Melchizedek, king of Salem (Jerusalem), _?_ Abraham after Abraham's rescue of Lot. (*greet*, present)

__________________ 16. King David _?_ the central location of the city of Jerusalem. (*see*, past)

__________________ 17. He _?_ Jerusalem the capital of the united kingdom of Israel. (*make*, past)

__________________ 18. After Rome destroyed Jerusalem in AD 70, control of the city _?_ into the hands of many different nations. (*pass*, past)

__________________ 19. Tensions between Arabs and Jews regarding control of Jerusalem most likely _?_ for years to come. (*exist*, future)

__________________ 20. Jerusalem _?_ as a reminder of God's provision for His people in the past. (*stand*, future)

THE PERFECT TENSES

Perfect tenses tell about actions that are completed, or perfected. Perfect tenses are formed by using the past participle along with some form of the helping verb *have*.

Tense	Helping Verb
present perfect	have/has
past perfect	had
future perfect	will have/shall have

Present Perfect Tense

The **present perfect tense** expresses a state of being or action that has been completed during the present time or one that began in the past and has continued to the present. This tense is made by combining the present tense of the helping verb *have* and the past participle of the main verb.

have/has	+	walked	=	have/has walked
(present tense)		(past participle)		(present perfect tense)

I *have walked* to the park many times.
She *has walked* to the library.

Past Perfect Tense

The **past perfect tense** expresses an action that was completed (or a state that existed) before a certain time or event in the past. The past perfect tense is formed using *had* (the past tense of the helping verb *have*) along with the past participle of the main verb.

had	+	walked	=	had walked
(past tense)		(past participle)		(past perfect tense)

Ricky *had walked* all the way home before his mom arrived.

Future Perfect Tense

The **future perfect tense** tells about an action that will be completed before a future time or event takes place. This tense is formed by taking *will have* or *shall have* (the future tense of *have*) and adding the past participle of the main verb.

will/shall have	+	walked	=	will/shall have walked
(future tense)		(past participle)		(future perfect tense)

Rosie *will have walked* twenty miles by the end of the week.

Practice the Skill

Complete each section with the given verb in the tense indicated.

______________________ 1. The first century Jews _?_ being under Roman rule. (*resent*, past)

______________________ 2. They _?_ that Christ would deliver them from Roman domination. (*hope*, past perfect)

______________________ 3. Some Jews today still _?_ forward to the coming of their Messiah. (*look*, present)

______________________ 4. By the time Christ returns, many people _?_ still looking for His coming. (*die*, future perfect)

______________________ 5. When Jerusalem fell in AD 70, God's people _?_ over various continents. (*scatter*, past perfect)

______________________ 6. Since that time, the Jewish people _?_ much pain and persecution. (*endure*, present perfect)

______________________ 7. Today, many Jews _?_ to their homeland. (*return*, present perfect)

______________________ 8. However, political unrest still _?_ the nation of Israel. (*threaten*, present)

______________________ 9. By the time they reach middle age, most Israeli men and women _?_ in the military. (*serve*, future perfect)

______________________ 10. Lasting peace _?_ to Israel only when Christ returns. (*come*, future)

Review the Skill

Write sentences using the tenses indicated. Use verbs other than state-of-being verbs wherever possible.

11. Tell about your most enjoyable vacation. (past)

12. Write a sentence about what you think you will do next week. (future)

13. Describe what you had done before your last birthday party ended. (past perfect)

14. Tell about the house you live in now. (present)

15. Write a sentence about one thing you plan to have accomplished by the time you are seventy. (future perfect)

16. Tell about your favorite Christmas tradition. (present perfect)

17. Tell about something you owned that was broken by you. (past)

18. Write one sentence about your favorite novel. (present)

19. Write about your favorite household chore. (present)

20. Tell about the job you intend to have when you grow up. (future)

Use the Skill

Write a five-sentence paragraph describing an issue that is important to you. Use a mixture of *past perfect*, *present perfect*, and *future perfect* tenses.

USING TENSES CONSISTENTLY
Writing Traits: Organization, Voice

Listen Up!

The following selection describes the life of a farm boy living during the Civil War. Read the mentor text and identify all the verbs.

MENTOR TEXT

Ellen Creighton and her nine-year-old son, Jethro, were planting potatoes in the half-acre just south of their cabin that morning in mid-April, 1861; they were out in the field as soon as breakfast was over, and southern Illinois at that hour was pink with sunrise and swelling redbud and clusters of bloom over the apple orchard across the road. Jethro walked on the warm clods of plowed earth and felt them crumble beneath his feet as he helped his mother carry the tub of potato cuttings they had prepared the night before. . . .

He filled a burlap pouch with the potato cuttings and hoisted it expertly to his thin shoulder where a batch of new freckles was just beginning to appear. The world seemed a good place to him that morning, and he felt ready to stride down the length of the field with a firm step and a joke on his lips.

—Irene Hunt, *Across Five Aprils*

Now that you have found the verbs, identify the tense of these verbs. Rewrite the paragraph, changing only half of the verbs to a different tense. Is the paragraph better or worse? How does the tense of the verbs affect the paragraph?

GRAMMAR TOOLBOX

Take Notes!

Using your own words, explain why writers need to use consistent verb tense.

Good writers are careful to use consistent verb tense in their writing. Since tenses communicate time, using different tenses when describing one event will confuse the reader. Consider this example:

> Jared *eats* two pieces of pie every night and *drank* a glass of milk.

Does the sentence describe an event that is currently taking place, or does it describe a past event? We cannot tell because it uses the present-tense verb *eat* and the past-tense verb *drank*. The writer's voice is inconsistent. The tense of one of these verbs needs to change in order to avoid confusing the reader.

> Jared *eats* two pieces of pie every night and *drinks* a glass of milk.
> Jared *ate* two pieces of pie every night and *drank* a glass of milk.

Partner Up!

Rewrite each sentence using consistent verb tense.

1. I don't eat my food until I first thanked God for my meal.

   ____

2. Because Patrick swam on the swim team, he will practice the butterfly stroke every day.

   ____

3. When his car broke down, Chris calls a tow truck.

   ____

Try It Out!

Think of a future event that you are looking forward to. Write a paragraph about that event as though it already happened. Use the past tense consistently.

PROGRESSIVE VERBS

Progressive verbs show an action happening over a period of time.

Jariah *is learning* to drive.
Trenton *was flying* his remote-controlled plane.

Each of the six tenses you learned about has a progressive form. It is formed by using a state-of-being verb as a helping verb and by adding *-ing* to the main verb. The table on page 93 shows how to form progressive verbs using the verb *read*.

Practice the Skill

Underline the complete verb in each sentence. Identify the tense of the verb.

________________ 1. In Matthew 10 Jesus is talking to His disciples.

________________ 2. Prior to this passage, He had been healing the sick and disabled.

________________ 3. He was preaching the gospel to them as well.

________________ 4. Here, He is instructing His disciples in their responsibilities.

________________ 5. They will be taking neither money nor extra clothes with them for their journey.

________________ 6. They will rely on God and the hospitality of others for their needs.

________________ 7. In this passage Jesus warns the disciples about the fear of man.

________________ 8. The Holy Spirit will give them the right words at the right time.

________________ 9. By the end of the disciples' lives, many people will have been persecuting them for Jesus' sake.

________________ 10. Ever since His command to His disciples, Christ has been equipping willing and obedient Christians.

	Forms of *be*	Example with *read* + *-ing*
Present Progressive	present tense of *be*	He *is reading* his Bible. I *am reading* my Bible. They *are reading* their Bibles.
Past Progressive	past tense of *be*	He *was reading* his Bible. They *were reading* their Bibles.
Future Progressive	future tense of *be*	We *will be reading* our Bibles.
Present Perfect Progressive	present perfect tense of *be*	We *have been reading* our Bibles before the service each Sunday.
Past Perfect Progressive	past perfect tense of *be*	We *had been reading* until the service began.
Future Perfect Progressive	future perfect tense of *be*	We *will have been reading* our Bibles for ten minutes when the service begins.

Review the Skill

Write in the blank the progressive form of each italicized verb. Do not change the tense of the verb.

______________________ 11. The Old Testament Messianic prophecies *speak* of Christ.

______________________ 12. In these passages, God *discloses* some facts about Christ's coming.

______________________ 13. In Genesis 3:15, God *promised* that one day the seed of the woman would vanquish the serpent.

______________________ 14. God *narrows* the scope of the promise with the call of Abraham.

______________________ 15. In his prophecy, Jacob *identified* the Messiah as a king.

______________________ 16. The Messiah *will come* from King David's line.

______________________ 17. In 2 Samuel 7:12–14, God *tells* David that the Messiah will be God's Son.

______________________ 18. This passage *asserts* Christ's deity.

______________________ 19. As time went by, the prophecies *revealed* Christ to the Old Testament saints.

______________________ 20. Someday, Christ *will return* for all the Old Testament believers who put their faith in the promised Messiah.

ACTIVE AND PASSIVE VOICE

If the subject of a sentence does something or is something, the verb of that sentence is considered **active**.

S-LV-PA: The hit *was* good.
S-InV: The crowd *cheered*.
S-TrV-DO: The runner *rounded* the bases.

If the subject of a sentence is acted upon, the verb of that sentence is considered **passive**.

Active: The baseball *broke* the window.
Passive: The window *was broken*.
Active: Julia *found* the ball and glass on the couch.
Passive: The ball and glass *were found* on the couch by Julia.

Notice that the verb forms in the passive sentences have changed to include a state-of-being verb that is used as a helping verb. The passive voice is always formed by a state-of-being verb and the past participle.

Practice the Skill

Underline the complete verb in each sentence. Identify each verb as *active* or *passive*.

__________ 1. Both barley and wheat were grown as main food sources in Palestine during Bible times.

__________ 2. Often they were combined into a flour mixture.

__________ 3. Barley was used mainly as feed for cattle, horses, and mules.

__________ 4. However, poor people ate barley as well.

__________ 5. Wheat was often exported to surrounding nations.

__________ 6. Barley harvest begins in the spring.

__________ 7. Wheat harvest usually follows four weeks later.

__________ 8. Harvests of both barley and wheat are mentioned in the Bible.

__________ 9. Ruth returned to Bethlehem at the beginning of barley harvest.

__________ 10. Gideon was threshing wheat at the time of his call.

Review the Skill

Rewrite each sentence, changing it from passive voice to active voice. Do not change the tense of the verb.

11. Shadrach, Meshach, and Abednego were captured by the Babylonians.

____

12. The Babylonian people were ruled by Nebuchadnezzar.

____

13. A golden idol was built by Nebuchadnezzar's men.

____

14. The idol was worshiped by everyone.

____

15. The king's command was not followed by Shadrach, Meshach, and Abednego.

____

____

16. Shadrach, Meshach, and Abednego were thrown into the fiery furnace by the king's men.

____

____

17. The guards were killed by the flames.

____

18. No fear of death was shown by the three men.

____

19. The Son of God was seen with the three men by Nebuchadnezzar.

____

____

20. The king's heart was softened by God.

____

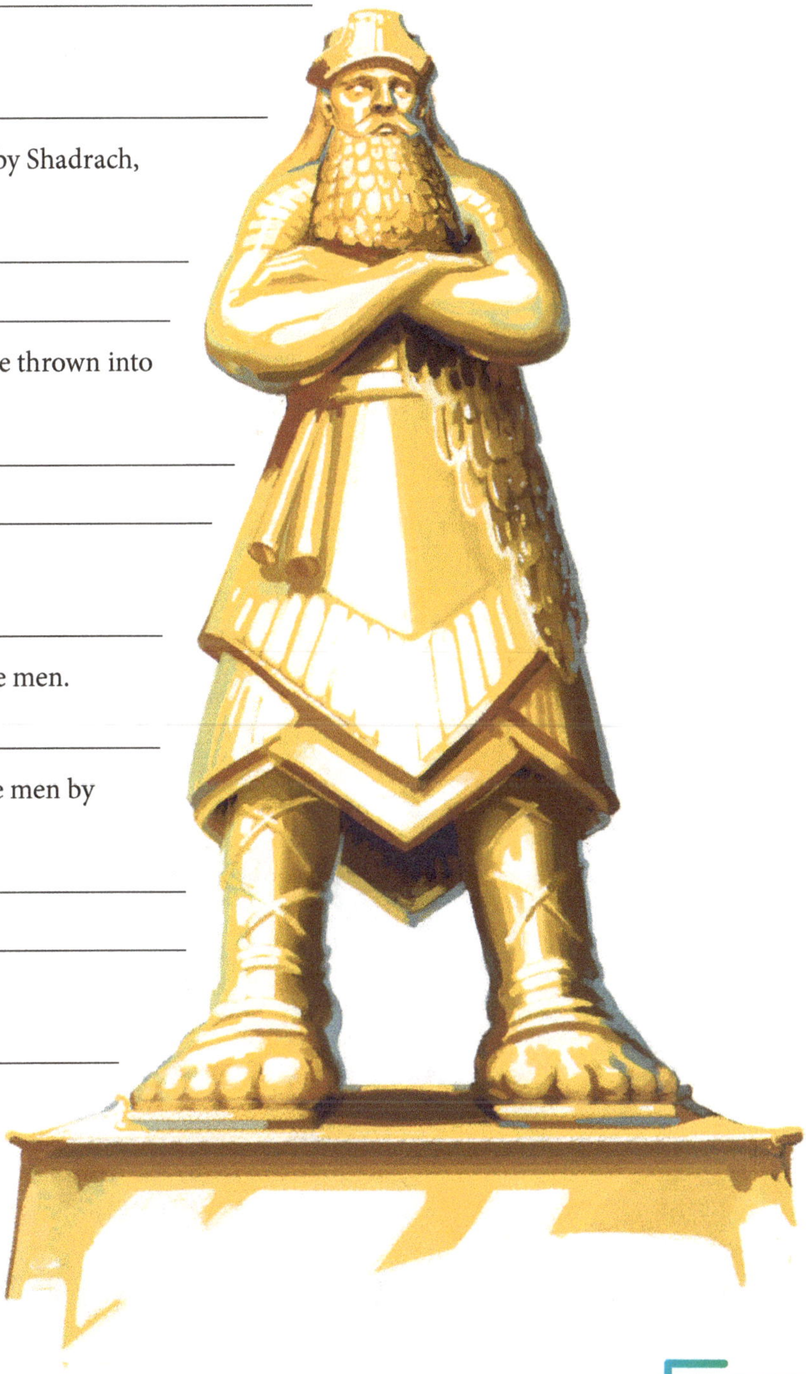

Use the Skill

Write a sentence to answer each question. Use active or passive voice as indicated in parentheses.

21. What happened to the car during the snowstorm? (active)

____

22. What happened during the orchestra's concert? (passive)

____

23. What happened when the family attended the fair? (active)

____

24. What do you do when you get locked out of your house? (active)

____

25. What happened when the lightning struck the tree? (passive)

____

26. What did the student say when asked where her essay was? (passive)

____

27. What happened when he bought a new car? (passive)

____

28. What unusual thing did the teacher tell you? (active)

____

29. What happened when the girl went to the amusement park? (active)

____

30. What happened during the basketball game? (passive)

____

USING ACTIVE AND PASSIVE VOICE
Writing Trait: Voice

Listen Up!

What was it like to be a Jewish person in Europe during the Nazi regime? The excerpt below gives us some understanding of how hard life was for Jewish people during that time. Read the excerpt, paying careful attention to whether each verb is active or passive.

MENTOR TEXT

In the late 1930s, the United States government could see the danger Jews were in. President Franklin Roosevelt and some members of Congress expressed concern, but little was done to change the immigration laws or bring refugees to the country in large numbers. Myron C. Taylor, who led the U.S. delegation to an international conference on political refugees in 1938, assured Americans that "our plans do not involve the 'flooding' of this or any other country with aliens of any race or creed." In 1939, the German ship *St. Louis*, which was carrying 933 refugees, was not allowed to land in the United States. Most of the passengers were already on the quota list but had not been fully processed. The ship was forced to return to Europe, and many of the passengers died during World War II.

Elise Radell, an eight-year-old German girl who was Jewish, was accepted by the United States. She remembered what happened to her home on November 9, 1938. The S.S., a German paramilitary group, "pushed us aside and came into the house. . . . they went about this utter destruction with axes. . . . [The] china closet was knocked all over and the pictures on the wall . . . and the furniture all just went. . . . The pillows were ripped and the feathers . . . just flew all over the house."

—Linda Barrett Osborne, *This Land Is Our Land: A History of American Immigration*

Does the author use active or passive voice more often?
Why do you think one voice is used more than the other?
What do you think are the advantages of using active voice? Passive voice?

Take Notes!

Use a T-Chart to list the rules for using active and passive voice.

When to Use Active Voice

Use active voice to create lively and strong writing. Passive voice is less concise because it uses more words, often making sentences awkward and unclear. Notice the difference between active and passive voice:

Passive Voice: He was first discouraged by the thought of all that work. Then he was reminded that he would be helped by God, and he was cheered up.

Active Voice: At first the thought of all that work discouraged him. Then he remembered that God would help him, and he cheered up.

When to Use Passive Voice

Even though active voice is better in most cases, in some instances, passive voice is useful.

- Use passive voice to avoid mentioning the doer of an action, especially when the doer is unimportant or unknown.
  The money was kept in the store's safe overnight.
  The doors to the Sunday School rooms are opened before 9:00 a.m. on Sunday.
- Use passive voice to be purposefully vague about who is responsible for committing the action. This is useful in bureaucratic writing when the writer wants to avoid accusing anyone in particular of something.
  The answers were copied off the paper.
  The game was lost.
- Use passive voice to emphasize the object of the action, especially when the object of the action is the subject of your writing. This often happens in journalistic writing.
  The bank was robbed last night.
- Use passive voice to emphasize the same subject for several verbs in a row. This will help your sentences flow more smoothly.
  Awkward: When parents ask children to help in the home, the children learn responsibility. If parents expect children to do their share, these children will also be more thoughtful as adults.
  Better: When children are asked to help in the home, they learn responsibility. If they are expected to do their share as children, they will also be more thoughtful as adults.
- Use passive voice to move certain words from the subject to the predicate. This is helpful if you have an awkwardly long phrase as a subject.
  Awkward: Parents, brothers and sisters, other relatives, and even friends teach the young child.
  Better: The young child is taught by parents, brothers and sisters, other relatives, and even friends.

Partner Up!

Read each sentence and explain whether it uses passive voice correctly. If it is incorrect, revise the sentence.

1. The bank was robbed last night.

____

____

2. It was decided by the congregation to take up a collection for the missionaries.

____

____

3. According to *The Maryland Gazette*, "The congressman has been accused of several crimes."

____

____

4. What was being said by the politician was found to be untrue by journalists.

____

____

Try It Out!

Think of an event that happened recently, either in school or in your personal life. Write about that event as a one-to-two-paragraph news article. Read your article aloud and identify when and why you used active and passive voice.

MOOD

Verbs can express different **moods**. The mood of a verb reflects the attitude of the writer. The three moods of verbs are **indicative**, **imperative**, and **subjunctive**.

Indicative mood is used for factual or declarative sentences.

> I *bought* my first car after I graduated from college.
> I still *drive* that car today.

Imperative mood expresses commands. Usually the subject *you* is understood but not expressed.

> *Take* out the trash.
> Luke, *look* both ways before you cross the street.

Subjunctive mood is used to express a wish or state a condition that is not true. These sentences often start with the word *if* and speak of something known to be untrue. Subjunctive mood uses the simple past form of the verb when making a statement about something in the present or future, and it uses the past perfect form of the verb when making a statement about something in the past.

> *Unknown factuality (not subjunctive):* If my dad *knows* that I broke the window, he will punish me.
> *Known to be untrue (subjunctive):* If my dad *knew* that I broke the window, he would punish me.

Practice the Skill

Identify the mood of each italicized verb as *indicative*, *imperative*, or *subjunctive*.

________________ 1. Please *study* the book of Hosea.

________________ 2. Hosea *lived* as a prophet of God during the reign of Jeroboam II.

________________ 3. God *told* Hosea to marry Gomer, who later left Hosea to pursue others.

________________ 4. If Hosea *had not married* Gomer, he would have disobeyed God.

________________ 5. This marriage *pictured* Israel's unfaithfulness to God.

________________ 6. Instead of divorcing Gomer, Hosea *restores* their relationship, just as God wanted to restore His relationship with Israel.

________________ 7. *Read* Hosea 6:6 to see what God expects from Israel.

________________ 8. I *find* Hosea to be a very interesting prophet.

________________ 9. If my pastor *were* to preach from Hosea, I would take careful notes.

________________ 10. *Tell* me of any good books you find on Hosea.

Review the Skill

Write sentences using the verbs and moods indicated.

11. go (imperative)

____

12. eat (indicative)

____

13. were (subjunctive)

____

14. watch (imperative)

____

15. sail (indicative)

____

16. had (subjunctive)

____

17. tell (imperative)

____

18. run (indicative)

____

19. came (subjunctive)

____

20. look (imperative)

____

CHAPTER REVIEW

Identifying Complete Verbs

Find the complete verb in each sentence. Write in the blank the letter that corresponds to the correct answer.

_______ 1. The Mississippi River has been considered one of the most important rivers in the United States.
- **A** has been
- **B** has been considered
- **C** considered

_______ 2. In the 1800s the river was regularly used as a means of transportation.
- **A** was used
- **B** was regularly used
- **C** regularly used as

_______ 3. The Mississippi River is steadily flowing from Minnesota into the Gulf of Mexico.
- **A** is steadily flowing
- **B** flowing
- **C** is flowing

_______ 4. On the border of Illinois and Missouri, the Illinois River and the Missouri River constantly flow into the Mississippi River.
- **A** constantly flow
- **B** flow
- **C** constantly flow into

_______ 5. Due to the muddiness of the Missouri River, the Mississippi also acquires a muddy appearance.
- **A** Mississippi also acquires
- **B** also acquires
- **C** acquires

Action and Linking Verbs

Underline the complete verb in each sentence. Identify each verb as (*A*) action or (*L*) linking.

_______ 6. The Mississippi River is a well-known river.

_______ 7. Mark Twain wrote about life on the Mississippi.

_______ 8. Some call the Mississippi "Old Man River."

_______ 9. The river can be one hundred feet deep in some places.

_______ 10. Sometimes the Mississippi floods after a heavy rain.

Sentence Patterns: S-InV, S-TrV-DO, and S-TrV-IO-DO

Identify the sentence pattern for each sentence. Write in the blank the letter that corresponds to the correct answer.

A S-InV
B S-TrV-DO
C S-TrV-IO-DO

_______ 11. Scouts traveled the Mississippi in exploration of the United States.

_______ 12. American Indians gave the Mississippi River its name.

_______ 13. The Mississippi flows from north to south.

_______ 14. Barges carry commercial products on the river.

_______ 15. The Mississippi provides commercial vessels an efficient transportation route.

Sentence Patterns: S-LV-PN and S-LV-PA

Identify the sentence pattern for each sentence. Write in the blank the letter that corresponds to the correct answer.

A S-LV-PN
B S-LV-PA

_______ 16. The Mississippi River appears murky in the southern states.

_______ 17. In the northern states, the river is a source of clear water.

_______ 18. The Gulf of Mexico is the final destination of the Mississippi River.

_______ 19. The Mississippi River grows deeper near the Gulf of Mexico.

_______ 20. Because of silt deposits, the land near the Gulf of Mexico has become a delta.

Verb Forms

Identify the correct verb to complete each sentence. Write in the blank the letter that corresponds to the correct answer.

_______ 21. When he was a boy, Duffee ? growing up near the Mississippi River.
- **A** enjoyed
- **B** is enjoying
- **C** will enjoy

_______ 22. By the time Duffee was twelve, he and his friend Darren already ? thousands of proud ships cruise down the rapid waters of the Mississippi.
- **A** has seen
- **B** see
- **C** had seen

_______ 23. Now that they are teenagers, Duffee and Darren ? their own boat for exploring the river.
- **A** wanted
- **B** want
- **C** had wanted

_______ 24. Duffee and Darren ? a sturdy raft in the next few days.
- **A** will build
- **B** building
- **C** have built

_______ 25. By next week, the boys ? far down the Mississippi in their light raft.
- **A** floated
- **B** will have floated
- **C** will float

Progressive Verbs

Complete each sentence with the given verb in the tense indicated.

_______________ 26. In the sweltering heat of the Mississippi, Duffee and Darren ? sluggishly on the water. (*drift,* past progressive)

_______________ 27. Later they noticed that the waters ? more rapidly than before. (*rush,* past progressive)

_______________ 28. Duffee exclaimed, "Darren, the water soon ? too fast for us to stop." (*move,* future progressive)

_______________ 29. A crewman on a large boat ? the boys, and he helped pull them from the river to the safety of the boat. (*watch,* past perfect progressive)

_______________ 30. By the time dinner is over, Duffee and Darren ? their family about their narrow escape for hours. (*tell,* future perfect progressive)

Active and Passive Voice

Identify the italicized verb as *active* or *passive*.

_______________ 31. The ship *moved* down the river.

_______________ 32. The ship *was steered* by the captain.

_______________ 33. During the night, the captain *was given* a warning.

_______________ 34. The safety of the ship *was threatened* by the shallow waters.

_______________ 35. The captain *steered* the ship safely through the dangerous area.

Verb Mood

Identify the mood of each underlined verb as *indicative*, *imperative*, or *subjunctive*.

_______________ 36. Mark Twain often <u>wrote</u> about life on the Mississippi River.

_______________ 37. <u>Read</u> about his characters' voyages on the Mississippi in *The Adventures of Huckleberry Finn.*

_______________ 38. Many people <u>enjoy</u> this book.

_______________ 39. If Mark Twain <u>were</u> alive today, he would be pleased to see so many people still enjoying his stories.

_______________ 40. <u>Visit</u> the Mark Twain home and museum if you are ever in Hartford, Connecticut.

CHAPTER 4

NOUNS

DO YOUR NOUNS TELL A VIVID STORY?

With over 100,000 words to choose from, nouns are by far the largest word group in the English language. The Trumpeter of Krakow, *written by Eric P. Kelly in 1928, uses vivid nouns to tell the story of a young man who gave his life to warn his countrymen about dangerous invaders. The author effectively uses concrete and proper nouns to help us picture what happened, where it happened, and to whom it happened. Abstract nouns are used to convey deep emotions and specific ideas in the story.*

DISCOVER!

MENTOR TEXT

It was in the spring of the year 1241 that rumors began to travel along the high-road from Kiev in the land of Rus that the Tartars of the East were again upon the march. Men trembled when they heard that news and mothers held their children close to their breasts, for the name "Tartar" was one that froze folks' blood in their veins. As the weeks went on, the rumors grew thicker and there began to come through to Poland, our land of the fields, the news that the country lands of the Ukraine were ablaze. Then it was heard that Kiev had fallen, then Lvov, the city of the Lion, and now there was naught between the savage band of warriors and the fair city of Krakow save a few peaceful villages and fertile fields.

—Eric P. Kelly, *The Trumpeter of Krakow*

Read the mentor text and complete the following exercise.
Underline the nouns in the mentor text. Choose a sentence from the mentor text and draw a picture to illustrate what the sentence describes. Use the nouns from the sentence to title your picture.

NOUN FORMS

Nouns Defined

A **noun** names a person, place, thing, or idea.

Person: carpenter, Mrs. Radford
Place: cornfield, Wrigley Field
Thing: snow, Washington Monument
Idea: friendship, patriotism

Noun Forms

Most nouns have four forms: singular, plural, singular possessive, and plural possessive. A **singular noun** indicates one person, place, thing, or idea. A **plural noun** indicates two or more persons, places, things, or ideas and is usually formed by adding *-s* or *-es* to the end of the word. A **possessive noun** shows ownership or belonging, telling who or what owns a thing.

Punctuation PowerUp
Use an apostrophe (') when making a noun possessive.

Possessive Noun Forms

Singular possessive: Add an apostrophe and *s* (*'s*) to the singular form of the noun (even if the singular form ends in *s*).

clock   clock's face
bus   bus's seats

Plural possessive: Add only an apostrophe (') to a plural noun that already ends in *s*. If a plural noun does not end in *s*, add an apostrophe and *s* (*'s*) to form the plural possessive.

governors   governors' luncheon
the Smiths   the Smiths' dog
mice   mice's nest

To form the singular possessive of a proper name ending in *s*, add an apostrophe and *s* (*'s*). *Jesus* and *Moses*, however, traditionally add only the apostrophe (').

Charles   Charles's opinion
Jesus   Jesus' love
Moses   Moses' brother

Practice the Skill

Rewrite each italicized phrase as an equivalent phrase containing a possessive noun.

1. John Chapman was one of *the famous pioneers of the Ohio frontier.*

2. Although he was part of *the population of Massachusetts* at birth, John Chapman spent most of his life in the Ohio region.

3. *The name of the frontiersmen* for John Chapman was Johnny Appleseed.

4. Johnny Appleseed earned his name because he traveled throughout *the northern and central parts of the Ohio wilderness* planting young trees and apple seeds.

5. As reimbursement for his seedlings and apple seeds, Johnny Appleseed would accept *the money of the people* or other items the pioneers offered.

6. *The wanderings of Johnny Appleseed* made him famous.

7. We know that he was not forgotten in *the memories of the pioneers.*

8. Johnny Appleseed helped meet *the needs of the settlers* by acting as a physician and using herbal medicine.

9. Also, during the War of 1812, Johnny Appleseed functioned as one of *the messengers of the frontier area.*

10. Johnny Appleseed was best known for his work with apple trees; these plants contributed to *the strength of the farming business* in Indiana and Ohio.

Review the Skill

Rewrite each phrase as an equivalent phrase containing a possessive noun.

11. the horse of the cowboy

____

12. the sod house of the family

____

13. the stalls of the horses

____

14. the squawk of the goose

____

15. the flight of the geese

____

16. the wagon of the Davises

____

17. the pond of the fish

____

18. the antlers of the deer

____

19. the games of the boys

____

20. the letter of the girl

____

Use the Skill

Brainstorm a list of five nouns related to social media. Include at least one singular noun, one plural noun, and one possessive noun. Write a short paragraph using the nouns you chose.

USING VIVID AND CONCRETE NOUNS
Writing Trait: Word Choice

Listen Up!

Eric Kelly helps the reader feel the building tension and dread in the town of Krakow through his effective description of their approaching enemy. Read the excerpt and note the author's vivid noun choices.

MENTOR TEXT

The Tartars came through the world like a horde of wild beasts. They left not one thing alive nor one green blade of wheat standing. They were short, dark men of shaggy beards and long hair twisted into little braids, and they rode on small horses which they covered with trophies that they had gained in war.

—Eric P. Kelly, *The Trumpeter of Krakow*

How did the author employ vivid nouns to make you picture the *who*, *what*, and *where* questions that nouns answer? Can you think of any nouns that could have been more vivid than the ones the author chose? Defend your choices.

Take Notes!

Explain the types of nouns in your own words. Provide 3–5 examples.

Nouns can be either concrete or abstract. **Concrete nouns** name people, places, and things that are *tangible*; that is, they are recognizable through one of the five senses (e.g., cat, bridge, field). **Abstract nouns** are *intangible*, meaning they are not directly identifiable by any of the five senses (e.g., loyalty, weakness, hope). Abstract nouns name ideas and concepts.

Vivid nouns are a type of concrete noun that makes writing clearer, more colorful, and more specific (*cat* [general]: *cheetah* [vivid]; *bridge* [general]: *drawbridge* [vivid]; *field* [general]: *cotton field* [vivid]). Choosing, whenever possible, nouns that are concrete and vivid will help to increase the clarity, meaning, precision, and power in your writing. Look at the following two sentences:

The mountain trees are beautiful and fragrant.
Mount Rainier's red cedars are beautiful and fragrant.

Which of these sentences provides a clearer picture? Using nouns that are too general could lead readers to come to imprecise or wrong conclusions. A *thesaurus* is a good resource for helping the writer pick out just the right word.

GRAMMAR TOOLBOX

A word of caution: Writers sometimes run the risk of sacrificing clarity or meaning in their compositions by choosing an uncommon or little-known word in an attempt to be creative. Make sure that the words you choose are familiar to your audience.

> The rugged western mesa stood like a rampart around the hamlet.
> The rugged western mountain stood like a protective wall around the village.

Which sentence provides a clearer meaning? In what ways might the other sentence leave the reader confused?

Partner Up!

Working with a partner, choose two vivid nouns to replace each underlined noun or phrase.

1. A <u>person</u> just gave me the most fascinating book on <u>animals</u>.
2. Waiting for my grandmother's <u>dessert</u> is always so hard!
3. The thirsty hikers could not wait to get to the <u>store</u> to have a <u>beverage</u>.
4. The varied hues of <u>color</u> made the <u>space</u> feel very cozy.
5. The <u>park</u> is beautiful and peaceful, yet it can be dangerous if you run into a <u>wild animal</u>.
6. All my <u>family members</u> on my father's side are adventurous and funny!
7. We are blessed to see the <u>water</u> and the <u>birds</u> just beyond our backyard every day.
8. God commands us to respect and obey our <u>government officials</u> as long as they do not require us to violate God's Word.
9. Yesterday I saw the most stunning <u>car</u> turn onto the <u>road</u>.
10. My heart was full of <u>strong emotion</u> when I saw the scared <u>child</u> crying.

Try It Out!

Write a paragraph about one of the following topics. Use vivid concrete nouns.

What is family?
Describe your personality using three objects.
What do you like to do during your summer vacation?

TYPES OF NOUNS

Noun Types

Common and Proper Nouns

All nouns are either common or proper. A **common noun** refers to a general person, place, thing, or idea. A **proper noun** is the name of a specific person, place, thing, or idea and begins with a capital letter.

	Person	Place	Thing	Idea
Common	daughter president	park church	drama oatmeal	philosophy era
Proper	Emily President Trump	Banff National Park First Baptist Church	*The Tempest* Quaker Oats oatmeal	Stoicism Roaring Twenties

Count and Noncount Nouns

Count nouns, nouns that can be numbered, can be singular or plural and are often preceded by a number or by definite or indefinite articles (*the, a, an*). They may also be preceded by the demonstrative pronouns *this, that, these*, and *those* or by the indefinite pronouns *every, each, either, neither, some, any*, and *enough*. (*Hint:* If you can use the word *much* or the phrase *amount of* with a noun, it is not a count noun.)

Noncount nouns, also called *mass nouns*, are almost always singular in form. Abstract nouns are often in the noncount noun category (*peace, hospitality, courage*). Noncount nouns are preceded by definite articles as well as the indefinite pronouns *some, any*, and *enough* and the singular demonstrative pronouns *this* and *that*.

Count noun: gallon
Noncount noun: water

Compound Nouns

Compound nouns are formed by combining two or more words. The meaning of a compound noun is often a unique combination of the meanings of the two original words. Compound nouns can be *closed* (one word), *hyphenated*, or *open* (two or more words).

To form the plural of a compound noun, change the most important word into its plural form. If you are unsure which part of the compound noun should be made plural, check a dictionary for the correct form.

book + shelf = bookshelf, bookshelves
great + aunt = great-aunt, great-aunts
father + in + law = father-in-law, fathers-in-law
police + officer = police officer, police officers
attorney + general = attorney general, attorneys general

Practice the Skill

Imagine that you are the narrator of the following sentences. Write in the blank a proper noun to replace the italicized word or phrase.

______________ 1. My family and I used to live in *a state* in New England.

______________ 2. In *a certain month* we moved to Vermont.

______________ 3. I miss our old house and *my neighbor*.

______________ 4. I met *a new friend* at school today, though.

______________ 5. My father is going to pastor the new church in *town*.

Identify each italicized noun as *count* or *noncount*.

______________ 6. The Conestoga wagon is a famous *symbol* of the American frontier.

______________ 7. Conestoga, Pennsylvania, was the *birthplace* of this covered wagon.

______________ 8. The high sides served as a means of moving large quantities of *freight*, and the curved *floor* prevented the cargo from shifting.

______________ 9. Conestoga wagons had wide-rimmed wheels to help them move through *mud*, but the wheels could be removed so that the wagons could serve as a *boat*.

______________ 10. Conestoga wagons, a product of Pennsylvania Dutch *inventors*, helped the frontier remain connected with places of *commerce* in the East.

Underline the singular compound nouns in each sentence. Write in the blank the correct plural form of each noun.

_______________ 11. The legendary cowboy of the American western frontier originated as the cattle business developed.

_______________ 12. Cowboys, who herded cattle on animals called a cow pony, guarded cattle as the animals grazed on the prairie grassland.

_______________ 13. Many men carried guns, such as the famous six-shooter, as they conveyed cattle to the railroad.

_______________ 14. Men would share stories around the fire or play pranks, with the new man being the target of the old-timer's practical jokes.

_______________ 15. The original cowpuncher faded into history shortly after the use of fences became common.

Review the Skill

Imagine that the narrator of the following sentences is describing an attack on a frontier stagecoach. Write in the blank a noun that completes the sentence. Use a variety of common and proper nouns.

____________________ 16. Last week, bandits tried to rob the ? stagecoach.

____________________ 17. The men were transporting two mail ? and some silver from the bank in Weston.

____________________ 18. As the coach approached Farson Crossing, three men with ? rode down from the surrounding rocks, but ? and his deputy were also approaching the area.

____________________ 19. Hearing the gunshots and knowing the stagecoach was due to pass ? at Farson Crossing, the sheriff and his deputy hurried into position.

____________________ 20. After the coach rushed through the pass, the sheriff and his deputy separated the ? from their target, and Deputy ? caught two of the robbers.

Identify each italicized noun as *count* or *noncount*.

____________________ 21. People today owe much of their *knowledge* of the Old West to William Frederick Cody, better known by his *nickname* Buffalo Bill.

____________________ 22. He earned this *nickname* hunting buffalo in Kansas to feed railroad workers.

____________________ 23. As a young *man*, Cody rode for the Pony Express, and later he acted as a *scout* for the US Army in several conflicts with the Indians.

____________________ 24. His *fame* grew as people read dime novels about his adventures; many would come to his Wild West *show*, which demonstrated life on the frontier.

____________________ 25. Cody worked hard to create an *image* of the West as a rough, exciting place to visit.

Underline the singular compound nouns (omit *Pony Express*).
Write in the blank the correct plural form of the underlined compound noun.

_______________ 26. The Pony Express provided mail service for the West in the early 1860s with a different sort of mailman.

_______________ 27. The Pony Express horses were much faster than the stagecoach, and a rider might be a daredevil, willing to ride through deserts and over mountains while facing wild animals and storms.

_______________ 28. Lonely young men in the West could now send notes quickly to their bride-to-be in the East.

_______________ 29. Even the middle class could afford to send mail quickly through the Pony Express.

_______________ 30. The Pony Express was replaced after only sixteen months by the telegraph, which could send messages at the touch of a fingertip.

Use the Skill

Write a paragraph about a vacation. Use at least two compound nouns, one proper noun, and one noncount noun.

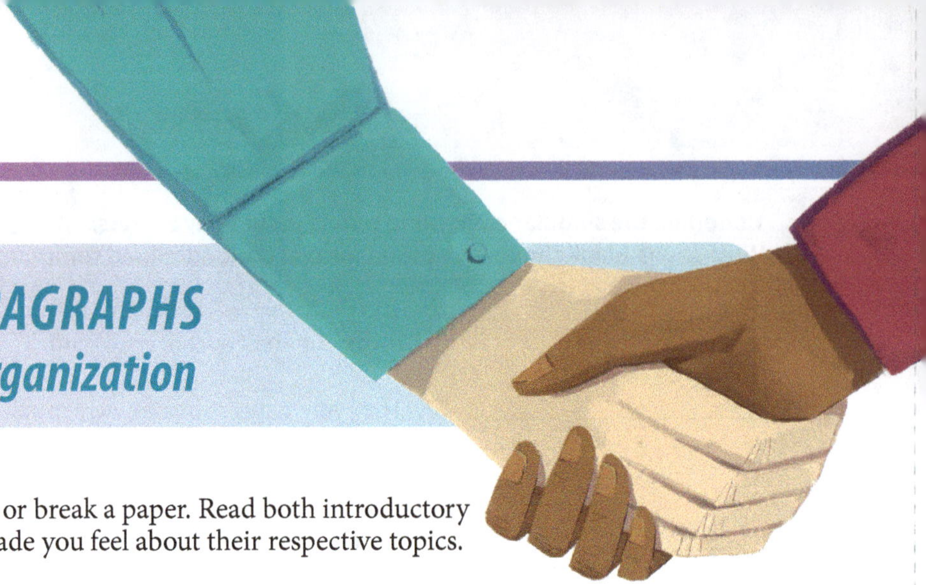

INTRODUCTORY PARAGRAPHS
Writing Traits: Ideas, Organization

Listen Up!
An introductory paragraph can make or break a paper. Read both introductory paragraphs; then discuss how each made you feel about their respective topics.

MENTOR TEXTS

Have you ever stood in a magnificent cathedral and gotten goose bumps listening to the rich, haunting sounds of male voices echoing through the imposing sanctuary? The poetic and beautiful psalms of the Bible sung in these ancient halls are not often heard in modern times or in the churches of North America. Called *plainsong*, this unique style of music, used mostly in the Middle Ages, employs only a single line of melody and has been used for both religious and nonreligious purposes.

This essay will be discussing the benefits of eating sauerkraut. First, it tastes really good! You will love it if you just give it a try. Made from cabbage and salt that has been sitting in a cabinet for weeks, sauerkraut is strong and tangy but really good for you. Nutritionists tell us that we should be eating a lot of fermented food, but most of us don't. Who wants to eat food that has gotten so old that it has fermented? I will tell you in this paper about its many health benefits.

Take Notes!
Describe in your own words the parts of an effective introductory paragraph.

Good introductions are crucial to successful essays. Like a first impression at school or work, a written introduction—good or bad—has the power to influence the reader by either drawing him in to read on and learn more or causing him to lose interest and stop reading altogether. An introduction is short, whether spoken or written. When you write an **introductory paragraph**, it needs to move quickly to keep your reader engaged. The functions of an introductory paragraph are threefold:

- to effectively grab the reader's attention with a hook (A **hook** is a sentence that is intended to grab the reader's attention right away, keeping him "hooked" to want to continue reading.)
- to provide background information or context that transitions into the thesis
- to present a concise thesis statement, clearly stating and explaining a topic or a position

WRITING TOOLBOX

The Hook

Type of Hook	Example	Example Sentence
Interesting fact or statistic	average human attention span = about eight seconds	The average person's attention span is approximately eight seconds.
Quotation	"Facts alone are wanted in life."	When writing an informational essay, remember, as Charles Dickens wrote in *Hard Times*, that "facts alone are wanted in life." Leave personal opinions out of the conversation.
Question	Would you want a stranger to take your hard-earned money?	Would you want a stranger to take the money from your paycheck out of your hand and pass it out to the first three people he sees on the street?

Background Information or Context

The sentences that follow the hook provide the reader with background information or context that will allow the reader to appreciate the author's position in the thesis statement. They help to stir up interest, build emotion, and provide a taste of what's to come. *Caution:* Do not give away too much information or include irrelevant details!

The Thesis Statement

The thesis statement comes last in the paragraph and tells the topic of the entire essay. Typically, the thesis statement is a single sentence. This sentence usually begins with the topic to be discussed or the position to be defended, followed by two or three phrases drawn from the two or three topic sentences in the body paragraphs. Be sure that the phrases from the body paragraphs are clearly identifiable. In an informative essay, make sure that the thesis statement contains no personal opinions.

Partner Up!

Read the second example paragraph at the beginning of the lesson and analyze how it fails to follow the guidelines for a good introductory paragraph: What is missing? What is included that shouldn't be? Is the topic of the essay clearly seen in the thesis statement? Discuss and mark the text's errors on a separate sheet of paper, and be ready to explain your assessment.

Try It Out!

Brainstorm ideas for an introduction to an essay that discusses a topic of interest to you. (Remember to keep your audience in mind.) Make sure you have sufficient knowledge of your topic without having to do research. Compose an introductory paragraph that includes an attention-grabbing hook, interest-building background information or context, and a concise thesis statement.

CHAPTER REVIEW

Identifying Nouns

Write in the blank the type of the underlined noun: *abstract*, *concrete*, *proper*, or *possessive*. More than one type may be required for some sentences.

_______________ 1. Mr. Stanley became a police officer because he wanted to protect his community.

_______________ 2. Though she didn't understand why, the young girl obeyed her mom's urgent command to put her bike away and come inside.

_______________ 3. Just like a mother who desires to guard her children, God's commands are given for our own protection.

_______________ 4. God commands our obedience for our own protection and happiness.

_______________ 5. Undaunted by the weather, the postman tenaciously continued to deliver his immense stack of letters.

_______________ 6. The <u>cats'</u> food bowl was nearly empty.

_______________ 7. The buildings swayed precariously with the <u>earthquake's</u> powerful motion.

_______________ 8. Possessing discernment when writing ensures that students' <u>essays</u> will be appropriate for their audience and pleasing to God.

_______________ 9. The <u>kindness</u> of the stranger was touching and inspiring.

_______________ 10. The front, side, and back doors of the house open with the same key, which keeps my <u>keychain</u> from being too heavy.

_______________ 11. Travis wrote in his journal on <u>Pastor Smith's</u> sermon, "Guarding Our Words."

_______________ 12. When the young soldier saluted the American flag, his heart swelled with <u>patriotism</u>.

_______________ 13. God encourages us in the <u>Bible</u> to be strong and courageous because He is with us always.

_______________ 14. Though you may think that <u>integrity</u> is old-fashioned, God will honor your display of the noble quality.

_______________ 15. The <u>quality</u> of your work should not suffer because you are excited about the upcoming winter break.

Common and Proper Nouns

Underline each common noun once and each proper noun twice.

16.–20. The last month of our calendar year is December. The name of the month comes from the word *decem* in Latin. Many people around the world celebrate Christmas on the twenty-fifth day. Other holidays in December include Hanukkah and the Feast of Saint Nicholas.

Types of Nouns

Identify the type of the underlined noun. Write in the blank the letter that corresponds to the correct answer.

_______ 21. The stack of textbooks in the office belongs to the new student.
- **A** compound
- **B** abstract
- **C** noncount

_______ 22. Thunder filled the sky with booms and cracks that not only shook the house but also shook our nerves.
- **A** compound
- **B** noncount
- **C** count

_______ 23. After the heavy rains, our crawlspace stayed flooded for nearly three days.
- **A** compound
- **B** abstract
- **C** noncount

_______ 24. My sisters-in-law took me out for a surprise birthday brunch.
- **A** abstract
- **B** noncount
- **C** compound

_______ 25. I don't think that the river will breach its bank, despite the deluge.
- **A** compound
- **B** count
- **C** abstract

Multiple Choice

Write in the blank the letter that corresponds to the correct answer.

_______ 26. Which form of *Jesus* is a possessive noun?
- **A** Jesus
- **B** Jesus'
- **C** Jesuses

_______ 27. What is the correct form of the following compound word?
- **A** carwash
- **B** car wash
- **C** car-wash

_______ 28. What is the most logical set of vivid nouns to replace the underlined words in the following sentence?

The large, gray <u>animal</u> lumbered through the <u>land</u> looking for a watering hole.
- **A** whale, forest
- **B** squirrel, sand dunes
- **C** African elephant, savanna

_______ 29. Choose the correct plural compound form of the words *attorney* and *general.*
- **A** attorney general's
- **B** attorney generals
- **C** attorneys general

_______ 30. Which set of nouns is all noncount nouns that can be made plural?
- **A** meat, sugar, cheese
- **B** happiness, journey, salt
- **C** jewelry, solid, weather

OF THE

CHAPTER 5

PRONOUNS

WHY USE PRONOUN SUBSTITUTIONS?

Nouns are foundational to a sentence. However, if nouns are repeated over and over, they can lose their effect and may even bore the reader. Pronouns can do anything a noun can do. They help the writer replace nouns rather than repeat them.

DISCOVER!

On the snow-covered morning of January 20, 1961, the newly elected president from Massachusetts, John F. Kennedy, challenged the nation in his inaugural speech. Read the mentor text, and look for the eighteen personal pronouns.

MENTOR TEXT

In the long history of the world, only a few generations have been granted the role of defending freedom in its hour of maximum danger. I do not shrink from this responsibility—I welcome it. I do not believe that any of us would exchange places with any other people or any other generation. . . .

And so, my fellow Americans: ask not what your country can do for you—ask what you can do for your country. . . .

With a good conscience our only sure reward, with history the final judge of our deeds, let us go forth to lead the land we love, asking His blessing and His help, but knowing that here on earth God's work must truly be our own.

—John F. Kennedy, Inaugural Address

What are the antecedents of the personal pronouns? Which are possessive? Which two words in the first paragraph are indefinite pronouns? Which two are acting as adjectives?

PRONOUNS AND THEIR ANTECEDENTS; PERSONAL PRONOUNS

Pronouns and Antecedents

Pronouns are words that substitute for nouns. Pronouns allow us to simplify our writing and speaking.

The **antecedent** is the noun or other pronoun that a pronoun replaces. An antecedent usually appears before the pronoun that replaces it.

> *Commuters* in California depend on **their** vast freeway system.
> The first *freeway* in California opened in 1940; **it** covered six miles from Pasadena to Los Angeles.

Personal Pronouns

Personal pronouns are the most-used type of pronoun. All personal pronouns have four characteristics: **person**, **number**, **gender**, and **case**.

	Singular (Number)		
	Subjective Case	Objective Case	Possessive Case
First Person	I	me	my, mine
Second Person	you	you	your, yours
Third Person			
Masculine (Gender)	he	him	his
Feminine (Gender)	she	her	her, hers
Neuter (Gender)	it	it	its

	Plural (Number)		
	Subjective Case	Objective Case	Possessive Case
First Person	we	us	our, ours
Second Person	you	you	your, yours
Third Person	they	them	their, theirs

Person tells whether the personal pronoun refers to the speaker(s), the person(s) spoken to, or the person(s) or thing(s) spoken of.

First Person: *My* cousins live in South Dakota.
Second Person: Have *you* ever visited Mount Rushmore National Memorial?
Third Person: *It* is a popular tourist attraction.

Number tells whether the personal pronoun is singular or plural.

Singular: Gutzon Borglum and *his* son Lincoln created the memorial.
Plural: *They* were talented sculptors.

Gender tells whether the personal pronoun is neuter, masculine, or feminine. Only the third-person singular pronouns change form to show a difference of gender.

Neuter: *Its* construction took fourteen years from 1927 until 1941.
Masculine: Gutzon Borglum died before seeing *his* masterpiece completed.
Feminine: Mrs. Borglum must have been proud of *her* family's work.

Case tells how the personal pronoun is being used in a sentence. *Subjective case* pronouns usually function as subjects and predicate nouns; *objective case* pronouns usually function as objects (objects of prepositions, direct objects, indirect objects); and *possessive case* pronouns often function as adjectives.

Subjective: Before Borglum began work on Mount Rushmore, *he* had started work on Stone Mountain in Georgia.
Objective: Today, people remember *him* as a master craftsman.
Possessive: Mount Rushmore is *his* best-known sculpture.

Practice the Skill

Underline each pronoun. Write in the blank its antecedent.

_______________ 1. Although the League of Nations assembled in 1920 to prevent aggression between countries, the rising dictators and their threat to world peace continued.

_______________ 2. Japan began its defiance of the League of Nations by taking Manchuria from China.

_______________ 3. Because no country was willing to stop the aggression, Japanese troops continued their invasion of China in 1937.

_______________ 4. The Italian dictator Mussolini defied the League when he led an invasion of Ethiopia in 1935.

_______________ 5. The League still did not use military force, but it imposed sanctions on Italy instead.

_______________ 6. Adolf Hitler also desired a powerful empire, so he pulled Germany out of the League of Nations.

_______________ 7. In an attempt to acquire more land, Hitler and his troops invaded Poland in September 1939.

_______________ 8. Because Britain and France supported Poland, they declared war on Germany two days later.

_______________ 9. While Germany invaded Poland in the west, Russian troops made their assault on Poland from the east.

_______________ 10. By the end of the 1930s, Germany and its forces appeared indestructible.

EXTRA!
9 A.M. EDITION Los Angeles Times 9 A.M. EDITION
WAR! GERMAN TROOPS INVADE POLAND
NAZIS BOMB WARSAW
British Mobilize Army and Fleet
Poles Spurn Berlin Terms; Troops Move
LATE BULLETINS
Reichstag Hears Hitler Defy Poles
Fighting Rages Along Border
Henry Tells of War Work
Italy Pledges Respect for Swiss Neutrality
Hitler Secludes Self in Room

Review the Skill

Write in the blank a pronoun to replace the italicized word or phrase.

______________ 11. Keith, did *Keith* know that the Allied retreat from Dunkirk was a miracle?

______________ 12. Most Americans know only part of the story. *Americans* all can be thankful to God for the outcome.

______________ 13. Many British and French men escaped with *the men's* lives because of a German military error.

______________ 14. Hitler normally receives the blame, but *Hitler* was only partly to blame.

______________ 15. Runstedt, a high-ranking German military official, called for *Runstedt's* soldiers to cease all front-line activity.

______________ 16. The Germans knew that *the Germans* must follow the authority of their leaders.

______________ 17. Because the port of Dunkirk was small, *the port* could not hold many troops.

______________ 18. Operation Dynamo was unique because many fishermen used *the fishermen's* own boats to rescue the soldiers.

______________ 19. *The rescue* became one of the most famous rescues of World War II.

______________ 20. The soldiers were brave; we salute *the soldiers*.

Use the Skill

Write ten sentences using the personal pronouns indicated in the parentheses. Use the pronoun chart on page 130 if needed.

21. Write a sentence about soldiers. (third person plural, objective case)

22. Describe your history book. (first person plural, possessive case)

23. Tell about a leader in World War II. (third person singular, masculine, subjective case)

24. Ask someone what his most memorable battle is. (second person singular, possessive case)

25. Write a sentence about a nurse's work. (third person singular, feminine, subjective case)

26. Describe seeing the campground with hundreds of soldiers. (first person plural, subjective case)

____

27. Tell about your first night in a foreign country. (first person singular, objective case)

____

28. Describe a doctor's work in a field hospital. (third person plural, objective case)

____

29. Ask someone about the most important battle in World War II. (second person singular, subjective case)

____

30. Tell about a soldier's welcome when he came home from the war. (third person singular, masculine, objective case)

____

USING THIRD PERSON FOR FORMAL WRITING
Writing Trait: Voice

Listen Up!
Read the mentor text. Is this article written in first, second, or third person? What proof can you give?

MENTOR TEXT

Icelandic horses may be itty bitty in size, but their personalities are giant. These mighty midgets are more intelligent, sociable, and curious than their taller counterparts. Here is their story.

The Icelandic horse is small, (52-56 inches tall and 730-840 pounds) and muscular. These tiny titans are the only horse breed in the world that can perform five **gaits** (ways of walking). Most breeds can perform only three or four gaits: walking, trotting, and cantering/galloping. Tölt is a gait unique to Iceland. It is an impressive, ultra-smooth trot. The horse lifts its front legs up high, and only one foot touches the ground at any time. The Icelandic horse is known for its sure-footedness and ability to cross glacial rivers and rough terrain. It is undaunted by high winds or snowstorms. It provides a steady ride on the often-uneven ground of Iceland. A fifth type of movement is the *skeið*, or flying pace. It is like a very rhythmic gallop that feels like flying. Not all Icelandic horses can perform these two gaits, but the ones that can are considered most valuable.

The spirited but gentle Icelandic horse is a hardy animal. It has a lifespan of 40 to 59 years. It is long-lived because it has no predators in Iceland, and it gets very few diseases. Its health stems from Iceland's "keep out and don't come back" policy. The government has not allowed foreign horses into the country for more than a thousand years, and an Icelandic horse that leaves the country cannot return. Thanks to these careful standards, this ancient race has survived in Iceland for 1,100 years without crossbreeding.

— Pat Betteley, "The Icelandic Horse: Small but Mighty"

Take Notes!
In your own words, describe when third person is used in writing. Make a cluster map to identify the characteristics of formal writing.

The choice of voice depends on the type and purpose of the writing. First- and second-person pronouns generally assume a familiarity with an audience. They can result in a more personal, conversational, sometimes opinionated tone. Slang, idioms, and fragments are often acceptable in such informal writing.

Academic writing, such as research, explanatory, and argumentative writing, generally uses third person, creating a more impersonal, authoritative tone. Slang, idioms, and fragments are not acceptable.

GRAMMAR TOOLBOX

A skillful writer needs to use first, second, or third person selectively. In order to choose an appropriate point of view for a piece of writing, a writer has to evaluate his relationship to his readers. Are they equals? Are the readers superiors? How well does the writer know them? A writer must also think about the purpose and context of his writing. Consider the difference between writing a friendly letter to a childhood friend and writing a letter introducing yourself to a prospective employer. How would the two letters differ in wording and tone? Ask yourself, "With whom am I communicating? What message do I want to send? How formal or familiar should I be?" Proverbs 25:11 tells us that we are demonstrating wisdom when we choose the right words for the right time.

Characteristics of Formal Writing

- Writes about someone or something by name or uses third-person pronouns with a clear antecedent

  Incorrect: **They** have not allowed foreign horses into the country for more than a thousand years. (*They* would have no antecedent.)
  Correct: The **government** has not allowed foreign horses into the country for more than a thousand years.

- Avoids first person; stays focused on facts and evidence

  Incorrect: **I** learned that the Icelandic horse is small, . . . and muscular.
  Correct: The **Icelandic horse** is small, . . . and muscular.

- Avoids second person; writes to a general audience

  Incorrect: Did **you** know that, thanks to these careful standards, this ancient race has survived in Iceland for 1,100 years without crossbreeding?
  Correct: Thanks to these careful standards, this ancient **race** has survived in Iceland for 1,100 years without crossbreeding.

Partner Up!

Rewrite the following sentences in third person, removing or replacing all first-person references.

1. My friends and I love to sing in the church choir.
2. We are preparing to sing in the Christmas cantata.
3. The conductor chose my friend and me to sing a duet.
4. He gave me a special recording to familiarize me with the song.
5. Our song was the very first song on the program.

Search for correct example sentences for each of the characteristics of third person writing in nonfiction pieces (newspaper, encyclopedia, etc.).

Try It Out!

Write an entry for an encyclopedia on a current event.

MORE PRONOUNS

Demonstrative Pronouns

The **demonstrative pronouns** *this*, *these*, *that*, and *those* point out persons, places, things, or ideas being discussed. These pronouns may function as subjects, predicate nouns, direct objects, indirect objects, and objects of prepositions. *This* (singular) and *these* (plural) point to things that are near, and *that* (singular) and *those* (plural) point to things that are farther away.

This is a fascinating story about Allied storage of wartime supplies.
The Allies needed *that* to prepare for the invasion of Normandy.
Munitions, weapons, and vehicles—all of *these* were vital to the success of Operation Overload.
Those were vital to the success of Operation Overload.

Interrogative Pronouns

The **interrogative pronouns** *who*, *whom*, *what*, *whose*, and *which*, like interrogative sentences, are used to ask questions.

Who first suggested an underwater pipeline?
Admiral Mountbatten's suggestion benefited *whom*?
For *what* did the Allies use the pipeline?
Whose was the idea for the acronym PLUTO (Pipeline Under the Ocean)?
Which of the European countries were connected by PLUTO?

Intensive and Reflexive Pronouns

The **intensive pronouns** and **reflexive pronouns** look the same but function differently. Both types are made by adding *-self* or *-selves* to certain pronouns.

	Singular	Plural
First Person	myself	ourselves
Second Person	yourself	yourselves
Third Person		themselves
Masculine	himself	
Feminine	herself	
Neuter	itself	

Reflexive pronouns function as direct objects, indirect objects, and objects of prepositions. They always refer to the same person, place, thing, or idea as the subject of a sentence. Therefore, the subject is the antecedent.

Direct Object: During the 1940s, many men removed *themselves* from the workforce to enter military service. (*Men* is the antecedent.)
Indirect Object: Women then gave *themselves* the responsibility of filling jobs in defense factories. (*Women* is the antecedent.)
Object of a Preposition: A working woman earned the nickname "Rosie the Riveter" for *herself*. (*Woman* is the antecedent.)

An intensive pronoun emphasizes its antecedent, a noun or pronoun already used in the sentence. Because an intensive pronoun does not function as part of the sentence pattern, it can be removed without changing the basic meaning of the sentence.

Norman Rockwell *himself* popularized the image of Rosie the Riveter with a magazine cover illustration.

Popular songs also mentioned Rosie *herself*.

The phenomenon of women in the workplace outlasted the war *itself*.

Practice the Skill

Underline the demonstrative and interrogative pronouns. Identify the pronoun as *D* (demonstrative) or *I* (interrogative).

_______ 1. What was the name of the German air force?

_______ 2. The name of that was the Luftwaffe.

_______ 3. The Luftwaffe commander for Germany was who?

_______ 4. Reich Marshal Hermann Goering was this.

_______ 5. The honor of top-scoring fighter ace in the war goes to whom?

_______ 6. Erich Hartmann earned this with 352 victories.

Underline the reflexive pronouns and intensive pronouns. Identify the pronoun as *Int* (intensive) or *R* (reflexive).

_______ 7. More than a thousand kamikazes gave themselves in the defense of Okinawa in 1945.

_______ 8. The kamikazes themselves flew their explosive-filled planes into targets.

_______ 9. However, the plane itself was also called a kamikaze.

_______ 10. The kamikaze pilot himself made the decision to sacrifice everything for the Japanese cause.

_______ 11. A kamikaze pilot would have a funeral for himself before flying on his mission.

Review the Skill

Write in the blank an appropriate demonstrative or interrogative pronoun to complete the sentence.

_______________ 12. _?_ bombers did the Germans use during World War II?

_______________ 13. One of _?_ was the Heinkel He 111.

_______________ 14. _?_ had the fastest planes during World War II?

_______________ 15. _?_ flew faster than any Allied interceptors?

_______________ 16. The Arado AR 234 B-2 could do _?_. However, Germany did not make many of them during the war.

_______________ 17. _?_ was nicknamed the Blitz because of its great speed.

_______________ 18. Of all the planes, _?_ were the hardest to shoot down.

_______________ 19. _?_ was Germany's strategy?

_______________ 20. The idea to use planes to destroy Britain's Royal Air Force was _?_ ?

_______________ 21. _?_ helped cause the defeat of the German Luftwaffe.

Write in the blank an appropriate reflexive or intensive pronoun to complete the sentence.

_______________ 22. Jeremy found _?_ in a precarious situation.

_______________ 23. Leah _?_ carried the medicine into the hospital.

_______________ 24. The gun seemed to get dirty all by _?_.

_______________ 25. We found _?_ unprepared for battle.

_______________ 26. Have you _?_ ever seen the general?

_______________ 27. Fred and José wrote the battle strategies _?_.

_______________ 28. Michelle rebuked _?_ for not writing Tom a letter.

_______________ 29. Stephen _?_ flew the plane faster than anyone else.

_______________ 30. Sara asked _?_ when Lance would be back from across the ocean.

_______________ 31. Justin _?_ lived in France for two years.

Use the Skill

Write one sentence for each pronoun of these pronoun types: demonstrative, interrogative, intensive, and reflexive. Challenge yourself to make them all about the same topic.

INDEFINITE PRONOUNS

Like most other pronouns, **indefinite pronouns** can function in any noun position. Unlike other pronouns, indefinite pronouns usually do not refer to specific persons or things. Indefinite pronouns often do not have obvious antecedents. Most indefinite pronouns are singular; some are plural; and some can be either singular or plural depending on how they are used.

Singular				
another	each	everything	neither	one
anybody	either	little	nobody	somebody
anyone	everybody	less	no one	someone
anything	everyone	much	nothing	something

Plural				
both	few	fewer	many	several

Singular or Plural					
all	any	more	most	none	some

Everyone was affected by food shortages during wartime.
Victory gardens provided vegetables for *many*.
All were careful not to waste scarce foods.
All of the food was distributed.

Practice the Skill

Underline the indefinite pronouns. Label each pronoun above the word: *S* (subject), *DO* (direct object), *PN* (predicate noun), or *OP* (object of the preposition).

1. The atom bomb is one of the nuclear weapons available for war.
2. All of these weapons receive their power from the changing of atoms into energy.
3. Torpedoes, missiles, and mines make up a few of these weapons.
4. In August 1945 mass destruction was caused by both of the bombs that were dropped.
5. Because the bomb dropped on Hiroshima killed over seventy thousand people, many disapproved of its use.
6. The end of the war caused seemingly everyone to rejoice.
7. Since that time, no one has used nuclear weapons in battle.
8. The threat of nuclear war is believed by most to keep peace among strong nations.
9. Some believe that nuclear weapons will eventually destroy the world.
10. Even though the countries with nuclear weapons have the advantage, nobody has used these weapons recently.

Review the Skill

Write in the blank an appropriate indefinite pronoun to complete the sentence.

_______________ 11. _?_ of my friends sleep late on Saturdays.

_______________ 12. My brother and I get up early on Saturdays. _?_ of us work around the house.

_______________ 13. _?_ of us ever misses our mother's great breakfasts.

_______________ 14. Later in the day, _?_ comes to our house.

_______________ 15. Every week _?_ invents a new game.

_______________ 16. Horsenappers, Pickle, and Foursquare are _?_ of our games.

_______________ 17. _?_ remembers all of our games.

_______________ 18. I still know _?_ of the rules to my favorite games by heart.

_______________ 19. Almost _?_ is enthusiastically accepted.

_______________ 20. _?_ loves Saturday afternoons at our house.

Use the Skill

Write a sentence for each of the following pronoun/case combinations.

21. *many*/subject

____

22. *everybody*/object of preposition

____

23. *each*/subject

____

24. *more* (plural)/direct object

____

25. *fewer*/direct object

____

26. *everyone*/indirect object

____

27. *some* (plural)/direct object

____

28. *more* (plural)/subject

____

29. *nothing*/subject

____

30. *both*/indirect object

____

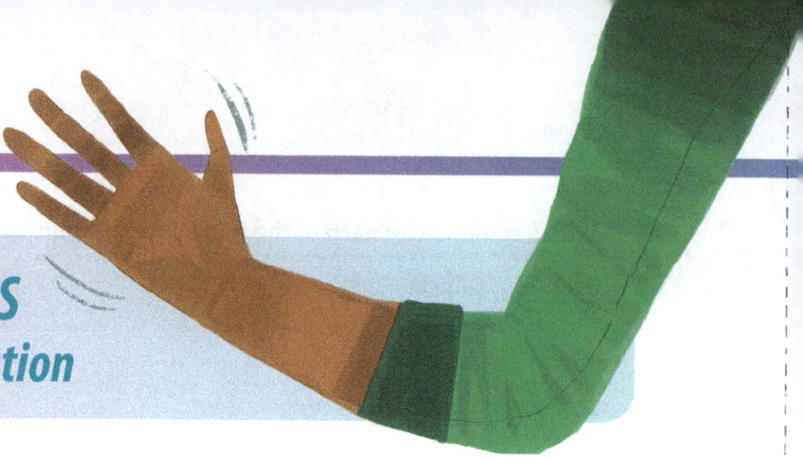

CONCLUSION PARAGRAPHS
Writing Traits: Ideas, Organization

Listen Up!
The mentor text for the introduction paragraph in Lesson 37 introduced the topic of plainsong. What was its topic sentence? Can you spot a version of the topic sentence in this corresponding conclusion paragraph?

MENTOR TEXT

Plainsong was influential for both religious and non-religious music in the Middle Ages. It also served as a predecessor to other forms of music. Without plainsong, the basis for many early musical forms would be absent.

Take Notes!
Make a three-column chart identifying and describing the conclusion paragraph patterns.

Description
Writing a good conclusion may be the most important part of any informative paper. It should leave the readers thinking about the main idea(s) and give them a feeling of completion.

Paragraph Patterns
There are different patterns for writing a conclusion paragraph that can be used alone or combined.

1. A conclusion paragraph can *restate* the main idea and *stress* the importance of the topic.

The mentor text above reemphasizes the importance of plainsong as introduced in the introduction paragraph. Notice how the topic sentence is reworded and restructured.

2. A conclusion paragraph can *restate* the main idea and *summarize* the supporting points.

Rewording and restructuring your topic statement and summarizing the key points made in the body is an effective way to tie all the ideas together. In the following rewritten conclusion, how is the main idea restated? What are the supporting points?

MENTOR TEXT

Medieval worship used a form of music called plainsong, which influenced the church music and the secular music of the time. It dominated because of its simple form, its adaptability, and the reverent atmosphere it created.

3. A conclusion paragraph can *ask* your audience a question(s).

A question is an effective strategy for keeping your audience engaged and thinking. Different kinds of questions can be used, such as leaving your audience with a general question that checks their comprehension, a question that challenges them to learn more, or a question that makes them think. What is the purpose for the question in this rewritten conclusion?

MENTOR TEXT

Medieval worship used a form of music called plainsong, which influenced the church music and the secular music of the time. After examining the importance of plainsong, one must wonder, "Can modern man truly appreciate this artistic genre of music?"

Selecting the paragraph pattern should not be done haphazardly. Your motivation in making that decision should be based on the pattern's purpose and appropriateness, not on its ease of use or cool effects. Which pattern would you consider to be more formal, which more informal? Which would best communicate to your audience that you care about what they think or what they take away? Be discerning.

Which Conclusion Pattern Should I Use?

1. Which is most appropriate for the purpose?
2. Which is most appropriate for the audience?
3. How formal does it need to be? Which best achieves that level of formality or informality?
4. Which best communicates my take-away message?

Partner Up!

Identify the pattern the following conclusion paragraph uses.
Rewrite the paragraph using one of the other patterns.

Setting aside a portion of every day to read will reap numerous benefits. Can you list them? Which imaginary world will you escape to next?

Try It Out!

Write a conclusion paragraph using the pattern you did not use in *Partner Up!*

CHAPTER REVIEW

Pronouns and Antecedents

Write in the blank a pronoun to replace the italicized word or phrase.

__________ 1. Heather says that *Heather's* favorite season of the year is summer.

__________ 2. In the summer, *Heather* enjoys teaching young children to swim.

__________ 3. Her brother Brent loves summertime because *Brent* gets a three-month break from school.

__________ 4. *Brent's* favorite summer activities are camping and hiking.

__________ 5. Brent enjoys hiking and camping only once in a while, because *hiking and camping* make his body very sore.

Personal Pronouns

Write in the blank the letter that corresponds to the correct answer.

_____ 6. _?_ took the youth group to camp. (first person plural, subjective case)
A Us
B You
C We

_____ 7. The boys unloaded the suitcases and put _?_ on the cots. (third person plural, objective case)
A our
B them
C it

_____ 8. Nancy waited on the boys to bring _?_ five suitcases. (third person feminine singular, possessive case)
A her
B our
C its

_____ 9. Did _?_ make up your cot yet? (second person singular, subjective case)
A they
B I
C you

_____ 10. The counselor told _?_ it was time for supper. (first person plural, objective case)
A our
B us
C them

Pronoun Types

Underline the personal, demonstrative, interrogative, intensive, and reflexive pronouns in the following sentences. Identify the pronoun as *P* (personal), *D* (demonstrative), *I* (interrogative), *Int* (intensive), or *R* (reflexive).

_______ 11. One summer, my family took a trip to the Ark Encounter in Williamstown, Kentucky.

_______ 12. That was one of my favorite vacations.

_______ 13. We arrived at the park after hours of traveling.

_______ 14. My sister asked Dad, "Who is going to buy the tickets?"

_______ 15. My father, however, had purchased them himself.

_______ 16. "Which bus is ours?" my brother asked.

_______ 17. My baby brother exclaimed, "This is the biggest boat I have ever seen!"

_______ 18. Our family made ourselves wonderful memories.

Indefinite Pronouns

Write in the blank an indefinite pronoun that could be a substitute for the underlined word(s).

________________ 19. In the summer, my friends and I play miniature golf; a portion of my friends always get lower scores than I get.

________________ 20. Out of all the players, Kelly is the best player.

________________ 21. My friends and I try to beat Kelly.

________________ 22. The majority of the scores total about fifty points.

________________ 23. My sister and my best friend defeated me.

More Pronouns

Write in the blank an appropriate pronoun of the type indicated.

________________ 24. In the weeks before school resumed, ? family bought much-needed school items. (possessive)

________________ 25. ? of us purchased school clothes and supplies. (indefinite)

________________ 26. My brother ? enjoyed this time more than the rest of us. (intensive)

________________ 27. ? list was always longer than ours. (possessive)

________________ 28. ? would have thought a boy would like shopping more than a girl would? (interrogative)

________________ 29. Oddly enough, ? was typical of our school shopping trips. (demonstrative)

________________ 30. My mother hid ? whenever we told her it was time to do some school shopping. (reflexive)

CHAPTER 6

RESEARCH SKILLS

HOW VALUABLE IS KNOWLEDGE?

Solve this problem. Research that topic. Answer this question. School is all about gaining and applying information and assessing the knowledge that you obtain. As you know, gaining this knowledge does not come through osmosis; it takes time and effort. What if you were given a test today over the most valuable knowledge you can possess—the knowledge of God? How would you fare? Perhaps you could answer some basic factual questions, but have you taken the time and made the effort to really know Him, "[i]n whom are hid all the treasures of wisdom and knowledge" (Colossians 2:3)? Knowing Christ by faith enables believers to start seeing all knowledge in its right perspective. A writer who knows God through Christ can begin to use other knowledge he gains for true Christ-expression, not just self-expression.

MENTOR TEXT

JIM ELLIOT
A LIFE OF SERVICE

Jim Elliot spent his youth preparing for missionary service, but there was nothing that could have prepared him for the eventual happenings of that fateful day.

"He is no fool who gives what he cannot keep to gain that which he cannot lose" sums up the motivation of Jim Elliot's life. Although only twenty-eight years old when he died, Jim Elliot remains one of the most famous and inspiring missionaries in modern history. As a result of his martyrdom, many people have been inspired to enter the foreign mission field. His own family later led to Christ the very people who killed him. Jim Elliot's devotion to Christ and the legacy he left remain an inspiration to Christians around the world.

The foundation for Jim Elliot's legacy was laid by his dedicated Christian parents. Jim's father "read the Scriptures daily to his children" and prayed with them regularly (Elliot 25). His mother, a chiropractor, worked from home, making raising her children her priority (Elliot 25). As a result of his parents' desire to obey the biblical admonition, "Train up a child in the way he should go" (*Authorized King James Version*, Prov. 22:6), Jim recognized that he was a sinner and trusted Christ as his Savior at a very young age. He began a disciplined devotional and prayer life. He learned to love God's Word so much that he would often cry when he read it (White 26). Because he loved God and His Word so much, he was faithful in witnessing for Christ.

Note that portions are quoted, followed by a cross-reference to the Works Cited. Why do you think that is necessary?

By the time Jim entered Benson Polytechnic High School, he was well on his way to sharpening the communication skills that would give him opportunities to speak into the lives of young people. A natural orator—someone who is "eloquent and skilled" ("Orator") at speaking—Jim joined his speech and debate team where he excelled in delivering persuasive messages (White 16). He also found valuable opportunities to share his views in his school newspaper's editorial page. His goal remained, however, to share Jesus with his friends (Elliot 28). Even if they did not agree with him, they liked his adventurous spirit, charm, and wit, and they valued his insights.

In 1945, Jim moved to Wheaton, Illinois, to attend Wheaton College. As he had always done, he continued his daily Bible study and prayer. His "mission field" expanded from evangelizing classmates to "talk[ing] to people in the train station about Christ", going on summer mission trips, preaching in prisons and evangelistic rallies, and teaching for Sunday school (Fickas).

In the summer of 1950, he completed linguistics studies at the Institute of Linguistics in Oklahoma and began making plans to go to the people of Ecuador. Upon reaching South America, he and four fellow missionaries used a Piper PA-14 plane, complete with a loudspeaker and baskets of gifts, to make contact with the unreached Auca Indians. They eventually established a camp near the tribe to make personal contact. On January 8, 1956, the men made what was to be their last radio transmission to the base. The call never came. A frantic search ensued by a group of neighboring missionaries and the United States

Air Force Air Rescue Service ("Go Ye and Preach the Gospel"). A few days later, the bodies of Jim and his fellow missionaries were found and buried in the jungle.

Although it would appear to many that Jim died too young, his entire brief life lives on as a legacy to many believers—an inspiration to live a life pleasing to God with a burning desire to share Christ. Even though Jim Elliot sacrificed the life that he could not ultimately keep, he did indeed echo Paul's sentiment that "to die is gain" (Phil. 1:21).

Works Cited

The Holy Bible. Authorized King James Version, The National Publishing Company, 1975.

Elliot, Elisabeth. *Shadow of the Almighty*. Harper and Brothers, 1958, pp. 25, 28.

Fickas, Tamara D. "Jim Elliot Biography." *Inspirational Christians*, 24 Apr. 2012, www.inspirationalchristians.org/evangelists/jim-elliot-biography/. Accessed 24 Mar. 2020.

"Go Ye and Preach the Gospel." *Life*, vol. 40, no. 5, 30 Jan. 1956, books.google.com/books?id=gT8EAAAAMBAJ&printsec=frontcover&source=gbs_ge_summary_r&cad=0#v=onepage&q&f=false. Accessed 24 Mar. 2020.

"Orator." *The American Heritage Dictionary*. Houghton Mifflin Harcourt, 5th ed., 2012, www.ahdictionary.com/word/search.html?q=orator. Accessed 24 Mar. 2020.

White, Kathleen. *Jim Elliot*. Bethany House Publishers, pp. 16, 26.

What consistency do you see with the use of punctuation in each entry?

Find in the mentor text each source listed under Works Cited.

Look back through the body of the piece. Why do you think some passages are cited but have no quotations?

RESEARCH QUESTIONS AND GATHERING INFORMATION

The idea of a research chapter may bring back memories of going to the library and finding more books than you can read or of finding more Google results than you know what to do with. There is good news, however. This chapter provides a process that is much more manageable.

First, begin with a general topic that interests you or is assigned by your teacher, and narrow the topic to a particular concept, time period, event, or person.

Formulating Research Questions

Turning a narrowed topic into a focused research question will give clear direction for exploring answers. The focused question should be narrow enough to be answered in the space and time given but broad enough to allow for analyzing supporting ideas using multiple sources. Asking questions beginning with *why*, *how*, or *which* generates more material than asking questions that begin with *who* or *what*.

Broad topic: planets
Narrowed topic: Pluto
Poor research question: Who discovered Pluto?
Better research question: Why is Pluto no longer considered a planet?

Broad topic: Benjamin Franklin
Narrowed topic: Franklin's electrical discoveries
Poor research question: What were Franklin's electrical discoveries?
Better research question: How have Franklin's electrical discoveries impacted our way of life today?

Practice the Skill

Substitute better research questions for the poor examples below.

1. Poor question: What percentage of Pluto is covered by water?

   Better question: ______________________________

2. Poor question: What is a dwarf planet?

   Better question: ______________________________

3. Poor question: What inventions did Benjamin Franklin create?

   Better question: ______________________________

4. Poor question: What political roles was Franklin appointed to?

   Better question: ______________________________

Complete the process, using topics of interest to you.

5. Broad topic: ______________

   Narrowed topic: ______________

   Research question: ______________

   ____

6. Broad topic: ______________

   Narrowed topic: ______________

   Research question: ______________

   ____

Gathering Information

Your next step is to create a research plan, a sort of working document for planning for and organizing your paper. Analyze the following sample research plan.

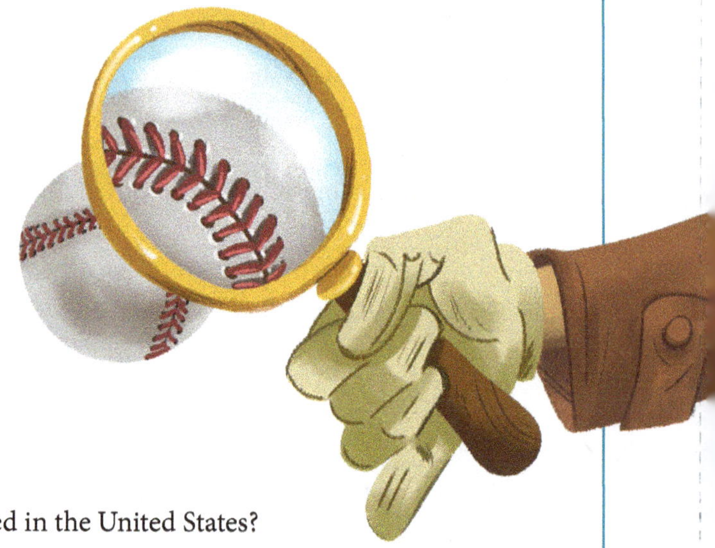

Research Plan

Research timeline:

2 days: Read sources.

2 days: Develop outline.

3 days: Write paper.

2 days: Revise paper.

1 day: Proofread paper.

2 days: Publish paper.

Broad topic: Baseball

Narrowed topic: The history of baseball

Research question: How did baseball get started in the United States?

Related questions: Where did the game concept come from?
Where did it start?
Who started it?
What was the first game like?
How has the game changed?

Sources needed/required:

3+ print (books, encyclopedias/reference books, magazines, newspapers)

2+ nonprint (internet sites, software, videos)

Search terms used:

1. where baseball began
2. how baseball began
3. history of baseball
4. baseball in the United States

Sources referenced and used:

Burns, Ken and Lynn Novick. *Baseball.* Public Broadcasting Service, Premiered Sept. 1994.

Nathanson, Mitchell Urbana. *A People's History of Baseball.* U of Illinois P, 2012.

Stamp, Jimmy. "A Brief History of the Baseball." *Smithsonian Magazine,* Smithsonian Institution, 28 June 2013, www.smithsonianmag.com/arts-culture/a-brief-history-of-the-baseball-3685086/. Accessed 24 Mar. 2020.

A wide range of sources needs to be located and recorded. These sources should provide enough detail and several perspectives in order to satisfactorily explain the answer to the research question. Record all sources, using MLA format (see Lessons 50–51); sources can always be deleted if they prove to not be useful. Too many are better than not enough.

The type of information needed will change depending on the question you are trying to answer; therefore, it is important to understand where to go to find all types of information.

Using Library Support

Above all, the library skills of maneuvering through shelf sources and using search tools must become a researcher's best friend.

Library Organization and Labels

Libraries use either the **Dewey Decimal System** or the **Library of Congress System** to arrange nonfiction books. The Dewey Decimal System categorizes books numerically according to ten divisions of knowledge with each division assigned one hundred numbers. For instance, 000–099 identifies general works; 800–899 identifies books on literature and rhetoric. The call number—the label on the book's spine—may also include the first three letters of the author's last name and a library section letter, such as *R* for *reference*.

The Library of Congress System divides all knowledge into twenty-one categories identified by a letter. Most categories are subdivided using two- or three-letter combinations with numbers. For instance, *BF 175* on a book's spine would identify a subcategory of books on psychoanalysis.

Types of Sources

Many paper sources are now also available in electronic form; they can be read on the internet, and many can also be downloaded for a period of time for reading offline. The library usually organizes them by section.

Audio-visual materials such as DVDs and CDs have a separate section.

Books fall into one of two categories: **fiction** or **nonfiction**. In research, nonfiction books, which present facts on virtually any topic, are useful for obtaining complete background or an in-depth analysis of an issue or topic.

Periodicals are materials published at regular intervals, such as monthly magazines or daily newspapers. Because they are published regularly, periodicals are an excellent source for current information about a wide variety of topics. Some online publications, such as newspapers, require a subscription. As opposed to general interest periodicals, scholarly journals are periodicals written by experts in a particular field and published by a credible publisher. These experts document original research and analysis of a focused topic by explaining facts, ideas, and methods and footnoting their sources.

Reference sources refer to materials used to find specific statistics, facts, or general background on a topic and are not generally read beginning to end. They serve as a good source for starting the research and polishing the finished product with more specific details. They often cite additional sources, which can help with further research. Common reference sources include almanacs, dictionaries, thesauruses, encyclopedias, and atlases. Bible commentaries and concordances supply biblical interpretation and references. **Bible commentaries** explain books of the Bible or the entire Bible, section by section or verse by verse. **Bible concordances** are alphabetical indexes to words and phrases found in the Bible. They are helpful for locating a specific passage or multiple passages on a specific subject.

Examples of online reference sources:

Almanac: farmersalmanac.com

Dictionary: merriam-webster.com

Thesaurus: merriam-webster.com/thesaurus

Encyclopedia: britannica.com

Atlas: worldatlas.com

Bible study tools: biblegateway.com and blueletterbible.org

Using Search Tools

Library Catalog

Libraries maintain computer catalogs of all library sources. The call number that appears on a book's spine will also appear in the library card-catalog entry. To use the computer catalog, you must know the author, title, or subject of the book you want to find.

The Great and Only Barnum: The Tremendous, Stupendous Life of Showman P. T. Barnum / by Candace Fleming; illustrated by Ray Fenwick.

BOOK | New York: Schwartz & Wade Books | 2009 | 151 p.: ill.: 25 cm

Language: English **Database:** BJU Mack and Music Libraries

Subjects: Circus owners; United States; Biography; Juvenile literature; Barnum, P. T. 1810–1891

Location	**Call No.**
Juvenile biography	JB-B B267f

Practice the Skill

Using the catalog entry, answer the following questions.

1. What is the complete title of the book? ____________________
2. Who is the book's author? ____________________
3. What company published the book? ____________________
4. Where was the book published? ____________________
5. In what year was the book published? ____________________
6. What is the book's call number? ____________________
7. Where is the book located in the library? ____________________
8. Under what subject headings would you find other books on the same topic? ____________________

The Internet

Search Engines

A search engine uses keywords entered to explore the internet for websites, web pages, and other resources related to a subject.

Online Websites

Websites are a collection of webpages about specific topics, organizations, or individuals. They contain information and links to other websites or webpages with related information. Websites ending in *.gov* or *.edu* are generally reliable; websites ending in *.com* or *.org* are often good but need to be chosen selectively. For finding the most accurate, useful information, the internet is generally not as helpful as catalog searching.

Searching Tips

The following tips will help you find and record the information you need, whether using the internet or a library for research.

1. Enter the most specific keywords related to the topic in the search bar. This will help to limit the search results generated by the query.
2. Use a variety of keywords in the searches.
3. Broaden or narrow the topic or research question if necessary.
4. For further research, keep a list of important words or phrases that may come up.
5. Make sure to record the source information before returning the book to the library or closing the webpage.

Practice the Skill

Using the sample research plan on page 160 as a model, complete a research plan for one of the research questions you wrote on page 159.

Make a list of five search terms; then use your library catalog and the internet to list a minimum of three sources relevant to the research question. Include at least one printed book, one website, and one periodical (print or online). Record as much of the following information as possible. Not all sources will contain all information.

- author(s)
- title of source
- container (a larger source from which the source comes, such as a magazine from which an article comes or a book from which a short story comes)
- other contributor(s) (editors [of the container], translators, illustrators, and the like)
- version (edition)
- number (volume)
- publisher
- publication date
- location (page numbers or URL)

EVALUATING AND INCORPORATING SOURCES

Before you begin gathering information from your sources, you must first check all your sources to make sure they are relevant and credible, or trustworthy. Relevant and credible sources will give strength to your paper's thesis and reinforce your credibility with your audience.

Evaluating Sources for Relevancy

Understandable and Related

Before you can begin citing a source, you need to be able to read and comprehend the material. Often, experts in their fields write with complex sentence structures and technical vocabulary, making the material difficult to understand.

It is also important that your source relates directly to the purpose of your paper. Does the content relate to your thesis statement? Without reading the whole document to check for relevance, you can try:

- Checking titles for possible connections to your paper's purpose
- Reading the introduction, abstract, or summary
- Skimming the table of contents or index

Current

Is the information up-to-date? When was it last updated? For some content such as science where new discoveries are constantly being made, obtaining the most current information is of utmost importance.

Evaluating Sources for Credibility

Primary or Secondary

Information will be from one of two types of sources: primary or secondary. **Primary sources** are factual results of research or firsthand accounts or records from a time period, place, or people. Examples include diaries, autobiographies, letters, historic documents, speeches, or records of scientific observations. **Secondary sources** provide existing research and are a good place to begin. They are secondhand descriptions, interpretations, or reviews of primary sources. Examples include biographies, book reviews, encyclopedias, or history books.

Fact, Opinion, or Bias

The purpose of a research paper is to report on existing factual information, not opinion or bias. **Facts** are information that can be proven true by observation or research. Examples might include, "Abraham Lincoln was the sixteenth president," or, "The history teacher graded all the tests."

Opinions are expressions of judgment or belief that differ from person to person. They may or may not be biased. Examples might include, "Abraham Lincoln was one of the best United States presidents," or, "The history teacher did not grade the tests fairly." In general, blogs and online forums are not reliable sources for a research paper. They reflect the opinions of the writers rather than objective facts. Statements beginning with "in my opinion," I believe that," or "in my mind" are clear warning signs.

Bias refers to the idea of *unfairly* promoting one side over another. The reader must be discerning. Journalists are often accused of bias when they frequently report favorably about politicians they personally like and unfavorably about politicians they disagree with. They might selectively choose facts and words to influence the reader toward a particular point of view. Sources that are selling something or that deal with controversial topics are often biased. Possible indicators of bias may include:

- The language tends to be dominantly positive or negative.
- The author depends more on emotion than logic.
- The author tries to change the reader's point of view.
- The author presents only facts that support his point of view.

Christ-expression requires us to discern researched content that is as free from opinion and bias as possible. Most research papers or books include not only facts but interpretation of those facts. In order to communicate the interpretation desired, researchers can choose which information to include and which to leave out, thus shaping the results of their research. The writer must compare findings of multiple sources for accuracy and agreement. A writer's compiled research is a reflection on the writer's integrity. It is up to him to sift through the many sources and present a work as credible and trustworthy as possible.

To determine how factual a source may be:

- Compare the source's content with other reliable sources.
- Check for in-text citations and a Works Cited or bibliography.
- Check for biased language or assumptions in delivering facts.

The writer also practices Christ-expression by making an effort to avoid bias. Although Christians are called to have and promote biblical convictions and beliefs, even believers' opinions can sometimes be biased because of their lack of knowledge or understanding of a given topic. A Christian writer must beware of promoting his beliefs and opinions in a biased, dishonest way. This caution begins with being self-critical, evaluating his own thinking and interpretation. He must beware of forcing borrowed facts to say what he wants them to say or prove what he wants them to prove. Including just enough facts to support his desired conclusion but leaving out nonsupportive facts is simply a form of dishonest bias. A writer can be deceptive while appearing to be objective. He needs to test the true intents of his heart (Prov. 21:2). Be discerning. Are you telling the whole truth and nothing but the truth?

Practice the Skill

Identify the two factual statements (*F*), two opinion statements (*O*), and one biased statement (*B*).

_______ 1. The school board is considering adopting a uniform policy.

_______ 2. "Our uniforms improve classroom discipline. Buy now before our sale ends!"

_______ 3. I think wearing uniforms is a good idea.

_______ 4. The blue-and-brown color combination is the best choice.

_______ 5. The school board decided on the blue-and-brown uniforms.

Use an internet search to find at least one factual, one opinionated, and one biased source.

Authoritative and Accurate

Sources should be written by an authority on a topic. Credible authors often include their credentials and are published by a recognized organization or publisher. Using a professional tone, they support their claims by citing and documenting other experts in their field. A writer should not assume the content of a seemingly credible source is always trustworthy. He should check out the accuracy of the content by comparing even an expert's claims to other credible sources.

The following checklist is a convenient tool for evaluating sources.

	Relevance and Credibility Checklist
Understandable and Related	❑ Does the information make sense? ❑ Does the information relate to the thesis?
Current	❑ Is the information up-to-date?
Primary or Secondary	❑ Is the information original data or a firsthand account, or is it second-hand interpretation of data?
Fact, Opinion, or Bias	❑ Is the content found in other reliable sources? ❑ Does the author give documented support for his conclusions? ❑ Does the author interact fairly with viewpoints contrary to his own? ❑ Does the author express bias?
Authoritative and Accurate	❑ Does the information come from an expert on the subject? ❑ Is the information accurate?

Practice the Skill

Use the Relevance and Credibility Checklist to find one source that is credible and one that is not. Show your sources to a partner and explain the decisions you made.

Common Knowledge

Common knowledge is widely known or easily proven and does not need documentation or its sources identified. Deciding what is common knowledge depends on the writer's audience. If the information is known or is easily accessible to most in your audience, it is considered common knowledge and requires no documentation; however, if it is not, it must be documented. For example, much of the information in the Jim Elliot mentor text is general knowledge that can be found in multiple sources and thus does not need to be documented. On the other hand, a piece written for your class on how hot air balloons fly is probably unfamiliar to most and would require borrowed, documented information.

Borrowed Knowledge

Most researched content will not be common knowledge but borrowed knowledge—the ideas, words, phrases, and sentences of another person. Stealing another writer's content without giving that person credit is a serious academic violation called **plagiarism**. Examples of plagiarism include using someone else's ideas without identifying whose they are, copying something from another writer with no citation and only changing a few words, or including exact words without quotation marks and citation. Plagiarism is considered a serious academic offense that can result in receiving a failing grade.

One of God's Ten Commandments is "Thou shalt not steal" (Exodus 20:15). When we think of God's prohibition against stealing, we tend to think of stealing physical property; but stealing intellectual property—a person's ideas, words, and creative expressions—without identifying the source is just as wrong. A writer that chooses to do so is not imitating his Creator in whose image he is created. He is revealing something about his character or lack thereof. Determine to obey God's command in Ephesians 4:28, "Let him that stole steal no more." The next part of this verse, "but rather let him labour, working with his hands the thing which is good," emphasizes the fact that practicing Christ-expression takes work, effort, and time. Every detail should be checked and rechecked.

How to Avoid Plagiarism

Plagiarism can be avoided by summarizing, paraphrasing, or quoting a source. Summarizing and paraphrasing are similar tasks for rewriting a passage in your own words without changing the meaning of the original passage. Understanding the difference between the process and the purpose for each is important when deciding how to use your sources.

Summarizing

Summarizing is used when you want to reduce a longer passage (e.g., chapter, article, book) to just the main ideas. For instance, for an article about a science experiment, you might relate the main steps in the experiment or just the final experiment result. If you are highlighting a famous person's speech, you might relate the main points or just the one big idea. Often, summarizing is useful for giving an overview of a source you will discuss in more detail. For instance, if you are researching an important historical figure, you might cite the title of a biography and give one statement describing its overall content approach.

Process for Summarizing:

1. Identify a specific passage in a text.
2. Read the entire text carefully.
3. Identify the main idea(s).
4. Rewrite the main idea(s) in your own words.
5. Check to make sure your words and structure are not similar to the original.
6. Be sure to mention the name of the source you are summarizing.

Paraphrasing

Depending on the subject, paraphrasing will often make up the bulk of a paper. Use it when you want to recount the ideas of a passage that are not significant enough to quote. Because you are relating what the passage said, the length of the paraphrase should be approximately the same as the original. Whereas *summarizing* the science experiment would hit the main steps or the final result, *paraphrasing* the experiment would involve a detailed explanation of each step of the process in your own words and with different sentence structure from the original. Paraphrasing a famous speech, you would explain each point and the speaker's supporting information. Paraphrasing is still borrowing; without citation, it is plagiarism.

Practice the Skill

Read the following passage from Britannica.com concerning Benjamin Franklin. Identify which of the passages following it is a summarized version and which is a paraphrased version.

> The experiment he suggested to prove the identity of lightning and electricity was apparently first made in France before he tried the simpler but more dangerous expedient of flying a kite in a thunderstorm. But his other findings were original. He created the distinction between insulators and conductors. He invented a battery for storing electrical charges. He coined new English words for the new science of electricity—*conductor*, *charge*, *discharge*, *condense*, *armature*, *electrify*, and others. He showed that electricity was a single "fluid" with positive and negative or plus and minus charges and not, as traditionally thought, two kinds of fluids. And he demonstrated that the plus and minus charges, or states of electrification of bodies, had to occur in exactly equal amounts—a crucial scientific principle known today as the law of conservation of charge (Hornberger and Wood).

Work Cited

Hornberger, Theodore and Gordon S. Wood. "Benjamin Franklin: American Author, Scientist, and Statesman." *Encyclopaedia Britannica*, Encyclopaedia Britannica, Inc., 2020, www.britannica.com/biography/Benjamin-Franklin/Achievement-of-security-and-fame-1726-5. Accessed 19 Mar. 2020.

1. More than likely France was the first to demonstrate lightning and electricity, not Benjamin Franklin with his classic kite-flying experiment. Franklin's original findings, however, include distinguishing between insulators and conductors and developing a battery for holding electric charges. As a result of his research, he is credited with creating English terms, such as *armature*, *charge*, *condense*, *conductor*, *discharge*, and *electrify*. Finally, he found that electricity was not two different fluids as others originally thought, but it was actually the excess or deficiency of one "fluid." As a result of this finding, he developed a scientific principle, critical to scientists today, known as the law of conservation: plus and minus charges have to exist in equivalent amounts (Hornberger and Wood).

    ____

2. Benjamin Franklin is credited with several original scientific discoveries having to do with electricity. He came up with original English terms for describing electrical processes and developed the law of conservation, critical to scientists today (Hornberger and Wood).

    ____

Direct Quotations

The writer's voice should dominate a paper. Quoting someone's exact words is using someone else's voice and should be done purposefully and sparingly. The writer should use quotes to distinguish between his own view and that of another author, to point out another author's position on a topic, to support a claim, or to call attention to powerful, memorable wording. Before quoting, the writer should ask: What is my purpose for quoting? Is the passage too long? Would a paraphrase work just as well? Would quoting just a sentence or a phrase be as effective?

Smoothly Incorporating Summaries, Paraphrases, and Quotes

Although you should have a thorough understanding of the subject of your paper, you are not an expert. You need to borrow the information and voices of experts to lend authority and credibility to your paper. Being able to smoothly transition from your voice to the voice of another and back is a mark of a skillful writer.

One of the best ways to make this transition happen is to introduce the borrowed information in the flow of your own words, using what are called *leads*.

Examples of leads for summaries or paraphrases:

Smith argued that . . .
Smith said that . . . to prove his point.
. . . according to Smith's study.

Examples of leads for quotations:

Smith emphasized his point by saying, ". . . ."
Smith stated, ". . . ," to prove his point.
". . . ," wrote Smith.

Review the Skill

Summarize and paraphrase a passage of at least ten sentences from one of the sources you listed in your research plan on page 165.

Use the Skill

Write a five-paragraph paper on your research question. Smoothly incorporate at least one summary, one paraphrase, and one quotation.

The Works Cited

After the paper is written, the sources cited at least once should be listed on a separate works-cited page that goes at the end of the paper. Modern Language Association (MLA) standard format specifies that this alphabetical list uses *hanging indentation*, indenting all lines half an inch except the first line of each entry.

On a works-cited page, the source information included in the following list should be ordered as indicated, with the specified punctuation separating each item. Apply correct rules for capitalization, italics, and quotation marks.

Examine the indentation, order, and punctuation in the following works-cited entry template:

author's last name, first name.(1) **title of source.**(2) **title of container,**(3) **other contributors,**(4) **version,**(5) **number,**(6) **publisher,**(7) **publication date,**(8) **location.**(9)

1. **Author's last name, first name:** A citation entry usually begins with the author's name when available. Variations of author citations may include:
   - **Two authors:** First author's last name, first name, the word *and*, plus second author's first name and last name.
   - **More than two authors:** First author's last name, first name, and the abbreviation *et. al.*
   - **Unknown author(s):** Begin entry with next available item on list (usually title of source).
   - **Authors of different sources share the same last name:** Alphabetize by the author's first name also. For instance, "Smith, John" would come before "Smith, Katherine" on the works-cited page.
   - **Editor(s) only; no author(s):** Begin entry with the name of the editor(s) in place of the author, followed by a comma and the word *editors*.

2. **Title of source:** The title is placed in quotation marks when part of a larger work or italicized when a single publication.

3. **Title of container:** The title of the container should be included if the source is a part of a larger whole. For instance, articles are contained in magazines, newspapers, journals, or encyclopedias; pictures are contained in books; books may be part of a series; stories might be contained in a collection.

4. **Other contributors:** Include this if editors or translators are listed in addition to the author or if recognition of illustrators or other contributors is relevant to your research.

5 **Version:** The version should be included if a source lists its edition or version.

6 **Number:** The number of a source should be included if it is a part of a numbered sequence. For instance, books, magazines, or journals may be part of a series or multivolume set.

7 **Publisher:** The publisher is the organization responsible for producing and distributing the work.

8 **Publication date:** The date of publication is written in day-month-year order depending on available specifics.

9 **Location:** To cite a source's location, include the page number(s) for a printed source or the URL (web address) or DOI (digital object identifier) for an online source. Exclude *https://* from the web address. If the publication is in a database (e.g., *JSTOR*), name this second container before the DOI. When citing a website, also provide the date of access in the location.

Geshki, Michael. "Reimagining Dinosaurs." *National Geographic*, Oct. 2020, pp. 38–49.

Moo, Douglas J. *The Epistle to the Romans*. The New International Commentary on the New Testament, edited by Gordon D. Fee, William B. Eerdmans Publishing, 1996, p. 65.

In-Text Citations

Although a works-cited page gives credit to the sources used, it is not enough. Whenever sources are quoted, summarized, or paraphrased, an in-text citation must be included that tells the reader what source the information came from and where in the source it came from. In order to not interrupt the flow of the text too much, sources are credited inside parentheses at the end of the sentence or at a natural pause in the sentence. The citation should come before any punctuation needed at that place in the sentence.

General Sources

In-text citations generally include the first word found in the corresponding full works-cited entry and the location, usually a page number. If the author's name is mentioned in the sentence, only the page number is needed in the parentheses.

In-text citations
The missionary reported that she is "still teaching online, regularly meeting and praying with church friends, and finding ways to brighten my neighbors' days by leaving pictures and encouraging notes in the hallways" (Belz 44).

Belz quotes the missionary: "I am still teaching online, regularly meeting and praying with church friends, and finding ways to brighten my neighbors' days by leaving pictures and encouraging notes in the hallways" (44).

Works-cited entry
Belz, Mindy. "Witnessing in Place." *World*, vol. 35, God's World Publications, May 2020, pp. 40–45.

If the works-cited entry lists no author and instead lists the title first, the title (or a shortened version of the title that includes the word used to alphabetize the works-cited entry) should be used.

In-text citation
Chapter 15 informs the reader that "the goal of the in-text citation is to provide enough information to lead your reader directly to the source you use while disrupting the flow of your argument as little as possible" (*MLA Handbook* 58).

Works-cited entry
MLA Handbook, 8th ed., The Modern Language Association of America, 2016, p. 58.

The same instruction applies to a website. If there is no author, the citation is the title of the article, the name of the website, or whatever word is used to alphabetize the entry in the works cited. No page number or other location is generally necessary for in-text citations of online sources.

Bible References

For in-text citations, the first time a Bible quote is included, note the translation, chapter, book, and verse. All additional quotes just need the reference unless a different translation is used.

In-text citation

Paul encouraged believers to "rejoice in the Lord alway; and again I say, Rejoice" (*Authorized King James Version*, Phil. 4:4).

Works-cited entry

The Holy Bible. Authorized King James Version, The National Publishing Company, 1975.

Slide-based Presentations

MLA suggests inserting a citation on each slide when borrowed information is used. A works-cited list should be included on a slide at the end of the presentation.

In-text citation

The exchange of goods between European explorers and Native Americans was called the Columbian Exchange (Baker).

Works-cited entry

Baker, Kathleen. "Columbian Exchange." *Christopher Columbus & European Exploration*, updated 25 June 2019, Prezi Inc., prezi.com/p/oqrvvr8ahhal/unit-2-cc-northwest-passage-columbian-exchange/. *Prezi.com*, Accessed 19 May 2020.

Interviews

Interviews conducted by the writer of the paper list the name of the person being interviewed, the label "Personal interview" in the section where the source's title would normally be listed, and the date the interview was conducted.

In-text citation
"I have taught computers for years; I cannot believe how fast the technology has changed" (Henry).

Works-cited entry
Henry, William. Personal interview. 19 Mar. 2020.

Interviews conducted by someone else and recorded in some fashion are generally listed in accordance with the type of source in which they appear.

In-text citation
In that interview he said, "[I]f the Bible is truth, God's eternal truth, we have to stand opposed to the false doctrine that is contrary [to] the Bible, regardless what label it may carry" (Jones).

Works-cited entry
Jones, Robert, III. Interview with Larry King. *Larry King Live*, Cable News Network, aired 3 Mar. 2000, www.cnn.com/TRANSCRIPTS/0003/03/lkl.00.html. Transcript. *CNN.com*, Accessed 20 May 2020.

Practice the Skill

Insert in-text citations into your five-paragraph paper. Then create a correctly formatted Works Cited for the sources you used. Exchange papers with a partner and check for correct formatting.

EXPLANATORY PARAGRAPHS
Writing Traits: Ideas, Organization

Listen Up!

Read the mentor text. What is this paragraph explaining? What quotation(s), summary/summaries or paraphrase(s) are incorporated?

MENTOR TEXT

How America Entered World War I

Originally known as "The Great War," World War I was one of the bloodiest wars in human history, but it was a war that America originally sought to avoid. When the war first began, President Woodrow Wilson called for "peace without victory," arguing that it would be more profitable to negotiate a lasting peace between the two alliances rather than joining the Allies to defeat the Central Powers (Wilson). However, two major events disrupted Wilson's plan. First, the Germans killed a number of Americans by sinking several unarmed ships, most notably the *Lusitania* ("The United States officially enters World War I"). While this outraged Americans and turned public opinion against Germany, an even more shocking action helped change Wilson's mind about remaining neutral. On January 16, 1917, British Intelligence intercepted an encoded message by German foreign minister Arthur Zimmerman encouraging Mexico to join the war and fight the United States (Carlisle 195–96). The combination of these two events caused Wilson to reluctantly ask Congress to declare war.

Works Cited

Carlisle, Rodney P. *World War I*. Infobase Publishing, 2007, pp. 195–96.

"The United States officially enters World War I." *History*, A&E Television Networks, 9 Feb. 2010, updated 3 Apr. 2020, www.history.com/this-day-in-history/america-enters-world-war-i. Accessed 12 May 2020.

Wilson, Woodrow. "Peace without Victory." 64th Congress, US Senate, 22 Jan. 1917, Washington, DC, Presidential Address.

Take Notes!

Identify the purpose for each of the explanatory paragraph parts.

A lot of the writing you are expected to do in school requires giving reasons for how or why something happened or continues to happen. Your purpose is to explain something well to a reader with little prior knowledge of or experience with what you are writing about.

The topic sentence should introduce a topic that can be explained satisfactorily in the length of a paragraph. The body should provide evidential support, such as borrowed knowledge from authorities, examples, figures, and statistics. Use transitions to logically guide the reader from one point to the next. The concluding sentence should summarize the main information explained in the paragraph.

Partner Up!

Choose one of the explanatory topics below or a topic of interest to you. Pick a topic you know a little about but need to do some additional research on. Find three to five sources. Brainstorm supporting evidence and number it in logical order. Insert possible transitions.

How are racecars built?
What makes a healthy snack?
How can exercise improve concentration?
Why are astronauts weightless in space?
What are some helpful ways to study for a math test?

Try It Out!

Write a paragraph, using the information you gathered and organized in *Partner Up!* Insert in-text citations and include a Works Cited at the end.

INTEGRITY
Truthful
honest
accurate

CHAPTER 7

INFORMATIVE

ESSAY

HOW DO I WRITE WITH INTEGRITY?

Your everyday written conversation shows who you are and what is important to you. It visually shows what is in your mind and heart. Academic writing, however, focuses on the accuracy of facts, vivid and concrete presentation, and the formal yet personal quality of your written voice. While writing with honor and leaving an inspiring and lasting impression on your audience is important for a successful essay, displaying Christ-like expression should be your top priority. Fortunately, all of this can be achieved with excellence while remaining true to your personal creative style. Characteristics of informative writing, such as truthful, relevant ideas infused with straightforward, precise language, will help you to be easily understood and keep your readers engaged. Organization that is logical, systematic, and efficient will help your voice to sound fluent and professional, while maintaining a personal style that is powerful and influential.

The mentor text is an example of an informative essay that provides information about essential preparations for a career as a national or state park ranger. As you read, pay attention to the presence of ideas, word choice, organization, voice, *and* sentence fluency.

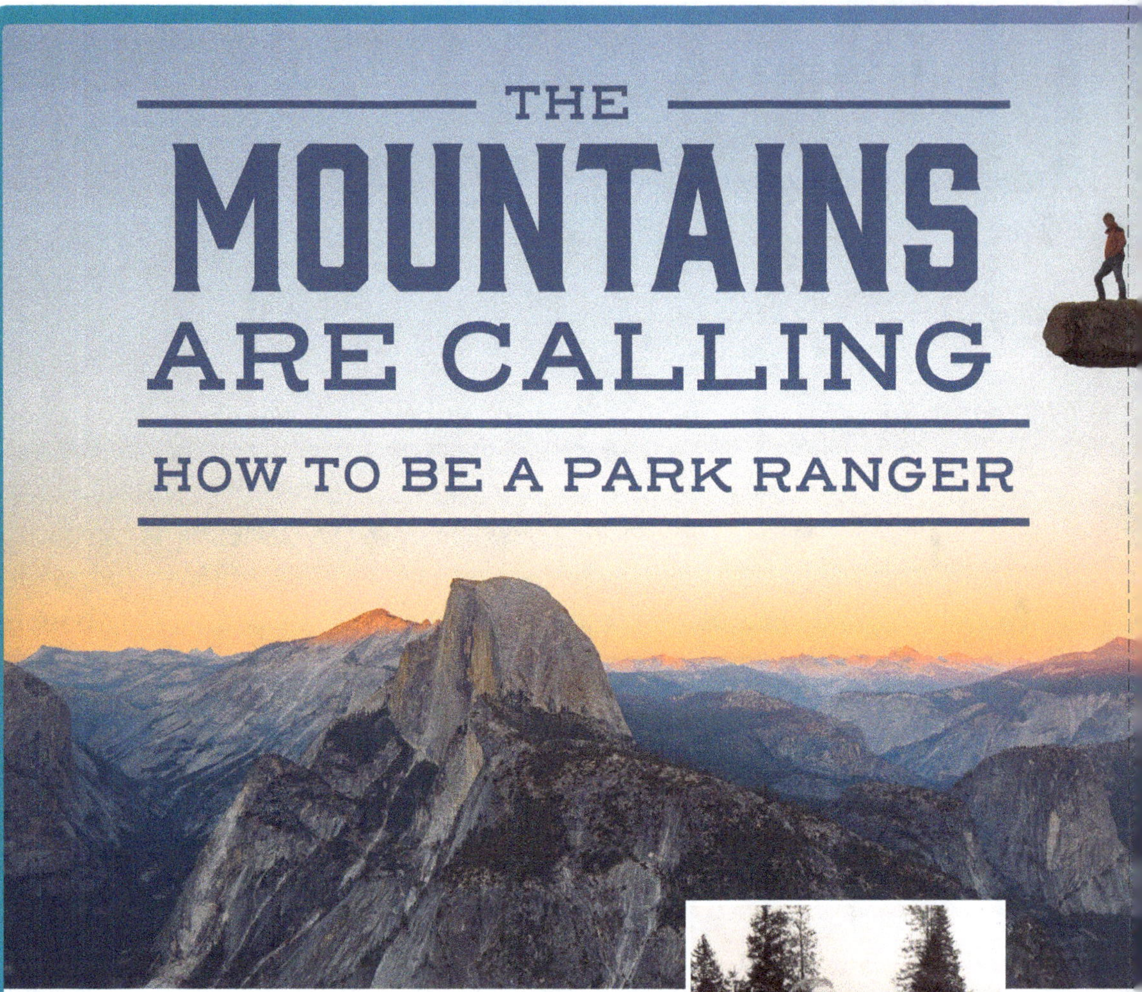

THE MOUNTAINS ARE CALLING

HOW TO BE A PARK RANGER

The hook is a statistic, quote, or question that grabs the reader's attention to interest them in what is to come.

The thesis statement should inform the reader of the topic and talking points of the essay or report.

"The mountains are calling, and I must go" is a now-famous reflection written by the early 20th century preservationist John Muir (Badè 385). As a philosopher, wildlife conservationist, and naturalist, Muir spent his life traveling, observing, and writing about the Yosemite Valley region. Like John Muir, many people today have chosen careers as park rangers because of their love for and desire to protect and enjoy nature. A student interested in becoming a park ranger should not wait to plan for this adventurous and rewarding career. A student can prepare for a career as a park ranger by doing volunteer work in middle school, gaining related job experience in high school, and earning a degree in college.

Volunteering is the easiest way for students to learn about a park ranger's job and to develop useful skills. A major part of a ranger's job is protecting public land, to ensure not only its beauty, but also its usefulness for generations to come. A ranger's duty, then, is to protect from what John Muir warns is the threat of "both axe and fire. . . [and] danger of extinction" (Muir 181). Students can look for opportunities to volunteer at wildlife rescue organizations, fisheries, and local animal shelters. These organizations are good places to receive valuable training in protecting and caring for animals and for the environments in which they live ("How to Become a Park Ranger"). Volunteering for these organizations will develop a student's awareness of conservation efforts. Membership in community youth organizations is another important opportunity for learning leadership and outdoor survival skills that are essential to a park ranger's job. Adventure activities, such as kayaking, canoeing, and hiking, help to build strength, endurance, and teamwork. These are important skills for a park ranger. Volunteering and participating in outdoor activities may help students decide if becoming a park ranger is truly something they want to explore.

As students enter high school, they should continue volunteering while also taking advantage of new opportunities available to them. Many places students volunteered at in middle school may offer part-time jobs to high school students. State parks can also provide valuable employment opportunities. Students can work in a park's visitor center or in the park office answering phones or doing other light office work. If, however, a student is interested in the law enforcement side of park ranger duties, he can check with his local police department. Many offer junior police academy summer programs. Remember, all work develops important character traits, such as faithfulness in attendance, diligence in work, and willingness to do whatever is asked. A good work ethic is something employers regard highly in their employees. Finally, most high schools offer career track programs or extracurricular activities that provide students with knowledge and training for potential careers. Diligence in pursuing high school employment opportunities helps to bring the student closer to his or her ultimate career goal.

A topic sentence is usually placed at the beginning of the paragraph. It should reflect the first issue in the thesis statement.

The concluding sentence should rephrase the topic sentence to neatly close the paragraph.

MENTOR TEXT

Students interested in park service should plan to complete their college degrees and pursue internships. First, students need to determine what kind of park ranger they want to be: an interpretive guide, focusing on education and tours, or a protective ranger, focusing on law enforcement. Although life and earth sciences are the most beneficial degrees, the NPS (National Park Service) accepts graduates from a wide range of majors ("Steps to Becoming a Park Ranger"). Other interesting majors that provide knowledge and skills for a park ranger include environmental studies, biology, criminal justice, education, public relations, and forestry management. Above all, most park rangers agree that pursuing internships is vital, providing opportunities for "on-the-ground experience, networking, and a host of unexpected opportunities" that cannot be attained in the classroom ("What Does It Take to Be a Park Ranger?"). No matter what college a student chooses, studying hard in classes, continuing volunteer work, and accepting internship opportunities will help prepare for a career.

A career in park ranger service really is a lifelong adventure in learning, and students can start preparing early with volunteer work in park or animal service. A passion for working outdoors opens a variety of employment opportunities to develop an interest in and knowledge of park ranger careers. Students who have completed their college degrees and valuable internships help to ensure their future as rangers. Inspiring and exciting, a park ranger's job is a new adventure every day. Who else hears the mountains calling?

The conclusion should begin with a rewording of the thesis statement, followed by a quick summary. It should end with a call to action or an inspiration.

Works Cited

Badè, William Frederic. *The Life and Letters of John Muir.* Houghton Mifflin, 1924.

"How to Become a Park Ranger." *Get Educated*, www.geteducated.com/career-center/how-to-become-a-park-ranger/. Accessed 19 Feb. 2020.

Muir, John. *Wilderness Essays.* Gibbs Smith, 2015.

"Steps to Becoming a Park Ranger." *Park Ranger EDU*, www.parkrangeredu.org. Accessed 4 May 2020.

"What Does It Take to Be a Park Ranger? Words of Wisdom from SCA Alumni (Part I)." *Student Conservation Association*, 18 May 2018, www.thesca.org/connect/blog/what-does-it-take-be-park-ranger-words-wisdom-sca-alumni-part-i. Accessed 20 May 2020.

Read the mentor text and complete the activity.

Identify the thesis statement, the topic sentences in the body paragraphs, and the restatement of the three topics in the conclusion.

How did the author connect the introductory hook with the final sentence?

Create Your Blueprint

As the successful and lasting construction of a boat or a house begins with a blueprint (i.e., a plan), so too does the construction of an effective informative essay. Refer to Lesson 2 which explains the importance of the planning stage for successful writing. As you develop your blueprint, create a research plan as explained in Chapter 6.

Establish Your Audience and Purpose

Consider and record the intended audience and purpose for writing your essay. Use the prompt below to get started.

Imagine that you are a professional in a field that interests you. Write an informative essay and prepare a slideshow presentation on your chosen career, explaining to your audience what they can do now and in the future to prepare for a career in that field.

Create a Cluster Map

Brainstorm three to five professions based on the writing prompt above, jotting down what you know about each one before you make a final choice.

Formulate a Research Question

Formulate one research question that will guide your thesis statement. This will be the starting point of your outline. For example, in the mentor text, the research question might have looked like this:

How can a student prepare now for a career as a park ranger?

Gather Sources, Take Notes, and Find Pictures

Your profession has been chosen. You formulated your research question. Now it is time to research the profession.

- Use general reference sources as a starting point.
- Access your local online library catalog system to find books, journals, magazines, and newspaper articles.

Remember to focus on maintaining your integrity and credibility in the sources you choose. Christians need to ask God to give them discernment as they evaluate every source they come across to determine its credibility.

- Interview a professional in the field or someone who has special knowledge of your topic.
- Take thorough notes, including complete citation information from each source you used.
- Find three to four pictures associated with your profession and print them. At the conclusion of this project, you will publish the essay in a slideshow presentation.
- Document the sources and pictures used in MLA format.

Tips for Conducting an Interview

- Research first!
- Brainstorm about 15 questions.
- Come prepared (pencil, paper, questions, recording device).
- Be on time!
- Take good notes.
- Ask brief, open-ended questions.
- Pause; allow the interviewee time to think.

Draft a Thesis Statement

Your thesis statement should identify your topic and the main points you plan to explain in your essay. Refer to the Writing Toolbox in Chapter 4 to help you craft your thesis statement.

- Identify the profession you selected.
- Make a claim or statement about your profession.
- List details that will form the topic sentences for the body paragraphs.

Write an Outline

Choose an organizational method and create a topic outline for your essay. List your main points and include facts and details as subpoints. Refer to Lesson 2 for examples of organizational methods and a sample topic outline.

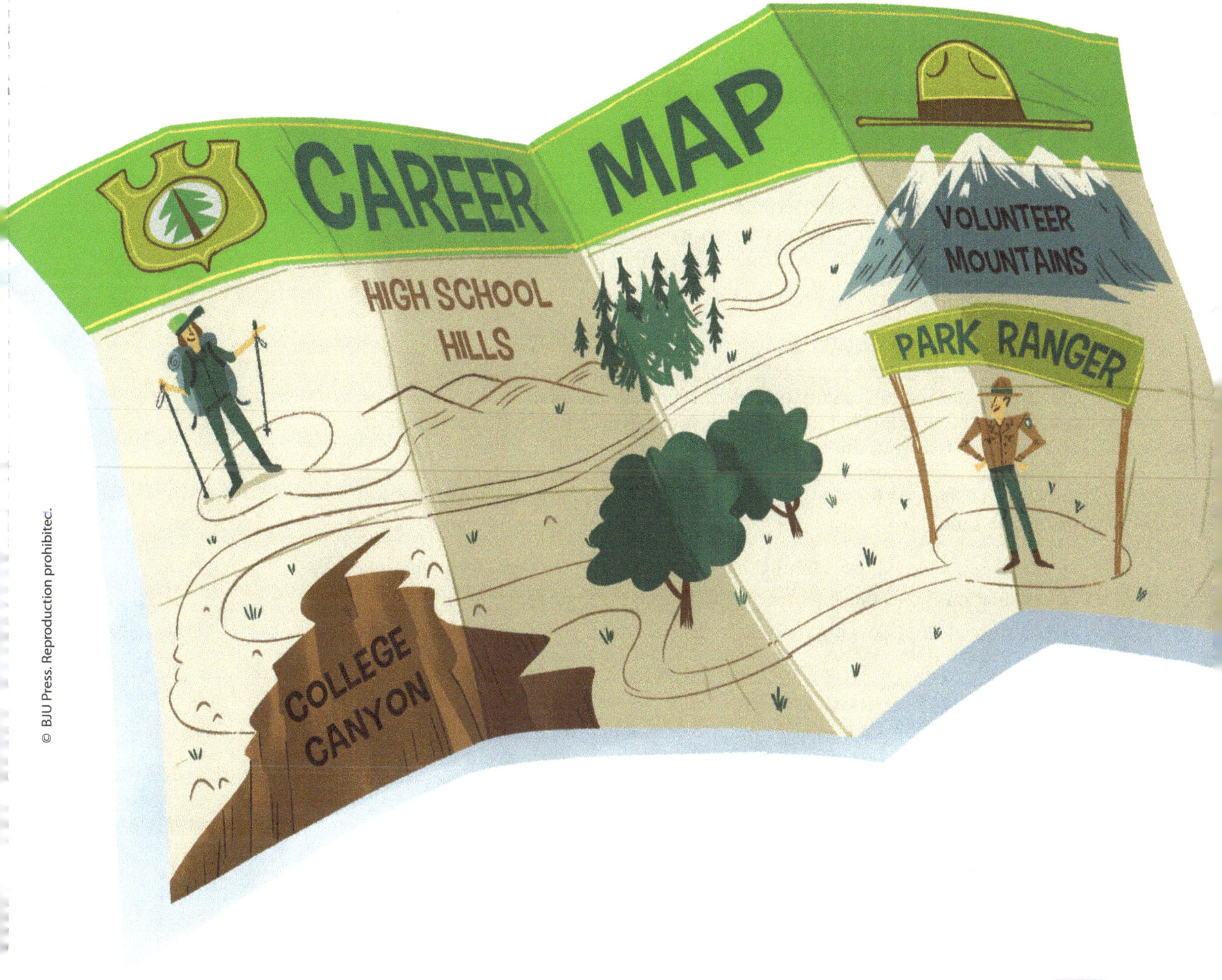

Draft Your Plan

The first draft of your essay is essentially a rough sketch of your thoughts on paper. It is simply turning all your notes and your outline into paragraphs. Focus on organizing ideas logically, as well as maintaining a **formal tone** (i.e., the use of third person pronouns studied in Lesson 41). Keep in mind as you draft your essay that the goal of informative writing is to present the facts in an unbiased format. If your essay includes personal opinion, you run the risk of attempting to persuade rather than inform. Keeping the audience in mind as you write your paper is a great way to hone your Christ-expression by showing empathy for others in your writing.

Draft the Introduction

The introduction is your opportunity to invite your audience to read your essay. Include an engaging hook that draws your reader in, along with interesting background information and a strong thesis. Refer to the Writing Toolbox in Chapter 4 to remind you how to construct a good introductory paragraph.

Draft the Conclusion

The conclusion should restate the points in your thesis and the main ideas of your paper, tying all the information together. Refer to the Writing Toolbox in Chapter 5 to remind you how to construct a conclusion paragraph.

Draft the Three Body Paragraphs

To draft the body of your paper, follow the outline you created in the planning stage. You can modify your outline during this stage if something does not seem to be working, but try to stick to your plan if possible. As you integrate your research into your draft, remember that you are practicing imitating God and Christ-expression by ordering your ideas logically and clearly. Refer to the Writing Toolbox in Chapter 6 for writing tips about explanatory paragraphs. Each body paragraph should have

- a topic sentence at the beginning that clearly reflects the thesis statement,
- explanation and example sentence(s) following the topic sentence, and
- transitional words and phrases within the paragraph and leading to the next paragraph's topic.

Prepare the Pictures

Gather and print the public images you have chosen for your slideshow. Place your pictures throughout your draft as you imagine them supporting your text during your presentation.

Draft the Works Cited

Use the formula given in Lessons 52–53 to create citations in MLA format for your works-cited page. Also, include accurate in-text citations. This is an important area for practicing being a young person of integrity and virtue: giving recognition to others' work (not plagiarizing, or taking credit for, work that is not your own).

REVISING

The revising stage is the heart of the writing process. Content (ideas, word choice, and organization), sentence fluency, and voice are your top priorities during this stage. Paying attention to formal tone, bias-free language, and facts that are clear, concise, and provable should also be part of your focus at this stage. Use the following checklist as a helpful guide for working through your revisions.

	Revising Checklist
Ideas	❑ Does my introduction contain the three required elements? ❑ Does my thesis contain the required elements? ❑ Do I include relevant and reliable facts in the body paragraphs? ❑ Does my conclusion contain all required elements?
Organization	❑ Does my essay contain five paragraphs (introduction, three body paragraphs, and conclusion)? ❑ Do I express my ideas in an easy-to-understand way (i.e., logically, clearly)? ❑ Do I use a clear organizational method to order my ideas?
Word Choice	❑ Do I provide too much explanation? Not enough? ❑ Do I make good use of strong verbs and vivid nouns?
Voice	❑ Is my language appropriate (i.e., no slang or contractions)? ❑ Do I include transitional words and phrases within paragraphs as well as between paragraphs? ❑ Does my language and style inspire my audience to keep reading?
Sentence Fluency	❑ Do I express my thoughts in complete sentences? ❑ Do I provide variety in sentence length and structure? ❑ Do my words and phrases have a good rhythm and flow?

Peer Reviews

Peer reviews provide an opportunity for someone unfamiliar with your paper to evaluate the overall readability of your draft and give you vital feedback: Are your ideas well represented and organized? Does your word choice reflect your voice while maintaining high academic standards? Does your writing read smoothly? A good peer review can address these important issues as a representative audience. The following steps should be used as a guide for a peer read.

- Read the essay aloud but without marking errors. Read to get the feel of the whole essay.
- Read the essay again silently, this time marking errors with proofreading symbols.
- Check for smoothness and overall readability.

Keep the Guidelines for Giving Feedback in Lesson 6 in mind as you discuss your classmate's work.

Discerning Listener Traits

- Look at the person who is speaking.
- Be sincerely interested and supportive.
- Don't interrupt.
- Listen for total meaning.
- Ask questions for clarification.
- Be ready to restate what the person is saying.

The proofreading stage is the last opportunity to improve your writing before presenting it to an audience. At this stage, the small details are important: spelling errors, word choice issues, grammatical misfires (i.e., capitalization, spelling, and punctuation), faulty sentence construction, and concept disorganization. You also need to confirm the accuracy of your in-text citations and Works Cited.

The first step in this process is reading the essay aloud to yourself. Reading aloud helps you listen for and locate awkward construction, omitted words, and other organizational issues. After the initial read-aloud, read your essay silently to yourself several times, focusing on one type of problem with each reading.

Finally, you should read your essay backward for a thorough spelling check. Though it may seem awkward, reading this way forces you to look at each word on its own merits. It is the best way to catch misspellings that may be overlooked when reading the words together as whole units of thought.

	Proofreader's Checklist
Conventions	❑ The essay follows the teacher's formatting guidelines and correct MLA format.
	❑ There are no spelling errors.
	❑ There are no grammar errors.
	❑ There are no errors in capitalization or punctuation.

After you have proofread your essay several times, it is a good idea to exchange papers with a classmate for a second peer read. Asking a classmate to proofread your essay provides an opportunity for fresh eyes to look for grammatical and conventional errors you may have missed.

PUBLISHING

As technology develops, the ways to publish essays and reports expand exponentially (i.e., in a rapidly growing way). In this final stage of writing, you are making preparations for sharing your essay with the teacher and for presenting it orally and visually to your classmates.

Finalizing your paper will be the first step in the publishing process of your informative essay. Use this short list as you prepare your final copy.

- Read and edit your paper one last time, making any necessary changes or corrections.
- Confirm that your Works Cited is formatted accurately and that all sources are noted.
- Type up a final copy of your paper. Print two copies.

Next, write your thesis statement and topic sentences on notecards to guide your oral presentation.

One of the ways to present the ideas from your research is through a slideshow presentation. Use the following list to help you present a visually engaging, attractive slideshow as well as one that is logically ordered and easy to read.

- Use technology skillfully and knowledgeably.
- Keep content to bullet points with limited text.
- Arrange content in logical order.
- Make sure words are clear and visible.
- Choose appropriate and consistent fonts.
- Limit fancy transitions between slides.
- Use animation purposefully and effectively.
- Use high-quality graphics (charts, graphs, photos, etc.).
- Use appropriate color.

Third, the most important part of a presentation is the presenter—you! Look over this list as you practice your presentation in front of a mirror, a family member, or on a recording device.

- Use an attention-getting introduction; tell the audience what they will learn.
- Demonstrate clear planning.
- Demonstrate complete and confident understanding of content—do not just read your essay to your audience.
- Use appropriate language for the purpose, audience, and topic.
- Plan a clear and purposeful conclusion.
- Demonstrate polished presentation etiquette.

Your role as a speaker does not end after your closing remarks. Once you have finished your presentation, you have the opportunity to interact with your audience in a question-and-answer format to ensure your message was delivered successfully. When an audience member asks you a question, you should repeat the question for understanding and ask for clarification if necessary. Keep your answers brief and clear, and be humble enough to admit that you do not know an answer. After you have answered a question, make sure that it was answered satisfactorily and always avoid getting into an argument over a difference of opinion or experience. Finally, give everyone a chance to ask a question; do not let one person dominate the question time.

Tips on Presentation Etiquette

- Maintain good posture.
- Use effective gestures; avoid distracting movements, such as hands in pockets.
- Engage in eye contact with all audience members.
- Speak with a clear and audible voice; use vocal variety.
- Use purposeful pauses; avoid verbal clutter: “um,” “uh,” “like.”

Your responsibilities while interacting with classmates not only include presenting your work but also being a good audience member during others’ presentations. As you know from your own experience, the presenter has put in a lot of effort to share his research with the audience. Make sure, as an audience member, you intentionally focus on the speaker and show sincere interest and support. Do not interrupt; rather, listen for understanding. You will need to be prepared to restate the speaker’s main ideas and ask thoughtful follow-up questions.

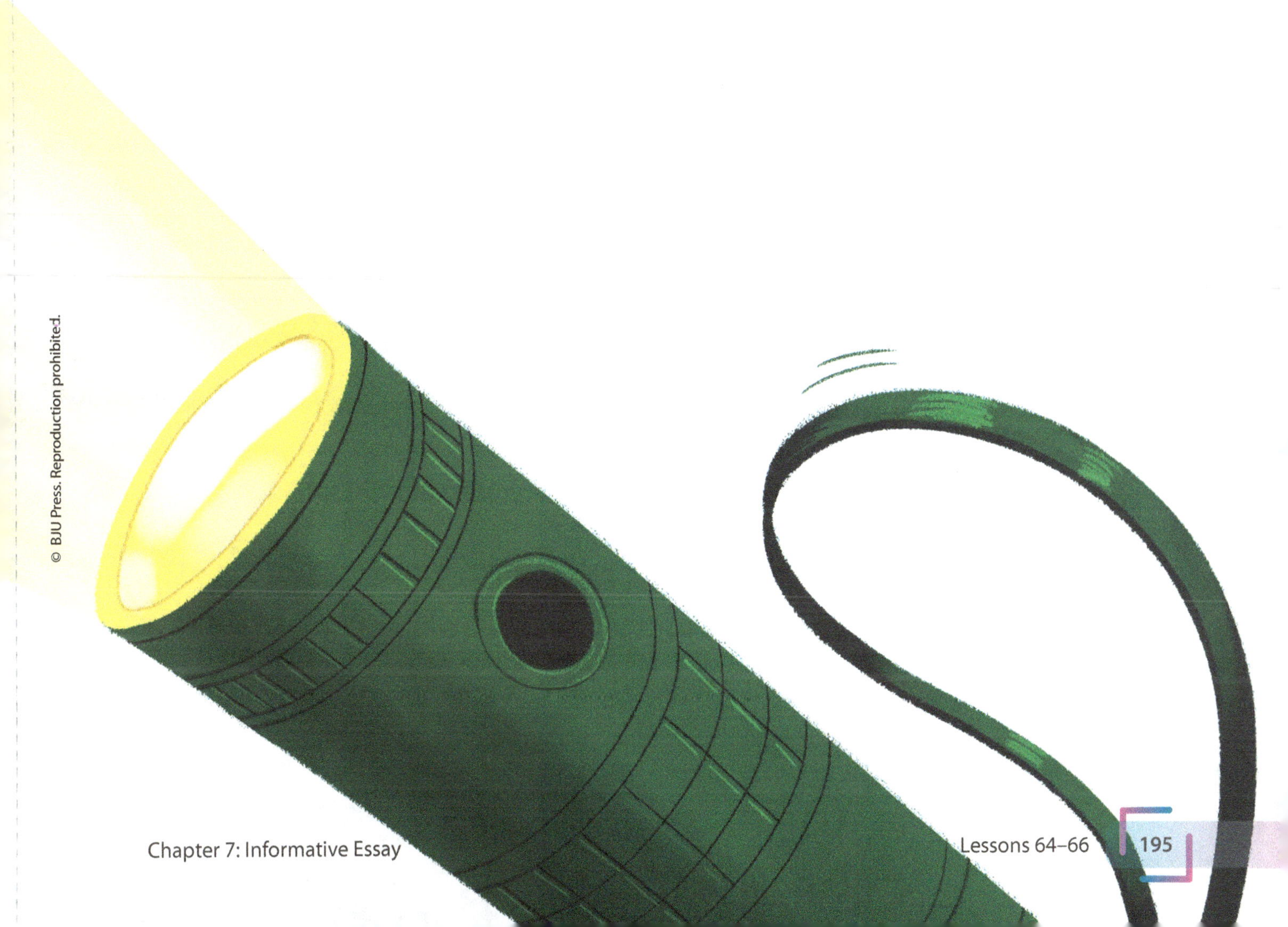

CHAPTER 8

ADJECTIVES

HOW DO DETAILS SHAPE PEOPLE'S IDEAS?

Think back to some favorable (or unfavorable) first impressions you have had of other people. Chances are, these impressions were shaped by the details you noticed about them—their body language, their tone of voice, or how much they smiled. In writing, these details are often revealed by adjectives. Adjectives are an important tool to help your reader visualize every detail you describe. Part of practicing Christ-expression is using adjectives well. Christians do not just use adjectives to sound interesting. They also use adjectives to make their communication precise, clear, and engaging. These are ways they can connect with the reader, whom they are commanded to love as their neighbor. They are showing their love by communicating with precision.

DISCOVER!

The famous fictional detective Sherlock Holmes is known for his incredible attention to detail and his ability to figure out what happened based on his observations. Read the selection below and see how many adjectives there are.

MENTOR TEXT

He was a large man with rounded shoulders, a massive head, and a broad, intelligent face, sloping down to a pointed beard of grizzled brown. A touch of red in nose and cheeks, with a slight tremor of his extended hand, recalled Holmes's surmise as to his habits. His rusty black frock coat was buttoned right up in front, with the collar turned up, and his lank wrists protruded from his sleeves without a sign of cuff or shirt. He spoke in a slow staccato fashion, choosing his words with care, and gave the impression generally of a man of learning and letters who had been ill used by the hands of fortune.

—Sir Arthur Conan Doyle, "The Adventure of the Blue Carbuncle" in *Jewel Cases*

What details do the adjectives add to the sentences? What would be lacking if the adjectives were removed?

ADJECTIVES AND ADJECTIVAL ORDER

A **modifier** is a word that describes another word. While the basic parts of a sentence (nouns and verbs) are always the most important words, modifiers make the meanings of these words clearer.

An **adjective** is a word that modifies a noun or pronoun. Adjectives give information and details that make a noun's meaning clearer. Adjectives tell *which one*, *what kind*, *how many*, or *whose* about the words they modify.

Which one? Shelby chose *this* topic.

What kind? She will research how technology is used in a *modern* classroom.

How many? Mrs. Gilroy will require *five* sources for the paper.

Whose? Taylor and Shelby enjoy *their* class.

Most adjectives come just before the nouns they modify. However, predicate adjectives come after a linking verb and describe the subject of a sentence.

The house was *drafty*.

The table is *large*.

To determine whether a word is an adjective, ask the adjective questions or use the adjective test frame below. Any word that will fit into the frame can be used as an adjective.

The ________ thing (or person) is very ________.
The *cold* water is very *cold*.
The *kind* boy is very *kind*.

Punctuation PowerUp

Coordinate adjectives are adjectives that modify the same noun separately. Sometimes, these adjectives need to be separated by a comma. Use a comma to separate these adjectives if you can reverse their order or if you can place the word *and* between the adjectives without changing the meaning.

I enjoy walking on this *clear*, *crisp* morning.

You need a comma between *clear* and *crisp* since you can put the word *and* between these adjectives.

I met the *new history* teacher.

You do not need a comma between *new* and *history* since you cannot put the word *and* between these adjectives.

Determiners

A **determiner** is a special kind of adjective because it signals that a noun is coming in the sentence. A determiner always comes before the noun it modifies and before any descriptive adjectives (those adjectives that fit into the adjective test frame). There are several kinds of determiners.

Articles

The words *a*, *an*, and *the* are called ***articles***, the most common type of determiner. *The* is a **definite article** because it points to a specific thing. *A* and *an* are **indefinite articles** because they point to nonspecific things.

Samuel picked up *a* leaf from the ground. (*any leaf*)
He was looking for *an* orange leaf. (*any orange leaf*)
His leaf was from *the* maple tree in the front yard. (*a specific tree*)

A is used before words that begin with a consonant sound. *An* is used before words beginning with a vowel sound.

Skylar brought *a* tray of brownies.
She also brought *an* apple pie.

Demonstratives

Certain words that sometimes function as pronouns can also sometimes function as determiners. The **demonstrative** words *this*, *that*, *these*, and *those* are determiners when they modify nouns. When a demonstrative functions as a subject, predicate noun, direct object, or object of the preposition in a sentence, it is a pronoun.

Determiner: How much did *that* car cost?
Pronoun: *That* is my favorite type of car.

Indefinites

Just as there are indefinite pronouns (see the list of indefinites on page 142), there are also **indefinite determiners**. The indefinites are determiners only when they modify nouns.

Determiner: I need to buy *some* milk from the store.
Pronoun: Do you have *some*?

Practice the Skill

Underline the adjectives. Draw an arrow from each adjective to the noun it modifies.

1. Modern schools are different from early schools.
2. The first students in America did not have nutritious meals at school.
3. Sometimes, three age groups shared a classroom.
4. Early schools lacked elaborate playgrounds for children.
5. The first students in American schools often traveled great distances to the school.
6. Many schools now provide bus transportation.
7. This transportation protects students from harsh weather.
8. Modern schools use air conditioners during warm weather.
9. Classrooms may have expensive computers or tablets for students to use.
10. Educational equipment has changed.

Identify the underlined determiner as *article*, *demonstrative*, or *indefinite*.

✓ article 11. Fred Rogers was a popular children's television host for over thirty years.

✓ indefinite 12. As a child, Rogers endured some difficulties, such as being shy and having asthma.

✓ demonstrative 13. When his family bought their first television set in the 1950s, Rogers immediately saw how this piece of technology could help children.

✓ article 14. When he became an ordained minister, his church sent him to minister to children through television.

✓ indefinite 15. Rogers eventually created *Mister Rogers' Neighborhood*, a television show watched by many children.

✓ ✗ demonstrative 16. During every episode, Mr. Rogers wore a sweater; these sweaters were made by his mother.

✓ ✗ indefinite 17. Mr. Rogers talked about difficult subjects that most children's programs did not address, such as divorce and death.

✓ ✗ article 18. In 1969 when black people were still not allowed to share a pool with white people, Mr. Rogers invited a black police officer to dip his feet in a wading pool with him on the show.

demonstrative 19. That episode taught children that people of all skin colors should be treated equally.

demonstrative 20. Mr. Rogers died in 2003, but those episodes he created are still enjoyed by children today.

Review the Skill

Underline the seventeen adjectives. Draw an arrow from each adjective to the noun it modifies.

Anne Mansfield Sullivan provides an excellent illustration of the commitment that teachers need. In 1887, Sullivan began educating Helen Keller, a deaf and blind student. Since previous experiences had allowed Sullivan to learn the manual alphabet, she was a promising candidate to be a tutor. Before beginning to teach Helen, Sullivan proved to be an exemplary student, though she faced painful surgeries to reestablish sight in her weak eyes.

Identify the underlined determiner as *article, demonstrative,* or *indefinite*.

article 21. The preeminent example of a master teacher is Jesus Christ.

indefinite 22. Jesus is an excellent example of a master teacher for many reasons.

demonstrative 23. Christ is omniscient. That characteristic perhaps best distinguishes Him as a master teacher.

indefinite 24. The best teacher must have complete understanding of each student.

article 25. Christ possesses the ultimate understanding of His students because He is their Creator.

article 26. Jesus taught His disciples based on an unlimited knowledge of their innermost thoughts as well as an accurate interpretation of their outward behavior.

demonstrative 27. Those other qualities that distinguish Jesus as an extraordinary teacher are His sinlessness and His perfect knowledge of truth.

demonstrative 28. Christ's divine nature keeps Him from making those errors made by an imperfect human teacher.

indefinite 29. Jesus was never an unfair judge of any students' performances or a poor example for His disciples to follow.

articles 30. Christ's instruction is perfect because He teaches His followers the Word of God.

Use the Skill

Revise each sentence to put the coordinate adjectives in the proper order. Insert or remove punctuation as needed.

31. My mom and I baked cinnamon, hot rolls yesterday.

32. We baked them in the muffin gray tin.

33. The hot sticky rolls tasted delicious.

34. Because I enjoyed them so much, my thoughtful loving mom baked me more the next day.

Write a paragraph about your favorite season. Include a sentence with each type of determiner in your paragraph.

COMPARING WITH ADJECTIVES

Sometimes a writer or speaker needs to compare two or more nouns. Comparisons are made by changing the form of the adjectives. Adjectives that can be compared answer the question *what kind?* and come just before the nouns they modify. These adjectives have three forms.

The **positive** form is the stem form of the adjective, the **comparative** form is used to compare two people or things, and the **superlative** form is used to compare three or more people or things. Adjectives add *er* or *more* to the positive form to make the comparative form and *est* or *most* to the positive form to make the superlative form. Nearly all one-syllable adjectives are compared with *er* and *est*. Some two-syllable adjectives take *er* and *est*, especially adjectives that end in *y*, *ly*, or *le*. Otherwise, expect the adjective to be compared with *more* and *most*.

Positive	Comparative	Superlative
fresh	fresher	freshest
friendly	friendlier	friendliest
amazing	more amazing	most amazing

Lauren was *busy* doing homework in her room. Mother was *busier* cooking dinner in the kitchen. Dad was *busiest* cleaning the entire house.

Mrs. Smith's apple pie was *delicious*, and Mrs. Thompson's coconut bars were even *more delicious*. However, Mom's chocolate cake was the *most delicious* dessert at the church picnic.

Irregular adjectives are adjectives that cannot be compared by adding *er/est* or *more/most* to the stem form. These adjectives often take entirely different forms to show comparison, or they may not change at all.

Positive	Comparative	Superlative
good	better	best
well	better	best
bad	worse	worst

Adjectives that can be compared will always fit the test frame. However, be sure to use the positive form of the word when using the test frame. Failure to use the positive form can result in an illogical sentence.

Incorrect: The *weariest* person is very *weariest*.

Correct: The *weary* person is very *weary*.

Absolute adjectives are adjectives that cannot be compared. An example of an absolute adjective is the word *dead*. A person or thing is either alive or dead. It cannot be deader or deadest. Other words that cannot be compared are *unique*, *perfect*, and *eternal*.

Practice the Skill

Underline the correct form of the adjective in parentheses to complete the sentence.

1. The Ivy League was formed because of a desire for a (big, biggest) football league.
2. The reputation of Ivy League schools is (prestigious, more prestigious) than that of other colleges.
3. The (more famous, most famous) Ivy League schools are Harvard, Yale, and Princeton.
4. Harvard is the (older, oldest) institution of higher learning in the United States.
5. The old brick buildings and spacious design make Harvard's campus (beautiful, most beautiful).
6. Yale, the second-oldest institution of higher learning in the United States, is (younger, youngest) than Harvard.
7. Yale has one of the (bigger, biggest) libraries in the world.
8. Yale has a (small, smaller) enrollment than most of the other Ivy League schools.
9. One of the (more interesting, most interesting) additions to Princeton's campus is the Plasma Physics Laboratory.
10. Although they are more famous, Ivy League schools are not necessarily (good, better) than other schools.

Review the Skill

Complete the sentence with the correct form of the adjective in parentheses.

______________ 11. An ? invention than today's teaching equipment, the chalkboard has been an instrument of learning since its first widespread appearance in Europe during the 1600s. (*old*, comparative)

______________ 12. A chalkboard, whiteboard, or smartboard exists in nearly every American school, even in the ? of all settings. (*poor*, superlative)

______________ 13. Teachers used to consider their chalkboards to be ? teaching devices. (*essential*, positive)

______________ 14. Was there a tool ? to a math teacher than the chalkboard? (*helpful*, comparative)

______________ 15. Chalkboards may have been the ? tool used in education. (*popular*, superlative)

______________ 16. The chalkboard was popular because it was ? . (*reliable*, positive)

______________ 17. The chalkboard was ? than other classroom equipment since it functioned even during a power loss. (*dependable*, comparative)

______________ 18. The chalkboard was perhaps the ? to maintain of all educational equipment. (*cheap*, superlative)

______________ 19. Traditional chalkboards appeared black or green, though some boards may have displayed ? pigments than others. (*dark*, comparative)

______________ 20. Chalkboards were once one of the ? classroom tools. (*good*, superlative)

USING ADJECTIVES TO EXPAND OR COMBINE
Writing Traits: Sentence Fluency, Organization

Listen Up!
Have you ever wondered what it would be like to grow up during the Great Depression? The passage below gives the reader an idea of what life was like during this difficult time. Read the text and see how many adjectives you can find.

MENTOR TEXT

The sideboard ran along most of the wall opposite the stove. In addition to the basin, numerous other bowls, buckets, and odds and ends decorated the long wooden shelf. In a small corner space where the wall and shelf failed to meet stood an old oak cupboard. Its door swung loosely on the hinge. A large rectangular table and five rickety chairs occupied the center of the room. Here the family ate, worked, and lounged whenever time allowed. The only other furniture was an old rocker, used mostly by Cassie, and a three-legged stool portable enough for the children to carry from place to place. It never remained in one place long. Rashana, two years older than Fletcher, had already claimed it this morning. She sat across the room folding a batch of freshly laundered clothes and stacking them neatly into a worn wicker basket. She glanced over at her brothers.

—Donnalynn Hess, *Dust of the Earth*

What descriptive details does this passage lose if you take out the adjectives? Would this passage be better or worse if you added five additional adjectives?

Take Notes!
Read the following passage and summarize the rules for expanding and combining with adjectives.

Expanding with Adjectives
To expand with adjectives, follow this simple process:

1. Identify the sentence pattern and locate the nouns.
2. Ask the adjective questions (Which one? What kind? How many? Whose?). What additional information would help to clarify the meaning?

3. Logically and clearly insert the answers.

   S **InV**
   Students cheered at the sight of snow.
   S **InV**
   What kind? The *excited* students cheered at the sight of *accumulating* snow.

When you expand with adjectives, be sure to use them effectively. Adjectives are like salt. Just as adding some salt flavors your food, adding some well-chosen adjectives can help expand a simple sentence into one that is more vivid and descriptive. However, too many adjectives, like too much salt, can clutter your writing and make it difficult to read.

To effectively use adjectives, you must first avoid adjectives that are overused and imprecise. Vague words, such as *big*, *nice*, and *hot*, not only fail to make your writing more descriptive, they actually make it boring. Instead, focus on using adjectives that are vivid and precise.

- Imprecise adjective: The opposing team panicked when a *tall* basketball player ran onto the court.
- Precise adjective: The opposing team panicked when a *towering* basketball player ran onto the court.

Although using descriptive adjectives makes your writing clearer, too many of them can make your writing complicated and difficult for the reader to follow. One way to avoid using too many adjectives is to replace adjectives with vivid nouns. Doing this will help show your reader what is happening rather than just tell your reader about what is happening.

- Wordy: The opposing team panicked when a *towering*, *golden-haired*, *tanned-skinned* basketball player ran onto the *spotless*, *gleaming* court.
- Precise: The opposing team panicked when a *giant* ran onto the court.

This does not mean that you should always replace adjectives with vivid nouns, but you should keep in mind that, like salt, adjectives should be used sparingly.

Combining with Adjectives

Not only can adjectives be used to expand sentences, but they can also be used to combine several short sentences. While short sentences can sometimes be effective, too many will make your paragraph sound choppy. The example below shows how adjectives in the second and third sentences can be combined with the first sentence to form a longer, better-sounding sentence.

- Choppy: The lady offered the child some candy. The child was crying. The lady was being kind.
- Better: The *kind* lady offered the *crying* child some candy.

Partner Up!

Expanding

Rewrite the following sentences, expanding each sentence with one or two vivid adjectives. Be sure to follow the steps listed in *Take Notes!* Then rewrite your sentences, replacing the adjectives with vivid nouns.

1. We climbed the tree.

____

2. He ran into the night.

____

3. The boy was punished.

____

4. I smelled the flower.

____

Combining

Using adjectives, combine the following sentences into one sentence.

1. The dog licked my face. The dog was friendly. The dog was brown.

____

2. The child was excited. He received a toy for his birthday. The toy was fun.

____

3. The student was relieved. His teacher told him he passed the class. The class was difficult.

____

4. The thieves were elusive. The sheriff finally caught them. The sheriff had to be persistent to catch them.

____

Try It Out!

Write a paragraph describing a favorite hobby or event. Use strong nouns and a few vivid adjectives.

MORE DETERMINERS

Possessives

A **possessive** is a noun or pronoun form that shows ownership. Most often, possessives function as adjectives. A possessive functioning as an adjective answers the question *whose?* about the noun it modifies.

Possessive Pronouns	Singular	Plural
First Person	my, mine	our, ours
Second Person	your, yours	your, yours
Third Person	its, his, her, hers	their, theirs

James's school has a good basketball team.
His school colors are gray and burgundy.
The players love *their* coach, Mr. McGlone.
They call themselves "*McGlone's* All-Stars."

If a possessive noun is modified by at least one other adjective, the possessive and its modifier form a **possessive phrase**. The entire phrase shows possession.

His sister's school plays softball instead.
Each parent supplies *his child's* bat and ball.

Independent Possessives

Sometimes a possessive noun or pronoun does not modify any noun in the sentence.

His little sister's school plays softball instead.
Hers plays softball instead.

In the second sentence above, the possessive pronoun *hers* does not modify any noun in the sentence. Instead, the word replaces the entire phrase *his little sister's school*. When a possessive acts in place of a noun or noun phrase, it is called an **independent possessive**. Independent possessives are not adjectives, because they replace nouns instead of modifying them.

Noun phrase: *Their coach* was the best.
Independent possessive: *Theirs* was an excellent teacher and leader.
Noun phrase: I can't find *my pencil*.
Independent possessive: May I borrow *yours*?

Practice the Skill

Underline the possessives. Identify each underlined word as *Adj* (adjective) or *IP* (independent possessive).

_______ 1. The stories of many men of faith are recorded in the Bible; however, these men's teachers are not well known.

_______ 2. Paul's was Gamaliel.

_______ 3. Luke's statement in Acts 5:34 describes Gamaliel as a "doctor of the law."

_______ 4. Gamaliel's expertise in the law was widely acknowledged.

_______ 5. His was a valued legal opinion.

_______ 6. The New Testament's record of Gamaliel shows that he was a man of courage.

_______ 7. Gamaliel's speech saved the apostles from death but not from punishment.

_______ 8. Theirs was a severe beating.

_______ 9. The apostles' delivery of the gospel was able to continue partly because of Gamaliel.

_______ 10. Although he did good things, Paul's teacher was probably a lost man.

Review the Skill

Revise the sentences below to include possessives or independent possessives.

11. The Sunday school movement was the idea of Robert Raikes.

12. Raikes had a job as a journalist for the *Gloucester*.

13. He once had an assignment to observe English prisons.

14. The prisons of England were full of children.

15. Many children worked in factories, and Sunday was the only day they had off.

16. These children often used the time they had off to get into trouble.

17. Raikes believed a school for children would lessen the opportunity for them to get into mischief.

18. The curriculum of the school included reading instruction, writing, arithmetic, morals, and manners.

19. The attempts of others at this type of work had failed in the past.

20. However, the attempt of Robert Raikes succeeded and eventually spread to other countries.

OTHER WORDS AS ADJECTIVES

A **modifying noun** is a noun or pronoun that acts as an adjective. Modifying nouns function as adjectives only when they describe nouns or pronouns.

Adjective: Southern Maryland Christian Academy has a great *theater* program.
Noun: Both Morgan and I will attend the *theater* on Friday.
Adjective: The tournament awards a best *speaker* trophy.
Noun: Either contestant could be named the best *speaker*.

Capitalization CheckPoint

As with proper nouns, capitalize proper adjectives.

Proper adjectives are adjectives that are made from proper nouns.

Many *Hawaiian* farmers grow pineapples.
Tacos are one of my favorite *Mexican* foods.
We usually visit my grandparents during *Christmas* vacation.
Have you heard the saying "*April* showers bring *May* flowers"?

Compound adjectives are adjectives that are composed of two or more words.

Snakes are a type of *cold-blooded* animal.
The *thirteen-year-old* prodigy performed a piano solo in Carnegie Hall.

Punctuation PowerUp

Put a hyphen between a compound adjective if it comes before the noun, but leave the hyphen out if the compound adjective comes after the noun.

The ill-conceived plan cost the company millions of dollars.
The plan was ill conceived and cost the company millions of dollars.

Practice the Skill

Identify the underlined word as *N* (noun), *P* (pronoun), or *Adj* (adjective). Capitalize any proper adjectives and put a hyphen between compound adjectives.

_______ 1. Elizabeth I's tutor was a well educated man named Roger Ascham.

_______ 2. Ascham was responsible for training the princess to become queen.

_______ 3. Ascham voiced his educational opinion in the *Schoolmaster*.

_______ 4. The subject of this was the education of the children of the british social elite.

_______ 5. One of ascham's famous topics was how to develop a harmonious individual.

_______ 6. His other book does not discuss education.

_______ 7. *Toxophilus* praises the sport of archery.

_______ 8. Archery fans find his book insightful and amusing.

_______ 9. That was the man who taught the future queen.

_______ 10. Ascham was also secretary to Elizabeth's sister, Queen Mary I.

Review the Skill

Identify the underlined word as *N* (noun), *P* (pronoun), or *Adj* (adjective). Capitalize any proper adjectives and put a hyphen between compound adjectives.

_______ 11. Plimoth Plantation is a reconstruction of a <u>well</u> <u>known</u> town.

_______ 12. <u>Many</u> students visit it while studying american history.

_______ 13. The people who work there act as though they were the first <u>settlers</u>.

_______ 14. They try to speak in the vernacular of <u>two hundred</u> years ago.

_______ 15. <u>That</u> requires a drastic change in their thought processes.

_______ 16. <u>Many</u> ask the actors questions about their kids.

_______ 17. The <u>actors</u> will give an answer about their goats and sheep.

_______ 18. Actors portraying <u>indian</u> braves come into the plantation to sell furs.

_______ 19. Barnyard smells and the aroma of homemade <u>bread</u> are overpowering.

_______ 20. Plimoth Plantation is a great place to learn <u>historical</u> facts.

Use the Skill

Choose a famous historical or natural landmark (Grand Canyon, Mount Rushmore, Statue of Liberty, etc.), and list at least two proper adjectives, modifying nouns, and compound adjectives that could describe your landmark. Then write a paragraph about the landmark using the words listed.

Plimoth Plantation

DESCRIPTIVE PARAGRAPHS
Writing Trait: Word Choice

Listen Up!

Since a reader cannot see what you see in your mind, your ability to describe well is incredibly important. In *Anne of Green Gables*, L. M. Montgomery paints a picture of the Lake of Shining Waters by using directional words to guide the reader's "eye." Notice in the first sentence you "see" Matthew and Anne driving over the crest of the hill. Think of a time you came to the top of a hill. Do you have the scene in your mind? What did you see? Highlight the directional words Montgomery uses to guide your eye.

MENTOR TEXT

They had driven over the crest of a hill. Below them was a pond, looking almost like a river so long and winding was it. A bridge spanned it midway and from there to its lower end, where an amber-hued belt of sand-hills shut it in from the dark blue gulf beyond, the water was a glory of many shifting hues—the most spiritual shadings of crocus and rose and ethereal green, with other elusive tintings for which no name has ever been found. Above the bridge the pond ran up into fringing groves of fir and maple and lay all darkly translucent in their wavering shadows. Here and there a wild plum leaned out from the bank like a white-clad girl tip-toeing to her own reflection. From the marsh at the head of the pond came the clear, mournfully-sweet chorus of the frogs. There was a little gray house peering around a white apple orchard on a slope beyond and, although it was not yet quite dark, a light was shining from one of its windows.

—L. M. Montgomery, *Anne of Green Gables*

Take Notes!

Read the following passage. Using your own words, explain how to use spatial order in writing.

When describing a location, use directional words, such as *above*, *in front of*, *next to*, or *between*, to show the logical progression in a setting. As you learned in Chapter 1, this method of organizing paragraph details is called spatial order (page 15). Using spatial order could mean describing something from the top to the bottom, the bottom to the top, right to left, left to right, or any other logical direction. Whichever method you choose, you should organize your details in a logical order to guide the reader's eye.

Partner Up!

Revise the paragraph below to include more concrete, specific details. Be sure to use spatial order as you describe the office.

The office was big. There was a lot of stuff on the walls. There were also a lot of cubicles with desks. Some of the cubicles were decorated. Other cubicles were bare. The carpet was worn.

Try It Out!

Use your words to paint a clear description of a room in your home. Brainstorm a list of items in that room you want to include in your description and where those items are. Write a description of this room using spatial order. Highlight the directional words you use. Share your description with another student.

CHAPTER REVIEW

Identifying Adjectives

Underline each adjective and draw an arrow to the word it modifies.

1. Many rules for teachers have changed since the days of 1872.
2. In that year teachers had many extra responsibilities.
3. Each teacher was required to bring a full pail of coal for the day's fuel and to clean the classroom chimneys.
4. His students' need for water and chalk were also the teacher's concern.
5. In addition to his responsibilities, a teacher's free time was different.
6. A normal class day consisted of ten hours in the school classroom before the teacher could relax by reading the Bible or good books at home.
7. A female teacher could not marry.
8. A male teacher could court for one evening each week.
9. If he attended church, he was allowed two evenings a week for courting.
10. A diligent teacher might get a raise of twenty-five cents a week after five years of teaching.

Determiners

Identify each underlined word as *article*, *demonstrative*, or *indefinite*.

✓ articles 11. Every morning, I enjoy a cup of coffee.

✓ indefinite 12. Many people around the world drink coffee every day.

✓ demonstrative 13. Although this drink is popular, more people drink tea.

✓ indefinite 14. Some people don't like coffee because of its bitter taste.

✓ articles 15. Others enjoy coffee only by changing the taste with different flavors and sweeteners.

Comparing Adjectives

Identify the correct form of the adjective in parentheses. Write in the blank the letter that corresponds to the correct answer.

✓ __A__ 16. "The Last Lesson," by Alphonse Daudet, is an _?_ story about a schoolboy's last French lesson. (*expressive*, positive)

- **A** expressive
- **B** more expressive
- **C** most expressive

✓ __B__ 17. When little Franz arrives late for class, he is surprised to find that his class is _?_ than he expected. (*quiet*, comparative)

- **A** quiet
- **B** quieter
- **C** quietest

✓ __B__ 18. Everyone looks sad, but the teacher, Monsieur Hamel, is the _?_ of them all as he informs the class that this will be their last lesson in French. (*sad*, superlative)

- **A** sadder
- **B** saddest
- **C** sad

✗ __C__ 19. School, his faithful teacher, and the French language become _?_ to Franz than ever before. (*important*, comparative)

- **A** most important
- **B** important
- **C** more important

✗ __B__ 20. Before Monsieur Hamel dismisses his class for the final time, he writes in his _?_ handwriting, "Vive la France!" (*large*, superlative)

- **A** large
- **B** largest
- **C** larger

Possessive Adjectives and Independent Possessives

Identify each italicized word as a *possessive adjective* or an *independent possessive*. Write in the blank the letter that corresponds to the correct answer.

A possessive adjective
B independent possessive

A 21. *Adam's* new classmate, Kai, is from Germany.

B 22. Kai's German grammar is much better than *his*.

A 23. They enjoy singing German songs with *their* German teacher, Frau Adams.

B 24. Their German singing is not as good as *hers*.

A 25. *Her* voice is clear and melodious.

Other Types of Adjectives

Identify each underlined word as *modifying noun, proper adjective*, or *compound adjective*.

modifying noun 26. Most United States citizens probably know Noah Webster as a famous <u>dictionary</u> maker.

proper adjective 27. In 1828 Webster gave colonial America the result of his life's work, a dictionary of the <u>English</u> language.

compound adjective 28. In addition to his dictionary, Webster produced the "<u>Blue-backed</u> Speller."

compound adjective 29. This was the <u>well-known</u> name for an educational textbook that Webster wrote.

proper adjective 30. This speller did much to standardize <u>American</u> spelling.

CHAPTER 9

ADVERBS

WHAT DOES NUANCE HAVE TO DO WITH ADVERBS?

Good writers write with nuance—they use just the right details, adding layers of color, emphasis, and precision to communicate their ideas clearly and effectively. Without those layers, the writer's message would be not only flat and uninteresting but could also be unclear or misleading. How does a writer add nuance to his writing?

DISCOVER!

Hugh Lofting wrote an adventurous tale of a doctor who discovers he can talk to animals. Doctor Dolittle's adventures are full of colorful, descriptive words. Without the use of well-placed adverbs, this imaginative tale would lack variety, emphasis, and precision—in short, it would lack nuance.

Read the mentor text below. See if you can find all the adverbs. How do they add nuance—depth of meaning and clarity of understanding—to the story? Read the story without the adverbs. In what ways would the story be less clear and less interesting if those adverbs were omitted?

MENTOR TEXT

And presently all these birds came down close, skimming over the water and the land; and the night-sky was left clear above, and the moon shone as before. Still never a call nor a cry nor a song they made—no sound but this great rustling of feathers which grew greater now than ever. When they began to settle on the sands, along the ropes of the ship—anywhere and everywhere except the trees—the Doctor could see that they had blue wings and white breasts and very short, feathered legs. As soon as they had all found a place to sit, suddenly, there was no noise left anywhere—all was quiet. . . .

When the ship moved out upon the water, those who stayed behind, Chee-Chee, Polynesia and the crocodile, grew terribly sad. For never in their lives had they known any one they liked so well as Doctor John Dolittle of Puddleby-on-the-Marsh.

—Hugh Lofting, *The Story of Doctor Dolittle*

ADVERBS

Adverbs modify verbs, adjectives, and other adverbs and answer certain questions about those words. Adverbs that modify verbs usually tell *when*, *where*, or *how* about those verbs. Adverbs that modify adjectives and other adverbs tell *to what extent* about those words.

When? We arrived *later*.

Where? Darcy waited *outside* for the rest of the group.

How? They proceeded *slowly* to the edge of the cliff.

To What Extent? Brandon felt *slightly* fatigued after the long trip.

Not is also an adverb. It shows negative meaning. Unlike other adverbs, *not* can be joined to a verb, usually as a contraction.

Gretchen will *not* participate in the upcoming regional debate.
She is *not* able to debate on the assigned topic.
She can*not* be expected to travel.
It is*n't* that she has*n't* prepared—she has broken her leg!

Many adverbs are made from other words. The most common way to form an adverb is to add *-ly* to an adjective. However, not all words ending in *-ly* are adverbs. Words like *lovely* and *friendly*, which are formed from a noun plus *-ly*, are adjectives and modify nouns or pronouns. Be sure to consider the word in the context of the sentence before determining whether it is an adverb.

Adjective	+*ly*	Adverb
slow	+***ly***	slow**ly**
quick	+***ly***	quick**ly**
clear	+***ly***	clear**ly**
fond	+***ly***	fond**ly**

Practice the Skill

Underline the adverbs. Draw an arrow from each adverb to the word it modifies.

1. Onesimus was a slave who wrongly ran away from his master, Philemon.
2. The slave somehow met the apostle Paul.
3. After his salvation, Onesimus quickly recognized his responsibility to his master.
4. Onesimus had become a servant and very close friend of Paul, and Paul did not want to separate from him.
5. The unusually small book of Philemon in the New Testament is Paul's letter to Onesimus's master.
6. Paul lovingly makes an appeal to Philemon for the forgiveness of Onesimus.
7. Paul sacrificially offers to pay any debts of his friend Onesimus.
8. Paul appeals quite humbly to Philemon by reminding him that all saved men are brothers in the Lord.
9. The story of Onesimus demonstrates the forgiveness that we receive freely in Christ.
10. Onesimus may have been graciously pardoned by his earthly master, but certainly his greatest pardon was the forgiveness of his sins in salvation.

Review the Skill

Underline the adverbs. Write in the blank the question that the adverb answers. Draw a line from each adverb to the word(s) it modifies.

______________ 11. Lew Wallace's book *Ben-Hur: A Tale of the Christ* tells the story of Judah Ben-Hur, a member of an important Jewish family, who unintentionally knocks a tile off the roof of his house onto a Roman leader.

______________ 12. Ben-Hur immediately is sent to row with slaves as punishment, and his mother and sister are imprisoned.

______________ 13. Messala, a Roman who was at one time a very close friend to Ben-Hur, refuses to help his former companion.

______________ 14. When Ben-Hur is providentially rescued from the galleys and placed in the favor of an important Roman named Arrius, he determines to find his mother and sister and have his revenge on Messala.

______________________ 15. Ben-Hur completely defeats and humiliates Messala in a chariot race.

______________________ 16. He has had his revenge against Messala but is quite bitter toward the Roman government that took his family's freedom.

______________________ 17. His mother and sister spent several years in a miserable prison cell and later joined a colony of lepers outside the city.

______________________ 18. Ben-Hur becomes one of the group that follows Jesus continually in His travels about the countryside in the hope that Jesus will lead the Jews in a fight against the Romans.

______________________ 19. Jesus compassionately heals Ben-Hur's mother and sister of their leprosy.

______________________ 20. Finally, Ben-Hur realizes after Jesus' death on the cross that true freedom from Rome must come from within, and he gives up his bitterness.

Use the Skill

Write five sentences about your favorite place. Use the adverbial elements from the list below.

- A **where** detail
- A **when** detail
- A **how** detail
- A **to what extent** detail
- The word **not**
- An ***–ly*** detail

DOUBLE NEGATIVES

In Standard English, we use only one negative word to make a sentence convey negative meaning. Using another negative word along with the adverb *not* is called a **double negative** and should typically be avoided in both speaking and writing. To correct a double negative, eliminate one of the negative words. Some common negative words are *barely, hardly, scarcely, never, no, none, not, nothing,* and *nowhere*.

Incorrect	Correct
I did*n't* eat *nothing* for breakfast.	I did*n't* eat *anything* for breakfast. I ate *nothing* for breakfast.
Joan had*n't* gone *nowhere* for vacation.	Joan had*n't* gone *anywhere* for vacation. Joan went *nowhere* for vacation.
Lori can*not* eat *no* peanuts.	Lori can*not* eat peanuts. Lori can eat *no* peanuts.
The candidates did*n't barely* get to speak.	The candidates *barely* got to speak.
The twins could*n't hardly* wait to go to the water park.	The twins *could hardly* wait to go to the water park.
None of the children *never* had cavities.	*None* of the children *ever* had cavities.
My grandmother ca*n't scarcely* climb the stairs after her knee surgery.	My grandmother *can scarcely* climb the stairs after her knee surgery.

Practice the Skill

Underline the double negatives. Write the correction in the blank. If the sentence is correct, write *C* in the blank.

______________ 1. Most vegetation does not normally make any light.

______________ 2. Some people may think there aren't no glowing plants.

______________ 3. Some scientists, however, don't find nothing strange about plants that emit light.

______________ 4. A few fungi are bioluminescent, but you might not never know that by seeing them in daylight.

______________ 5. The glowing Japanese moonlight mushroom isn't safe for anyone to eat.

______________ 6. America's poisonous jack-o'-lantern mushroom produces light, so you do not need to go nowhere exotic to see a luminous mushroom.

______________ 7. Fungi cannot emit no blinking light like fireflies can.

______________ 8. Luminous fungi don't produce flashing lights—only steady blue, green, or yellow glows.

______________ 9. Someone not knowing no better may say such fungi don't make enough light to be photographed at night, but they do.

______________ 10. No one will find anything useful about bioluminescence if scientists don't study it more.

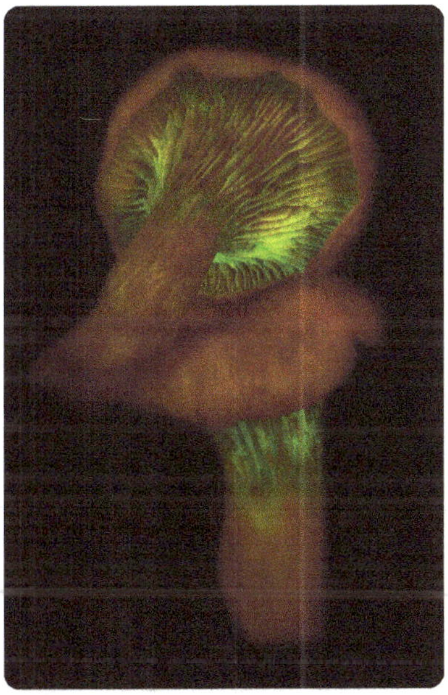

Review the Skill

Underline the double negatives. Write the correction in the blank. If the sentence is correct, write *C* in the blank.

______________________ 11. Lilies aren't never purchased as often as roses, but they are just as beautiful.

______________________ 12. Lilies should not ever be grown in dark soil but in light soil with excellent drainage.

______________________ 13. Most lilies do not grow nowhere but in the Northern Hemisphere.

______________________ 14. If you never study lilies, then you will not never know some of a lily's characteristics.

______________________ 15. Some kinds don't produce no flowers.

______________________ 16. Some cannot grow nowhere but in a woody area.

______________________ 17. We eat some lilies.

______________________ 18. Many people do not never know that garlic and asparagus are part of the lily family.

______________________ 19. Some species, such as the Madonna lily and regal lily, don't like no shade, but other species don't like sun.

______________________ 20. Lilies have no fewer than two thousand species.

ADVERB POSITIONS

Adverbs that modify adjectives or other adverbs come just *before* the word or words they modify.

> The water is *somewhat* cool.
> The weary hiker drank it *very* quickly.
> He was *so* sleepy that he wanted to stop.
> After the hike, his muscles were *exceedingly* sore.

Adverbs that modify verbs, however, are usually *movable* throughout the sentence, although moving the adverb changes the emphasis of the sentence. Typically, adverbs that can change position in the sentence are adverbs of frequency, time, and manner. They can be placed in the following positions:

- at the beginning of the sentence
- in the middle of the sentence (before or in the middle of the verb phrase)
- at the end of the sentence

> *Soon* the group will leave the campsite.
> The group will *soon* leave the campsite.
> The group *soon* will leave the campsite.
> The group will leave the campsite *soon*.

When writing, be careful to place adverbs where they will best give the emphasis that is desired in a sentence.

Practice the Skill

Write in the blank an appropriate adverb.

_______________ 1. ? Scott Carpenter blasted off from the platform on a beautiful day.

_______________ 2. He peered ? out the window of the spacecraft.

_______________ 3. Earlier he had been ? involved with the control of his ship.

_______________ 4. He ? had time for some observation.

_______________ 5. He had ? watched his jettisoned escape tower zip away.

_______________ 6. He ? looked around.

_______________ 7. He could ? see billowy bands of cumulus clouds.

_______________ 8. The clouds stood ? between him and the earth.

_______________ 9. We can imagine that he was awed by the ? expansive view.

_______________ 10. Had we been there, we would be ? moved by the loveliness of the world beneath us.

Review the Skill

In each of the following sentences, insert a caret (^) in each place where the adverb at the left sounds natural. You will insert more than one caret for most of the sentences.

11. *often* The story of the prodigal son reminds us about forgiveness.

12. *rashly* In this story the younger son asks for his inheritance from his father.

13. *sadly* His father divides the money, and his son leaves home.

14. *foolishly* This son squanders his money in riotous living.

15. *soon* All of his money is spent, and he needs food.

16. *eventually* He returns home.

17. *joyfully* His father welcomes him and forgives him instantly.

18. *seemingly* The father forgives before his son asks for forgiveness.

19. *not* The father did scold but rejoiced at his son's return.

20. *similarly* God forgives us when we do wrong but are penitent.

Use the Skill

Rewrite the following descriptive paragraph, inserting adverbs where they are most useful. Choose four adjectives to modify and four verbs to modify.

Winter is a beautiful time of year when fireplaces are lit, cozy blankets are draped over legs, and mugs of hot cocoa froth steamy and welcoming between huddled hands. Daylight's visits are shorter, and nights are long and cold. Winter is a season that reminds us that, although things look dark and bleak, the next season is coming, and our hearts ready themselves for the burst of spring color and warmth when fireplaces are cooled, blankets are folded away, and hot cocoa mugs are replaced with glasses of cooling iced tea. The sun shines longer and warmer, and moods brighten and cheer.

COMPARING WITH ADVERBS

Like adjectives, many adverbs have comparative and superlative forms. The **positive** form is the most basic form, the form that appears in a dictionary entry. The **comparative** form is used in comparing *two* actions or qualities; the **superlative** form is used when comparing *three or more* actions or qualities. Many short, **regular** adverbs use the suffixes ***-er*** and ***-est*** to form their comparative and superlative forms. Other adverbs, including those that end in *-ly*, use the words ***more*** or ***most*** to form their comparative and superlative forms.

Positive	Comparative	Superlative
soon	soon**er**	soon**est**
abruptly	**more** abruptly	**most** abruptly

Irregular adverbs, however, must be formed in different ways.

Positive	Comparative	Superlative
well	better	best
badly	worse	worst

When there is uncertainty, consult a dictionary to provide the correct form of any adverb.

Many adverbs, like some adjectives, are not compared. To make comparisons with these would not make sense. Among others, these include some very common adverbs: *not*, *daily*, *now*, *very*, *really*, *almost*, and *here*.

Practice the Skill

Underline the correct form of the adverb in parentheses.

1. Zacchaeus was one of the (higher, highest)-ranking publicans in the city of Jericho.
2. He was a wealthy man because of his (shamefully, more shamefully) dishonest business practices.
3. When Zacchaeus heard that Jesus was coming through his town, he tried (earnestly, more earnestly) than anyone else to see Him.
4. Because Zacchaeus was not very tall, he cleverly climbed a tree so that he could see (better, best) than everyone else.
5. Although Zacchaeus was amazed to see Jesus, he was (more, most) amazed that Jesus recognized him and called him by name.
6. When Jesus called out, "Zacchaeus, make haste, and come down; for to day I must abide at thy house" (Luke 19:5), it was the (more, most) wonderful dinner invitation that Zacchaeus had ever received.

7. Many people were surprised that Jesus would (gladly, more gladly) visit the home of a despised sinner.

8. Of all the people who heard Jesus that day, Zacchaeus probably showed his love (better, best) when he promised to restore any stolen money fourfold and to give half of all he owned to the poor.

9. The religious people were probably even (more, most) skeptical when Jesus granted Zacchaeus the gift of salvation.

10. Though Christ looks at our outward good works, He looks (closely, more closely) at the heart for true repentance like that of Zacchaeus.

Review the Skill

Write in the blank the correct form of the adverb in parentheses.

______________________ 11. Any discussion of forgiveness must _?_ include the cross. (*eventually*, positive)

______________________ 12. Through His death, Christ demonstrated forgiveness _?_ than anyone else. (*completely*, comparative)

______________________ 13. His own people cried _?_ for His death. (*loudly*, positive)

______________________ 14. He _?_ endured cruel suffering. (*bravely*, positive)

______________________ 15. He suffered _?_ when God the Father turned His back on Him as He carried the sins of the world. (*intensely*, superlative)

______________________ 16. Death came _?_ than the crowd expected. (*soon*, comparative)

______________________ 17. They might have _?_ witnessed a long ordeal that ended only when a soldier broke the legs of the prisoner. (*eagerly*, comparative)

______________________ 18. Before He died, though, Christ asked His Father _?_ to forgive those who had put Him on the cross. (*publicly*, positive)

______________________ 19. Christ's love extended _?_ than the people's hatred. (*far*, comparative)

______________________ 20. _?_ Christ's death provided the forgiveness of sins that His people need to go to heaven. (*importantly*, superlative)

Use the Skill

Write sentences using the sets of words below. Use the comparative or superlative form of the adverbs in parentheses as it fits the sets provided.

21. Lucy/works/Catherine. (*diligently*)
22. Baker County Ensemble/sings/ensembles in the region. (*beautifully*)
23. daughter/cooks/mother (*well*)
24. house cats/hunt/dogs (*fiercely*)
25. (noun)/(verb)/(noun) (*soon*)

USING ADVERBS TO EXPAND OR COMBINE

Writing Traits: Sentence Fluency, Organization

Listen Up!

The feeling of impending doom: that is exactly what the rats are feeling in the story of Doctor Dolittle when they get that sudden tingle in their tails. Read the mentor text to see how the author effectively uses adverbs to add understanding and tell his story with precision.

MENTOR TEXT

"We always know," answered the rat. "The tips of our tails get that tingly feeling—like when your foot's asleep. This morning, at six o'clock, while I was getting breakfast, my tail suddenly began to tingle. At first I thought it was my rheumatism coming back. So I went and asked my aunt how she felt—you remember her?—the long piebald rat, rather skinny, who came to see you in Puddleby last Spring with jaundice? Well—and she said *her* tail was tingling like everything! Then we knew, for sure, that this boat was going to sink in less than two days; and we all made up our minds to leave it as soon as we got near enough to any land. It's a bad ship, Doctor. Don't sail in it any more, or you'll be surely drowned."

—Hugh Lofting, *The Story of Doctor Dolittle*

What adverbs did you find that added specific details to the story? In what ways do the adverbs expand your understanding of the story?

Take Notes!

Read the following passage and summarize the rules for expanding and combining with adverbs.

Expanding with Adverbs

To expand with adverbs, follow a process similar to the process used to expand with adjectives:

1. Identify the sentence pattern and locate the verbs.
2. Ask the adverb questions (Where? When? Why? How?)
3. Logically and clearly insert the answers.

S InV
The child smiled at the clown.
How: The child smiled *shyly* at the clown.

Combining with Adverbs

Study the relationships between two or three short sentences to see if any of the sentences answer an adverb question.

> The clown rode the tricycle in the parade. The clown rode yesterday. The clown rode awkwardly.
> *Yesterday*, the clown *awkwardly* rode the tricycle in the parade.

Overused Adverbs

Overused, imprecise adverbs that do not add clarity or understanding should be avoided, or at least used sparingly. Here are a few to avoid or use rarely:

Interestingly: This word is used to awaken the audience or reader to what "interesting" idea is imminently coming, but often fails to deliver. Overusing this word and then disappointing the reader will cause you to lose credibility and even trust. Best to stay away from this one.

Significantly: Typically, when reading something of significance, the reader does not need that significance pointed out to him. The importance of the message should be self-evident.

Obviously: This adverb often can feel like an insult to a reader or an audience. What if the topic, concept, or message was not obvious to them? A writer runs the risk of alienating his audience by writing a word that makes him sound superior or sarcastic.

Actually: This word tends to be more of a filler when one doesn't actually have a whole lot to add to a sentence and doesn't actually know how or what they actually want to say. (Get the point?)

Literally: This adverb too tends to be used as a filler and should be avoided as often as possible. Typically used to add emphasis, this adverb ends up literally subtracting from the intelligence of the message. It is *literally* distracting.

Very: This is possibly one of the most used, yet most ineffective, adverbs. Meant as an intensifier, the word has, for all intents and purposes, lost its effectiveness. For instance, look at the phrase *very calm*. Expanding the feelings evoked by using a word like *calm* can be easily done. Say instead: *tranquil*, *hushed*, *quiet*, *serene*, or *relaxed*. The adverb *very* usually adds unwelcome wordiness to one's writing.

A Special Note about Modifying Absolutes

In formal and academic writing, it is best to avoid using intensifying adverbs to further strengthen **absolute** adjectives. They are strong enough on their own. When used in everyday conversation or informal writing, however, you may occasionally use intensifying adverbs for special emphasis's sake. Look at the following examples:

> An **utterly** impossible circumstance
> A **somewhat** (or **more**, **very**, **pretty**) unique story
> An **entirely** (or **somewhat**) complete set

Partner Up!

Add adverbs to combine or expand the following sentences. Avoid the adverbs in the overused adverbs list. Be creative!

1. The family took a trip to their mountain cabin. They were snowed in.

____

____

2. My mom went to the store to get some milk. It was busy. The milk shelves were empty.

____

____

3. The thunderstorm blew into town. It was unexpected. The whole neighborhood lost power.

____

____

4. The caterpillar inched. It ate a large, green leaf.

____

____

Try It Out!

Write a paragraph describing your favorite summer activity. Use vivid nouns with colorful adjectives, strong verbs, and nuanced adverbs.

COMMON PROBLEMS

Adverb or Adjective?

Because both adjectives and adverbs are modifiers, they are easily confused with one another. Speakers and writers sometimes incorrectly use an adverb where an adjective is necessary or an adjective in the place where an adverb should go. To choose the correct modifier, you need to know the function of the word being modified.

- Use an adjective to modify a noun or pronoun.
- Use an adverb to modify a verb, an adjective, or another adverb.

S LV PA
The three-year-old appears **slight** for his age.

S LV PA
The toddler seems **slightly** thin.

Other words that are particularly confusing are the words ***good*** and ***well*** and ***bad*** and ***badly***. Remember to keep the following ideas in mind:

Good is an adjective.

S LV PA
The steak tasted **good**.

Well is an adverb.

S TrV DO
The chef seasoned the meat **well**.

Bad is an adjective.

S LV PA
The child's behavior was **bad** during the recital.

Badly is an adverb.

S InV
After the disturbance, the musician performed **badly**.

COMMON PROBLEMS (CONTINUED)

Comparative or Superlative?

As you have already learned, many adjectives and adverbs have comparative and superlative forms that show degrees of comparison. Be careful to use these forms correctly. The comparative form compares two things. The superlative form compares three or more things.

Comparative

Incorrect: Of the two brothers, Ben does his work most promptly.
Correct: Of the two brothers, Ben does his work more promptly.

Superlative:

Incorrect: The little boy was the faster walker of his whole family.
Correct: The little boy was the fastest walker of his whole family.

Double Comparisons

Be careful of incorrectly using double comparisons. Just like double negatives, the use of double comparisons distracts from the meaning and clarity of the sentence.

Incorrect	Correct
More wiser/most wisest	Wiser/wisest
More happier/most happiest	Happier/happiest
More worser/most worstest	Worse/worst
More better	Better

Practice the Skill

Identify each underlined word as *adj* (adjective) or *adv* (adverb).

_______________ 1. Giant sequoias are <u>huge</u> trees of the redwood family that are <u>largely</u> uncommon.

_______________ 2. Giant sequoias, also called the Sierra redwoods, grow <u>only</u> in part of California's Sierra Nevadas.

_______________ 3. <u>Sometimes</u> giant sequoias are over three hundred feet tall and about a hundred feet around.

_______________ 4. In fact, records of bark over a foot thick <u>currently</u> exist.

_______________ 5. <u>Many</u> redwoods grow in Sequoia National Park, which was established in 1890.

Underline the incorrect adjective or adverb. Write in the blank the correct modifier. If the sentence is correct, write *C* in the blank.

__________ 6. Pitcher plants are carnivorous plants that catch insects good.

__________ 7. These plants are probably not as well-known as the Venus flytrap.

__________ 8. Special leaves on the plant look like small pitchers and collect rainwater good.

__________ 9. The top edge of this pitcher is a red, nectar-rich rim that does not function bad at drawing insects.

__________ 10. The insect's chance of escape does not look well once it has fallen off the nectar-covered, waxy edge into the pitcher's depths.

Underline the correct adjective or adverb from the choices in parentheses.

11. Among all early botanists, Gregor Mendel is perhaps the (more, most) famous.
12. Mendel was a nineteenth-century monk whose scientific work receives recognition (more, most) often than his religious endeavors.
13. Of all research in genetics up to that time, Mendel's contributions were the (more significant, most significant).
14. Since all of Mendel's laws are important, it is hard to say which ranks (higher, highest).
15. Though not fully recognized for his work while alive, Mendel provides a (good, best) example of the lasting results that hard work can bring.

Review the Skill

Label the sentence patterns. Underline each adjective once and each adverb twice. Draw an arrow from each adjective or adverb to the word it modifies.

16. Botany introduces us to wondrously diverse plants.

17. The parasitic mistletoe grows naturally on host trees.

18. Mistletoe becomes easily visible on leafless trees.

19. Mistletoe actually pierces the tree's bark and gets nourishment without being in the soil itself.

20. Mistletoe can be seriously destructive to trees, and apple trees are frequently unfortunate victims.

Write in the blank the correct modifier to complete the sentence: *good, well, bad,* or *badly*.

______________ 21. One _?_ example of an interesting plant is the Venus flytrap.

______________ 22. The Venus flytrap is a carnivorous plant that can survive _?_ in low-nitrogen soil.

______________ 23. Spiny hairs that work like bars on a leaf's edge make the closed leaf a _?_ snare.

______________ 24. Small insects that would make a _?_ meal escape through the closed leaves.

______________ 25. Before the leaf reopens in one to two weeks, juices from the plant digest an insect _?_ .

Underline the incorrect comparative or superlative word(s) and write the correct word in the blank.

______________ 26. Compared to other edible fungi, truffles are generally much more expensiver.

______________ 27. People do not raise truffles on farms because, compared to all other environments, these fungi do the most well in the wild.

______________ 28. Despite their other locations, truffles seem to appear most frequentest among the roots of beech and oak trees.

______________ 29. Of all countries, France is more wider known for its large truffle harvest.

______________ 30. Pigs and dogs can find truffles more easiest than humans because with their strong sense of smell, they can detect the plants that grow about twelve inches underground.

COMPARE AND CONTRAST PARAGRAPHS

Writing Traits: Ideas, Organization

Listen Up!

Have you ever heard of weighing the pros and cons of doing something? Being able to weigh two or more ideas or things based on their similarities and their differences is an important writing skill. In the mentor text below, the author took the ideas he gathered about hunting and fishing and organized them into two paragraphs. The first paragraph discusses the similarities between the two activities. The second paragraph explains the differences between the two activities.

Read the following mentor texts about two outdoor activities. List the examples that support the topic sentences for each paragraph (in the first, to compare; in the second, to contrast).

MENTOR TEXT

Hunting and fishing are two popular outdoor sports that attract people for many of the same reasons. First, both activities are a wonderful way to enjoy the great outdoors, and both offer a healthful and economic way to get food. Second, both sports are especially attractive for those who enjoy being out in nature for hours or even days at a time. Third, both hunting and fishing require a lot of patience. People who like quiet, still hours that start very early in the morning may enjoy these activities. Moreover, a hunter or a fisherman can easily spend most of his day out in the woods or on the lake and have little-to-no success. Finally, both hunting and fishing require specific equipment. Both activities not only require state-issued licenses but also require proper personal gear and supplemental tools to promote success. Whatever a person's interests, an outdoor enthusiast could find one or both of these adventurous sports exciting.

Although hunting and fishing are often grouped together because of their similarities, there are differences that sometimes make one more appealing than the other to different people. For example, unlike hunting, fishing does not require a person to kill the animal he catches. For this reason, an animal lover or a squeamish person may prefer fishing. Similarly, fishing is generally less messy. It takes much more time and effort to process (i.e., gut and clean) most animals taken by hunting than it does to gut and clean a fish. Another difference lies in the tools used to obtain the animal. Fishing materials are non-lethal and require little training. Hunting materials are dangerous and require careful and diligent training before obtaining a license. Finally, cost differences are vast. The cost for a hunting rifle and ammunition or a bow and arrows can easily reach hundreds or thousands of dollars. A fishing pole and some tackle, on the other hand, can be purchased for less than one hundred dollars. In choosing an outdoor sport like hunting or fishing, a person needs to consider all sides to see which one sounds more interesting and suitable.

WRITING TOOLBOX

Take Notes!

Write what you see as the difference between the terms *compare* and *contrast* and define each of them in your own words. Make a short list of important elements for the compare and contrast paragraphs.

People often use the term *compare* when they want to talk about similarities and differences between two things. It is important to note, however, that comparing two things is different from contrasting them. To **compare** is to see what is the same about two things or ideas. To **contrast** two things or ideas is to see what is different between them. Learning how to analyze in this way makes a person a better critical thinker and develops discernment in decision making. Christians should focus on precision and logic in their opinions and ideas. This focus on Christ-expression ensures that they communicate love and truth to their neighbors and honor God through their integrity.

Here are two important steps to take when preparing to write compare and contrast paragraphs:

1. Make a simple list of all the things you can think of to describe the activity, thing, or idea.

2. Organize that list into a graphic organizer, visually separating the similarities and differences.

Partner Up!

Brainstorm and write a list of all the similarities and differences you can think of for one of the topics listed. Organize your list into a graphic organizer that visually separates that list into similarities and differences.

- Cold weather vs. hot weather
- Flowers vs. weeds
- Cruise ships vs. cargo ships
- Messaging vs. person-to-person conversation
- Campaign speeches vs. church sermons
- E-books vs. traditional books

Try It Out!

Write a paragraph either comparing or contrasting the topic you developed in *Partner Up!* Make sure to write a topic sentence that broadly describes the topic. Write at least three sentences that give examples for comparing or for contrasting. Write a strong concluding sentence that summarizes the topic sentence.

CHAPTER REVIEW

Identifying Adverbs

Underline each adverb in the following paragraph.

1.–10. Jesus told the story of a servant whose lord compassionately forgave him a great sum of money. Out of gratitude for this unusually generous pardon, the servant should have always tried to forgive others. He went instead to another servant who owed him a small amount of money and treated him harshly. When the lord heard of this, he quickly commanded that the servant be tormented until he could fully pay what he owed. Jesus was trying to teach His disciples that they should freely and completely forgive each other since God had graciously forgiven them.

Modified Words

Identify the type of word modified by each italicized adverb. Write in the blank the letter that corresponds to the correct answer.

A verb
B adverb
C adjective

_______ 11. The story of Joseph and his brothers is *very* familiar to most Christians.

_______ 12. After throwing him into a pit, Joseph's brothers sold him to slave traders, whose ways were probably *extremely* foreign to him.

_______ 13. Joseph *rather* quickly became a slave and a prisoner.

_______ 14. Because of his trust in God's providence, Joseph *faithfully* remembered that God had a perfect plan for his life.

_______ 15. Despite their cruel treatment, Joseph quite *willingly* forgave his brothers.

_______ 16. In fact, Joseph *completely* surprised his brothers by his acts of kindness.

_______ 17. They feared his anger, yet he treated them *truly* graciously.

_______ 18. Joseph gave his brothers *much* better treatment than they deserved.

_______ 19. In the same way, God *lovingly* grants forgiveness to anyone who asks.

_______ 20. Though such forgiveness seems *nearly* impossible, with God's help all Christians can treat each other in a similar way.

Positive, Comparative, and Superlative Adverbs

Write in the blank the correct form of the adverb in parentheses.

_______________ 21. The Lord forgives ? . (*fully*, positive)

_______________ 22. David knew ? than most about the Lord's forgiveness. (*well*, comparative)

_______________ 23. David sinned ? against the Lord. (*grievously*, positive)

_______________ 24. David ? begged the Lord for forgiveness. (*remorsefully*, positive)

_______________ 25. David prayed ? for cleansing than he ever had before. (*fervently*, comparative)

_______________ 26. Though God chastened David in other ways, David perhaps suffered ? when the Lord took his infant son. (*intensely*, superlative)

_______________ 27. David ? praised the Lord for restoring his soul. (*joyfully*, positive)

_______________ 28. Among the many biblical examples of repentance and forgiveness, David's story probably comes to mind ? (*frequently*, superlative)

_______________ 29. Only believers should rest ? in their forgiveness because they know the one true God. (*confidently*, positive)

_______________ 30. Because God is faithful to forgive penitent sinners, His people should praise Him ? than those who are not believers. (*often*, comparative)

Double Negatives

Underline the double negatives and write a correction in the blank.

_______________ 31. Jesus tells His followers that they should not forgive nothing their enemies do to them.

_______________ 32. People must remember that they are not no better than their enemies, and they will also need someone to forgive them someday.

_______________ 33. If a Christian's enemy finds no help nowhere, the Christian should do whatever he can to help, showing a forgiving attitude.

_______________ 34. Jesus said that Christians should not render evil to no one.

_______________ 35. The Savior, who is the greatest example of a forgiving attitude, asked God to forgive His enemies while He was on the cross, because they did not hardly realize what they were doing.

CHAPTER 10

PHRASES

ARE YOU EVER LEFT WITH QUESTIONS?

Have you ever read an article or listened to someone relate an experience and found yourself asking questions such as why?, when?, where?, how?, *or* what kind? *These details communicate a full picture to the reader or listener. Many times, prepositional phrases fill in those details.*

DISCOVER!

In her autobiography, Helen Keller describes her passion for boating in the summer. Read the excerpt. Even though Helen is blind and deaf, how does she steer the boat?

MENTOR TEXT

More than once in the course of my story I have referred to my love of the country and out-of-door sports. When I was quite a little girl, I learned to row and swim, and during the summer, when I am at Wrentham, Massachusetts, I almost live in my boat. Nothing gives me greater pleasure than to take my friends out rowing when they visit me. Of course, I cannot guide the boat very well. Some one usually sits in the stern and manages the rudder while I row. Sometimes, however, I go rowing without the rudder. It is fun to try to steer by the scent of watergrasses and lilies, and of bushes that grow on the shore. I use oars with leather bands, which keep them in position in the oarlocks, and I know by the resistance of the water when the oars are evenly poised. In the same manner I can also tell when I am pulling against the current. I like to contend with wind and wave. What is more exhilarating than to make your staunch little boat, obedient to your will and muscle, go skimming lightly over glistening, tilting waves, and to feel the steady, imperious surge of the water!

—Helen Keller, *The Story of My Life*

Reread the excerpt, putting parentheses around the prepositional phrases. What questions do the prepositional phrases answer? How do they help you see how Helen steers her boat?

PREPOSITIONS AND THEIR PHRASES

Prepositions

A **preposition** is a word that shows the relationship between its object and another word in the sentence. The **object of the preposition** is the noun or pronoun that follows the preposition. All prepositions have objects.

We looked *in* the haystack for the needle.
We looked *on* the haystack for the needle.
We looked *under* the haystack for the needle.
We looked *near* the haystack for the needle.
We looked *beside* the haystack for the needle.

In each of these sentences, a different preposition links the verb *looked* to the object of the preposition *haystack*. The preposition shows how the verb is related to the object of the preposition. Notice how the change in preposition changes the meaning of the sentence.

Commonly Used Prepositions				
about	behind	except	on	to
above	below	for	onto	toward
across	beside	from	out	under
after	between	in	outside	until
against	beyond	inside	over	upon
among	but	into	past	with
around	by	like	since	within
at	down	near	through	without
before	during	of	throughout	

Prepositional Phrases

A preposition and its object together form a **prepositional phrase**. Any modifiers of the object are also included in the phrase. By itself, the object is the simple object of the preposition. The object and its modifiers together are the complete object of the preposition.

The toy octopus (*with only seven arms*) was injured (*in a battle*) (*against the garbage disposal*).

This example contains three prepositional phrases. Each one consists of a preposition followed by a noun phrase (the object and its modifiers). The preposition *with* shows the relationship between its complete object, *only seven arms*, and the subject, *octopus*. The preposition *in* shows the relationship between its complete object, *a battle*, and the verb, *was injured*. The preposition *against* shows the relationship between its complete object, *the garbage disposal*, and the previous simple object of the preposition, *battle*.

Some prepositional phrases contain compound objects.

> The boat was tossed (*by the wind and sea*).

In the prepositional phrase *by the wind and sea*, both *wind* and *sea* are simple objects of the preposition *by*.

Preposition or Adverb?

Some of the same words that are used as prepositions can also be used as adverbs. To determine whether a word in a sentence is a preposition or an adverb, look for an object of the preposition.

> The swimmer swam *around* the buoy.
> The swimmer swam *around* for thirty minutes.

Around is a preposition in the first sentence because it is followed by the object *buoy*. In the second sentence, *around* is an adverb that tells how the swimmer swam, and it has no object. (*For thirty minutes* is a prepositional phrase and cannot be the direct object.) Every preposition must have an object.

Practice the Skill

Underline the prepositions.

1. The sea level fluctuates with the changing tides.
2. Oceanographers say that sea level is halfway between high and low tide.
3. The currents are the lifeblood of the ocean.
4. Currents tie together remote regions and carry warmth toward the frigid poles.
5. Ocean currents affect the climate, the ecosystem, and even the seafood in particular regions of the world.

Place parentheses around the prepositional phrases. Underline the simple objects of each prepositional phrase.

6. Fish can live in freshwater or saltwater.
7. Their body temperatures change with their environment.
8. A fish has sensory organs on its sides.
9. A fish's sense of smell is strong.
10. A female fish releases many eggs during spawning season.
11. Some fish release seven million eggs at one time.
12. Some fish have lived over fifty-five years.
13. A characteristic of all fish is fins.
14. Scientists are still learning about fish's migratory patterns.
15. For almost all fish, their fins are located on their sides.

Identify the underlined word as *prep* (preposition) or *adv* (adverb).

_______ 16. The table toppled over.

_______ 17. The rocket shot over the moon.

_______ 18. The bird flew up in the air.

_______ 19. The smoke curled up the chimney.

_______ 20. He was running in the rain.

_______ 21. The dog lay behind the car.

_______ 22. The jogger fell behind in the race.

_______ 23. The camper placed a sweater around his shoulders.

_______ 24. The new sailor ran aboard the ship.

_______ 25. The mixture was consistent throughout.

Review the Skill

Underline the prepositions.

26. In the late 1760s, David Bushnell experimented with underwater explosives to use against the English navy.
27. Eventually, Bushnell formulated the idea of a submarine with a screw that would get the torpedo near its target; he began building one.
28. On an August night in 1776, Sergeant Ezra Lee of the Continental army climbed into the world's first submarine.
29. The machine functioned perfectly, but the submarine's screw could not break through the English warship's hull.
30. Although the first mission was a failure, today David Bushnell is called the father of the submarine.

Place parentheses around the prepositional phrases. Underline the simple object of each prepositional phrase.

31. Beginning in 1998, an underwater exploration team documented eight ancient ships in a fifty-five-mile radius at the bottom of the Mediterranean Sea.
32. Five of the wrecks were of Roman origin, and three were from North Africa.
33. The depth of these shipwrecks has kept them largely undisturbed by storms.
34. Until recent times, divers could examine only those ships that were found no deeper than two hundred feet.
35. With the help of a remotely operated vehicle (ROV), archaeologists can uncover artifacts at 2,800 feet.
36. Like a diver, an ROV can map the site of a wreck and retrieve artifacts.
37. An elevator with a mesh net lifts artifacts to the scientists in the boat.
38. The team removed only a few artifacts from six of the ships.
39. They left the rest for further exploration.
40. As technology advances, more ancient time capsules will be discovered beneath the ocean's surface.

Identify the underlined word as *prep* (preposition) or *adv* (adverb).

_______ 41. In the late 1800s, the age of the sail was giving way <u>to</u> the age of the steam-powered boat.

_______ 42. The demand <u>for</u> shipmasters such as Captain Joshua Slocum was waning.

_______ 43. But Captain Slocum had been sailing the sea too long to spend the rest of his life <u>on</u> land.

_______ 44. In 1894 he decided to do what no seaman had done before: sail <u>around</u> the world by himself.

_______ 45. On April 24, 1895, Captain Slocum set <u>off</u> in his little sloop.

_______ 46. Captain Slocum would often lash the helm to hold a steady course, set the sail, and go <u>below</u> to read *Life of Columbus*.

_______ 47. Since no one else was <u>around</u>, Slocum would sing a sea chantey to ward off loneliness.

_______ 48. Crossing the Atlantic <u>during</u> the summer was relatively easy compared to what lay ahead.

_______ 49. It took Captain Slocum twice as long to cross the Strait <u>of</u> Magellan as it did to cross the whole Atlantic Ocean.

_______ 50. On June 27, 1898, three years, two months, and two days <u>after</u> the beginning of his journey, Joshua Slocum became the first man to sail around the world alone.

FUNCTIONS OF PREPOSITIONAL PHRASES

Some prepositional phrases operate as adjectives and modify nouns. These prepositional phrases are called **adjectival prepositional phrases**.

Megan saw the birthday present *with the red bow*.

She noticed the gift card *under the red bow on the present*.

The present *from her grandmother* was a surprise.

Each of the prepositional phrases in the examples modifies the noun that it follows: *with the red bow* modifies *present*; *under the red bow* modifies *card*; *on the present* modifies *bow*; and *from her grandmother* modifies *present*. An adjectival prepositional phrase usually comes just after the noun it modifies.

Other prepositional phrases function as adverbs and modify verbs. These phrases are called **adverbial prepositional phrases**.

Wendy and Felice jumped *onto the trampoline*.

Felice lost her expensive watch *under the trampoline*.

In desperation, the friends searched *among the weeds for an hour*.

Each of the prepositional phrases in the examples modifies the verb of the sentence. *Onto the trampoline* modifies *jumped*, telling where about the verb; *under the trampoline* modifies *lost,* telling where about the verb; *in desperation*, *among the weeds*, and *for an hour* all modify *searched* telling how, where, and how much/to what extent about the verb. Notice that adverbial phrases can appear just about anywhere in the sentence: at the beginning, at the end, or next to the words they modify.

Practice the Skill

Underline the adjectival prepositional phrases once and the adverbial prepositional phrases twice. Draw an arrow to the word each modifies.

1. In 1849 the New York Yacht Club built the *America* to display America's shipbuilding prowess.
2. The Club members entered a competitive yacht race for profit.
3. They sailed across the ocean for a competition.
4. The Royal Yacht Squadron in England opened its annual regatta yacht race to include the *America*.
5. In August of 1851, the ship was positioned at the starting line.
6. Three hours later the *America* in first place sailed across the finish line.
7. The *America* gained the impressive reputation of the fastest yacht.
8. The *America*, later named *CSS Memphis*, served during the Civil War.
9. The Confederate army sank the ship so that it would not be captured by the Union army.
10. The submerged ship was recovered by the US navy and renamed the *America*.

Review the Skill

Underline the adjectival prepositional phrases once and the adverbial prepositional phrases twice. Draw an arrow to the word each modifies.

11. The mystery of the *Mary Celeste* has baffled seamen and land dwellers.

12. On November 7, 1872, Captain Benjamin Briggs, his family, and a seven-man crew set sail.

13. All of the crewmen were excellent seamen.

14. Captain Briggs's wife brought her sewing machine and some toys in a toy box.

15. In December the *Dei Gratia* spotted the *Mary Celeste* between the Azores and Portugal.

16. The captain of the *Dei Gratia* hailed the *Mary Celeste.*

17. Not a soul was found on board.

18. No signs of violence were evident.

19. Some signs of a quick departure were evident.

20. Their fate remains a mystery to this day.

Use the Skill

Write two sentences with adjectival prepositional phrases and two sentences with adverbial prepositional phrases. Show your sentences to a partner and explain the location and function of your phrases.

USING PREPOSITIONAL PHRASES TO EXPAND OR COMBINE

Writing Traits: Sentence Fluency, Organization

Listen Up!

Read this true account of Ida Lewis, a teenage lighthouse keeper in the mid-nineteenth century.

MENTOR TEXT

On the afternoon of March 29, 1869, Zoradia Lewis was doing what she did many times each day, gazing out a window of the lighthouse on Lime Rock Island in Newport, Rhode Island. Choppy waves leapt to meet sheets of rain. The sun struggled to light the sky over Narragansett Bay. And yet, she could swear she saw an overturned boat with two men clinging to its slippery sides. Zoradia called her daughter, Ida.

Ida ran outside without pausing to grab a coat or boots. She and her younger brother Hosea pushed their lifesaving skiff into the surf. Again and again, the waves forced the little boat back to shore. Ida would not give up, and finally pulled the oars hard enough to launch. Despite the rough seas, they made steady progress. Though Ida weighed just over a hundred pounds, her arms were incredibly strong from years of rowing on the bay.

When they neared the overturned sailboat, Ida maneuvered the skiff so that the back, or stern, faced the men. While Hosea held the boat steady with the oars, Ida extended a pole to one man and pulled him over the stern. While he flopped on the floor, gasping for air, she reached for the second man. Once he also was safely on board, she struck out for the lighthouse.

Ida had rescued two soldiers, Sergeant James Adams and Private John McLaughlin. She and Hosea helped them into their home, where Zoradia had a roaring fire waiting. The soldiers could not believe that a woman had saved them. Once they recovered and returned to nearby Fort Adams, they spread the word. Newspapers and magazines took up the story. Suddenly, Ida was famous.

—Timothy Tocher, "Ida Lewis, the Heroine of Lime Rock Lighthouse"

Focusing on the first paragraph, what information do the prepositional phrases add that is essential for meaning?

Take Notes!

List the steps for expanding a sentence. Summarize the process for combining sentences.

In chapters 8 and 9, you practiced expanding and combining sentences with the modifiers, adjectives and adverbs. For what purpose(s) are sentences expanded? For what purpose(s) are sentences combined? What strategies can be used? Since prepositional phrases function as adjectives and adverbs, they too can be used to expand and combine. Changing the placement of prepositional phrases will help you achieve sentence fluency—varying your sentence structure and rhythm.

Expanding with Prepositional Phrases

To expand with modifiers, follow this simple process:

1. Identify the sentence pattern.
2. Ask the adjective questions (Which one? What kind? How many? Whose?). What additional information would help to clarify the meaning?
3. Ask the adverb questions (Where? When? How? Why?). What additional information would help to clarify the meaning?
4. Logically and clearly insert the answers.
   - Adjectival prepositional phrase:
     The sun struggled to light the sky.
     The sun struggled to light the sky *over Narragansett Bay* (which one?).
   - Adverbial prepositional phrase:
     She and Hosea pushed their skiff.
     She and Hosea pushed their skiff *into the surf* (where?).

Combining with Prepositional Phrases

Short sentences can be included in a paragraph for emphasis. For instance, the sentence "Suddenly, Ida was famous" highlights Ida's quick rise to fame. However, strings of short sentences often sound choppy and defeat the goal of fluency. Try combining pairs of short sentences instead. Study the relationship between two sentences to see if one sentence answers any of the adjective or adverb questions.

Note the choppiness of the following mentor text rewrite and how turning the sentences into prepositional phrases aids fluent reading.

> Zoradia Lewis was doing what she did many times each day, gazing out a window. It was on March 29, 1869. It was in the afternoon. She looked out the window of the lighthouse. The lighthouse was on Lime Rock Island. Lime Rock Island was in Newport, Rhode Island.
>
> *On the afternoon* (when?) *of March 29, 1869* (which one?), Zoradia Lewis was doing what she did many times each day, gazing out a window *of the lighthouse* (which one?) *on Lime Rock Island* (where?) *in Newport, Rhode Island* (where?).

Partner Up!

Expand

Write four sentences each with different sentence patterns and label the sentence patterns. Brainstorm a list of prepositional modifiers for each pattern, both adjectival and adverbial.

Example: The fisherman (S) caught (AV) many fish (DO).	inside the small skiff (adj) with a strong jerk (adj) over the bow of the skiff (adv/adj)

Combine

Combine the sentences using adjectives, adverbs, and prepositional phrases as modifiers. Include at least two prepositional phrases in each of your new sentences. Add or delete words as necessary but keep the same meaning.

1. Ida often used her skiff. She often used it for fishing. She fished along the coast.
2. Skiffs are small open boats. They have flat bottoms. They have a pointed bow. They have a flat stern.
3. Now, some skiffs are used for racing. Skiffs have single rowers or outboard motors. These races are often a part of a regatta.

Try It Out!

Write a paragraph about one of your favorite activities. Include one sentence for each sentence pattern and use at least one prepositional phrase in each sentence.

APPOSITIVE PHRASES

Appositives

An **appositive** is a word that renames a noun or pronoun. It usually follows the noun or pronoun it renames.

Helen's neighbor *Margaret* enjoys playing in the community orchestra.
She plays a more difficult instrument, the *French horn*.

An appositive can often be switched with the noun or pronoun it follows.

Margaret, *Helen's neighbor*, enjoys playing in the community orchestra.
She plays the French horn, *a more difficult instrument*.

Appositive Phrases

An **appositive phrase** consists of an appositive and its modifiers. These modifiers may include other phrases.

The French horn, *a more difficult instrument*, contributes a clear, mellow sound.
Margaret enjoys playing in the community orchestra, *a group of volunteer musicians*.

Restrictive and Nonrestrictive Appositives

Restrictive appositives are essential to understanding the meaning of a sentence. They do not require a comma.

Helen's neighbor *Margaret* enjoys playing in the community orchestra.

Margaret is referred to as **restrictive** because it is essential to understanding which neighbor is playing in the orchestra. A comma is not needed.

Nonrestrictive appositives are not necessary to understand the meaning of a sentence. They require commas.

Margaret, *Helen's neighbor*, enjoys playing in the community orchestra.

In this sentence, *Helen's neighbor* is not necessary because the name of the neighbor has been identified. It is referred to as **nonrestrictive** and is set off with commas. Removing the appositive set off with commas will not hinder the reader's understanding of who is playing in the orchestra.

Punctuation PowerUp

An appositive phrase placed at the beginning of a sentence renames or further identifies the subject of the sentence. It is typically nonrestrictive and requires a comma.

A professional musician, Margaret still practices hours a week.

Nonrestrictive appositives may also be set off with dashes or parentheses. The use of one or more dashes (depending on the placement of the appositive within the sentence) will emphasize the appositive. The use of parentheses will minimize it.

Margaret's hours of practice help to prepare her for the orchestra's final performance—*Saturday Night in the Park*.

Practice the Skill

Underline the appositives and appositive phrases.

1. A middle-school orchestra director, Mr. Simms practices weekly with the musicians.
2. The orchestra's performance will be this Saturday, August 5.
3. Mr. Simms selected the first-chair violin player, Patty Bryant.
4. The first violins, the largest orchestra section, plays the main melody part in one of the pieces.
5. The bass clarinet, a player to the left of the director, is preparing a fun accompaniment to a melody part.
6. A piece with four movements, *Violin Concerto No. 1 in A Minor* is a difficult piece for some of the orchestra's musicians.
7. The trumpets play my favorite part in the piece *Also sprach Zarathustra*.
8. A group of five instrumentalists, the trumpets make a bold sound when they stand to play.
9. One of the trumpet players Albert becomes red in the face when he hits those high notes.
10. Mr. Simms works on unifying the tempo (the speed of the piece).

Review the Skill

Underline the appositives and appositive phrases. Insert commas as necessary.

11. *Peter Pan* was written by J. M. Barrie Scottish novelist and playwright.
12. Peter Pan Barrie's fictional character has been featured in a wide variety of media.
13. In 1904, *The Boy Who Wouldn't Grow Up* a play about Peter Pan was performed on stage.
14. The production included "Pirate's Song" and "Plank Around" the songs in the script.
15. The father of the Darling children George Darling was played by the same person who played Captain Hook.
16. Like *The Boy Who Wouldn't Grow Up*, the play *Peter and the Wolf* has also been adapted for orchestration.
17. The sounds of the clarinet, the bassoon, and the horns correspond with the movements of certain characters the cat, the grandfather, and the wolf.
18. A string quartet's lively rhythms represent Peter's adventure a carefree jaunt in the woods.
19. The hunter's shots sharp and loud sounds are portrayed by the kettle and bass drums.
20. *Peter and the Wolf* the orchestral performance has helped many a child to distinguish among the sounds of orchestra instruments.

Use the Skill

Write a descriptive or explanatory paragraph about a musical experience you have had. Incorporate a minimum of three appositives or appositive phrases. Include at least one restrictive and one nonrestrictive phrase. Challenge yourself to vary the appositive locations.

ANECDOTES
Writing Trait: Ideas

Listen Up!

Read this humorous anecdote. What characteristics of a short story does it have? How is it different from a short story?

MENTOR TEXT

Two young engineers applied for a single position at a computer company. They both had the same qualifications. In order to determine which individual to hire, the department manager asked both applicants to take a test.

Upon completion of the test, both men had missed only one of the questions. The manager went to the first applicant and said, "Thank you for your interest, but we've decided to give the job to the other applicant."

"And why would you be doing that? We both got nine questions correct," argued the rejected applicant.

"We have based our decision not on the correct answers, but on the question you missed," said the department manager.

"And just how would one incorrect answer be better than the other?" the rejected applicant inquired.

"Simple," said the department manager. "Your fellow applicant put down on question number five, 'I don't know.' You put down, 'Neither do I.'"

—Michael E. Hodgin, "Almost Identical Answers"
from *1002 Humorous Illustrations for Public Speaking*

Take Notes!

Use a Venn diagram to compare and contrast a story with an anecdote.

Anecdotes are short accounts of interesting or humorous incidents. Writers use this technique to illustrate, persuade, or make a point stick in a reader's or listener's mind. You may remember how important it is to trust God because your pastor told a real-life story illustrating the importance of trust. You may remember to make a decision based on a story your parents shared about their childhood. These anecdotes help make a point meaningful and memorable.

The New Testament records multiple examples of believers "bearing witness"—testifying to what they knew of God or had experienced from God. For instance, the woman at the well told the townsfolk about meeting the true Christ: "Come, see a man, which told me all things that ever I did: is not this the Christ?" (John 4:29). In John 12:17, the people who experienced the raising of Lazarus from the dead told of Jesus' resurrection power to others.

WRITING TOOLBOX

Believers should look for opportunities to "bear witness" in their writing to what Christ has done in and through them. To make his witness believable, a believer must first of all be living a consistent Christian life before others. Second, his purpose should accurately point to Christ and not draw attention to himself or even the story itself. Last, but certainly not least, his motive should be one of sincere love and concern for the person with whom he is sharing.

Perhaps you are thinking that anecdotes are just short stories. "I've been writing short stories forever," you say. "Why do I need a whole workshop about telling stories?" Stories and anecdotes do have some commonalities. Both have a setting, at least one character, a problem, and a conclusion. Anecdotes, however, have these distinct differences. They

- occupy the length of one or two paragraphs.
- tell of a single moment in time.
- begin with a quick reference to a setting. For instance:
  I pushed the swing in the park.
  The grocery cart got away from me and rolled down the aisle.
- start as close to the peak of the action or the challenge as possible.
- may or may not use a line or two of dialogue.
- may or may not end with an explanation of its purpose or meaning.

Partner Up!

In *Try It Out!* you will be writing an anecdote illustrating either a fear you have, a quality or characteristic you possess, or something you have learned. Brainstorm and select a topic and possible personal events to illustrate your selected topic. For your selected topic, sketch out chronological details, keeping the following list of characteristics in mind.

Story Characteristics	Anecdote Characteristics
setting	occupy the length of one or two paragraphs
character(s)	tell of a single moment in time
problem	begin with a quick reference to setting
dialogue	start as close to the peak of action or challenge as possible
conclusion	may or may not use dialogue
	may or may not end with an explanation of purpose or meaning

Try It Out!

Create an anecdote based on the prewriting you did in *Partner Up!* Read your anecdote to your partner. Take turns analyzing the message your anecdote is communicating. What is its purpose? What overall impression does it make? Is it constructive? Does it reflect Christ-likeness?

CHAPTER REVIEW

Prepositional Phrases

Place parentheses around the prepositional phrases. Underline the simple object of each prepositional phrase.

1. Approximately fifteen million people in the United States have a hearing impairment.
2. For many people, their hearing impairment is not severe.
3. Those who suffer from mild hearing loss can often have normal hearing with the use of a hearing aid.
4. Two million people with some form of hearing impairment are completely deaf.
5. Because of prenatal defects, some people's auditory systems are damaged before birth.

Prepositions and Adverbs

Identify each italicized word as a preposition or an adverb. Write in the blank the letter that corresponds to the correct answer.

A preposition
B adverb

_______ 6. Ludwig van Beethoven began losing his hearing in his twenties, and his hearing continually declined *past* his thirtieth birthday.

_______ 7. Most of Beethoven's music was written *before* his total loss of hearing.

_______ 8. He grew more melancholy and reclusive as the years went *by*.

_______ 9. As the end of his life drew *near*, Beethoven became completely deaf.

_______ 10. He did not cease to write music; instead, Beethoven composed some works that were more beautiful than any he had ever written *before*.

Adjectival and Adverbial Prepositional Phrases

Identify each italicized phrase as adjectival or adverbial. Write in the blank the letter that corresponds to the correct answer.

A adjectival prepositional phrase
B adverbial prepositional phrase

_______ 11. Some people acquire hearing loss *in their teenage or adult years.*

_______ 12. Prolonged exposure *to extremely loud noises* will most likely cause hearing loss.

_______ 13. Most deaf people in America can learn to communicate well *through sign language.*

_______ 14. Many people without hearing loss learn sign language so that they can interpret speech *for the hearing impaired.*

_______ 15. A deaf person can send and receive phone messages *by texting.*

Appositives and Appositive Phrases

Underline the appositives and appositive phrases.

16. Andrew Foster was born in 1925 to a coal-mining family in Ensley, a community in Birmingham, Alabama.
17. At the age of eleven, Andrew contracted the disease spinal meningitis and was left deaf.
18. He had a desire to minister to deaf children, specifically African children, from the time he heard a missionary speak in Sunday School.
19. He completed his final high-school class, a correspondence course, and applied to colleges.
20. The first black student to graduate from Gallaudet University, Andrew went on to get a master's degree from Seattle Pacific Christian College.

Restrictive and Nonrestrictive Appositives

Underline the appositives and appositive phrases. Insert commas as necessary.

21. Andrew arrived in Africa in the year 1957.
22. Andrew Foster founded Christian Mission for the Deaf African a mission for the deaf.
23. In multiple countries, Andrew established thirty or more deaf schools the first of their kind in many African countries.
24. Gallaudet the university he attended named the campus auditorium after him.
25. Foster has been honored with the title Father of Deaf Education in Africa.

CHAPTER 11

NARRATIVE WRITING

HOW CAN I USE MY STORY TO COMMUNICATE TRUTH?

Have you ever wondered why Jesus told stories? Although He could have always preached sermons, Jesus often told stories because storytelling is a powerful way to communicate truth. If Christians are to practice Christ-expression, they should imitate Christ's method of communication by learning the art of storytelling and using this skill to teach truth to others.

As you read the mentor text, look for techniques the narrator uses to make the story come alive to the reader. How does the author use this tale to communicate truth?

A Man and His Two Motherless Sons

by Mrs. Cora Bray Buckner Karr, from *Come Go with Me: Old-timer Stories from the Southern Mountains*, collected by Roy Edwin Thomas

What is the conflict? How is it introduced?

What is the setting?

Note the use of dialogue. What can you tell about the characters from the way they talk?

I know one time, we was just all little kids. And they come a man and two little boys. And they was a-foot. They was going somewhere to see if he could find work. And they had buried his wife on the way. In 1902.

They stopped at our house. Mother fixed their dinner. Course, we didn't have too much food then. Our father had died.

And the man said, "Missus, I don't have no money to pay for food."

Mother said, "You don't need no money to have dinner with us." She said, "I was getting dinner, and you're welcome to eat. We don't live high, but we have plenty to eat, what we want."

Course, she had stuff canned in glass jars, and stuff dried, to eat.

And one little boy—we was sitting out in the yard, us kids and them two little boys—and they was telling us about burying their momma, on the road. The oldest one said, "She got sick and died, on the road. We had to bury her and leave her by the side of the road."

Us kids thought that was terrible. We didn't see how anybody could do that.

But there was no other way.

And that man was real—the best I can remember—he was such a humble guy. He was a little frail-looking man. And I think he had tuberculosis.

Note the use of description. What details about the man does the narrator give us?

MENTOR TEXT

And I said, "Do you have any money?" to one of the little boys. I was about twelve or thirteen, and the boys, I guess, were about eight and ten.

He said, "Uh-uh. I never did have no money."

I said, "I've got some. I'll give it to you." I just had two pennies.

But I ran in the house and got them pennies, and gave them to him.

Wy, I was so happy! Because he didn't have no money, and I had two pennies. After they left, I told my mother, "Momma, I gave that little boy my pennies."

She said, "Well, honey, in the sight of God, that's just as much as a thousand dollars. It's all you had."

That made me feel better, you know. I thought, now, I had done a good deed.

I'm satisfied that little boy never forgot that. No, he never. And I never did.

It seems like, sometimes, I'd just think, Oh, if I knew where he was, I'd send him some money.

Course, he was a grown man by then. But he always stayed the same, he always stayed little in my sight.

I never did know; we never did hear from the family. And the father he'd kind of promised Mother he would write back, when he got to his destination. But he never did. I guess the poor guy didn't have anything to do it with.

Or maybe he couldn't write. For all I know, he couldn't.

I don't know where they were from. I don't remember that. But they was sure a pitiful-looking sight.

What lesson did the narrator learn from this experience?

How is the story paced? Is it fast paced, or is it slow and reflective?

What do you think is the theme of the story? How does the author reveal the theme throughout the story?

INTRODUCING THE NARRATIVE ESSAY

The Power of Stories

Take a moment to imagine what it would be like to go for a month without hearing or telling any stories. Life would be rather boring if you ever experienced this. If you are like most people, you probably tell and hear several **narratives** every day. You might do this by listening to family and friends talk about what has been happening to them recently, sharing your own recent experiences with your family and friends, reading a book or article, or watching television or videos on the internet. Much of your education consists of learning about different narratives. You study fictional and nonfictional stories in English class, you read stories from different cultures in history class, and you learn about the most important stories in Bible class. Even your math teacher might tell stories to illustrate his point.

God Himself is very interested in narratives. The Bible is filled with stories that we need to know if we want to have a relationship with Him. Additionally, God is so interested in the narrative of each individual that He even knows the number of hairs on every head (Matthew 10:29). Because we are created in God's image, stories and storytelling are fundamental parts of our identity.

Not only are narratives entertaining, but they also have a powerful effect on people. When Harriet Beecher Stowe revealed the evils of American slavery through her novel *Uncle Tom's Cabin*, she changed many people's minds about this wicked practice, and her story significantly contributed to the eventual emancipation of slaves. Her story's influence was so great that when Abraham Lincoln met her, he allegedly said, "So you're the little woman who wrote the book that started this great war." What stories have affected your life and caused you to think differently about the world?

Storytelling Techniques

There are four main techniques that are important to every narrative: dialogue, description, pacing, and reflection. To write a powerful story, you need to learn how to use them effectively.

Dialogue refers to a conversation between characters. Using dialogue helps *show* the reader what is happening rather than just *telling* about a situation.

Description refers to words that create a vivid image for the reader. Good descriptions often include details that appeal to the senses or emotions.

Reflection refers to the writer sharing lessons learned or conclusions drawn about the story. This normally takes place at the end of a story.

Pacing refers to the speed at which the reader is moved from event to event. Fast-paced stories can excite the reader and create suspense. Slow-paced stories invite the reader to reflect more deeply on the story. How quickly or slowly your story is paced depends on its purpose. Although your pacing can have some variation, an important rule is to be consistent. Do not suddenly swing from one extreme to another, or your readers will be confused.

Looking at the Experts

To write a good narrative, you should study well-written stories in order to see what makes them so effective. Read the mentor text carefully and answer the following questions:

- What is the story's purpose?
- How does the writer capture the reader's interest at the beginning of the story?
- What is the **conflict**, or main problem, in the story? How does the conflict build? How is the conflict resolved at the end?
- How does the author use the techniques of dialogue, description, pacing, and reflection to add interest?

As you study this mentor text, take careful note of the techniques that make it a good story. Try to incorporate these techniques into your own writing as you write your narrative.

Writing with Purpose

In this chapter, you will be writing a story in which you tell the reader about an event that happened in your life. However, not all personal stories are worth telling. As you learned in Chapter 1, your paper will not have value unless it has an ultimate purpose. For example, telling about a time when you ate a bowl of cereal will not be interesting or helpful to your readers unless there is a reason for telling this story. Choose one of the following writing assignments to focus the purpose of your narrative.

- Write a story that entertains the reader. This type of story normally informs the reader about an event that is funny or unique. Entertaining stories are an effective way to communicate a truthful idea.
- Write a story that teaches the reader an important life lesson (e.g., hard work brings its own rewards, cheaters never prosper, etc.).
- Write a story promoting a particular product or service by sharing your experience (e.g., athletic shoes, ATVs, etc.).
- Write a story to demonstrate that a problem is real or that a specific solution to a certain problem is the correct one (e.g., cyberbullying is dangerous, wearing a seat belt is the best way to prevent injuries in an accident, etc.).

Consider Your Audience

As mentioned in Chapter 1, you must always consider your audience before writing. The way you would tell a story to a first grader would be very different from the way you would tell it to an adult. Consider who your audience is, what they already know, and what interests them. Let your audience inspire you to tell them an engaging, relatable story.

Choose Your Topic

Sometimes the hardest part of writing a narrative is simply choosing what you want to write about. Try out the following activities to help you choose a topic.

Make a List

Write down a list of interesting events, experiences, and memories. To refresh your memory, try the following:

- Look at personal pictures of you and your friends and family.
- Go through your social media history.
- Skim your school's yearbooks.
- Ask friends and family members about their favorite memories of you.

Ask Questions

Ask yourself the following questions and write down your answers:

- What was the best day of my life? What was my worst day?
- What was one of the funniest events that ever happened to me?
- What have I done that has gotten me into trouble?
- What was my favorite vacation?
- What obstacles have I overcome? How did I overcome them?

Brainstorm

Do a brainstorming session with your classmates so everyone can share interesting life events. Take good notes, and be on the lookout for inspiration for your own narrative.

Narrow Your Topic

Look back at the information in Lesson 2 on narrowing your topic. When you have some good topic ideas, evaluate the scope of each one. Are any of your topics too broad to cover in your story? For example, it would be very difficult to cover your entire seventh-grade experience in just a few paragraphs. Try to focus on an event that happened within a twenty-four-hour period.

Gather Information

Unlike informative papers, personal narratives do not require you to gather much information. However, you may want to look at any available photos or videos of the event and talk to several people who experienced the event with you to make certain you are remembering the details correctly.

Determine Your Story's Elements

Each narrative has several major elements. Before you begin your narrative assignment, you need to think through each of these elements of your story. Use the following graphic organizer to guide your thinking.

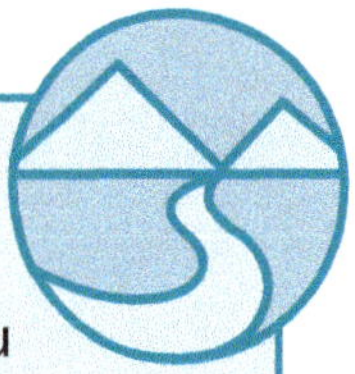

Setting

Where does your story take place? How would you describe this place to someone who has never been there?

Characters

What should your readers know about you to understand your story? What character traits do you need to bring out? Think through the general storyline. What motivated you and the others involved to take action (or refrain from acting)?

Theme

What overall idea are you trying to communicate through your story? Look back to your story's purpose to answer this question.

Conflict

What is the main problem in this story? How does this conflict grow throughout the story and get resolved at the end? The main conflict can be serious or trivial. It can also be a conflict that you have had with yourself, with someone else, or with an impersonal force, such as bad weather or a difficult task.

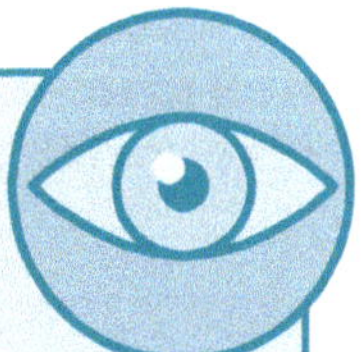

Point of View

You can tell your story in **first person** by referring to yourself directly (e.g., "One day, I went to the store"), or you can use **third person** by telling about yourself from an outside narrator's perspective (e.g., "One day, John went to the store").

As you plan out your elements, keep in mind that part of Christ-expressive writing is being intentional with your story. Christians should not just be interested in entertaining their readers or gaining their approval, but they should also use their story to communicate a central theme or message that they believe will benefit their readers. It is therefore important that you ask yourself how these elements point to the main theme of the story.

Developing a Framework for the Plot

The **plot** simply refers to the events that happened in the story. Each plot has a beginning, middle, and end. Use the following framework to plan your plot:

Beginning

- Include an attention-getting opening sentence.
- Introduce the setting, main characters, and conflict.

Middle

- List a clear sequence of events.
- Show how the conflict grows to a climax.
- Develop the plot and characters through dialogue and vivid descriptions.
- Engage your reader and build suspense through pacing.

End

- Show the resolution of the conflict.
- Finish with a memorable ending that causes the reader to reflect on the theme of the story.

DRAFTING

Now that you have finished planning, it is time to put your plan into action and write your story. Draft your story in one sitting, writing quickly without making corrections. When you finish, set your draft aside for a time before revisiting it. Here are some writing tips to help you through each section of your narrative.

Beginning

- Grab your reader's attention in the first sentences with relevant dialogue, questions, facts, definitions, or quotes. This is very important because it is your reader's first impression of your story. Since one of your primary goals is to communicate a message that will benefit your reader, you need to capture his attention from the beginning to motivate him to read your entire story and think about your message.
- Introduce your setting, characters, conflict, and any important background information. Be careful to avoid an "information dump"—adding so many details that the reader becomes overwhelmed or confused.
- Establish yourself as the narrator. Use first-person or third-person point of view.

Middle

- Sequence your plot clearly, omitting events unnecessary to your story. Climb toward the peak of suspense.
- Be sure your pacing is appropriate and does not have too much variation.
- Bring characters to life. Make them convincing. You can develop your characters by directly describing them or by indirectly showing the reader who they are by their words and actions.
- Include details, vivid verbs, and descriptions that appeal to the senses. Remember, your audience is living the experience through your account.
- Use clear, logical transitions between the different sections of your story. Refer to the chart on page 17.

End

- Resolve the conflict and conclude your story, wrapping up any loose ends.
- Finish with a personal reflection, a lesson learned, or a conclusion drawn from the event.

Self-Evaluation

Now that you have written your draft, it is time to take a fresh look at what you have written. Read your narrative aloud to yourself. Did you find your story easy to follow? If you stumbled in certain areas or had a hard time understanding what you wrote, your reader will struggle as well. This is an opportunity to evaluate your story. Make sure you are logically telling a story that communicates an important theme. Remember that a key component of Christ-expression is to create in *imitation* of our Creator. Ask yourself whether your creative writing exhibits the consistency, coherence, truth, and beauty that reflect the God who created all things.

Next, look at your characters. Are their actions consistent with their personality? Your reader will find your narrative more interesting if you show what kind of people your characters are through action and dialogue rather than just describing them.

Finally, look at the purpose of your story. Is your purpose clearly achieved? Do you successfully communicate a theme to the reader?

As you review your story, use the revising checklist to guide your revision.

	Revising Checklist
Ideas	❑ Do I introduce all the necessary storytelling elements (setting, conflict, etc.)? ❑ Is my theme apparent throughout my story? ❑ Are my characters realistic and convincing? ❑ Do I show what is going on through action and dialogue rather than just telling the reader about what is happening? ❑ Does my conclusion reflect on the theme and bring a satisfactory resolution to the conflict?
Organization	❑ Does my narrative have a solid beginning, middle, and end? ❑ Do I tell what happened in a reader-friendly way (i.e., logically, clearly)?
Word Choice	❑ Do I describe the setting and characters sufficiently so that my audience can visualize what I want them to see but not so extensively that I run the risk of losing my audience with too many details? ❑ Do I use details, vivid verbs, and descriptions that appeal to the senses or emotions?
Voice	❑ Do my descriptions and dialogue realistically portray my characters? ❑ Am I consistently using a writing style that is engaging, inspiring my audience to continue reading?
Sentence Fluency	❑ Is my story appropriately paced? ❑ Do I provide variety in sentence length and structure? ❑ Do I include varied transitional words and phrases for smoothness and rhythm?

Peer Evaluation

By now, you should already be familiar with the process of peer evaluation. Choose a peer who is unfamiliar with the story you are telling. Try to ask someone to read your paper who has not yet done any peer evaluations for your previous work. Better yet, have several different peers read your paper and give feedback. Remember to follow the peer review guidelines in Lesson 6.

You have revised for the first five traits of writing, and it is now time to focus on making certain your paper follows proper writing conventions. Be sure to follow the proofreading strategies listed in Lesson 7.

While you should use proper spelling and grammar in most papers, narratives are a little different. When a person writes a story, he may use poor grammar or spelling in character dialogue or narration in order to portray the character realistically. Your mentor text shows how **colloquial language**, the language of everyday conversation, can be used to effectively portray a character. Similarly, the dialogue in Mark Twain's novels often includes incorrect grammar because the characters he created either lacked education or spoke in a regional dialect. Proofreading a narrative, therefore, does not necessarily mean checking your story for proper spelling and grammar. You might choose to use informal or colloquial language, but you should only do so to accomplish a specific purpose. Remember that the main reason why good writers typically use correct spelling and grammar is that they want their readers to understand their message. Be careful to not sacrifice clarity in your efforts to create realistic dialogue.

Creating a Digital Storytelling Video

To publish this particular assignment, you will be presenting your story as a digital storytelling video. The purpose of this part of your assignment is to create a video in which you read your story while providing accompanying visuals. Consider the following questions when choosing visuals to go along with your story:

1. Am I choosing the right type of visual? A diagram would probably work well for an informative essay, but it might not be the best fit for a personal narrative. Photos and illustrations are typically good options for narratives.
2. Are my visuals appropriate for my audience? Make sure the visuals you choose are ones that your audience would be interested in. For example, you do not want to choose visuals that look like they came out of either a preschool storybook or a college textbook if your audience is your peers.
3. Do my visuals accurately portray my story? If your story is about a hiking trip to the Smoky Mountains, you will want to make sure you use a picture of those particular mountains, not the Rockies or some other mountain range. Your visuals should reinforce what you say in your story, or your audience might become confused.

Since this is a personal narrative, you may not have pictures of the actual event you are describing. This does not mean you cannot add visuals. For example, a story about a day of fishing on the Chesapeake Bay could include pictures of the type of boat you were on, the bay itself, and the type of fish you caught. Be creative! Remember, many people find illustrations to be the most interesting part of a story. A storytelling video will make your narrative come alive to your audience.

Evaluating Your Peers

During the presentations, you will do peer evaluations. Be sure to follow the guidelines for giving helpful suggestions on page 26. Speaking in front of others is one of the hardest things for many people to do. Practice Christlike discernment by checking the tone of your review before you share it with a classmate. Are your comments constructive and encouraging? Are there any negative comments that you can reframe to avoid coming across as demeaning? Remember to also be gracious and willing to listen when receiving feedback on your own presentation.

When you are finished, reflect on your presentation. Identify at least two things you did well and at least one thing you would like to improve in your next presentation.

CHAPTER 12

VERBALS

"BORING!" IS THIS A READER'S RESPONSE TO YOUR WRITING?

Modifiers are an essential tool for preventing your writing from becoming boring. They allow you to paint a precise picture that your reader can visualize. Your toolbox of modifiers presently includes adjectives, adverbs, prepositional phrases, and appositive phrases. In this chapter, you will add participles and infinitives to your toolbox, giving you many additional options. Be selective. Pick just the right brush or tool to paint the clearest picture. No excuse for "boring"!

DISCOVER!

Joseph Kim, a North Korean refugee, tells of his journey to fulfill the American Dream. Underline any infinitives or infinitive phrases you recognize.

MENTOR TEXT

In 2004, Congress passed the North Korean Human Rights Act to grant political refuge to North Koreans. . . . By 2011, only 122 North Korean refugees had come to this country. One of them was Joseph Kim, who immigrated when he was seventeen. His father had died of starvation, and his mother and sister disappeared trying to escape to China. At fifteen years old, he fled to China and was helped by a humanitarian organization to come to the United States.

"I had to do anything to survive," said Kim, who swam across a river to get to China. "I just didn't understand why it was happening to me. I couldn't even blame it on someone else. . . . [In] North Korea there's nothing I could blame or ask. I couldn't find answers." Kim was placed in a foster home in Virginia with children from Myanmar. "My dream . . . is to go to college," he said. "I like to play soccer a lot. Some say my hobby is studying but that is not true. I like to eat. I like to hang out with friends." In 2013, Kim told a reporter, "I did not come here by myself. I had hope, but hope by itself is not enough, many people helped me along the way. . . . This is my message to you. Have hope for yourself but also help each other. Life can be hard for everyone, wherever you live. . . . [You] may . . . change someone's life with even the smallest act of love."

—Linda Barrett Osborne, *This Land Is Our Land: A History of American Immigration*

PARTICIPLES AND THEIR PHRASES, PRESENT AND PAST

Verbals are special verb forms that are not used as verbs but rather function as other parts of speech. Because a verbal retains some of its verb qualities (shows action, can be modified by an adverb, and may have complements), it is sometimes mistaken for a normal verb. However, verbals function in sentences just like nouns, adjectives, or adverbs. The three types of verbals are participles, gerunds, and infinitives.

Participles

A **participle** is a verbal that acts as an adjective. Because it retains some of its verb qualities and functions as an adjective, it can be modified by an adverb.

The skillfully *rappelling* mountain climber descended safely.
(*Rappelling* is a participle modifying the noun *mountain climber*. *Skillfully* is an adverb modifying *rappelling*.)

The noisily *buzzing* bumblebee startled the boy.
(*Buzzing* is a participle modifying the noun *bumblebee*. *Noisily* is an adverb modifying *buzzing*.)

The bumblebee pursued the rapidly *fleeing* boy.
(*Fleeing* is a participle modifying the noun *boy*. *Rapidly* is an adverb modifying *fleeing*.)

Present Participles

The **present participle** consists of the first principal part of a verb plus *-ing*. Like any adjective, a participle often comes before the word that it describes or modifies.

The *hurrying* student almost dropped her library books.
(*Hurrying* is a present participle modifying the subject *student*.)

Sometimes other adjectives come between the participle and the noun or pronoun it modifies.

The *hurrying* Algebra student bent over to pick up the library books.

Punctuation PowerUp

A participle at the beginning of a sentence modifies the subject and is set off by a comma.

Hurrying, Reba almost dropped her books.

Past Participles

The past participle is the same as the third principal part of a verb. Past participles often end in *-d*, *-ed*, *-t*, or *-en*. Like the present participle, the past participle expresses the action of a verb and describes a noun or pronoun.

> The dental hygienist used a *filled* syringe to numb the area around the tooth. (The syringe was *filled* by someone.)
>
> The *chipped* tooth needed repair. (The tooth was *chipped* by someone or something.)
>
> The *dimmed* lights calm many patients. (The lights were *dimmed* by someone.)

Participial Phrases

A **participial phrase** includes the participle, its modifiers, and any words that complete it. Participial phrases function as adjectives. They may come before or after the noun or pronoun they modify.

> Miguel, *tapping at the window*, woke his family.
>
> *Tapping at the window*, Miguel woke his family.

Punctuation PowerUp

When the participial phrase comes first in the sentence, it is set off by a comma.

A participial phrase that follows the noun it modifies is not set off with (a) comma(s) unless it is nonrestrictive.

Practice the Skill

Underline the present participles. Draw an arrow from each underlined participle to the noun it modifies. Two sentences do not contain a present participle.

1. In addition to man, the earth is full of many interesting creatures.
2. One such animal is the amazing freshwater lungfish.
3. Today, six species of lungfish inhabit the earth's waters.
4. Slow-moving, the waters of South America, Africa, and Australia are habitats for lungfish.
5. The lungfish has a special lunglike breathing organ.

Underline the past participles. Draw an arrow from each underlined participle to the noun it modifies.

6. One of the most picturesque creatures is the endangered snow leopard.
7. A grown snow leopard may reach a length of six or seven feet.
8. Snow leopards' beautiful tails account for roughly three feet of their total recorded length.
9. The snow leopard's gray fur is dappled with blackish leopard's spots.
10. These cats dwell among the snow-swept steeps of the Himalayan and Altai Mountains as well as among other mountain ranges of central Asia.

Underline the participial phrases. Draw an arrow from each underlined participle or participial phrase to the noun it modifies. Identify each underlined participle or participial phrase as *present* (present participle) or *past* (past participle). Insert commas as necessary. Two sentences do not contain a participle.

________________ 11. Panda ants found in Chile, South America are a unique insect of God's creation.

________________ 12. Resembling both a panda and an ant panda ants are neither.

________________ 13. These ants have been nicknamed "panda" because of their coloring.

________________ 14. Called "ants" because they have six legs they are technically wasps.

________________ 15. Panda ants having soft, thick fur have also been called "velvet ants."

________________ 16. The panda ants' appearance pleasing to the eye may trick the naïve observer.

________________ 17. A naïve person handling panda ants with bare hands may be sorry.

________________ 18. Someone stung by a panda ant experiences sharp pain.

________________ 19. Because six or more stings have been known to kill a cow, the female ant has earned the additional nickname, "cow killer."

________________ 20. Males lacking stingers cannot be blamed!

Review the Skill

Underline the present participles. One sentence does not contain a present participle.

21. The exciting life of a river otter is filled with fun.
22. Ironically, river otters are afraid of the water when they are very young.
23. Swimming parents sometimes carry their babies on their backs.
24. After much practice with their parents, otters become amazing swimmers.
25. Because fishing otters find food quickly, they have much time for leisure and play.

Underline the past participles. One sentence does not contain a past participle.

26. A skunk's defense leaves an impression on uninformed enemies.
27. An alarmed skunk will warn its enemy to stay away.
28. The approached skunk will lift its tail high in the air.
29. The skunk will aim toward the eyes of a fearless enemy.
30. A sprayed victim endures burning eyes and smelly clothes.

Underline the participles and participial phrases. Insert commas as necessary. Two sentences do not contain a participle.

31. Among the many creatures created by the Lord certain birds have been extremely helpful to man.
32. Known for its gorgeous songs the canary has enjoyed popularity as a domestic bird for years.
33. However, canaries also have served as indicators of threatening fumes and harmful gases in mines.
34. Because of its susceptibility to contaminated air, the canary has saved lives during war because the bird's death alerted men to the presence of airborne poisons.
35. Another one of man's flying allies is the carrier pigeon.
36. Navigating carrier pigeons depend partly on the sun for their sense of direction.
37. These messengers aided long-distance communication before the invention of the telegraph and during the world wars.
38. The falcon has been hunting with humans since before Christ's birth.
39. The peregrine falcon diving as fast as 180 miles per hour illustrates the swiftness of these birds.

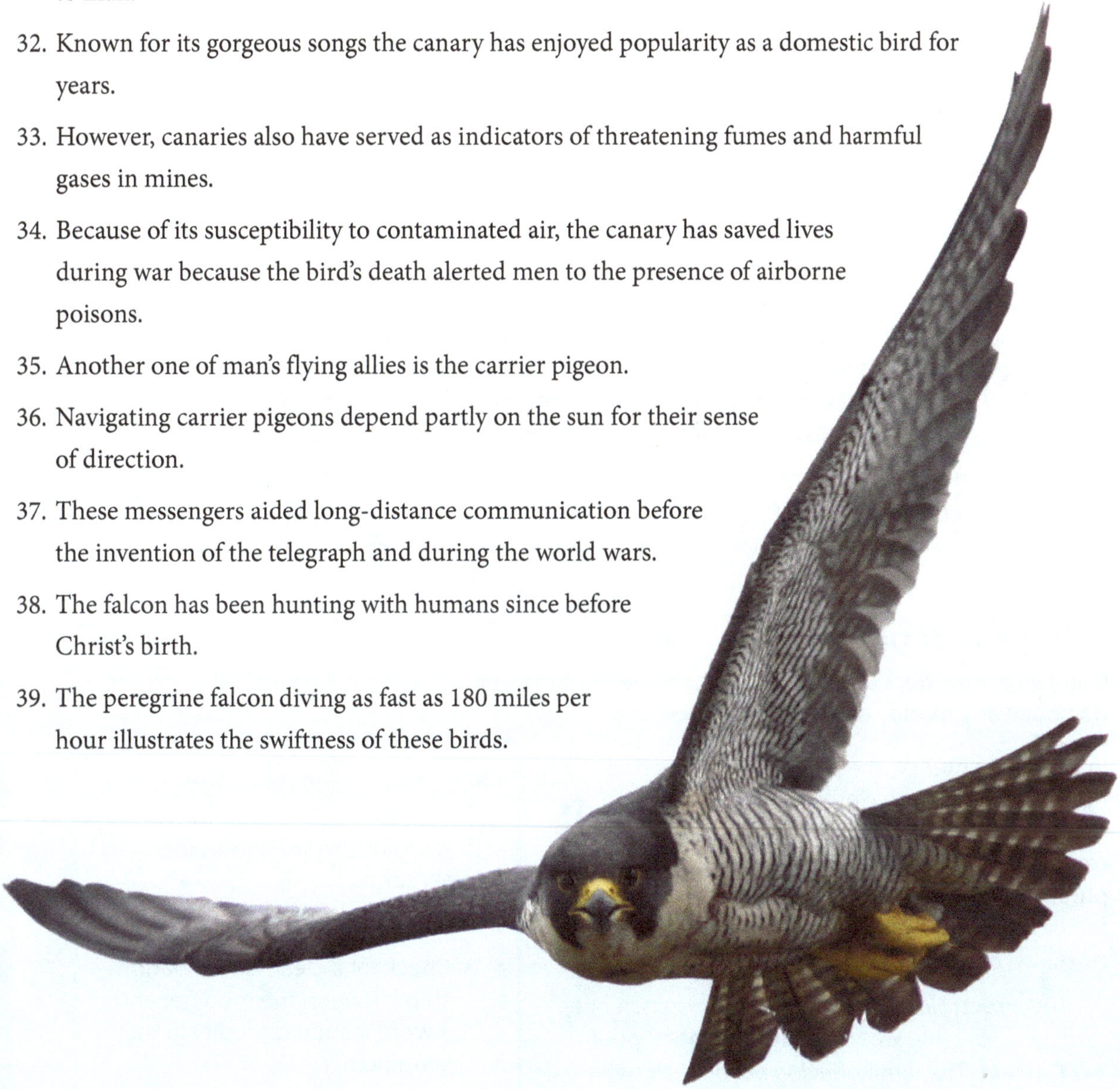

MISPLACED AND DANGLING MODIFIERS

Misplaced Modifiers

Misplaced modifiers are verbals or verbal phrases placed too far away from the word they are intended to modify in the sentence. Misplaced modifiers can be corrected by moving the modifier closer to the word modified.

In the first sentence, the participial phrase is too far from the intended noun, *destination*. The result is that the modifier appears to modify *signs*, communicating an unintended message. Moving the participial phrase *chosen months ago* close to the noun it modifies clarifies the meaning.

Incorrect: The family saw multiple signs *chosen months ago* for their vacation destination.

Correct: The family saw multiple signs for their vacation destination *chosen months ago*.

Sometimes a misplaced modifier can distort the intended meaning, often leaving a humorous picture in the reader's mind. For example, the arrangement of the first sentence leads the reader to think the minivan was tired from traveling for hours! However, it was the family that was tired from traveling for hours. Moving the participial phrase makes that meaning clear.

Incorrect: They were finally able to scramble out of the minivan *tired from traveling for hours*.

Correct: *Tired from traveling for hours*, they were finally able to scramble out of the minivan.

Dangling Modifiers

Dangling modifiers usually dangle at the beginning or end of a sentence and do not clearly modify any word in the sentence.

In the first sentence, the participial phrase does not modify the noun closest to it, *beeline*, nor does it modify any noun in the sentence. This problem can be corrected by adding a subject the dangling phrase can logically modify. Adding the subject *the family* identifies who was putting on their swimsuits.

Incorrect: *Having put on their swimsuits*, a beeline was made for the motel pool.

Correct: The family, *having put on their swimsuits,* made a beeline for the motel pool.

To check for misplaced or dangling modifiers:

1. Identify all modifiers in the sentence.
2. Identify the words they modify.
3. Check for a clear, close relationship between the modifier and a word it should modify in the sentence.
4. Use one of the strategies in the lesson to fix the problem.

Practice the Skill

Underline the misplaced participial phrases.

1. The family pored over travel brochures checking on activities to do and attractions to see.
2. Mom made a final list of selected family-friendly activities jotting down all the suggestions.
3. The family spent one day at the water park sliding down the tube and body slides.
4. Two-by-two the kids rode the exhilarating, fast-water tube pitching this way and that.
5. Timothy chose to sit out the second tube ride shaken by the hurling power of the water.
6. Timothy tried paddleboarding instead of tubing, summoning a lot of courage.
7. Playing in the wading pool, Mom entertained two-year-old Charlie.
8. Suzanne and Christopher chose to try out their new goggles fascinated by the waves in the wave pool.
9. Dad took pictures of Suzanne and Christopher with his camera dodging waves in the wave pool.
10. The day was a great start to a fabulous vacation spent at the water park.

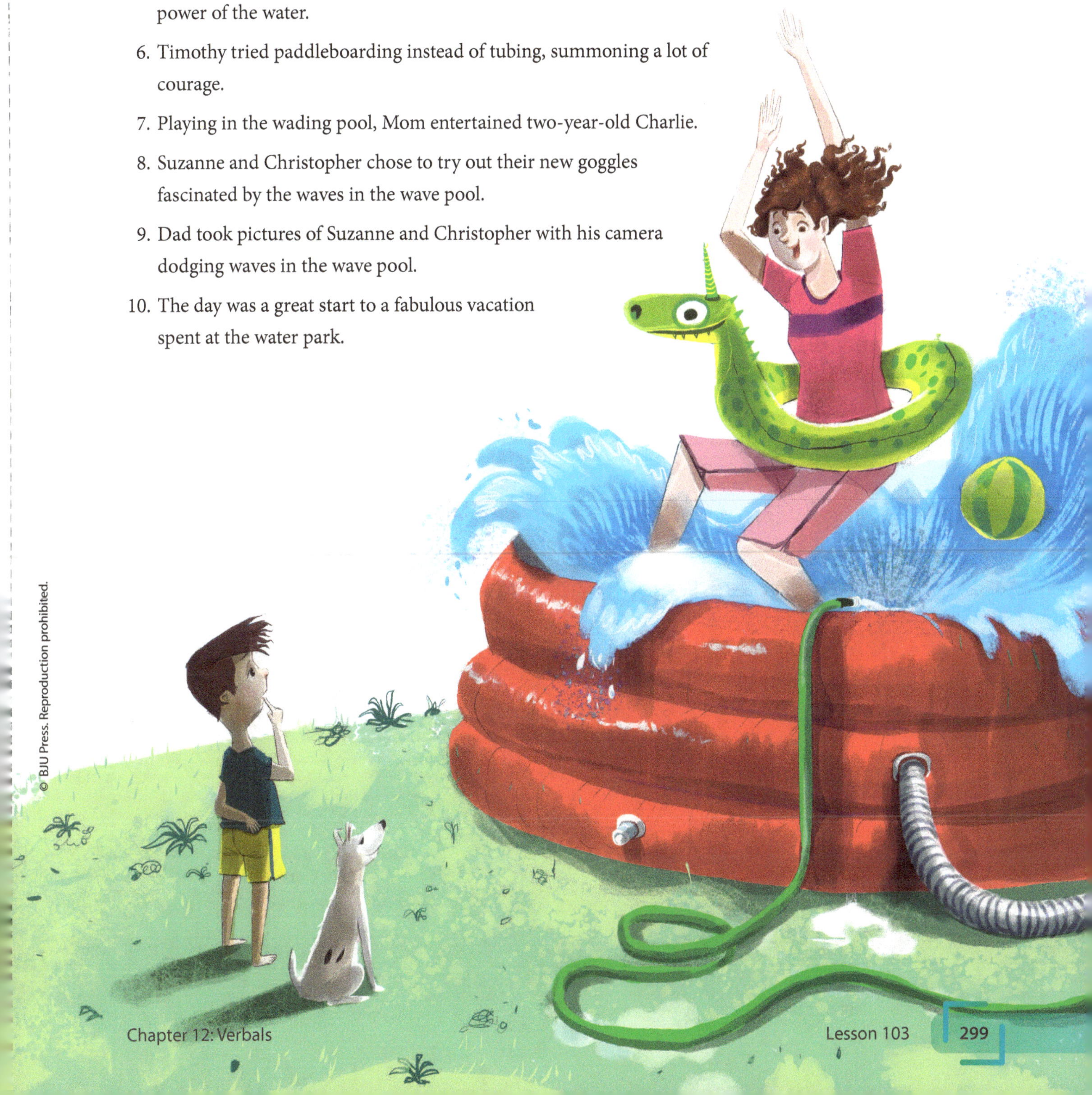

Underline the dangling participial phrases.

11. Several whole days were spent at the beach, bringing all the beach gear and sunblock.
12. The warmth from the sun was enjoyed, lying in the beach chairs.
13. Pouring water into the castle moat, the buckets were filled many times.
14. Having built a castle, the ocean waves were watched washing it away.
15. Running down the beach, the kite flew high in the sky.
16. The boogie boards hit the surf, racing toward the waves.
17. Sitting under the beach umbrella, the book's pages turned lazily.
18. The water was splashed in the air, playing along the seashore.
19. Collecting seashells, hermit crabs were observed scurrying along the beach.
20. The beach gear was loaded in the minivan, having watched the magnificent sunset.

Review the Skill

Rewrite the sentences in numbers 1–10 by relocating the misplaced modifiers to show a clearer relationship with the words they modify. Underline the relocated modifiers. Insert commas as necessary.

21. ______________________________

22. ______________________________

23. ______________________________

24. ______________________________

25. ______________________________

26. ______________________________

27. ______________________________

28. ______________________________

29 ______________________________

30. ______________________________

Rewrite the sentences in numbers 11–20 by adding a noun for the dangling modifiers to modify. Insert commas as necessary.

31. ______________________________

32. ______________________________

33. ______________________________

34. ______________________________

35. ______________________________

36. ______________________________

37. ______________________________

38. ______________________________

39. ______________________________

40. ______________________________

USING PARTICIPIAL PHRASES TO EXPAND OR COMBINE

Writing Traits: Sentence Fluency and Organization

Listen Up!

Ernie Pyle, Pulitzer Prize-winning World War II correspondent, describes one night during the London Blitz. Find the participles that help you visualize London as a result of the blitz.

MENTOR TEXT

Later on I borrowed a tin hat and went out among the fires. That was exciting too, but the thing I shall always remember above all the other things in my life is the monstrous loveliness of that one single view of London on a holiday night – London stabbed with great fires, shaken by explosions, its dark regions along the Thames sparkling with the pinpoints of white-hot bombs, all of it roofed over with a ceiling of pink that held bursting shells, balloons, flares and the grind of vicious engines. And in yourself the excitement and anticipation and wonder in your soul that this could be happening at all.

—Ernie Pyle, "A Dreadful Masterpiece"

Take Notes!

Outline the processes for expanding and combining with participles and participial phrases.

So far, you have collected a number of tools for expanding and combining sentences—all for the purpose of creating better fluency and logical organization in your writing. Since participles function as adjectives, they can serve as another expanding/combining tool.

Expanding with Participles and Participial Phrases

The same simple process you have used for expanding sentences works as well for participles and participial phrases.

1. Identify the sentence pattern.

   S InV
   The bicycle was taken to the shop.
2. Ask the adjective questions. (Which one? What kind? How many? Whose?) What additional information would help to clarify the meaning?
3. Logically and clearly insert the answers.

   Which bicycle? The *broken* bicycle was taken to the shop.
   The bicycle *broken from the fall* was taken to the shop.

   What kind of shop? The bicycle was taken to the *cycling* shop.
   The bicycle was taken to the shop *engaged in fixing bicycles*.

Combining with Participles and Participial Phrases

You have learned that when a short, choppy sentence modifies a noun in a preceding sentence, a single adjective or adjectival prepositional phrase can often be used to combine the two sentences. Participles and participial phrases provide another option.

Shane was delivering newspapers. The newspapers were newly-published.

Shane was delivering *newly-published* newspapers.

The second sentence identifies what kind of newspapers Shane was delivering. In the combined sentence, the second sentence has been reduced to a participle, *newly-published*, placed near *newspapers*, the word it modifies.

Shane fell off the bike. Shane was waving to a friend.

Waving to a friend, Shane fell off the bike.

The second sentence identifies what kind of action Shane was doing. In the combined sentence, the second sentence has been reduced to a participial phrase, *waving to a friend*, placed near *Shane*, the word it modifies.

Shane and his bike landed in the ditch. The ditch was filled with water from the recent rain.

Shane and his bike landed in the ditch *filled with water from the recent rain*.

The second sentence identifies what kind of ditch Shane fell into. In the combined sentence, the second sentence has been reduced to a participial phrase, *filled with water from the recent rain*, placed near *ditch*, the word it modifies.

Partner Up!

Expanding with Participles and Participial Phrases

Using the verb in parentheses, expand each sentence by inserting a participle or participial phrase. In your newly-created sentence, underline the participle or participial phrase. Draw an arrow from it to the word it modifies. Insert commas as necessary.

1. Shane retrieved his bicycle from the ditch. (*embarrass*)

____

2. Shane pushed his bicycle to his house. (*damage*)

____

3. Shane told his parents about his accident. (*surprise*)

____

Combining with Participles and Participial Phrases

Rewrite the first sentence, inserting participles or participial phrases made from the second and third sentences. Insert commas as necessary. Draw an arrow from each participle or participial phrase to the word it modifies.

4. Shane walked to the cycling shop to retrieve his bicycle. Shane was breathlessly anticipating what his bicycle would look like. His bicycle was rebuilt.

____

____

5. Shane paid the cycle-shop owner for his work. Shane used his newspaper money. The shop owner was very skilled.

____

6. Shane tipped the cycle-shop owner. He was very pleased with the cycle-shop owner's work. The shop owner was surprised.

____

Try It Out!

Write three sentences about one of your favorite possessions (book, hoverboard, piece of jewelry, etc.). Use a minimum of one participle or participial phrase per sentence.

GERUNDS AND THEIR PHRASES

Gerunds

A **gerund** is a verbal that functions as a noun. Because it retains some of its verb qualities, it can be modified by adverbs; because it functions as a noun, it can also be modified by adjectives.

Skillful rappelling requires concentration.

I enjoy leisurely walking.

Like participles, gerunds use the same form of the verb as the present participle: the first principal part plus *-ing*. However, their functions are entirely different: the participle is an adjective; the gerund is a noun. As a noun, the gerund can function in any of the noun positions: subject, direct object, indirect object, predicate noun, or object of the preposition.

Subject: *Staring* is impolite.
Direct object: Shelby enjoys silent *reading* and creative *writing*.
Indirect object: Sandra gave *studying* regularly careful thought.
Predicate noun: Her favorite activity is online *shopping*.
Object of the preposition: We learn best by *doing*.

Gerund Phrases

A **gerund phrase** includes the gerund, its modifiers, and any words that complete it. It functions as a single noun.

Adj **Prep**
Gayle's favorite hobby is *vegetable gardening in her backyard*. (*Vegetable gardening in her backyard* is the gerund phrase acting as the predicate noun.)

Adv **Prep**
Hope must pay more attention to *studying diligently for exams*. (*Studying diligently for exams* is the gerund phrase acting as the object of the preposition *to*.)

Practice the Skill

Underline the gerunds. Two sentences do not contain a gerund.

1. Some people are living without knowledge of certain African animals.
2. Finding information about Africa's bush baby may be difficult.
3. The animal's other name, the *galago*, might make researching tricky.
4. Wondering about the bush baby's peculiar name is common.
5. Perhaps crying gave the galago its other name, because the animal can sound like a child.
6. Because of its large ears and eyes, a galago's specialties are hearing and seeing.
7. This nocturnal creature spends much of its time in jumping.
8. This method of moving is the galago's way of travel in the tree limbs.
9. Of course, the galago also gives eating plenty of attention.
10. Insects, lizards, and fruit form part of the diet of the galago, which inhabits Africa's forests.

Place parentheses around the gerund phrases. Underline the gerunds.

11. Living in Lapland's winter environment is natural for reindeer.
12. By possessing antlers, female reindeer resemble the males.
13. People have succeeded in reindeer taming.
14. Relying on the reindeer is a way of life for people in Lapland.
15. People in Lapland have given much attention to domesticating reindeer.
16. A domesticated reindeer's job is working for its owner.
17. Pulling is relatively easy for reindeer.
18. Reindeer make the transporting of goods easier and faster.
19. The male reindeer enjoys fighting for control of a herd.
20. The Laplanders also practice cheesemaking with reindeer milk.

Identify each italicized word as *G* (gerund) or *P* (participle).

_______ 21. The raccoon likes the *making* of his home in a hollow tree.

_______ 22. Curious raccoons enjoy *exploring.*

_______ 23. *Rummaging* through garbage cans, raccoons acquire quick meals.

_______ 24. Raccoons have nimble fingers for the *opening* of containers and even doors.

_______ 25. A quick *pinching* by the raccoon's paw results in the catch of a crawfish.

_______ 26. The raccoon often dunks its food into water before a session of ravenous *indulging.*

_______ 27. In cold climates, *sleeping* raccoons spend most of the winter in their dens.

_______ 28. A raccoon's success in *hunting* is important for its survival.

_______ 29. Raccoons are sometimes identifiable at night by their *glowing* eyes.

_______ 30. These curious animals especially enjoy *finding* shiny objects like coins or bits of metal.

Review the Skill

Underline the gerunds. Identify each gerund's function as *S* (subject), *DO* (direct object), *IO* (indirect object), *PN* (predicate noun), or *OP* (object of the preposition). One sentence does not contain a gerund.

________ 31. A beaver's favorite activity is constructing.

________ 32. Regular and careful grooming keeps a beaver's fur clean.

________ 33. Beavers give cleaning an important role in their busy routine.

________ 34. Beavers enjoy lying in anthills; the ants' feasting on parasites in their fur cleans the beaver.

________ 35. Chopping down trees with their teeth keeps them from growing beyond a comfortable length.

________ 36. Beavers in danger slap their tails on the water in warning to other beavers.

________ 37. Before winter, the beaver will be storing bark for food.

________ 38. Diving is the beaver's way of escape from predators.

________ 39. Did you know that beavers are capable of holding their breath for several minutes?

________ 40. Beavers' best-known activity is building.

Place parentheses around each gerund or gerund phrase. Underline each gerund.

41. Swimming is one of a grizzly bear's favorite pastimes.
42. Grizzly bears enjoy eating berries and honey.
43. Another favorite pastime of the grizzly is catching fish.
44. Teaching her cubs is an important job for the mother bear.
45. The winter season makes hunting for food more difficult.
46. Bears survive the cold months by resting for long periods of time.
47. By carefully digging, the mother makes a warm home for her new baby cubs.
48. A mother may spank her cubs as a way of disciplining them.
49. Young cubs are very curious, and their inquisitive wandering can sometimes get them into trouble.
50. A mother grizzly's highest priority is protecting her young cubs.

Underline the gerunds and participles. Identify each underlined word as *G* (gerund) or *P* (participle). Draw an arrow from each participle to the word it modifies. Label each gerund's function as *S* (subject), *DO* (direct object), *IO* (indirect object), *PN* (predicate noun), or *OP* (object of the preposition).

_______ 51. Seeing Eye® dogs are faithful and valuable assistants to their blind owners.

_______ 52. Dogs such as golden retrievers and Labrador retrievers serve by guiding.

_______ 53. Also, many of these highly trained animals are German shepherds.

_______ 54. Dogs preparing for positions with sightless owners undergo rigorous lessons for many months.

_______ 55. Guide dogs must master the skill of accurately judging for distance and space.

_______ 56. For example, the dog must decide whether a hanging sign, much taller than his own head, is high enough for his owner's safe passage.

_______ 57. Disobeying is necessary if the owner gives dangerous instructions unknowingly.

_______ 58. Warning of things such as curbs and steps is also vital.

_______ 59. The intelligence shown by these dogs is truly remarkable.

_______ 60. In fact, one guide dog has received attention for bringing her owner's pajamas when the owner fell asleep on his couch.

INFINITIVES AND THEIR PHRASES

Infinitives

Unlike participles and gerunds, which each have only one function—adjective or noun—the **infinitive** is a verbal that can function as either a noun, adjective, or adverb. The simple infinitive of a verb consists of the word *to* followed by the first principal part of the verb. When it functions as an adverb or adjective, it can be modified by an adverb. When it functions as a noun, it can be modified by an adjective.

S TrV DO
Noun: Joanna loves *to paint.*

S LV PN
Adjectives: Dan is the person *to ask.*

S InV
Adverb: We go there *to eat.*

Remember, *to* plus a verb is an infinitive; *to* plus a noun or pronoun is a prepositional phrase.

After the speaker finished, we decided *to leave.* (*to* + verb = infinitive)
Arden went *to school.* (*to* + noun = prepositional phrase)

Infinitive Phrases

An **infinitive phrase** includes the infinitive, its modifiers, and any words that complete it. It functions as an adjective, adverb, or noun.

Adjective: The road *to reach our destination* was washed out by the rain.

Adverb: We crossed the bridge *to get to the other shore.*

DO
Noun: We need *to walk quickly.*

Practice the Skill

Underline the infinitives and infinitive phrases. Three sentences do not contain an infinitive or infinitive phrase.

1. Canada geese are distinct because of their desire to mate for life.
2. Sometimes two ganders will decide to fight for the affection of a female goose.
3. During incubation, the goose's eggs need to remain in the nest for twenty-five to thirty days.
4. Both parents' instinct is to protect the nest carefully.

5. After the eggs are hatched, the goslings are extremely susceptible to danger, and the parents must be alert constantly.
6. The male goose clears the water of potential dangers before the newly hatched goslings are allowed to dive in.
7. During the winter, geese travel together to a warm place to survive.
8. Canada geese are known for their intense loyalty to each other.
9. A Canada goose will not desert its partner, even if it must abandon its flight to warmer regions for the winter.
10. Geese have often sacrificed their own lives to protect each other from predators.

Review the Skill

Underline the infinitives. Identify each infinitive as *N* (noun), *adj* (adjective), or *adv* (adverb). One sentence does not contain an infinitive.

_______ 11. The hedgehog is an especially interesting animal to study.

_______ 12. Some people think that hedgehogs are similar to porcupines.

_______ 13. To survive, a threatened hedgehog transforms itself into a spiky ball of spines.

_______ 14. Because of this defense, hedgehogs have few foes to fear.

_______ 15. Hedgehogs like to eat.

_______ 16. One of the hedgehog's primary nighttime goals is to hunt.

_______ 17. It consumes worms, bugs, and more to live.

_______ 18. To navigate, the hedgehog uses its nose and ears.

_______ 19. Hedgehogs generally live alone; their usual reason for socializing is to mate.

_______ 20. For North Americans, hedgehogs are difficult to encounter because they are not native to North America.

Underline the verbals (not the entire verbal phrase). Identify each verbal as *P* (participle), *G* (gerund), or *I* (infinitive). If the verbal is a modifier, draw an arrow from the verbal to the word it modifies.

_______ 21. Some people do not like barking dogs.

_______ 22. However, barking is not a problem with basenjis.

_______ 23. The unique basenji can be difficult to find.

_______ 24. Unlike other dogs, the basenji does not have the ability to bark.

_______ 25. Though usually silent, this dog can make a sound similar to yodeling.

_______ 26. These noises and whines are the basenji's barking.

_______ 27. Ironically, the basenji likes to work as a herd dog, even without a true bark.

_______ 28. The basenji has a job to complete, so it wears a bell around its neck.

_______ 29. The bell's ringing alerts everyone to the basenji's location.

_______ 30. Consequently, the mostly muted basenji still finishes the job.

Use the Skill

The following narrative tells of a young boy's yearning for a pet. His mother has taken him to the local animal shelter where they survey their choices. Use an infinitive or infinitive phrase to complete each sentence.

31. Sawyer entered the pound ______________________________.

32. After standing inside for a few moments, Sawyer decided ______________________________.

33. The man said the pound had many dogs and puppies ______________________________.

34. ______________________________ made Sawyer feel sad.

35. Sawyer suddenly offered ______________________________.

USING INFINITIVES TO EXPAND OR COMBINE

Writing Traits: Sentence Fluency, Organization

Listen Up!

"The circus is coming to town!" This familiar call rang out all over the land, attracting huge crowds to pack circus tents. Perhaps one of the greatest circus showmen was P. T. Barnum. His Greatest Show on Earth toured the United States and eventually Europe from the last of the 19th century through the first half of the 20th century. Find the "to" phrases in the last sentence of the first paragraph. Which one is a prepositional phrase? Which one is an infinitive phrase?

MENTOR TEXT

Barnum had dedicated his life to amusing people. His goal, wrote historian Philip B. Kunhardt, was "to awaken a sleeping sense of wonder to help open the eyes of his fellow citizens to the amazing diversity of the human and the natural world." To do this, he had introduced them to the rare, the strange, the beautiful, and the exotic.

Startling inventions! . . .

Fossils, mummies, and three-headed snakes!

All this and much, much more had been Barnum's contribution to nineteenth-century America.

—Candace Fleming, *The Great and Only Barnum*

GRAMMAR TOOLBOX

Take Notes!

Outline the process for expanding with infinitives and infinitive phrases. Record and annotate each sample sentence in the Combining with Infinitives and Infinitive Phrases section.

Infinitives and infinitive phrases used as adjectives and adverbs are yet another tool for expanding and combining sentences with the now familiar processes.

Expanding with Infinitives and Infinitive Phrases

Infinitives as Adjectives

1. Identify the sentence pattern.

   S **LV** **PN**
   "The circus is coming to town!" was a familiar call.

2. Ask the adjective questions. What additional information would help to clarify the meaning?

   What kind of call?

3. Logically and clearly insert the answer.

   "The circus is coming to town!" was a familiar call *to ring out all over the land.*

Infinitives as Adverbs

1. Identify the sentence pattern.

   S **LV** **PN**
   "The circus is coming to town!" was a familiar call.

2. Ask the adverb questions. What additional information would help to clarify the meaning?

   Why did the call ring out?

3. Logically and clearly insert the answer.

   "The circus is coming to town!" rang out all over the land *to attract huge crowds to pack circus tents.*

Combining with Infinitives and Infinitive Phrases

Infinitives as Adjectives

Study these two sentences. What is the relationship of the second sentence to the first?

P. T. Barnum became a millionaire. He was one of the first in the United States.

Now analyze the two sentences combined. What is the relationship between these two sentences? How are they combined?

P. T. Barnum became one of the first men in the United States *to become a millionaire.*

Infinitives as Adverbs

Study these two sentences. What is the relationship between these two sentences? How can you combine them?

> Barnum moved to New York City in 1834.
> He wanted to publish a newspaper and run a boarding house.

Now analyze the two sentences combined. What is the relationship between these two sentences? How are they combined?

> Barnum moved to New York City in 1834 *to publish a newspaper and run a boarding house.*

Partner Up!

Expanding with Adverbial and Adjectival Infinitive Phrases

Expand each sentence by creating an infinitive with the verb in parentheses. Use the infinitive as the indicated part of speech. In your newly-created sentence, draw a line under the infinitive or infinitive phrase and draw an arrow to the word modified.

1. The circus was taking place in the convention center. (*attend*, adjective)

 ____

2. Tom and his friend Nathan couldn't wait. (*go*, adverb)

 ____

3. Nathan purchased the popcorn. (*eat*, adjective)

 ____

Combining with Adverbial and Adjectival Infinitive Phrases

Turn the second sentence into an infinitive modifying a word in the first sentence. Use it to complete the first sentence. Draw an arrow from the infinitive back to the word it modifies.

4. Barnum overcame adversity many times.
 Barnum's goal was success.

 ____

5. Thrilling and delighting middle-class families was his desire.
 Barnum's desire drove his ambition.

 ____

6. Barnum and his troupe received an invitation.
Queen Victoria invited them to entertain in Buckingham Palace.

____

Try It Out!

Choose a paragraph you have previously written and expand it by adding verbal modifiers. Make sure your additions help to develop the picture you are communicating.

CHAPTER REVIEW

Participles

Underline the participles. Draw an arrow to the noun or pronoun the participle modifies. Identify each participle as *present* (present participle) or *past* (past participle).

_______________ 1. Earthquakes are frightening and damaging natural disasters.

_______________ 2. Shifting rock plates deep in the earth usually cause the severe shakes that occur during an earthquake.

_______________ 3. The results of an earthquake are often ruined homes and collapsed buildings.

_______________ 4. Fires begun by the earthquake damage can also be a serious hazard.

_______________ 5. The very landscape of an area can be changed by a single ravaging earthquake.

Dangling and Misplaced Modifiers

Underline the participial phrases. Identify each participial phrase as *D* (dangling) or *M* (misplaced). Rewrite the sentence correctly.

_______ 6. The San Francisco earthquake of 1906 caused much death and destruction resulting in a disastrous fire.

____

____

_______ 7. Originating in Chile, many countries felt the Chilean earthquake of 1960.

____

_______ 8. Having made the list of devastating earthquakes, parts of the Alaskan landscape were changed in 1964.

____

____

_______ 9. Many towns were destroyed and many killed in 2004 devastating Indonesia and multiple Asian countries.

____

____

_______ 10. Working underground, China's earthquake in 2008 trapped coal miners.

____

Gerunds

Underline the gerunds. Identify each gerund's function as *S* (subject), *DO* (direct object), *IO* (indirect object), *PN* (predicate noun), or *OP* (object of the preposition).

_______ 11. An earthquake usually begins near an opening between the earth's rock plates.

_______ 12. Sometimes the sliding of the plates places too much stress on the rocks.

_______ 13. The dangerous result is often the cracking of the rock plates.

_______ 14. The epicenter designates the beginning of an earthquake on the earth's surface.

_______ 15. The breaking of the earth's crust starts at the epicenter and moves outward.

Differentiating Between Participles and Gerunds

Underline the gerunds and present participles. Identify each underlined word as *G* (gerund) or *P* (participle).

_______ 16. Seismographs are used by scientists for gauging earthquakes.

_______ 17. The measuring scale scientists use is the Richter scale.

_______ 18. Any earthquake registering over a 7.0 on the Richter scale is potentially very destructive.

_______ 19. The moment magnitude scale is used for earthquakes ranking above a 7.0.

_______ 20. The recording of a 9.5 earthquake on the coast of Chile broke the record for the strongest recorded earthquake on the moment magnitude scale.

Infinitives

Underline the infinitives in the paragraph.

21.–25. The damage caused by earthquakes can be devastating to towns and cities. During a quake, the ground itself has been known to rise into the air. The shaking causes homes to collapse and buildings to tumble. To add to the destruction, broken power lines may cause fires. Earthquakes in the ocean cause powerful waves called tsunamis to hit the coasts, causing severe flooding. Earthquakes are among the most severe and terrifying natural disasters.

Participles, Gerunds, Infinitives

Underline the verbals (not the entire verbal phrase). If the verbal is a modifier, draw an arrow to the word it modifies. If the verbal functions as a noun, identify its function as *S* (subject), *DO* (direct object), *IO* (indirect object), *PN* (predicate noun), *OP* (object of the preposition).

_______ 26. The San Andreas Fault, located generally along the coast of California, is the source of numerous earthquakes.

_______ 27. On April 18, 1906, at 5:13 a.m., San Francisco residents were awakened by a dreadful rumbling.

_______ 28. The most destructive action of the 1906 earthquake was the starting of a fire that lasted three days and devastated most of the city.

_______ 29. Minutes before game three of the 1989 World Series, an earthquake struck Candlestick Park. To evacuate was difficult for the thousands of spectators.

_______ 30. Sliding plates along the fault in California are the cause of these destructive earthquakes.

CHAPTER 13

CLAUSES AND SENTENCES

WHAT KIND OF STRUCTURE ARE YOU BUILDING?

Single-family homes. Towering corporate skyscrapers. Multifamily apartment buildings. The sky's the limit on the variety of structures that can occupy a plot of land. As long as the foundation is sure, the architect can focus on building according to the needs of the occupants, adding interest and creativity wherever he can. In the first twelve chapters of this textbook, you have learned how to build a solid grammatical foundation for compositions; your grammar toolbox is full, and now you are ready to build your composition—your structure. Are you going to create a simple cabin or a complex castle? Consider the needs of your audience, and then let your imagination help you create variety and interest in your composition.

Keep in mind that sentence pattern *refers to the functions of individual words in a sentence.* Sentence structure *refers to the arrangement, or construction, of the words in a sentence to make different kinds of sentences, such as simple, compound, complex, or compound-complex.*

DISCOVER!

Kenneth Grahame, the author of the beloved classic The Wind in the Willows*, mastered the art of structuring his sentences with variety, providing fluency for his readers and engaging his audience. Read the excerpt. Note the structure of the sentences. Are they engaging? Do they flow smoothly and provide interest?*

MENTOR TEXT

When at last they were thoroughly toasted, the Badger summoned them to the table, where he had been busy laying a repast. . . . Conversation was impossible for a long time; and when it was slowly resumed, it was that regrettable sort of conversation that results from talking with your mouth full. The Badger did not mind that sort of thing at all, nor did he take any notice of elbows on the table, or everybody speaking at once. As he did not go into Society himself, he had got an idea that these things belonged to the things that didn't really matter.

—Kenneth Grahame, *The Wind in the Willows*

INDEPENDENT AND DEPENDENT CLAUSES

Basic Sentence Structure

All sentences are constructed of phrases and clauses. A **phrase** is a group of related words that may or may not contain a subject or a verb. Previous lessons have introduced verb phrases, prepositional phrases, and verbal phrases. Do they all have subjects or verbs? No; all of them, however, serve a specific function within a sentence. Look at the phrases in the following example to find their functions.

Fanny Crosby's inspiration *has given* the world several hymns *about God's love*.

A **clause**, on the other hand, is a group of related words that contains both a subject and a predicate. If the clause expresses a complete thought, it can stand alone, making it an **independent clause**. If the clause contains both a subject and a verb but does *not* express a complete thought, it cannot stand alone. Therefore, it is called a **dependent clause** (sometimes called a *subordinate clause*). A dependent clause relies on the independent clause for its meaning. When a dependent clause is written as if it were a stand-alone sentence, it is called a *fragment*.

Punctuation PowerUp

Use a comma after a dependent clause when it begins a sentence.

The cat scratched the good chair in the living room *when its owners were away*.

The first clause, *The cat scratched the good chair in the living room*, is an independent clause because it can stand alone as a sentence. The second clause, *when its owners were away*, is a dependent clause because it cannot be used alone as a sentence.

Practice the Skill

Identify each italicized group of words as *P* (phrase), *IC* (independent clause), or *DC* (dependent clause).

_______ 1. *Music in western cultures is characterized by several basic elements* including pitch, rhythm, melody, harmony, and timbre.

_______ 2. The basic elements of music work together *to make music enjoyable*.

_______ 3. *Even though a musical tone has a definite pitch*, listeners perceive it differently depending on which instrument plays it.

_______ 4. The rhythm adds character to a piece of music because a composer can vary *the time signature and accent* according to his preference.

_______ 5. *The melody, or tune, of a piece* is usually what most people remember.

_______ 6. Whenever a composer repeats a melody throughout a piece of music, *he creates a theme.*

_______ 7. A composer develops harmony *if he writes two or more notes to be played simultaneously.*

_______ 8. Tone color is another term *for the timbre of music*, which permits the listener to identify the instrument making the sound.

_______ 9. Because of the variety of types of instruments, *composers can manipulate the timbre* as they arrange music for a group.

_______ 10. *Although the music within western cultures varies widely*, audiences respond to its broad appeal.

Underline each subject once and each verb twice. Place parentheses around each dependent clause.

11. Because a harp has forty-seven strings, it produces more tones than any other stringed instrument.
12. Since the modern harp stands about seventy inches tall, a harpist sits during a performance and rests the harp against her right shoulder.
13. A harpist uses the foot pedals on the pedestal so that she can control the pitch of the strings.
14. The pitch of the strings rises while the performer depresses the pedal.
15. The harp is a national symbol in Ireland, where the instrument first appeared during the eighth century.

Review the Skill

Underline each subject once and each verb twice. Place parentheses around each dependent clause.

16. Even though most people drive their own cars to work, people in large cities often take the train.
17. Trains are convenient because you do not have to find or pay for a parking space.
18. If the train is not an option in an area, people will often choose taxis or alternative ride-sharing services.
19. While people are using alternative ride-sharing services more, other modes of public transportation like buses and even bicycles are still popular.
20. Although manned transportation services are the norm now, people should watch for self-driving transportation options!

SUBORDINATING CONJUNCTIONS

Subordinating Conjunctions

A **subordinating conjunction** joins a dependent clause to an independent clause. Subordinating conjunctions establish a close relationship between the two clauses. Essential to the sentence, the subordinating conjunction cannot be removed without affecting the meaning of the sentence.

after	as though	provided	until
although	because	since	when
as	before	so	whenever
as far as	even if	so that	where
as if	even though	than	whereas
as long as	if	though	wherever
as soon as	in order that	unless	while

Two independent clauses:

The little dog crawled under the fence.

He became scared.

Parallel structure (with coordinating conjunction):

The little dog crawled under the fence, *and* he became scared.

The little dog crawled under the fence, *so* he became scared.

Nonparallel structure (with subordinating conjunction):

When the little dog crawled under the fence, he became scared.

Because the little dog crawled under the fence, he became scared.

The little dog became scared *because* he crawled under the fence.

Notice in the parallel sentences that the coordinating conjunction joins two clauses of equal importance. Both carry equal weight.

In the nonparallel sentences, the addition of the subordinating conjunction joins the two clauses, but it also forms a nonparallel relationship between them, making one more "important" than the other. In these sentences, the independent clause communicates the *primary* idea of the sentence, while the other clause (the dependent clause) communicates an idea that is *secondary* or *explanatory* to what the independent clause is saying.

SUBORDINATING CONJUNCTIONS (CONTINUED)

Preposition or Subordinating Conjunction?

Some words can be used as either a preposition or a subordinating conjunction. The word is used as a preposition when a noun or pronoun follows as the object of the preposition. The word is used as a subordinating conjunction when followed by a subject and a verb (i.e., a clause). Be careful not to confuse the two functions.

Words that can be used as prepositions or subordinating conjunctions include *after*, *as*, *before*, *since*, and *until*.

After: *After* the shameful performance, some of the audience complained.
The actors asked for extra time to practice, *after* the people heard about the poor performance.

As: He works *as* a waiter.
As his customers finished dinner, he started to clean up his station for the night.

Before: It will be some time *before* summer.
Before I buy my summer clothes, I will wait for the summer sales.

Since: My dog has been missing *since* late October.
Since my sweet poodle went missing, I have been melancholy.

Until: Fireflies wait to emerge *until* dusk.
We will not go outside to catch fireflies *until* we eat dinner.

Practice the Skill

Underline the subordinating conjunctions.

1. Some worker bees forage for pollen, while other bees guard the queen.
2. Honeybees, in order that the hive may be kept clean, have a type of worker bee called an undertaker.
3. Whenever bees die of old age or disease, the undertaker bees quickly carry out the little corpses to protect the health of the colony.
4. Temperature controller honeybees keep the hive at a cool and constant temperature all summer, while they maintain a warm and cozy temperature throughout the winter.
5. Even though all the bees contribute to the success of the hive by tending the nursery and making honey, the queen bee is vital for the preservation of the colony.

Identify each italicized word as *P* (preposition) or *SC* (subordinating conjunction). If the word is a preposition, circle its object. If the word is a subordinating conjunction, underline the subject once and the verb twice in the dependent clause.

_______ 6. *Since* ancient times, honey has been considered an important healthy food source.

_______ 7. *Because* allergists believe in the healing properties of honey for seasonal allergy relief, people will often go to local farmers' markets to buy their honey.

_______ 8. *After* the worker bees find good flowers for collecting pollen, they go back to the hive and do a "waggle dance," a special little jig informing the other bees of the location of the flowers.

_______ 9. A convenient way to get a small amount of honey out of the jar without making a mess is *with* a honey drizzler.

_______ 10. *Though* most people like sweeteners, not everyone likes the taste of honey.

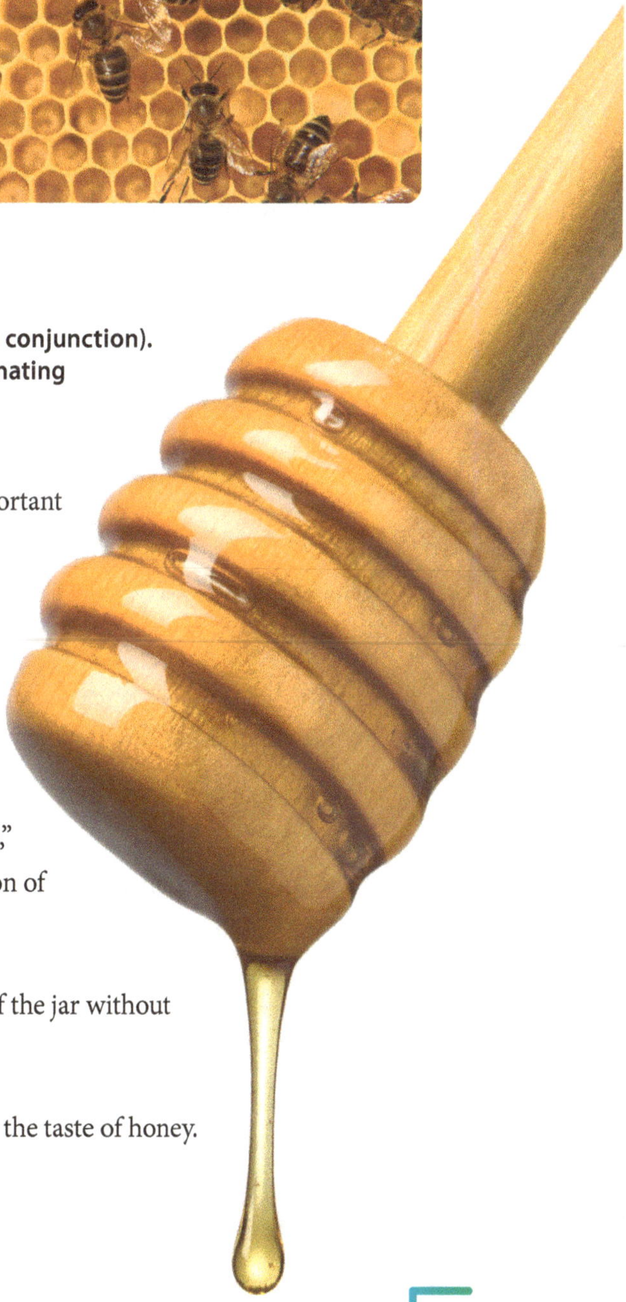

Review the Skill

Underline the subordinating conjunctions.

11. Castles, though they were constructed so long ago for practical purposes, hold a mysterious, romantic, and exciting attraction to people around the world today.
12. While all castles are majestic and impressive, one castle in Germany stands out above the rest.
13. The Neuschwanstein castle in Bavaria, Germany, is probably the most recognized and photographed of all the castles in the world, since it has been the inspiration and model for family theme parks.
14. The original castle was to be the magnum opus of infamous King Ludwig II, until he went mad, abandoned his castle, and was deposed of his kingly duties.
15. Even though the eccentric king isolated himself from his family and shunned his advisers, he had a long friendship with the famous composer Richard Wagner and used the composer's operas as inspiration for the art throughout his castle.
16. The towering fortress is built on the precipice of the Bavarian Alps where the expansive vista is nearly unmatched.
17. Mad King Ludwig, as he was disdainfully called, undoubtedly was crowned king too young.
18. Because his personality grew increasingly morbid, he was eventually declared insane, and he abandoned his unfinished castle.
19. Whereas the circumstances surrounding his life and downfall are controversial, he doubtless led a strange and extravagant life.
20. The moonstruck monarch is long gone, although his stunning castle stands still in its fairy-tale grandeur in the mountains of Bavaria.

Identify each italicized word as *P* (preposition) or *SC* (subordinating conjunction). If the word is a preposition, circle its object. If the word is a subordinating conjunction, underline the subject once and the verb twice in the dependent clause.

_______ 21. Oberammergau, a beautiful little Bavarian town in southeastern Germany, has put on a Passion play *since* 1634.

_______ 22. The play began *when* the residents of the village were facing the rapidly approaching bubonic plague in the mid-seventeenth century.

_______ 23. The townspeople, scared of the raging pandemic, made a promise to God to perform a play about Christ's crucifixion *if* He would spare their town.

_______ 24. *After* the bacterial menace subsided, they were grateful that no lives were lost in their tiny village.

_______ 25. The people of Oberammergau have honored their promise and have produced and performed the play every ten years *since* 1634.

_______ 26. Over two thousand people actively participate in the play, *whether* they are acting on stage, singing in the choir, playing in the orchestra, or working backstage.

_______ 27. With the performance lasting over five hours, attendance is a day-long commitment; in 2010, it continued *after* sunset.

_______ 28. The audience is so mesmerized and emotionally gripped by the performance *that* they do not mind sitting those long hours.

_______ 29. *Although* the performance is a dramatization of the last and hardest week of Jesus' earthly life, living-picture scenes from the Old Testament show the relationship between the Old Testament and the coming of the New Covenant.

_______ 30. *Until* 2020, when the world was gripped by another health pandemic, the play had only been cancelled three times in over 370 years: once during a religious upheaval, once during World War I, and once during World War II.

ADJECTIVE CLAUSES AND RELATIVE PRONOUNS

Adjective Clauses

An **adjective clause** is a dependent clause used as an adjective. Adjective clauses modify nouns or pronouns just like simple adjectives or adjectival phrases do. Usually an adjective clause comes immediately after the noun or pronoun it modifies. An adjective clause answers the same questions about a noun that a single adjective or an adjectival phrase answers: *which one*, *what kind*, *how many*, and *whose*.

Simple Adjective: My *favorite* hymn at church is "God Moves in a Mysterious Way" by William Cowper.

Adjectival Phrase: A favorite hymn *of my mother's* is "Amazing Grace."

Adjective Clause: The hymns *that my church sings* are worshipful prayers.

Relative Pronouns

Most adjective clauses contain **relative pronouns**; like all pronouns, these words take the place of nouns or noun phrases. They are called *relative* because they relate the adjective clause to a word in the independent clause. This word is the antecedent of the relative pronoun.

that	which	
who	whom	whose

S **TrV** **DO** **S** **TrV** **DO**
Lisa was fertilizing the *rosebush*. Her mom planted the *rosebush* last week.

S **TrV** **DO** **DO** **S** **TrV**
Lisa was fertilizing the *rosebush* **that her mom planted last week**.

The relative pronoun *that* takes the place of the second *rosebush*. *That* also relates the adjective clause to the independent clause. The whole adjective clause, *that her mom planted last week*, modifies the antecedent *rosebush*.

Relative pronouns do more in a sentence than simply relate the dependent clause to the independent clause. A relative pronoun may also function as a subject, object, or possessive adjective *within* the dependent clause.

S **TrV** **DO**
Subject: The man ***who*** *conducts our school orchestra* also plays the cello.

DO **S** **TrV**
Direct object: His cello is one ***that*** *he received from his great-grandfather*.

S **InV**
Possessive adjective: The parents ***whose*** *students play in the orchestra* may attend a free concert next Thursday.

S LV PA

Object of preposition: The hand-carved instrument ***that*** *he is so fond of* is quite valuable.

Look again at the sentence below:

S LV PN DO S TrV

His cello is one ***that*** *he received from his great-grandfather*.

First, notice that the sentence pattern of the adjective clause may be different from the sentence pattern of the independent clause. The sentence pattern of this independent clause is S-LV-PN; the sentence pattern of the adjective clause in the same sentence is S-TrV-DO. Second, notice that the word order within the adjective clause may be inverted. The clause *that he received from his great-grandfather* has the direct object *that* coming before the subject *he*.

When a relative pronoun acts as the object of the preposition, it may be either the first or second word in the clause. The fourth sentence above is another example of inverted order in a dependent clause.

S S LV PA LV PA

The hand-carved instrument ***that*** *he is so fond of* is quite valuable.

It could also be written this way:

The hand-carved (S) instrument *of* ***which*** (S) *he* (LV) *is so* (PA) *fond* (LV) is quite (PA) valuable.

This version of the sentence puts the preposition and object of the preposition in their normal order. Usually either way of stating the sentence is grammatically correct.

Sometimes a relative pronoun is understood (omitted) when it is the direct object or object of the preposition in the dependent clause.

This is a hymn (*that*) I will sing in church. (*understood DO*)
The hymn writer is one (*whom*) I had never heard of. (*understood OP*)
The church (*that*) I attend is near our house. (*understood DO*)

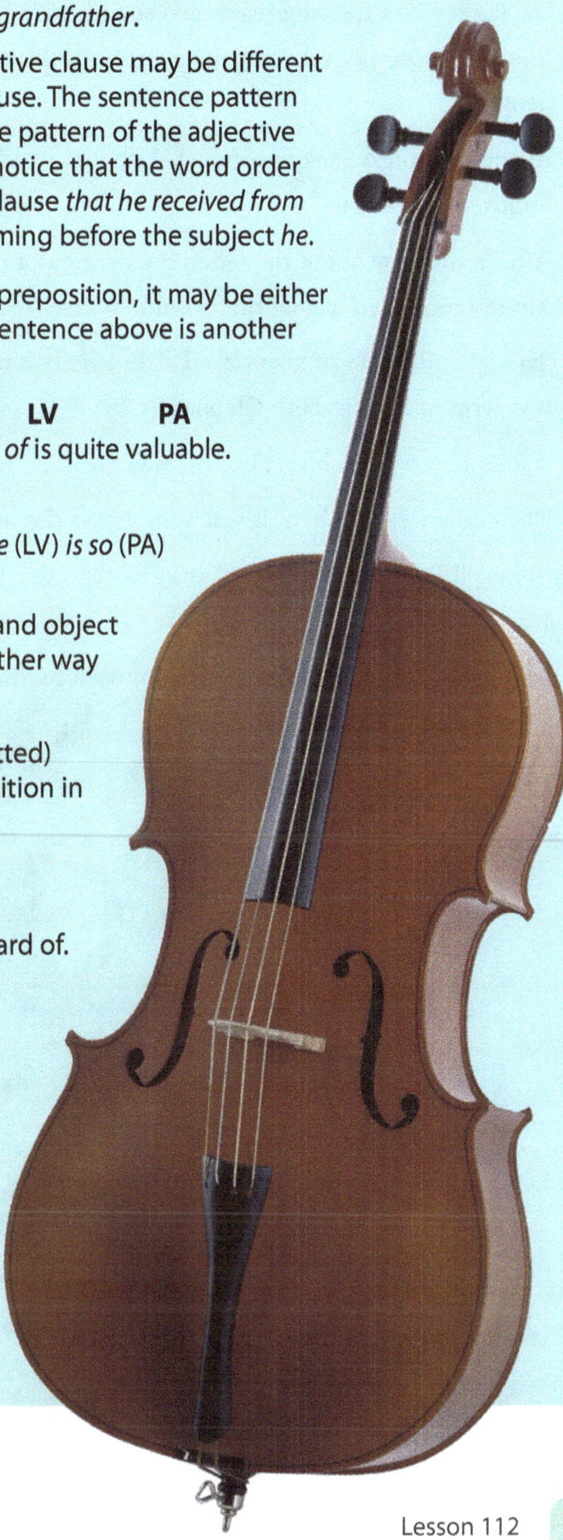

Practice the Skill

Underline each relative pronoun. Place parentheses around each adjective clause.

1. Many of the hymns that are a part of our church music today were written in the nineteenth century.
2. During the time after the Civil War, Ira Sankey was the best-known song leader who ministered in large revival meetings.
3. Ira Sankey was the congregational song leader for D. L. Moody, whose revival campaigns attracted thousands of people.
4. At the meetings, Sankey conducted choirs, which consisted of hundreds of people.
5. After a message about the Good Shepherd at a revival meeting, Moody requested a song that would emphasize the message.
6. Sankey pulled out of his pocket "The Ninety and Nine," which was written by Elizabeth Clephane.
7. Ira Sankey, whose musical talent was great, composed the music to this song during his solo.
8. The audience for whom it was sung loved the new song.
9. "There'll Be No Dark Valley" and "Faith Is the Victory" are other songs that were composed by Ira Sankey.
10. Many famous hymns that were composed by Ira Sankey are still sung today.

Review the Skill

Underline each relative pronoun. Place parentheses around each adjective clause. Identify the relative pronoun's function within the clause as *P. adj.* (possessive adjective), *OP* (object of the preposition), *S* (subject), or *DO* (direct object).

_______ 11. The history of classical composers, whose music is either instrumental or vocal, goes back to ancient Greece.

_______ 12. Soloists, for whom some composers wrote, may also have had instrumental accompaniment.

_______ 13. The conductor, who directs the orchestra, rehearses all pieces with the musicians repeatedly before an actual performance.

_______ 14. Churches that musicians composed for helped the growth of Western classical music.

_______ 15. Plainsong, which churches of the day used in their services, has one melody throughout the entire piece.

_______ 16. Churches sang the psalms, which are lyrical poems, to plainsong until around the ninth century.

_______ 17. Ludwig van Beethoven, who eventually went deaf, specialized in piano sonatas, string quartets, and symphonies.

_______ 18. Beethoven, whose works manifest great power and range, wrote mainly during the classical period.

_______ 19. The neoclassical movement, which began in the early 1900s, modeled its music after composers from earlier centuries.

_______ 20. Since the 1950s, nontraditional elements have appeared in the pieces that modern composers have produced.

Use the Skill

Using the relative pronoun in parentheses, combine each set of simple sentences to form a complex sentence. Be sure to place the adjective clause after the word it modifies.

21. Joseph Henry Gilmore had his hymn published in an unusual manner. Gilmore wrote "He Leadeth Me." (*who*)

____

____

22. While preaching a message on Psalm 23, Gilmore was impressed by the words "He leadeth me." The words are in verse two. (*which*)

____

____

23. Gilmore wrote a poem about Psalm 23:2. The Lord had blessed Gilmore with great writing ability. (*whom*)

____

____

24. He later forgot about the poem. He had written the poem and given it to his wife. (*that*)

____

____

25. Before he preached on a Sunday three years later, he was looking through a hymnbook and found his own poem. The poem had been set to music by William Bradbury, a popular composer. (*which*)

____

____

ADVERB CLAUSES

An **adverb clause** modifies a verb or an adjective in an independent clause. Adverbial dependent clauses are introduced by a subordinating conjunction that acts as an adverb and answers adverb questions (*where, when, why, how, to what extent*). Since this type of clause is introduced by a subordinating conjunction, it cannot stand alone.

The mother hugged her college-bound daughter *as if she might not see her ever again*.

As soon as the car drove up the driveway, the dogs ran expectantly to the side door, wagging their tails.

Practice the Skill

Place brackets around each adverb clause and underline the subordinating conjunction that introduces it. Write in the blank the word(s) the clause modifies.

_______________ 1. People have always struggled to get out of bed in the morning, since blankets are so soft and warm.

_______________ 2. Roosters have proved themselves to be poor alarm clocks because the feathered alarm, raspy and jarring, can sound at all hours of the night.

_______________ 3. The ancient Greeks created an alarm clock with a mechanical bird that whistled when water filled the clock's cavity.

_______________ 4. In eighteenth-century America, a clockmaker named Levi Hutchins developed a special alarm on his clock because he liked to get an early start on his work, usually before the sun rose.

_______________ 5. The early-bird clockmaker's special alarm sounded at four o'clock in the morning before the rest of the family wanted to be up.

__________________ 6. In the early twentieth century, the British would tap or knock on their clients' windows or doors whenever they needed a reminder to rise and shine.

__________________ 7. Because alarm clock users have grown too accustomed to traditional alarm sounds, companies have developed increasingly ingenious—and annoying—devices to get people out of their beds.

__________________ 8. People who balk at climbing out of their warm blankets when they hear their alarms sound may want to try the flying alarm clock.

__________________ 9. Some quirky alarm clocks require puzzle assembly if a person wants his alarm to stop sounding.

__________________ 10. Unique alarm clocks may be a fun novelty, but their value is only profitable as long as the sleepyhead responds and gets out of bed!

Review the Skill

Place brackets around each adverb clause and underline the subordinating conjunction that introduces it. Write in the blank the word(s) the clause modifies.

______________ 11. Teenagers who are habitually late will suffer hard consequences along with a damaged reputation unless they learn early to get up with an alarm clock.

______________ 12. Jack's eighth grade teacher had planned a special overnight class trip in order that the students could enjoy a break from the long semester, but the destination required an early start.

______________ 13. After he failed to set his alarm clock, Jack leapt from his bed and rushed through his morning routine, forgetting to put on his shoes or pack his overnight bag.

______________ 14. His mom tried to get him to the school on time because she knew that the tour bus would not wait for stragglers.

______________ 15. His mom approached an often-policed section of the road too fast and tried to slow down as soon as she realized her mistake.

______________ 16. In her rush, Jack's mom did not pay attention to her speedometer, so the police officer's radar detected her elevated speed when she passed him.

______________ 17. Jack's mom realized, while she was driving, that the tell-tale blue lights of a police car were flashing in her rearview mirror.

______________ 18. Jack gasped when he discovered his bare feet and his missing overnight bag.

______________ 19. Jack heard his mom on her phone apologize to her boss since she would be missing an important meeting.

______________ 20. Jack understood if he had not been lazy setting his alarm clock, he would have been spared the negative consequences that affected not only him but also his mom.

Use the Skill

Using the subordinating conjunction in parentheses, complete each sentence with an adverbial clause.

21. I decided that I did not like sailboat racing (*after*)

____

____

22. Social media and gaming devices can worry parents (*because*)

____

____

23. The young girl ran to her favorite tree on the top of the quiet hillside (*so that*)

____

____

24. I made sure to write down all my homework assignments (*before*)

____

____

25. Food will often taste strange (*if*)

____

____

USING CONJUNCTIONS TO EXPAND OR COMBINE

Writing Trait: Sentence Fluency

Listen Up!

The Wonderful Wizard of Oz is a fantastic story that sweeps its readers away on a colorful and unforgettable adventure. The author crafts his sentences masterfully to keep his readers engaged and eager to turn each page. Read the following excerpt, noting the author's use of coordinating and subordinating conjunctions to expand and combine sentences to create easy-to-read paragraphs. What combined sentences did you find in the selection? Do you think those combined sentences produce fluency that makes reading easy?

MENTOR TEXT

She bade her friends good-bye, and again started along the road of yellow brick. When she had gone several miles she thought she would stop to rest, and so climbed to the top of the fence beside the road and sat down. There was a great cornfield beyond the fence, and not far away she saw a Scarecrow, placed high on a pole to keep the birds from the ripe corn.

Dorothy leaned her chin upon her hand and gazed thoughtfully at the Scarecrow. Its head was a small sack stuffed with straw, with eyes, nose and mouth painted on it to represent a face. An old, pointed blue hat, that had belonged to some Munchkin, was perched on this head, and the rest of the figure was a blue suit of clothes, worn and faded, which had also been stuffed with straw. On the feet were some old boots with blue tops, such as every man wore in this country, and the figure was raised above the stalks of corn by means of the pole stuck up its back.

—Frank Baum, *The Wonderful Wizard of Oz*

Take Notes!

Summarize the goal (purpose) of using coordinating and subordinating conjunctions to combine and expand sentences. Tell how combining or expanding sentences with conjunctions provides meaning and clarity.

Expanding

Sometimes ideas can be further developed by expanding the structure of a sentence. In past grammar toolboxes, you expanded the meaning of sentences by adding modifying elements such as single adjectives, adverbs, prepositional phrases, and appositives. In this chapter, you are expanding sentences by using subordinating conjunctions and relative pronouns to add dependent clauses (which are also modifying elements). Dependent clauses add fluency and meaning to paragraphs.

GRAMMAR TOOLBOX

Combining

The skill of combining sentences is important for showing a single relationship that exists within several sentences. Using conjunctions is an effective tool for combining separate, yet related, thoughts.

> The beach is an exciting vacation spot.
> The beach is also a good place to relax.
> People visit the beach during the warm summer months.

How could these sentences be combined to show a relationship among the sentences?

Partner Up!

Follow the steps for each set of sentences to expand and combine. Use single adjectives, adverbs, and prepositional phrases in all the sentences to add details to individual words.

1. Use a coordinating conjunction and a subordinating conjunction.

   The dog and the cat were friends.
   They had depended on each other.

2. Use a relative pronoun in a dependent clause.

   The storm uprooted an oak tree.
   The tree was two hundred years old.

3. Use a present tense *-ing* verb in the first clause and place the subject in the second clause.

   The photographer drove to the small island beach.
   The photographer knew the light and scenery would be perfect.

Try It Out!

Rewrite the following paragraph about walking in the woods. Combine the sentences with coordinating and subordinating conjunctions to make the paragraph read fluently. Use adjectives, adverbs, descriptive phrases and clauses, and appositives to expand or combine the sentences. Remember to use variety to add fluency.

I took a walk in the woods yesterday. The daylight was beginning to fade. I went walking with my mom and my little brother. We heard the water from the brook. My brother did not see the water. He stepped in the edge of the water and got his flip-flop stuck. My mom laughed. She helped him get out of the mud. The sun began to set. We heard bullfrogs bellow at the water's edge. The crickets also began to chirp. We heard the evening song of the birds. It was very peaceful. The fireflies came out. The mosquitos were biting. The bats were flying. They were eating the mosquitos. We walked back home. We were very happy.

SIMPLE AND COMPOUND SENTENCES

Simple Sentences

A **simple sentence** is made up of one independent clause. It must contain a verb and its subject. However, some sentences have compound parts. A simple sentence may have a compound subject, a compound predicate, or both.

Simple Sentences	
with one subject and one verb	**Many ancient hymns ministered** to early believers.
with a compound subject	**The tunes** and **words** are still sung today.
with a compound predicate	**Composers wrote** and **sang** the second-century hymns.
with a compound subject and a compound predicate	**The music** and the **words honored** and **glorified** our Lord.

Compound Sentences

A **compound sentence** consists of two or more independent clauses joined together, usually by either a semicolon or a comma and coordinating conjunction.

Compound Sentences	
Simple Sentences	**Compound Sentence**
Heather plays the trumpet. She cannot play the piano.	Heather plays the trumpet**, but** she cannot play the piano.
Simple Sentences	**Compound Sentence**
Vernon Charlesworth penned the words to "A Shelter in the Time of Storm." Ira Sankey wrote the music.	Vernon Charlesworth penned the words to "A Shelter in the Time of Storm"**;** Ira Sankey wrote the music.

Just like simple sentences, compound sentences can have compound parts.

Compound Sentences with Compound Parts	
Compound Sentence	Lisa baked a cake, but I frosted it.
with a compound subject	Lisa and I ate some cake, and we drank a glass of milk.
with a compound predicate	Lisa washed and dried our cake plates; I put the remains in the refrigerator.
with a compound subject and a compound predicate	Lisa and I sat and talked afterwards, for we were exhausted. Lisa and I sat and talked afterwards, and the dog and cat came and sat on our laps.

Practice the Skill

Underline the coordinating conjunctions. Identify each sentence as *S* (simple) or *Cd* (compound).

_______ 1. Francis Scott Key wrote the words to America's national anthem, "The Star Spangled Banner."

_______ 2. The song was very popular shortly after 1812, but it did not become the official national anthem until 1931.

_______ 3. During the War of 1812, the American William Beanes was a prisoner on a British ship.

_______ 4. Aboard the ship, John Skinner and Francis Scott Key negotiated for his release.

_______ 5. The British agreed to Beanes's release, but they were preparing for an attack on Fort McHenry.

_______ 6. They held all three men aboard the ship until the end of the battle.

_______ 7. Scott, Skinner, and Beanes stayed up all night with great concern for their country.

_______ 8. At sunrise, the men detected the Americans' perseverance, for their flag still flew over the fort.

_______ 9. The turmoil of the night and the grand sight of the flag in the morning inspired Francis Scott Key's words to "The Star-Spangled Banner."

_______ 10. Francis Scott Key loved his country, and his beloved flag waves proudly over his grave today.

Review the Skill

Identify each sentence as *S* (simple) or *Cd* (compound). Label the sentence patterns above the appropriate words in each sentence.

_______ 11. Godly women wrote many of our favorite hymns.

_______ 12. Charlotte Elliott lived with her brother, for she was very ill by the age of thirty.

_______ 13. In 1836 she wrote "Just As I Am" and later wrote over one hundred other hymns.

_______ 14. William Bradbury wrote the tune, but it originally accompanied words to a different song.

_______ 15. Thomas Hastings later put Bradbury's tune with the words of "Just As I Am."

Fanny Crosby

_______ 16. Elliott wrote the words as a testimony of her relationship with the Lord, yet this song has blessed thousands around the world.

_______ 17. Another well-known song is "Nearer, My God, to Thee."

_______ 18. Sarah Flower Adams wrote the words, and her sister arranged the music to this popular song.

_______ 19. The band aboard the *Titanic* played this song; it comforted many passengers.

_______ 20. Contributions by other female hymn writers come from Fanny Crosby, A. Katherine Hankey, and many more.

COMPLEX AND COMPOUND-COMPLEX SENTENCES

Complex Sentences

A **complex sentence**, like a compound sentence, also consists of at least two clauses. However, a complex sentence contains one independent clause and one or more dependent clauses.

S S TrV DO
John and Charles Wesley wrote many powerful songs,
S TrV TrV DO
although they did not arrange the music.

S S LV PN TrV DO
Charles Wesley**, who was also a preacher, **wrote "O for a Thousand Tongues."

Determining whether a sentence is compound or complex requires analyzing the clauses. If a clause contains a subordinating conjunction or a relative pronoun, it is dependent. If a clause does not contain a subordinating conjunction or a relative pronoun, it is independent. Two or more independent clauses make a **compound sentence** and are usually joined by a *coordinating conjunction with a comma* or by a *semicolon*. One independent clause and one or more dependent clauses joined by a *subordinating conjunction* or a *relative pronoun* make a **complex sentence**.

Compound: (Our tour group visited London)**, and** (we saw Westminster Abbey.)
Complex: [**Since** most of the Abbey's architecture is Gothic,] (it is generally considered a Gothic structure.)
Compound: (The Abbey is a burial site for many famous persons)**, yet** (it is also a place of coronation for English monarchs.)
Complex: (Westminster Abbey,) [**even though** it is not the largest cathedral in London,] (has been the site of every English coronation since Norman times.)

COMPLEX AND COMPOUND-COMPLEX SENTENCES (CONTINUED)

Compound-Complex Sentences

A **compound-complex sentence** is the most highly developed sentence structure. Like its name indicates, this sentence structure is constructed of two or more independent clauses (a compound sentence) and one or more dependent clauses.

Compound: (Some strolled to Henry VII's chapel)**, but** (I hurried to the Poet's Corner.)
Complex: [**Because** it would probably be my only chance,] (I was eager to see the markers of my favorite Victorian authors.)
Compound-complex: (Some strolled to Henry VII's chapel)**, but** (I hurried to Poet's Corner) [**because** I wanted to see the markers of my favorite Victorian authors.]

	Independent Clauses	Dependent Clauses	Examples
Simple	1	0	It rained on Monday.
Compound	2+	0	It rained on Monday, but it was clear on Tuesday.
Complex	1	1+	Though it rained on Monday, it was clear on Tuesday.
Compound-Complex	2+	1+	Though it rained on Monday, it was clear on Tuesday, and the rest of our vacation week was clear and dry.

Practice the Skill

Place parentheses around each independent clause. Place brackets around each dependent clause and circle the subordinating conjunction or relative pronoun that introduces the dependent clause. Identify each sentence as *S* (simple), *Cd* (compound), *Cx* (complex), or *Cd-Cx* (compound-complex).

_______ 1. Because writers often consult different sources, they may produce accounts with some contradictory details about a hymn's origin.

_______ 2. However, each account testifies of God's presence in the hymn writer's life.

_______ 3. Charles Wesley wrote many of his hymns so that others would manifest courage and faith in the Lord.

_______ 4. Wesley's hymns pay tribute to Jesus Christ, who is the Savior, Companion, and Friend of believers; and they also provide encouragement to believers in their Christian walk.

_______ 5. Although his brother John wanted no changes to Charles's songs, many of the songs were altered.

_______ 6. Even though Charles Wesley wrote six stanzas to "Rejoice, the Lord Is King," most modern hymnals include only four.

_______ 7. In 1747 Charles fell in love with Sarah Gwynne, yet he did not propose until two years later.

_______ 8. Charles Wesley died on March 29, 1788.

_______ 9. He was still writing hymns on his deathbed.

_______ 10. Wesley wrote his last hymn as he was near death; the hymn was a poem of praise to the Lord.

Review the Skill

Identify each sentence as *S* (simple), *Cd* (compound), *Cx* (complex) or *Cd-Cx* (compound-complex).

_______ 11. Poet's Corner in Westminster Abbey is a favorite destination for many literature enthusiasts.

_______ 12. Some British writers, because they have contributed significantly to the nation's culture, have been buried within the Abbey itself, but some are buried on the grounds around the Abbey.

_______ 13. Although British actors, clergymen, and musicians are buried or memorialized in Poet's Corner, most of those buried here are writers, playwrights, and poets.

_______ 14. C. S. Lewis, who wrote the beloved children's series *The Chronicles of Narnia*, has a memorial stone in the Abbey, but Lewis's famous friend J. R. R. Tolkien is not memorialized on the property yet.

_______ 15. Over a dozen monarchs have been interred within the cloistered walls.

_______ 16. Today, people come to see the beautiful architecture, yet many come when they can also participate in worship services.

_______ 17. Young Princess Elizabeth, after her father died, became the next monarch, and her coronation was held at the Abbey in 1953.

_______ 18. After a British soldier died during World War I, his unidentified body was found and interred in a special grave in the Abbey.

_______ 19. The grave in the Abbey is called the grave of the Unknown Warrior, whereas the tomb in the United States is called the Tomb of the Unknown Soldier.

_______ 20. Although it is hundreds of years old, Westminster Abbey attracts visitors of all ages to its halls, for it is imposing in stature and fascinating in history.

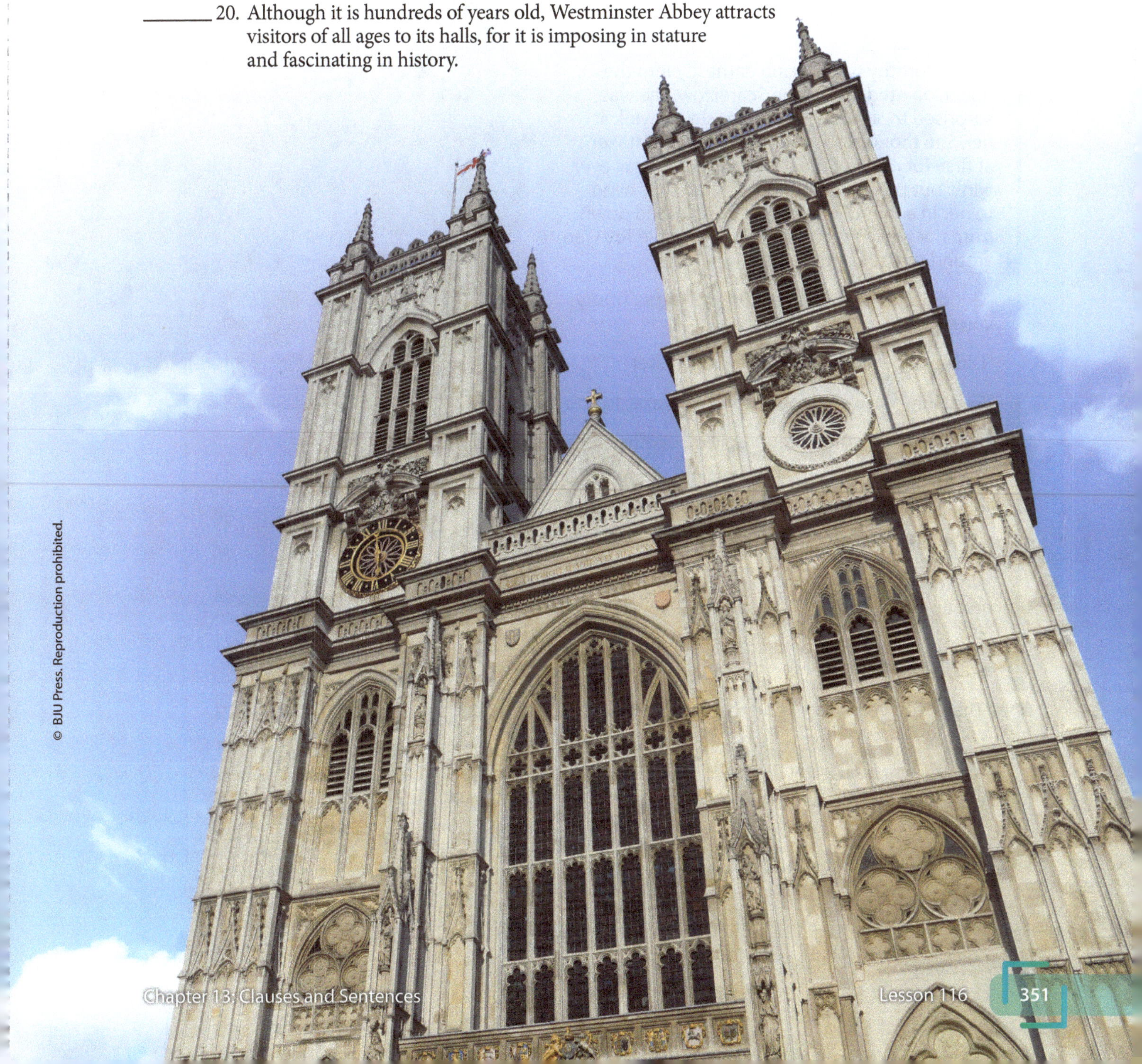

USING SENTENCE VARIETY
Writing Trait: Sentence Fluency

Listen Up!

Frank Baum showcases sentence variety in *The Wonderful Wizard of Oz.* Read the mentor text and notice how he uses the different sentence structures to create a fluid and interesting scene where Dorothy is introduced to the Scarecrow.

MENTOR TEXT

While Dorothy was looking earnestly into the queer, painted face of the Scarecrow, she was surprised to see one of the eyes slowly wink at her. She thought she must have been mistaken, at first, for none of the scarecrows in Kansas ever wink; but presently the figure nodded its head to her in a friendly way. Then she climbed down from the fence and walked up to it, while Toto ran around the pole and barked.

"Good day," said the Scarecrow, in a rather husky voice.

"Did you speak?" asked the girl, in wonder.

"Certainly," answered the Scarecrow; "how do you do?"

"I'm pretty well, thank you," replied Dorothy, politely; "how do you do?"

"I'm not feeling well," said the Scarecrow, with a smile, "for it is very tedious being perched up here night and day to scare away crows."

"Can't you get down?" asked Dorothy.

"No, for this pole is stuck up my back. If you will please take away the pole I shall be greatly obliged to you."

Dorothy reached up both arms and lifted the figure off the pole; for, being stuffed with straw, it was quite light.

"Thank you very much," said the Scarecrow, when he had been set down on the ground. "I feel like a new man."

Dorothy was puzzled at this, for it sounded queer to hear a stuffed man speak, and to see him bow and walk along beside her.

—Frank Baum, *The Wonderful Wizard of Oz*

GRAMMAR TOOLBOX

What sentence structures do you see used in this selection? Do you agree with the author's use of the different structures? Would you have constructed any of those sentences differently? In what way?

Take Notes!

Identify the structure of each sentence in this section and tell what makes each one effective.

William Cowper wisely said that variety is the spice of life. Variety adds interest and zest, but not only to life. In writing, variety gives rhythm and flow to sentences and paragraphs. Short sentences are good. They add emphasis. They add power. Sometimes sentences should be combined, and equal ideas should be given equal attention. Some ideas, while they are necessary to a sentence, are not equal in importance to others. When you compose an essay or narrative, you must consider your audience, and you must write to your audience's ability to respond to your message. The practice of using all the sentence structures in writing serves to sharpen your skills as a writer and ensure that your audience will keep coming back for more.

Partner Up!

Create variety in the following sentence groups, using the sentence structures learned in this chapter. Use what you have learned in previous grammar and writing toolboxes to include phrases and word variety.

1. I enjoy reading.
   My favorite genre is science fiction. (Or choose your favorite genre.)
   I love C. S. Lewis's *The Space Trilogy*. (Or choose a favorite story or series.)

2. We all admire someone.
   God gives us examples to follow.
   I admire my mom. (Or choose another person to write about.)
   Her example of [steadfastness, integrity, kindness, tenaciousness, etc.] inspires me.

Try It Out!

Compose a paragraph using all four sentence structures. Choose from the following topics. Include vivid nouns, strong verbs, descriptive prepositional phrases, colorful adjectives, and nuanced adverbs.

- Your favorite item in your room; why it is your favorite
- What you learn about God from a rainbow, a rain shower, or a walk in the woods
- Your favorite holiday and what makes it special

CHAPTER REVIEW

Types of Clauses

Identify each italicized group of words as *IC* (independent clause), *DC* (dependent clause), or *P* (phrase).

_______ 1. *Because a rose is one of the most beautiful flowers*, it is a favorite of many flower lovers.

_______ 2. The three main classes *of cultivated roses* are old roses, perpetual roses, and the ever-blooming hybrids.

_______ 3. Since old roses bloom only once a year, *flower lovers watch carefully for them in early summer.*

_______ 4. Perpetual roses bloom *in early summer* and in fall.

_______ 5. The ever-blooming hybrids bloom almost constantly *during the growing season.*

_______ 6. *Because roses come in diverse shades of pink, red, yellow, and white*, the perfect color can be found for almost any occasion.

_______ 7. *The most popular garden roses are the hybrid roses*, which are bred from two different varieties.

_______ 8. The climbing and rambler roses were given their names *because they climb trellises and fences.*

_______ 9. Even after they reach full maturity, *some miniature roses have flowers the size of a nickel.*

_______ 10. Unfortunately, thorns are attached to the stems *of many roses.*

Simple, Compound, Complex, and Compound-Complex Sentences

Identify each sentence as *S* (simple), *Cd* (compound), *Cx* (complex), or *Cd-Cx* (compound-complex).

_______ 11. *Daisy* comes from the Old English word for *day's eye.*

_______ 12. It is called this because some daisies, like a human eye, close at night and open at dawn.

_______ 13. While the center of the daisy is made of tiny disk flowers, the outside is made of petal-like ray flowers.

_______ 14. The oxeye daisy, which is one of the most common flowers, has a center of tiny yellow flowers, and that center is surrounded by delicate, white petals.

_______ 15. A daisy blossom normally measures about two inches.

Adjective Clauses

Place parentheses around each adjective clause. Underline the relative pronoun once and the word modified twice.

16. A violet has petals that are heart shaped.
17. Violets, whose blossoms are among the most beautiful of all flowers, grow in most of the world.
18. The United States, which is home to one hundred species of violets, contains only one-fifth of the total variety of violets.
19. Violets come in many colors, but blue and purple are the colors that I like best.
20. The violet, which is the flower for March, is also the state flower of four states.

Adverb Clauses

Using the subordinating conjunction in parentheses, complete each sentence with an adverbial clause.

21. Carnations are popular flowers to give. (*because*)

____

22. High school students give carnations to each other. (*whenever*)

____

23. A carnation's stem length can reach three feet. (*after*)

____

24. My mom has a beautiful flower garden. (*where*)

____

25. We enjoy the colorful flowers in the kitchen for many weeks. (*after*)

____

CREDIBLE

CHAPTER 14

AGREEMENT

WHY IS CREDIBILITY IMPORTANT?

In Chapter 6, you evaluated different sources for credibility. As you may recall, credible sources are ones that are trustworthy. The more credible a source is, the more you can trust its information. Similarly, every person is judged by others on his credibility (or lack thereof). In order for people to trust that what you are writing is true, you must first sound like a knowledgeable person who can make a clear, logical case for what he believes. Doing this imitates the character of God, the Author of all truth.

DISCOVER!

Using correct subject-verb and pronoun-antecedent agreement is an important part of sounding credible. To illustrate this, read the following description of some explorers' fictitious journey down to the center of the earth. Identify every mention of the verb was.

MENTOR TEXT

It was a sort of wild and savage staircase, without bannister or fence. A rope fastened above, near the surface, would certainly support our weight and enable us to reach the bottom. . . . Each of us could now descend by catching the two cords in one hand. When about two hundred feet below, all the explorer had to do was to let go one end and pull away at the other, when the cord would come falling at his feet. In order to go down farther, all that was necessary was to continue the same operation. . . . Going down appeared to me easy enough; it was the coming up again that now occupied my thoughts.

—Jules Verne, *Journey to the Center of the Earth*

Replace every instance of the verb was *with the verb* were *and read the passage again. How does it sound? Can you identify the problem you have created?*

SUBJECT-VERB AGREEMENT

Subject-Verb Agreement

In every clause, the verb must agree with its subject in number. A singular subject must have a singular verb; a plural subject must have a plural verb. When both the subject and the verb have the same number, the subject and the verb agree.

Singular: The girl *hikes* the trail daily. She *hikes* the trail daily.
Plural: The girls *hike* the trail daily. They *hike* the trail daily.

A noun usually forms a plural by adding *-s* or *-es* to the singular form (one *girl*, two *girls*). A verb, however, usually forms a singular by adding *-s* or *-es* (girls *hike*, girl *hikes*). This form change affects present-tense verbs with singular subjects in the third person (singular nouns and *it*, *he*, and *she*). Except for past-tense state-of-being verbs (*was* and *were*), past-tense and future-tense verbs do not show number.

Subject-Verb Agreement with Helping Verbs

State-of-Being, *Have*, and *Do*

If a verb consists of a helping verb(s) and a main verb working together, the first helping verb must agree with the subject. State-of-being verbs as well as the verbs *have* and *do* are the only helping verbs that change form to agree with a singular or plural subject. Notice the change from *is* to *are*, *has* to *have*, and *does* to *do*.

Singular: He *is helping* his father.
Plural: They *are helping* their father.
Singular: He *has helped* his father.
Plural: They *have helped* their father.
Singular: He *does help* his father.
Plural: They *do help* their father.

Remember that only the first helping verb in the complete verb shows agreement. Even *have*, *do*, and state-of-being verbs do not change form when they come later in the complete verb.

Singular: He *should have helped* his father.
Plural: They *should have helped* their father.
Singular: He *will be helping* his father.
Plural: They *will be helping* their father.

Practice the Skill

Underline the simple subject. Underline the verb in parentheses that agrees with the subject.

1. Grand Canyon National Park (contains, contain) one of the most beautiful canyons in the world.
2. The Grand Canyon's width (varies, vary) from less than one mile to eighteen miles.
3. The Colorado River (flows, flow) through the canyon.
4. Desert cacti (grows, grow) throughout the park.
5. Trees (lines, line) the north rim.
6. Many animals (makes, make) the park their home.
7. About four million tourists (visits, visit) the Grand Canyon every year.
8. Most visitors (views, view) the canyon from the south rim.
9. The north rim (begins, begin) ten miles away at the opposite side of the canyon.
10. The trail across the canyon (takes, take) visitors at least two days to hike.

Underline the simple subject. Underline the verb in parentheses that agrees with the subject. Identify the verb you chose as *V* (main verb) or *HV* (helping verb).

_______ 11. Big Ben (is, are) the famous bell in the clock tower in the Houses of Parliament in London.

_______ 12. It (has, have) a diameter of 2.7 meters and a height of 2.2 meters.

_______ 13. Big Ben (was, were) first rung in 1850.

_______ 14. It (was, were) installed during Sir Benjamin Hall's term as commissioner of works.

_______ 15. Sir Hall (was, were) nicknamed Big Ben; the members of Parliament named the bell after him.

_______ 16. The bell (does, do) have a clock connected to it.

_______ 17. The clock (is, are) famous for its accuracy.

_______ 18. Before 1913 it (was, were) wound manually.

_______ 19. Since then, an electric motor (has, have) been its power.

_______ 20. Londoners (does, do) still hear Big Ben ring today.

Review the Skill

Underline the simple subject. Underline the verb that agrees with the subject.

21. William Randolph Hearst's Hearst Castle (lies, lie) about halfway between Los Angeles and San Francisco in San Simeon.
22. This magnificent house (overlooks, overlook) the Pacific Ocean.
23. Its furnishings (comes, come) from all over the world.
24. Greek statues (surrounds, surround) the outdoor swimming pool.
25. The indoor swimming pool (recreates, recreate) a Roman bath.
26. The main dining room (looks, look) like the banquet hall of a medieval castle.
27. Tourists (imagines, imagine) the shouts from one end of the table to the other.
28. Many famous people (appears, appear) on the list of guests that have stayed at the mansion.
29. Wild animals (lives, live) in a zoo on the property now but roamed the grounds freely when Hearst was alive and inviting his famous guests.
30. Hearst Castle (demonstrates, demonstrate) how far a man will go to get the best of everything.

Complete the sentence with the correct form of the verb in parentheses.

________ 31. The Leaning Tower of Pisa _?_ a bell tower for that city's cathedral. (*state-of-being*)

________ 32. _?_ the Leaning Tower of Pisa really lean? (*Do*)

________ 33. The tower _?_ leaned several feet to the side. (*have*)

________ 34. People _?_ wondered why the tower leans as it does. (*have*)

________ 35. One suggestion _?_ that the architects built the tower to lean on purpose. (*state-of-being*)

________ 36. _?_ most experts agree that the ground was simply not firm enough for a good foundation? (*do*)

________ 37. They _?_ the idea that the builders did what they could to compensate. (*have*)

________ 38. Tourists _?_ challenged by the climb to the top of the tower. (*state-of-being*)

________ 39. A climber really _?_ feel as if he is leaning to the side as he makes his way up the 294 steps. (*do*)

________ 40. _?_ the Italian citizens want to save their tower? (*do*)

SUBJECT-VERB AGREEMENT WITH INDEFINITE PRONOUNS

Agreement with Indefinite Pronouns

Indefinite pronouns do not usually refer to specific persons or things. Most indefinite pronouns are singular; some are plural; and some can be either singular or plural, depending upon the meaning of the sentence. An indefinite pronoun used as a subject must agree in number with the verb.

Singular: *Everybody likes* bananas.
Plural: *Many like* apples even more.

Always Singular				
another	each	everything	neither	one
anybody	either	less	nobody	somebody
anyone	everybody	little	no one	someone
anything	everyone	much	nothing	something

Always Plural				
both	few	fewer	many	several

Singular or Plural					
all	any	more	most	none	some

To determine whether the indefinite pronoun in a sentence is singular or plural, examine the way it is used. Often a prepositional phrase will give a clue to the indefinite pronoun's meaning and number.

Singular: *All* of the library *has been* remodeled. (*All* is singular because it refers to one library.)
Plural: *All* of the books *are* new. (*All* is plural because it refers to several books.)

Practice the Skill

Underline the simple subject. Underline the verb in parentheses that agrees with the subject.

1. Everyone in my family (likes, like) to go on vacation.
2. All of us (has, have) visited Niagara Falls.
3. Many of the tourists (visits, visit) the falls yearly.
4. Some of the tourists (likes, like) to view the falls from the river on the *Maid of the Mist* tour.
5. However, most of the people (observes, observe) the churning water from the railings along the river's edge.
6. No one (wants, want) to go over the falls in a canoe.
7. Each of the falls (has, have) a name.
8. One (is, are) called the American Falls.
9. Another (is, are) known as the Horseshoe Falls.
10. Both (is, are) very beautiful.

Review the Skill

Underline the simple subject. Underline the verb in parentheses that agrees with the subject.

11. Few (visits, visit) Easter Island, located far west of the country of Chile.
12. Of those who do, no one (approaches, approach) without realizing that there is something different about this place.
13. Everyone (notices, notice) immediately that huge statues cover the surface of the island.
14. All of the statues (looks, look) out over the Pacific Ocean.
15. Most of them (is, are) twelve- to fifteen-feet tall and weigh about twenty-two and one-half tons.
16. Some of the figures (is, are) as tall as thirty-two feet and weigh as much as 101 tons.
17. Each (has, have) a large head with a pointed chin and long ears.
18. Many (questions, question) how the early islanders could have moved the statues.
19. Several (has, have) proved by experiment that it is relatively easy for a group to carry a statue using ropes.
20. Nobody (has, have) yet explained why the statues are there, though, or why they are looking toward the ocean.

Use the Skill

Write a one-paragraph story telling about an experience or a scene witnessed at a public place, such as an amusement park, concert, grocery store, airport, restaurant, or church. Include at least three indefinite pronouns used as subjects.

SUBJECT-VERB AGREEMENT IN UNCLEAR CONTEXTS

Agreement with Compound Subjects

When a compound subject is joined by *and* or *both-and*, the verb is plural.

Plural: Bob *and* Bill *are* twins.
Plural: *Both* hiking *and* climbing *are* their favorite activities.

When the compound subject is joined by *or*, *nor*, *either-or*, or *neither-nor*, the verb agrees with the subject that is closer to it.

Plural: George *or* the boys *buy* milk at the store.
Singular: The girls *or* Martin *bakes* delicious desserts.
Plural: *Neither* punch *nor* the mints *are* on the table yet.
Singular: *Either* cookies *or* cake *makes* an excellent party dessert.

Intervening Phrases, Predicate Nouns, and Inverted Order

Intervening Phrases

Often words come between the subject and the verb in a sentence. These intervening, or interrupting, words can cause the reader to lose track of the subject. Always find the true subject of the sentence in order to make the verb agree with it.

One common interrupter is the **negative phrase**. The verb of the sentence must agree in number with the subject, not the words in the negative phrase.

The *horses*, not the cow, *are* in the field.
The *cow*, not the horses, *is* in the barn.

Prepositional and appositive phrases are other common interrupters. If a prepositional or appositive phrase comes between the subject and the verb, it does not affect the agreement of the subject and the verb (though it might make the agreement clearer). The verb must agree in number with the subject and not with the object of the preposition or the appositive.

Prepositional phrase: The two *men* in the photograph *surf* the waves.
Appositive phrase: The *Pacific Ocean*, the largest ocean in the world, *has* some of the best waves for surfers.

Predicate Nouns of a Different Number

In sentences containing a linking verb, occasionally the subject and the predicate noun may not have the same number. One may be singular; the other may be plural. The verb must agree with the subject, not with the predicate noun.

Randall's *contribution* to the hike was bottles of water.
Sammy's *shoes* are a type of sandal.

SUBJECT-VERB AGREEMENT IN UNCLEAR CONTEXTS (CONTINUED)

Inverted Order

Sometimes the verb comes before the subject in a sentence or between the helping verb and the main verb.

V S
Singular: On the closet floor *is* my storage *place* for shoes.

V S
Plural: Where *are* your *shoes*?

HV S V
Singular: *Has he found* my shoes yet?

Remember that inverted order often happens when the words *there* or *here* introduce a sentence and come before the verb. *There* or *here* is almost never the subject of the sentence. The verb must instead agree with the delayed subject.

V S
Singular: There *is* a *puzzle* on the table.

V S
Plural: Here *are* several *pieces* of the puzzle.

Practice the Skill

Underline the simple subject. Underline the verb in parentheses that agrees with the subject.

1. Either the Painted Canyon of North Dakota or the Black Hills of South Dakota (is, are) good places to visit on a trip west.
2. Both Mount Rushmore and Rushmore Cave (is, are) special points of interest in South Dakota.
3. Either Washington or Roosevelt (is, are) my favorite sculpture on Mount Rushmore.
4. Both Jefferson and Lincoln (is, are) also beautifully carved.
5. Neither John Quincy Adams nor Woodrow Wilson (is, are) one of the US presidents on the face of Mount Rushmore.
6. Both Gutzon Borglum and his son (was, were) the supervisors of the sculpturing of Mount Rushmore.
7. Neither my sister nor my brothers (was, were) familiar with Gutzon Borglum.

8. Neither Borglum nor his son (was, were) able to finish all of the sculptures.
9. Either Washington or Jefferson (was, were) designed and carved first.
10. Both government money and private donations (was, were) helpful in funding the million-dollar project.

Underline the simple subject. Underline the verb in parentheses that agrees with the subject.

11. Why (was, were) the Eiffel Tower built?
12. It (was, were) built in celebration of the one hundredth anniversary of the French Revolution.
13. There (is, are) twelve thousand metal parts and 2.5 million rivets in the Eiffel Tower.
14. At the top of the tower (is, are) the lantern and the radio antenna.
15. The most unpopular part for tourists (is, are) the steps; therefore, most tourists choose the elevator.
16. There (is, are) over seven thousand tons of iron that make up the tower.
17. All of the workers on the scaffolding (was, were) safe.
18. How long (was, were) they working on the project?
19. The tower, except for the elevators, (was, were) completed in twenty-six and one-half months.
20. Here (is, are) a picture of the Eiffel Tower.

Review the Skill

Underline the simple subject. Underline the verb in parentheses that agrees with the subject.

21. Determination and a little time (is, are) the main requirements for creating a city.
22. Either skeptics or a believer (agrees, agree) with this statement when faced with the example of Brasília, the capital of Brazil.
23. Rio de Janeiro and São Paulo (is, are) cities on the coast of Brazil, but before 1960 not much activity took place in the country's interior.
24. Either the constitution of 1898 or Juscelino Kubitschek (is, are) primarily responsible for a new capital in the heart of the countryside.
25. Three years and many workers (was, were) enough to turn an empty plot of land in the wilderness into a modern city.
26. Neither a decent road nor raw materials (was, were) close to the construction site, so airplanes had to fly in supplies.
27. Fans and critics (argues, argue) over the attractiveness of the city's modern architectural design.
28. The National Congress buildings and the cathedral especially (attracts, attract) attention.
29. Neither pedestrians nor cars (has, have) to share space with trucks because each group has its own roads.
30. The population of the city and its importance in the country (grows, grow) as time passes.

Underline the simple subject. Underline the verb in parentheses that agrees with the subject.

31. Where (is, are) the Great Wall of China?

32. Across northern China from the Pacific coast to the Gobi Desert (extends, extend) the wall.
33. The Great Wall, not the Pyramids, (is, are) the longest structure ever built.
34. Estimates of the wall's length (varies, vary), but the figure is generally around four thousand miles.
35. Why (does, do) the wall exist?
36. The original purpose of the wall (was, were) to join several smaller walls into one long defense against northern invaders.
37. The joined walls of this structure (is, are) a highway more than an obstruction, though.
38. The width of the wall (allows, allow) ten men or five horses to travel side by side across its top.
39. Tourists, not an army, (walks, walk) on the wall today.
40. Parts of the wall (has, have) crumbled due to age and exposure to the elements, yet the Great Wall is still an amazing architectural achievement.

Use the Skill

The paragraph below contains five subject-verb agreement errors. If a verb does not agree with its subject, cross out the incorrect verb and write the correct verb above it.

41.–45. Are many of you able to swim? Sometimes people have trouble with this skill. Inability or fear keep them out of the water. Nobody sink in the Dead Sea, though. The salt content of the water are so high that everything living floats. In fact, while most seas contain about five percent salt, the Dead Sea has as much as twenty-five percent. How do the water become so salty? Although fresh water empties into the sea from nearby mountains and the Jordan River daily, much of it evaporates, leaving salt and other minerals behind. Saltiness and depth is the sea's claim to fame. At 1,286 feet below sea level, the Dead Sea is the lowest inland body of water on earth.

VISUAL REPRESENTATIONS
Writing Trait: Ideas

Listen Up!
Look at these pictures quickly without reading the captions and jot down your initial impression of each one. Then read the captions. To what extent are your initial impressions of the pictures different from what the captions say? How do the captions guide the way you think about each picture?

The highlight of Jeremy's day is helping his grandmother cook.

Ever since her dog survived major surgery, Julia treasures every moment she can spend with her pet.

Tom was a little nervous as he tried ghost pepper pizza for the first time.

Take Notes!
Summarize the ways in which photos and captions communicate information.

Effective Visuals
You have probably heard of the expression, "A picture is worth a thousand words." There is much truth in this statement. Pictures have been a method of communication from the beginning of time. Ancient languages, such as cuneiform and hieroglyphics, began by relying on pictures for communication; and Chinese, one of the oldest languages in the world, still uses pictures in its writing. Even after writing as we know it became predominant, pictures still had a large influence on society. In the 1800s, Thomas Nast used political cartoons to help bring down powerful but corrupt leaders; and after photographs were invented, photojournalism became a significant way to influence the public. As influential as words are, one can make the case that using pictures is many times a better way to express one's ideas.

Below are some of the main ways in which visuals communicate their messages to the viewer:

1. **Visuals generate interest.** Looking at pictures is more interesting to the average person than reading text. This is important because you cannot communicate information unless there are people interested in receiving it. Using pictures is a good way to gain people's interest and motivate them to pay attention to your message.

2. **Visuals provide nonverbal communication.** When you write, you are only using verbal communication, the words in the English language. However, much of human communication is nonverbal. For example, the raised eyebrow your parent gives you when you begin to misbehave is just as much of a warning as if they actually spoke to you. Pictures can provide these nonverbal messages, and many times, this type of communication is more powerful than any words that can be spoken.

3. **Visuals stir up emotion.** Although it is possible to become emotional when reading a description of an event, seeing a picture arouses people's emotions much more quickly and easily.

4. **Visuals help with the retention of a message.** For many people, it is easier to remember something they saw rather than something they heard or read about.

5. **Visuals communicate across cultures.** One major problem with using words to communicate is that there are so many different languages. Visuals, however, have the power to break this barrier and communicate to everyone, no matter what language he speaks.

Effective Captions

A caption is a short comment providing information concerning what is happening in a picture. A caption is located close to the picture so viewers will read it after looking at the photo. Although visuals are a powerful way to communicate, adding a caption gives the viewer information that he would not otherwise know, and it can guide the viewer to think about the photo in a specific way. Captions generally answer the following questions:

1. Who or what is in the picture?
2. What is happening?
3. Where is it?
4. Why is it happening?

Partner Up!

Select a picture that communicates a story or a significant idea. This could be a picture you found or one you took yourself. Then, write a caption giving context to the picture. Be sure to follow the guidelines in *Take Notes!*

Try It Out!

Using the caption as guidance, write a paragraph about the picture you chose in *Partner Up!* You may choose to write an anecdote, descriptive paragraph, explanatory paragraph, or any other type of paragraph that you used in a previous toolbox.

PRONOUN-ANTECEDENT AGREEMENT

Agreement with Personal Pronouns

Number of Personal Pronouns

Like subjects and verbs, pronouns and their antecedents must agree in number. If the antecedent is singular, the pronoun referring to it must also be singular.

The *runners* began to filter toward the starting line. *They* were eager for the race to begin.

The finish line was a yellow *tape*. *It* stretched from one side of the road to the other.

Gender of Personal Pronouns

Unlike verbs, pronouns show gender as well as number. Pronouns are either masculine, feminine, or neuter. Pronouns and their antecedents must agree in gender as well as number.

Masculine: *Mr. Gaines* held one end of the tape tightly; *he* was prepared for the rush of winners. (The masculine pronoun *he* replaces *Mr. Gaines*.)

Feminine: *Hannah* leaned forward with *her* heart pounding. (The feminine pronoun *her* replaces *Hannah*.)

Neuter: The *race* was about to start. *It* would be an exciting competition. (The neuter pronoun *it* replaces *race*.)

If the antecedent clearly refers to a person but does not refer to a specific gender, use a singular masculine pronoun.

Unclear gender: Each *spectator* held *his* breath in anticipation.

When referring to animals, use masculine or feminine pronouns if the context indicates the animal's gender.

Feminine: The *jaguar* fed *her* hungry cubs first.

If, however, the context does not indicate the animal's gender, use neuter pronouns.

Neuter: The *jaguar* fished using *its* large paws.

Compound Antecedents

If the antecedent is compound, look at the conjunction joining the parts of the antecedent. If the nouns are joined by *and* or *both-and*, the pronoun must be plural.

Plural: Tom *and* Evan are participating in *their* state fair.

If the nouns are joined by *or*, *nor*, *either-or*, or *neither-nor*, the pronoun must agree with whichever noun is closer to it.

Plural: *Neither* Jack *nor* the girls were in *their* booths at lunchtime.

Singular: *Either* the boys *or* the animal handler will appear on stage for *his* award.

Practice the Skill

Complete the sentence with a pronoun that agrees with its antecedent. Underline the antecedent of the missing pronoun.

_______ 1. Numerous inventions testify to _?_ creators' attentiveness to the details of everyday life.

_______ 2. Velcro is such an invention; _?_ came from a man's attempt to copy part of God's handiwork.

_______ 3. Surprisingly, Velcro came about as a result of cockleburs that a Swiss man encountered while _?_ was hunting.

_______ 4. George de Mestral became intrigued by the burs' adhering to _?_ clothes and to _?_ Irish Pointer.

_______ 5. Upon studying the cocklebur seeds under magnification, de Mestral found _?_ to be surrounded by hooklike attachments.

_______ 6. De Mestral eventually duplicated nature's design, and nylon Velcro was introduced in the 1960s as a result of _?_ efforts.

_______ 7. Nylon was the choice material because people knew _?_ to be strong.

_______ 8. Under the right conditions, Velcro is strong enough to support the weight of a person when _?_ is suspended.

_______ 9. Velcro has been especially useful in children's products, and many sports products have been improved by _?_ as well.

_______ 10. Today, baby products, shoes, certain toys, and blood-pressure cuffs display the ingenuity of George de Mestral as well as _?_ determination to make Velcro a reality.

Underline the correct pronoun from the choices in parentheses. Write in the blank the number of the pronoun you chose. If the pronoun is singular, write its gender as well.

__________________ 11. The ancient Greeks and Romans used an abacus to solve (his, their) arithmetic problems.

__________________ 12. Chinese students and their teachers would call (his, their) counting device a *suanpan*.

__________________ 13. Neither Greek mathematicians nor a Roman schoolboy could complete work as quickly without an adding machine to help (him, them).

__________________ 14. Wooden disks or plastic beads are placed on rods on which (it, they) can slide.

__________________ 15. The beads or disks are moved so that (it, they) indicate numerical values.

__________________ 16. A calculator can help with accuracy, and (it, they) can solve in a few minutes a problem that would normally take days.

__________________ 17. Students now can use calculators on phones to calculate (his, their) arithmetic.

__________________ 18. Today a business or a student would use a calculator to make (his, their) work easier.

__________________ 19. Neither businessmen nor scientists would find using an adding machine easier for (him, them) than pressing the buttons of a calculator.

__________________ 20. Either graphing calculators or a computer software package can solve difficult problems, and (it, they) can save hours of work.

Review the Skill

Write in the blank a pronoun that agrees with its antecedent.

_______ 21. Alexander Graham Bell knew that _?_ enjoyed working in the communication field.

_______ 22. _?_ most famous invention is the telephone.

_______ 23. Though _?_ was deaf herself, Mabel Hubbard, Bell's wife, founded the Aerial Experiment Association.

_______ 24. _?_ deafness inspired many of Bell's experiments.

_______ 25. Although people made fun of Bell's invention, _?_ soon realized the usefulness of the telephone.

_______ 26. _?_ ridicule did not stop Bell's work in both the communication and aeronautics fields.

_______ 27. _?_ persevered because he believed communication was the key to most problems.

_______ 28. You and I often forget the hard work that surrounded Bell's efforts; _?_ take much of modern technology for granted.

_______ 29. If you own a smartphone, you can do much more than just talk on _?_ phone.

_______ 30. Because we have the telephone, _?_ lives are quite different from those of our ancestors.

If the italicized pronoun does not agree with its antecedent, write the correct pronoun in the blank. If the sentence is correct, write C in the blank.

_______ 31. Almost every child who has played with LEGO bricks will admit that *their* opinion of the toy is favorable.

_______ 32. LEGO brick inventor Ole Kirk Christiansen busied himself with both carpentry and toy manufacturing, but *they* were not equally enjoyable to him.

_______ 33. The Danish carpenter decided to choose between toys and carpentry because *its* dual demands on his time did not suit him.

_______ 34. When he made plastic LEGO toys, Christiansen did not know whether his life or his finances would remain the same, and *it* certainly did not.

_______ 35. Not one person could claim that *they* would have guessed the family fortune to be several billion dollars.

_______ 36. Many people wonder whether the company has really sold more than one hundred billion blocks; *he* just cannot believe these statistics.

_______ 37. Neither one's creativity nor his enjoyment suffers when he plays with LEGO bricks; instead, *their* level usually increases.

_______ 38. In Billund, Denmark, LEGOLAND is quite popular, and *it* thrills visitors.

_______ 39. LEGOLAND's model of Chief Sitting Bull is a crowd favorite. *Their* structure of over one million blocks amazes visitors.

_______ 40. If you visit, you will find both the Statue of Liberty model and the Parthenon model memorable; *it* will not disappoint you.

PRONOUN-ANTECEDENT AGREEMENT WITH INDEFINITE PRONOUNS

Number of Indefinite Pronouns

Although the antecedent of a personal pronoun is usually a noun, it is sometimes an indefinite pronoun. The personal pronoun always has the same number (singular or plural) as its antecedent.

Singular: *Either* will submit *his* proposal.
Plural: *Several* believe *their* inventions to be the best.
Singular: *Everyone* has a different concept for *his* invention.
Plural: *Many* are prepared to present *their* designs.

For an indefinite pronoun that can be either singular or plural, consider the meaning of the sentence to determine the number of the pronoun. If the indefinite pronoun refers to only one thing, the personal pronoun should be singular. If the indefinite pronoun refers to more than one thing, the personal pronoun should be plural. Often a prepositional phrase gives a clue to the number of the indefinite pronoun.

Singular: *Most* of the floor was protected by *its* cover.
Plural: *Most* of the inventions were in *their* assigned spaces in the gymnasium.
Singular: *Some* of the spilled algae made *its* way onto the uncovered part of the gym floor.
Plural: *Some* of the students didn't realize that *their* projects could make a huge mess.

Refer to the chart of indefinite pronouns on page 362 if you are unsure whether a certain indefinite pronoun is singular or plural.

Gender of Indefinite Pronouns

Indefinite pronouns themselves do not show gender. However, sometimes the context of a sentence may indicate gender for an indefinite pronoun. Choose a personal pronoun that will agree with its indefinite pronoun in both number and gender.

Neuter: *One* of the frogs remained in *its* tank.
Masculine: *Each* of the brothers brought *his* own rags to help clean up.
Feminine: *Another* of the girls ran to get *her* teacher's mop.

If the context of a singular indefinite pronoun does not specify gender but clearly refers to people and not animals or objects, use a singular masculine pronoun. Do not use a plural personal pronoun to refer to a singular indefinite pronoun.

Incorrect: *Someone* thought to get *their* camera.
Correct: *Someone* thought to get *his* camera.
Incorrect: *Everyone* did *their* best to repair the damage to the invention.
Correct: *Everyone* did *his* best to repair the damage to the invention.

Practice the Skill

Write in the first blank an object of the preposition. Write in the second blank an appropriate pronoun that agrees with its antecedent.

1. Each of the __________________ began __________________ science project.
2. One of the __________________ demonstrated __________________ volcano.
3. Many of her __________________ stepped back for __________________ safety.
4. Each of the __________________ tried to hide __________________ fear.
5. The volcano exploded! A few of the __________________ who were standing nearby acquired wet, thick splotches on __________________ clothing.
6. Something in the back of the __________________ set off the fire alarm because of __________________ smoke.
7. Everybody in the __________________ walked outside to __________________ class's meeting place.
8. After several minutes, most of the __________________ were allowed back into __________________ rooms.
9. Five of the __________________ had been able to finish __________________ presentations.
10. Some of the __________________ would have to finish __________________ on Friday.

If the italicized pronoun does not agree with its antecedent, write the correct pronoun in the blank. If the sentence is correct, write C in the blank.

_______ 11. Each of the students really enjoyed *their* science experiments.

_______ 12. Everyone thought that the electricity experiment was *his* favorite one.

_______ 13. Most of the students experimented with combining *their* own chemicals.

_______ 14. Not many thought that *his* sulfur compound smelled very good.

_______ 15. Every one of the frogs looked shriveled in *their* formaldehyde.

_______ 16. One of the girls finished *their* project early.

_______ 17. All of the students gathered insects for *their* large science project.

_______ 18. Anyone who could not collect all *his* bugs did not receive a high grade.

_______ 19. Nobody handed *their* assignment in late.

_______ 20. Few considered science *his* least favorite subject in school.

Review the Skill

Correct the sentences that contain an agreement error by underlining the incorrect pronoun and writing the correct pronoun in the blank. If the sentence does not contain an agreement error, write *C* in the blank.

_______ 21. Some of today's parents use Gerber Baby Food to feed his children.

_______ 22. Dan and Frank Gerber began to produce baby food in 1928, and now his products appear in over sixty countries.

_______ 23. Neither Dan nor his father Frank lost his courage when it was suggested that they produce soft-style food for babies.

_______ 24. None of the Fremont Canning Company employees could predict whether its jobs would last long.

_______ 25. When Dan's wife Dorothy suggested the canned food, she had no idea that many around the world would someday buy such a product and even read the label in his own language.

_______ 26. Neither losses nor disaster resulted despite their potential to occur.

_______ 27. The improved choices and other advantages of the food were popular, and they created a demand for the item.

_______ 28. The Fremont Canning Company became successful making baby food. Now nearly everyone sees Gerber on the shelf of their local supermarket.

_______ 29. Either fruit or vegetables are available to those who would like to use it.

_______ 30. In some countries, you can find Gerber foods made from seaweed, since some children like to eat them.

Use the Skill

Write in the blank a pronoun that agrees with its antecedent. Underline the antecedent of the missing pronoun.

_______ 31. According to Jim Winner, necessity is the mother of invention. _?_ turned a bad experience into a successful business venture.

_______ 32. After losing _?_ new Cadillac car, Winner looked for a solution to car theft.

_______ 33. Winner invented the Club steering-wheel lock and helped popularize _?_ use.

_______ 34. Neither the ignition key nor door locks proved that _?_ could stop crooks.

_______ 35. Winner consulted law enforcement officers and a former robber while working on the device; _?_ input helped Winner develop this invention.

_______ 36. The Club steering-wheel lock makes a car or truck impossible to steer, thus lessening _?_ appeal to thieves.

_______ 37. Its features are designed so that even a busy mother can protect _?_ parked car.

_______ 38. Thanks to Winner's ingenuity, we now have another option for securing _?_ vehicles.

_______ 39. You can even purchase a Club steering-wheel lock for _?_ bike.

_______ 40. Everyone who buys this product wants to protect _?_ vehicle.

ARGUMENTATIVE PARAGRAPHS
Writing Traits: Ideas, Voice

Listen Up!
Read the mentor text below. To what extent does this paragraph change your mind about the benefits of learning to play an instrument? Explain your answer.

MENTOR TEXT

The Benefits of Playing an Instrument

Although not necessary for building a successful career, every student should learn to play an instrument because this knowledge has other valuable benefits. First, learning an instrument teaches perseverance. A student cannot become proficient with any instrument unless he spends quality time practicing his instrument, learning to read music, and studying the basics of music theory. Since this process takes great effort and patience, music students will learn to persist through these challenging tasks they face. Additionally, learning an instrument builds confidence. Since music recitals are the product of almost every music class, a student learns at an early age how to overcome his fear of an audience and confidently perform in front of others. This will benefit most students who will probably be required at some point in their lives to speak or perform in front of others. Most importantly, learning an instrument helps turn a student into a well-rounded individual, a person with a wide range of knowledge and experience. Knowing the difficulty of playing an instrument helps students develop a stronger appreciation for music, and it opens the door for them to explore different genres and even compose their own music. Therefore, while music may not have a direct effect on a student's career, learning to play an instrument helps a student develop several life skills that help him become a more resolute, confident, and well-rounded individual.

WRITING TOOLBOX

Take Notes!

Read the following information and list the components of an argumentative paragraph.

Components of an Argumentative Paragraph

Generally, the term *argumentative* refers to something negative. Nobody likes to be around an argumentative person. If your parents or teachers ever accused you of being argumentative, they were probably implying that your behavior needed to change. Although there are certainly bad ways of being argumentative, the basic idea of an argument, making the case for what you believe, is actually a good thing. Making an argument is often beneficial and even needed, as long as you do it with a Christlike purpose and approach. It is often necessary to make a case for the truth and humbly try to persuade others who might believe an error. This is especially true for Christians whom God commands to make clear, logical arguments for why people should trust Christ as Savior. I Peter 3:15 tells Christians to be ready to defend what they believe yet do so with gentleness and respect.

Argumentative writing begins with a thesis statement that clearly defines the author's position about a controversial issue. The author then proceeds to give different reasons and examples for why his position is correct. These reasons and examples could include statistics, research findings, case studies, or the opinions of credible people. Finally, the author ends with a concluding sentence that points back to the thesis statement and gives closure to his argument.

Writing an Argumentative Paragraph

1. Choose a topic that is controversial, something that people have different opinions about (Should schools have uniforms?, Is homework helpful or harmful?, etc.).
2. Decide which position you wish to take on the issue. Jot down several reasons that support your position.
3. Begin your paragraph with your thesis statement, the claim you are making about the issue.
4. Support your thesis statement with facts and examples.
5. Finish with a concluding sentence that summarizes your argument and points the reader back to your thesis statement.

Partner Up!

Pretend you have a friend who doubts whether God exists. Plan a paragraph that makes a case for the existence of God. Make a list of reasons that could convince someone that God exists.

Try It Out!

Take the list you created in *Partner Up!* and write a paragraph arguing for God's existence. Be sure to follow the guidelines listed in *Take Notes!* Remember, your goal is to have organized reasoning and argue in a way that shows gentleness and respect.

CHAPTER REVIEW

Agreement

The paragraph below contains five subject-verb agreement errors. If the verb does not agree with its subject, cross out the incorrect verb and write the correct verb above it.

1.–5. My family moved west last year to help settle the Northwest Territory. We spent many days and weeks building our farm. Our farm contain many different types of animals and buildings. My father add new buildings every time we have a little extra money. Our barns rise high in the sky. They look very large. We keeps hay, animals, and equipment in our barns. Sometimes I sleep in the hayloft, but my mother lets me sleep out there only when it is warm outside. My favorite activity are to gather corn in the fields at harvest time. During the first week after harvest, my mother make corn pudding.

Helping Verbs

Complete the sentence with the correct form of the verb in parentheses.

_______ 6. _?_ you know who led the Continental army during the Revolutionary War? (*do*)

_______ 7. Our teacher _?_ written a book on George Washington. (*have*)

_______ 8. _?_ colonies win their independence from Great Britain after the Revolutionary War? (*do*)

_______ 9. George Washington _?_ known as the first president of the United States. (*state-of-being*)

_______ 10. _?_ you ever studied Washington or the Revolutionary War? (*have*)

Agreement with Indefinite Pronouns

Underline the verb in parentheses that agrees with the subject.

11. One of the first permanent settlements in America (was, were) Jamestown.
12. All of the colonists in the new settlement (was, were) led by Captain John Smith.
13. Several of the histories (records, record) some of the difficulties the first colonists encountered during those first few years.
14. Some of the history books (show, shows) that the first representative legislature, the House of Burgesses, met in Jamestown in 1619.
15. Many of the historical facts about our country (help, helps) us understand our heritage.

Agreement with Compound Subjects

Underline the verb in parentheses that agrees with the subject.

16. Elliot and Harrison (reviews, review) their notes before each test.
17. Neither Elliot nor Harrison (remembers, remember) that the Gold Rush began in 1848.
18. Either the test or the quizzes (contains, contain) important facts about the colonial period.
19. Pioneers and prospectors (was, were) significant in building the towns of the Old West.
20. Either a river boat or a covered wagon (was, were) used as a settler's main form of transportation.

Agreement: Intervening Phrases, Predicate Nouns, and Inverted Order

Underline the simple subject. Underline the verb in parentheses that agrees with the subject.

21. The students in the elementary school (walk, walks) along the same trail the Cherokees walked in 1838.
22. Many of the students (imagine, imagines) the suffering that took place along the Trail of Tears.
23. The Cherokees' biggest trial (was, were) the many deaths that occurred along the trail.
24. Where (do, does) the Cherokees live today?
25. There (is, are) many American Indians living in the southwestern states.

Agreement with Personal Pronouns

Write in the blank a pronoun that agrees with its antecedent.

_______ 26. Hannah, a godly woman with no children, prayed desperately that God would give _?_ a son.

_______ 27. The Lord blessed Hannah, and _?_ was given a son.

_______ 28. Hannah named her son Samuel; _?_ name means "asked of God."

_______ 29. Samuel's parents knew that he was a special child, and _?_ dedicated him to the Lord.

_______ 30. During _?_ many years in the temple, God was preparing Samuel for an important ministry to the whole nation of Israel.

Agreement with Indefinite Pronouns

Identify the pronoun that agrees with its antecedent. Write in the blank the letter that corresponds to the correct answer.

_______ 31. Later in Samuel's life, God gave him an assignment, and _?_ was very important.
- **A** it
- **B** they
- **C** them

_______ 32. Samuel's job was to inform someone of _?_ being chosen as the king of Israel.
- **A** their
- **B** her
- **C** his

_______ 33. Neither King Saul nor his son Jonathan would be able to retain _?_ claim to the throne.
- **A** his
- **B** their
- **C** its

_______ 34. No one was more surprised than David about _?_ being chosen as the future king.
- **A** his
- **B** its
- **C** their

_______ 35. Most of the Israelites were excited to see Samuel anoint _?_ new king.
- **A** its
- **B** their
- **C** his

CHAPTER 15

ARGUMENTATIVE WRITING

HOW DOES MEDIA INFLUENCE ME?

Every day the average person spends hours absorbing some sort of media. This normally includes watching television, listening to the radio, spending time on the internet, or reading magazines and other materials. By doing this, people encounter thousands of different ideas that influence the way they think about the world. Many times, media's influence is so subtle that people do not even realize their thinking is being changed. Even though the Bible was written long before electronic media was invented, God's Word still speaks about this issue. Christians are called to not simply allow themselves to be influenced by the world's opinions but to evaluate all the ideas they encounter and reject anything that goes against biblical teaching (2 Corinthians 10:5). As you are taught to critically analyze media in this chapter, try to apply the skills you learn to all the ideas you encounter in your culture.

Look at the advertisement in the mentor text. How does it make you feel? Has it influenced your thinking in any way? Why or why not? Next, read the ad critique. Do you agree with the writer's thoughts about the ad? Has the writer changed your initial thoughts or made you think about the ad differently? Explain your answer.

A Critique of the Advertisement "Hot Cross Buns"

How does the author give the reader context for the ad?

What is the author's opinion of the ad?

"Hot Cross Buns" is a print advertisement whose goal is to raise awareness of child safety in automobiles. The ad contains a picture of a girl playing the tuba along with the following caption: "If you love them enough to listen to 'Hot Cross Buns' for two hours straight, then surely you'll check to make sure they're correctly buckled in the back seat." The ad is sponsored by the National Highway Traffic Safety Administration and the Ad Council, a nonprofit group whose mission is to produce and promote campaigns to improve daily life. The ad's target audience is those responsible for the child's safety while in the vehicle—parents. This advertisement is effective due to its simplicity, its creativity, and its emotional and moral appeal.

One important part of any advertisement, especially a print advertisement, is that it must be simple. Most people will not have the time or patience to read an ad that has too many words or pictures. An ad like this might also be featured on a billboard, and people will be unable to read it if it has too many words. This ad is effective because the reader can understand the message with just one glance. It has only one picture and a twenty-nine-word caption underneath. This simplicity enables people to read and understand the advertisement before losing interest.

Not only should an ad be simple, but it must also be creative in order to attract the attention and interest of the reader. This ad engages the targeted audience by first portraying a situation relatable to many parents. It is not uncommon for parents to listen to their children spend hours practicing an instrument. Since parents can relate to this situation, they become interested in this ad and want to continue reading to understand its message.

The most effective part of this ad is its emotional and moral appeal. It first appeals to parents' natural feelings of love for their children. While parents might find it annoying to hear the same song repeatedly, they tolerate it because they love their children and want to see them succeed. The ad also appeals to their moral instinct by showing that if parents love their children enough to tolerate inconveniences for their sakes, they should be willing to make sure their children are safely buckled in the car. A parent who reads this ad can easily understand that following this advice is the right thing to do.

Many print ads are uninteresting and easy to overlook, but "Hot Cross Buns" effectively uses simplicity and creativity in addition to emotional and moral appeal to influence its audience. While this ad is very well done, it would be even better if the picture showed a child practicing and a parent who is obviously tired of listening to the music. This would make the message more humorous and relatable. However, even without this change, this advertisement will most likely help parents understand the importance of ensuring their children's safety while they are in a vehicle.

How does the author use logical arguments to prove his opinion of this ad?

How does the author bring his argument to a close? What suggestions does he make for how the ad could be better?

INTRODUCING THE ARGUMENTATIVE ESSAY

Advertisements and You

Advertisements are a common part of modern life. You encounter ads on billboards, on television, in magazines, and on the internet. Your reaction to those ads might range from expressing annoyance because you think an ad is obnoxious to enjoying one so much that you watch it with your friends or share it on social media.

Every year, companies, governments, and organizations spend hundreds of billions of dollars coming up with ads that try to persuade you to buy their product, vote for their candidate, or follow their advice. As of this writing, the most money a company paid for a single commercial was 33 million dollars!

The reason people spend so much money on ads is that they are a powerful tool to influence you. Companies would not invest millions of dollars in this industry if it did not persuade many people to buy their product. Perhaps you can remember a time when you wanted something because you saw it on a commercial. While this influence might not seem bad, realize that, like any other communicator, the creators of such ads are influencing your worldview. Many times, advertisements can promote unbiblical ideas. Look at the different unbiblical ideas and motives a smartphone company could use in their advertisements.

Greed: "You should buy this new smartphone, even if you don't need it."
Pride: "You deserve to have this smartphone."
Discontentment: "Tired of your old smartphone? Buy this new one!"
Poor financial decisions: "You should own this expensive smartphone today. If you can't afford it, you can just buy it on credit."

Although the messages above are normally not stated this clearly, they are often subtly implied. It is very important that Christians practice discernment when watching or reading advertisements. They should identify and evaluate the ideas that ads present and reject any ideas that contradict a biblical worldview.

Advertising Techniques

Because you frequently encounter influential advertisements, it is important that you learn how to analyze and critique an ad. Advertisements are not put together haphazardly. Advertisers rely heavily on various techniques to influence their audience. On the following page are several popular advertising techniques.

Emotional Appeal

Instead of making a logical argument, many ads focus on addressing the way customers feel about an issue. Ads may address common needs and wants, such as the desire to look nice and be accepted by others, or they may address common fears, such as accidents, sickness, and death.

Example: "Don't be another victim. Buy Acme locks, and get the security you need for your home."

Bandwagon Effect

Have you ever done something just because everybody else was doing it? Advertisers know that being like everyone else is a natural desire for humans, so they create ads that make you feel that you should buy their product because everybody else is doing it.

Example: "Join the millions of people who use Acme locks."

Facts and Statistics

Using statistics makes the product seem factually reliable and gives customers confidence in the quality of the product.

Example: "Over 90% of security officers recommend Acme locks."

Endorsements

Customers are often influenced by celebrities whom they admire. A company therefore may pay a celebrity to promote their product.

Example: "When Superbowl champion quarterback John Smith leaves his multimillion-dollar mansion, he relies on Acme locks to keep his house safe."

Perfect vs. Miserable Lifestyle

Advertisements always portray those who use their products as people who are successful. The actors using the product in a commercial always appear to be smart, happy, or beautiful. On the other hand, those who do not use the advertiser's product are shown to be frustrated or miserable. This sends the audience the message that using the product will lead to success and happiness.

Example: "Jane used to be afraid to go on vacation for fear of being burglarized, but with Acme locks, she now has no problem being gone for weeks."

Special Offers

Companies frequently promote special offers, particularly around a holiday when people tend to spend more money. Special offers make the customer feel that they need to buy the product now so they can get a good deal.

Example: "Take advantage of this limited-time offer: buy one Acme lock now and get a second one free!"

Practice the Skill

Look at the advertisement and determine which advertising technique is being used. Then use the Worldview Checklist to evaluate the ad.

Worldview Checklist

1. Discernment: Is the ad appropriate for its audience?
2. Virtue: Is the ad being honest in its persuasive strategy?
3. Logic: Does the ad use effective reasoning?

Your Assignment

For this chapter, you will choose an ad for a product you are familiar with and write an argumentative essay evaluating and critiquing its message and techniques. You may choose to evaluate a print ad or a commercial. The purpose of your paper is to make a logical case for why your ideas about the ad are correct. In order to do that effectively, you must first learn the basic characteristics of argumentative writing.

Characteristics of Argumentative Writing

Like an advertisement, an argumentative essay uses different techniques to persuade the audience of the author's point of view. However, while an advertisement focuses greatly on appealing to both logic and emotions, argumentative writing, like informative writing, focuses only on appealing to logic. The author can appeal to logic by using the following:

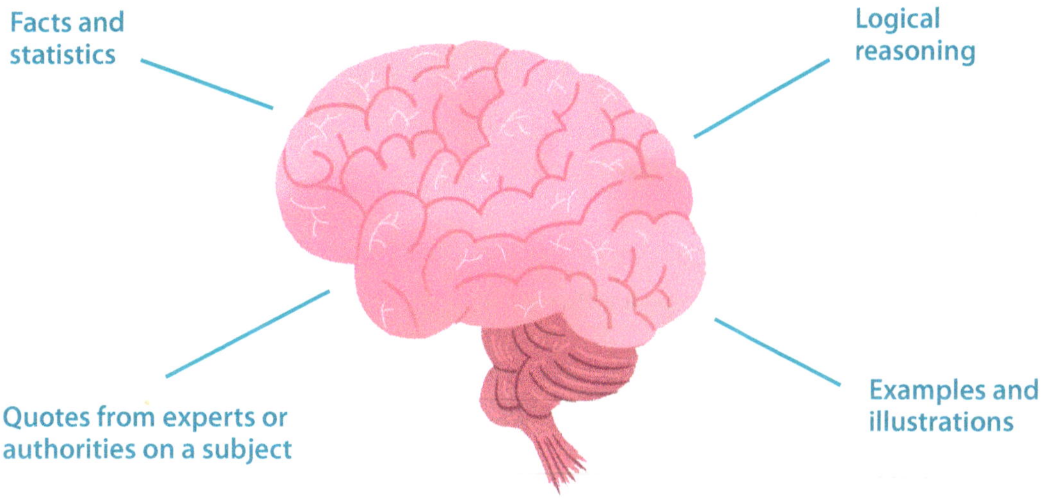

Practice the Skill

Look at the mentor text on pages 390–91 and identify which argumentative technique it uses. How does its argumentative technique help persuade the reader?

Planning Your Paper

In order to successfully write an ad critique, plan your paper by following these steps.

Step 1: Analyze the Ad

Study the ad and write a summary of it. Then, use the worldview themes to answer the following questions:

Logic

- What is the product? Describe it in two or three sentences.
- What does the ad claim about the product? What specific evidence does the ad use to support its claim?

Virtue

- What techniques does this ad use to influence its audience? Do these techniques encourage unbiblical ideas or motivations?
- Is the evidence presented factually, or is it exaggerated or embellished?

Discernment

- Who is the ad's targeted audience? Would another audience be more appropriate?
- What aspect of the ad grabs your attention (quotes, color, visuals, etc.)?
- What adjectives are used to sell the product?

Step 2: Write a Thesis Statement

What is the main idea you want to communicate about this ad? How can you put that idea into one sentence? Your thesis statement must be your personal belief about the effectiveness and value of the ad. Was it convincing? Did it have certain strengths or flaws? Look at the mentor text for a model of how to form a good thesis.

Step 3: Write an Outline

Use the following format to create your outline:

I. Introduction
  A. Purpose for the advertisement
  B. Summary of the advertisement content
  C. Sponsoring company, what it does, its reputation, its history
  D. Target audience
  E. Thesis statement: personal opinion on the effectiveness and value of the advertisement

II. Body
  A. Paragraph for argument one
  B. Paragraph for argument two
  C. Paragraph for argument three

III. Conclusion
  A. Restatement of the thesis statement
  B. Recommendations for improving the advertisement (if any)

Keep in mind that the arguments you are presenting in the body of your paper are meant to convince the reader that your point of view is correct. To make your paper as convincing as possible, you can start with your weakest argument and work toward your strongest argument. This arrangement will help you build a strong case for your argument.

DRAFTING

PLANNING DRAFTING REVISING PROOFREADING PUBLISHING

Drafting Your Paper

Once you have outlined a strong argument, you are ready to begin drafting your paper. Compose your draft just as you did when writing your previous compositions. If you make a spelling or grammar mistake while writing, make a note but keep on working. Wait until the next two stages to fix your mistakes. Keep in mind that you are making your argument in the *body* of your paper. Because of this, you might find it easier to write the body first and add the introduction and conclusion afterward.

Remember that good Christ-expressing writing demonstrates love for one's neighbor. It does this by following the worldview themes of logic, virtue, and discernment. Your writing should show discernment in the words you choose to communicate to your neighbor, honesty in communicating your point of view, and orderliness in structuring your communication to make sense to others and not just to you.

Using Third Person

In the narrative essay you were allowed to write using first person (*I*, *we*). In this more formal paper you should use third person (*he*, *she*, *it*, *they*). Using third person will make the essay sound more credible and professional.

It is now time to revise your draft. As with other writing assignments, part of the revision process includes conducting peer reviews. Use the questions below to evaluate both your draft and your peer's draft.

1. Read your paper aloud to yourself.
2. Ask yourself the questions in the Revising Checklist as you read.
3. Read your essay to a classmate. Let him tell you how it sounds to his ear. Allow your classmate to read your essay to himself and make suggestions.

	Revising Checklist
Ideas	☐ Does my introduction contain the five required elements? ☐ Does my thesis contain the required elements? ☐ Do I include relevant and reliable facts in the body paragraphs? ☐ Does my conclusion contain the two required elements?
Organization	☐ Does my essay contain five paragraphs (introduction, three body paragraphs, and conclusion)? ☐ Do I express my ideas in an easy-to-understand way (i.e., logically, clearly)? ☐ Do I use a clear organizational method to order my ideas?
Word Choice	☐ Do I provide too much explanation? Not enough? ☐ Do I make good use of strong verbs and vivid nouns?
Voice	☐ Is my language appropriate (i.e., no slang or contractions)? ☐ Do I include transitional words and phrases within paragraphs as well as between paragraphs? ☐ Do my language and style inspire my audience to keep reading?
Sentence Fluency	☐ Do I express my thoughts in complete sentences? ☐ Do I provide variety in sentence length and structure? ☐ Do my words and phrases have a good rhythm and flow?

PROOFREADING

PLANNING | DRAFTING | REVISING | PROOFREADING | PUBLISHING

Now that you have revised the major ideas in your paper, it is time to focus on the sixth writing trait: conventions. It is important that you check carefully to ensure you have no mistakes in spelling, mechanics, or grammar. Such mistakes distract the readers from the ideas you are presenting and damage your credibility, making it less likely that your readers will be persuaded by your paper. Use the following checklist to guide you as you proofread your essay.

	Proofreader's Checklist
Conventions	❑ The essay follows the teacher's formatting guidelines and correct MLA format. ❑ There are no spelling errors. ❑ There are no grammar errors. ❑ There are no errors in capitalization or punctuation.

PUBLISHING

PLANNING | DRAFTING | REVISING | PROOFREADING | PUBLISHING

Now that your critique is finished, you have the opportunity to present your final work to your peers and hear your peers present their work to you. Be sure to follow the presentation checklist below.

- Display your ad and briefly explain why you chose this ad for your project.
- Demonstrate clear planning.
- Demonstrate confidence and understanding of your content.
- Use appropriate language for the purpose, audience, and topic.
- Demonstrate polished presentation etiquette.
- When finished, give your peers time to ask questions about your presentation.

In addition to presenting your critique, remember to be a good audience member when you are listening to and critiquing other students' presentations. Keep in mind that Christ-expression is not limited to writing. It includes how you listen and speak to others. Love for God should motivate Christians to love each other by listening well, respecting other people's points of view, and motivating others with positive and constructive criticism. When you are critiquing others' presentations, be sure to praise the things they have done well and kindly point out the ways they can improve.

CHAPTER 16

PRONOUN USAGE

WHAT'S THE USE OF PRONOUNS?

As useful as they are, pronouns can be surprisingly tricky little substitutes. Overusing pronouns can leave a reader bored and confused, and problem pronouns can cause frustration. Writers should take care to use pronouns appropriately to aid the reader's understanding.

DISCOVER!

Jules Verne, the famous French science-fiction writer, uses pronouns effectively to be clear and concise. In this excerpt from A Journey to the Center of the Earth, *the professor, Henry, and Hans start their treacherous and exciting descent into the mysterious world inside the earth. How would your reading be affected if you replaced the pronouns with nouns?*

MENTOR TEXT

"Now," said my uncle, as soon as he had completed this important preparation, "let us see about the baggage. It must be divided into three separate parcels, and each of us must carry one on his back. I allude to the more important and fragile articles."

My worthy and ingenious uncle did not appear to consider that we came under that denomination.

"Hans," he continued, "you will take charge of the tools and some of the provisions; you, Harry, must take [. . .] arms. I will load myself with the rest of the eatables, and with the more delicate instruments."

"But," I exclaimed, "our clothes, this mass of cord and ladders—who will undertake to carry them down?"

"They will go down of themselves."

"And how so?" I asked.

"You shall see."

—Jules Verne, *Journey to the Center of the Earth*

CLEAR PRONOUN REFERENCE

A pronoun must clearly refer to its antecedent. When the antecedent is clear, the resulting sentence is meaningful. When the antecedent is ambiguous or remote, the resulting sentence will be either puzzling or misleading. Both ambiguous and remote pronouns can be corrected by rewriting the sentence to make the antecedent clear.

A pronoun is **ambiguous** when it has more than one noun that is a possible antecedent.

Unclear: When Nick whispered to Bruno, he looked confused.
Clear: Nick look confused when he whispered to Bruno.
Clear: When Nick whispered to him, Bruno looked confused.
Unclear: Maggie told Becca that her friends were planning a party.
Clear: Maggie told Becca, "Your friends are planning a party."
Clear: Maggie told Becca, "My friends are planning a party."

A pronoun is **remote** when it is too far removed from its antecedent, and the reader loses the connection, or relationship, of the pronoun to its antecedent.

Unclear: Jill sat contentedly on her boat's hull looking at her colorful new mainsail in the early morning sun. She had ordered a new sail two weeks ago to replace the tattered, faded one. Now *it* flapped carelessly in the salty breeze.

Clear: Jill sat contentedly on her boat's hull in the early morning sun. Two weeks ago, she had ordered a colorful new mainsail to replace the faded old one. Now *the colorful new sail* flapped carelessly in the salty breeze.

Unclear: Jill loved to sail her catamaran. Whenever she could, her best friend Laura would go with her and work the jib while she worked the mainsail and the rudder. On sunny Saturday mornings, *she* would go to the boatyard and drag the boat to the water's edge where she would get the rigging set up and wait in the salty sea breeze for *her* friend to arrive.

Clear: Jill loved to sail her catamaran. Whenever she could, her best friend Laura would go with her and work the jib while Jill worked the mainsail and the rudder. On sunny Saturday mornings, *Jill* would go to the boatyard and drag the boat to the water's edge where she would get the rigging set up and wait in the salty sea breeze for *Laura* to arrive.

Practice the Skill

Underline the ambiguous pronoun in each sentence. Write in the blank what you think the pronoun is referring to.

1. The people of Hawaii elect a governor and a lieutenant governor, and they appoint the Supreme Court justices, circuit court justices, and members of the governor's cabinet.

   ____

2. In the Hawaiian government, the governor appoints a judge. He must meet certain qualifications set down by the Hawaiian constitution.

   ____

3. The government collects an income tax as well as a business volume tax, and it is returned to companies for construction and grants.

   ____

4. The county of Honolulu includes Oahu; it has a very unusual government system.

   ____

5. The Hawaiian constitutional convention wrote a very simple and clear governing document, and it instituted an organized government.

   ____

Underline the remote pronoun in each sentence. Write in the blank what you think the pronoun is referring to.

6. Pearl Harbor, an old military base located near Camp H. M. Smith, is surrounded by a deep-water lagoon. James Cook could not reach it though because of the reef blocking his way.

   ____

7. Rule by the upper class has been replaced by the labor movement. The government, however, is still trying to retain some control over them.

   ____

8. The Democratic Party has grown bigger than the Republican Party. Famous and powerful financial donors have helped, but it still struggles to win some elections.

   ____

9. Cities and counties in the island state fight the federal bureaucracy in order to determine the control of schools, but change is very difficult for them.

   ____

10. Kamehameha wanted to gain control of Hawaii from his rival, Kalanikūpule, and with his troops, soundly defeated the local chiefs, and they became governors of the islands.

   ____

Review the Skill

Rewrite the sentence to correct the unclear pronoun-antecedent relationship. If the sentence is correct, write *C* on the line.

11. In Shakespeare's play *King Lear*, he decides to divide his kingdom among his three daughters.

12. King Lear and his courtier, Kent, meet with the daughters, and he has a foolish contest to determine which girl loves her father best.

13. Goneril declares that her love is inexpressible just before Regan claims single devotion toward their father. She says that her love cannot be put into words.

14. After her older sisters have spoken, Cordelia simply tells Lear that she loves him only as much as duty requires from a daughter.

15. After Kent tells the angry king that Cordelia's love is genuine, he banishes him from the kingdom.

16. Kent faithfully follows his king; however, delusions are weakening the king's mind, and he is forced to disguise himself.

17. King Lear and the disguised Kent intend to live with the king's daughters Goneril and Regan, but through increasing deception and manipulation, the play reveals that they are extremely selfish and cruel.

18. The king realizes that his youngest daughter Cordelia and his faithful courtier are honest and that Goneril and Regan are treacherous and manipulative. The doomed Lear deeply regrets his cruelty to them.

19. After Kent is recognized by Lear, he is overcome by grief.

20. While watching the king die, Kent sees from Lear's tragic life that fulfilling duty and being honest are more important than empty flattery.

INDEFINITE ANTECEDENTS OF PERSONAL PRONOUNS

Occasionally a pronoun that has no definite antecedent is used in writing. The antecedent for a pronoun like this is understood, much like the subject of an imperative sentence is understood. An indefinite pronoun like *someone* or *everybody* is intended to be indefinite and to refer to no specific individual or group. However, personal pronouns such as *they*, *it*, or *you* are normally expected to have clear antecedents and to refer to definite individuals or groups.

Indefinite *they*

In written English, *they* should be used only with a definite antecedent. Usually a specific noun or pronoun can be supplied in place of the indefinite *they*.

Indefinite *they*: In Alaska *they* are used to cold weather and snow.
Correct: In Alaska *people* are used to cold weather and snow.
More precise: *Alaskans* are used to cold weather and snow.
Indefinite *they*: During school *they* conduct fire drills.
Correct: During school *the administration* conducts fire drills.

Indefinite *it*

It should not be used as an indefinite pronoun in the phrase "it says." Use the specific name of the source of information instead.

Indefinite *it*: In our school newspaper *it* says that the walk-a-thon raised over one thousand dollars.
Correct: Our school *newspaper* says that the walk-a-thon raised over one thousand dollars.

It should also not be used to refer to an implied idea. Pronouns should refer to nouns present in the passage.

Indefinite *it*: Joe won the contest, and *it* surprised me.
Correct: I was surprised that Joe won the contest.
Correct: Joe's victory in the contest surprised me.

Indefinite *you*

In informal speaking and writing, the personal pronoun *you* is often used as an indefinite pronoun to refer to people in general. *You* is also sometimes used to refer to the listener or reader when instructions are being given. Avoid using *you* as an indefinite pronoun in formal speaking or writing.

Informal: The chapel speaker said *you* should memorize Scripture regularly.
Less informal: The chapel speaker said that a *person* should memorize Scripture regularly.
Most formal: The chapel speaker said that *one* should memorize Scripture regularly.
Informal: Be careful to handle all chemicals with *your* gloves.
Formal: *One* must be careful to handle all chemicals with *his* gloves.

Practice the Skill

Write in the blank the letter of the sentence that has no problem with pronoun reference.

_______ 1. **A** The legend of King Arthur says that he became the king of Britain by pulling a sword from a stone.
B In the legend of King Arthur, it says that he became the king of Britain by pulling a sword from a stone.

_______ 2. **A** In Britain, the people were joyful when Arthur married Princess Guinevere.
B In Britain, they were joyful when Arthur married Princess Guinevere.

_______ 3. **A** When Guinevere and Arthur were married, it was an important event for the country.
B Guinevere and Arthur's wedding was an important event for the country.

_______ 4. **A** Camelot is the most famous city of the legend.
B They say that Camelot is the most famous city of the legend.

_______ 5. **A** In Camelot, you could see the famous Knights of the Round Table.
B In Camelot, one could see the famous Knights of the Round Table.

_______ 6. **A** The men were the strongest and best in Britain, and it was a symbol of justice and bravery.
B The men were the strongest and best in Britain, and the Round Table was a symbol of justice and bravery.

_______ 7. **A** The people of Britain all considered Sir Lancelot to be the greatest knight of them all.
B They all considered Sir Lancelot to be the greatest knight of them all.

_______ 8. **A** If you read the story, you will read of Lancelot's promise to be loyal to Arthur.
B If one reads the story, one will read of Lancelot's promise to be loyal to Arthur.

_______ 9. **A** Arthur may have been a real person, but most of it is just fascinating legend.
B Arthur may have been a real person, but most of the story is just fascinating legend.

_______ 10. **A** The legend of Arthur forms the basis for innumerable stories; everyone should read some of them.
B The legend of Arthur forms the basis for innumerable stories; they should read some of them.

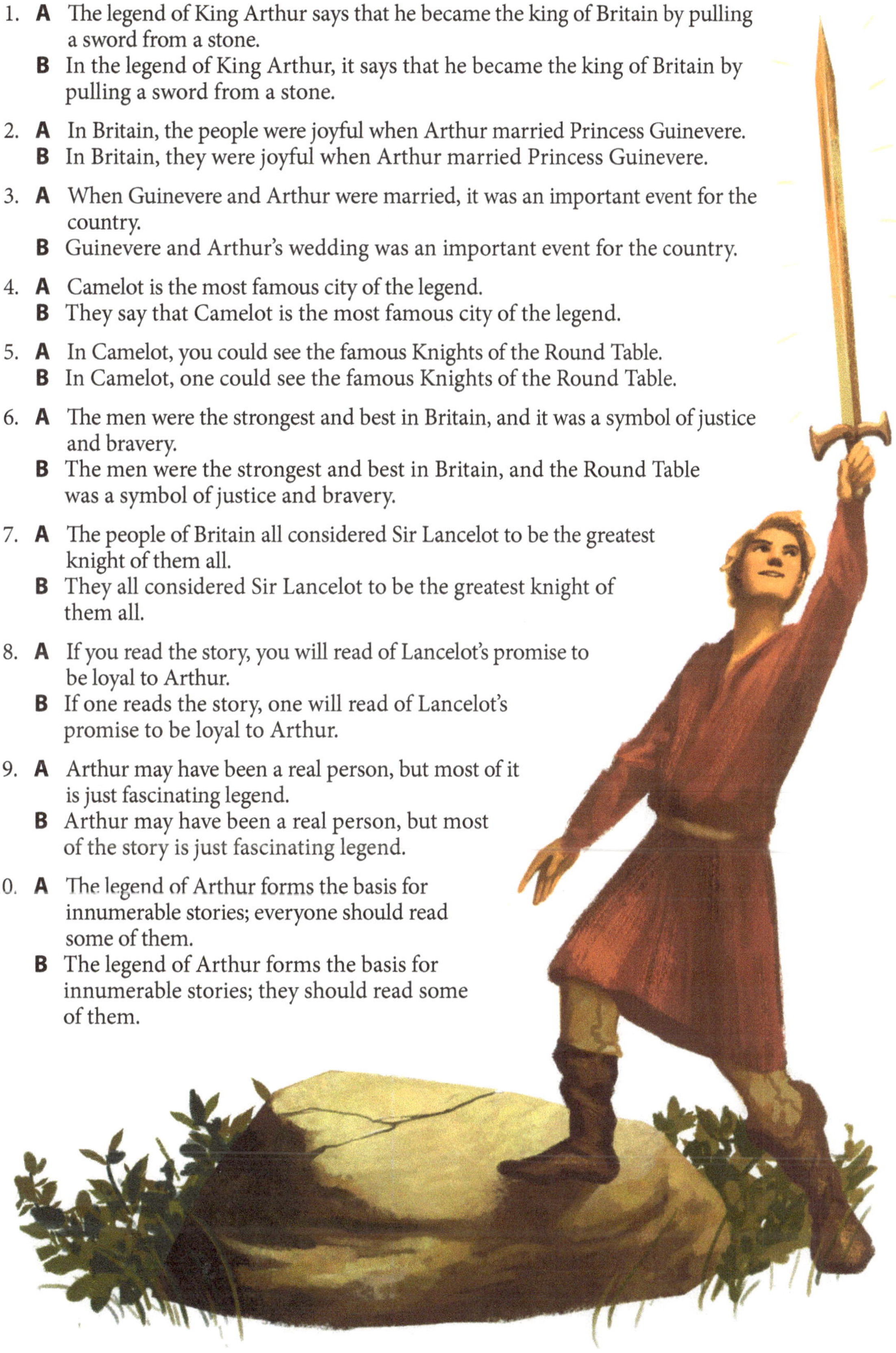

Review the Skill

Rewrite the following sentences to make the pronoun-antecedent relationship clear. If the sentence is correct, write *C* on the line.

11. Our British literature teacher believes that you should be familiar with the history of England.

12. In our literature book it says that the first Tudor ruler was Henry VII.

13. Henry VIII influenced the history of England by separating the Church of England and the Roman Catholic Church. He made the monarch the head of it.

14. Henry VIII is remembered for his pleasure-seeking lifestyle, his cruelty, and his six wives.

15. The first three of Henry's six wives were Catherine of Aragon, Anne Boleyn, and Jane Seymour. She gave birth to Edward VI.

16. Henry VIII also had two daughters, Mary and Elizabeth. When Edward VI died, she became queen.

17. They did not want Catholic Mary to become queen.

18. Mary distrusted Elizabeth, so she avoided her.

19. Mary Queen of Scots was Elizabeth's cousin. She had her tried and executed for high treason.

____

____

20. Elizabeth never married but used her single status to her advantage.

____

____

USING SUBJECTIVE AND OBJECTIVE CASE PRONOUNS CORRECTLY

Subjective Case

Use the **subjective case** for pronouns functioning as subjects or predicate nouns.

Subject: *I* went to the awards ceremony.
We enjoyed the presentations.
They had good seats.

Predicate Noun: "May I speak with Judge Saunders?" "This is *she*."
The driver of that car is *he*.
The club members are *they*.

Informal speech does not insist on the latter part of the rule. Expressions such as "It's me" or "That's her" are generally accepted in most conversations. However, formal written or spoken communication requires "It is I." This problem can sometimes be avoided. For example, when a telephone caller asks to speak with John, he could answer simply, "This is John."

Compound Subjects and Compound Predicate Nouns

Use the same rules for compound subjects and predicate nouns as you use for single subjects and predicate nouns.

Single: *I* brought a friend to the ceremony.
Compound: *Peyton and I* brought a friend to the ceremony.
Single: The president of the class was *I*.
Compound: The copresidents of the class were *Roger and I*.

If you are unsure which pronoun case to use in a compound, try dropping the other part of the compound. The correct choice will usually be clear.

Objective Case

Use the **objective case** for pronouns functioning as direct objects, indirect objects, or objects of prepositions.

Direct object: Great Britain governed the Australian colonies until the mid-1800s.
Great Britain governed *them* until the mid-1800s.

Indirect object: The Parliament of the United Kingdom granted local governments self-legislation.
The Parliament of the United Kingdom granted *them* self-legislation.

Object of preposition: Today Australians have a voluntary cooperation with the British.
Today Australians have a voluntary cooperation with *them*.

Compound Objects

Use the same rules for compound objects as you use for single objects.

Single: I visited *her* in Australia last summer.
Compound: I visited *Olivia and her* in Australia last summer.

If you are unsure which pronoun case to use in a compound, try dropping the other part of the compound. The correct choice will usually be clear.

Using *We* and *Us* Correctly

Occasionally, the pronouns *we* and *us* need to be used in combination with nouns. Remember to use the subjective case pronoun *we* for subjects and the objective case pronoun *us* for objects. Dropping the noun from the sentence will help you choose the pronoun with the correct case.

Subjective: *We* earned good grades on the test.
Objective: *Us* earned good grades on the test.
Correct: *We* students earned good grades on the test.

Subjective: The teachers expected this result of *we*.
Objective: The teachers expected this result of *us*.
Correct: The teachers expected this result of *us* students.

Using *Who* and *Whom* Correctly

The pronouns *who* and *whom* are often used to ask questions. *Who* is the subjective case form. *Whom* is the objective case form.

Subject: *Who* was on the phone?
Direct Object: *Whom* did the detective recognize?
Object of Preposition: She wanted to speak to *whom*?

Sometimes you may find it helpful to rearrange interrogative sentences into normal sentence order to see sentence patterns more clearly.

Original: *Whom* did the detective recognize?
Rearranged: The detective did recognize *whom*?

You may also want to rearrange some dependent clauses to see the sentence pattern.

Original: The suspect, *whom* the detective recognized, was ready to cooperate.
Rearranged: the detective recognized *whom*

Practice the Skill

Underline the correct pronoun from the choices in parentheses.

1. Do (you, he) remember when the Czech Republic was formed?
2. (Her, She) and (I, me) watched a video about it online.
3. Public dissatisfaction caused the communist leaders to lose power. (They, Them) resigned in 1989.
4. Because of tension between the Czechs and Slovaks, the leaders of the country had to make a decision. In 1992 (them, they) decided to split Czechoslovakia into two nations, the Czech Republic and Slovakia.
5. The Czech Republic became an independent country on January 1, 1993. (They, It) is a parliamentary democracy.

Underline the correct pronoun.

6. Peter Alekseyevich was a powerful Russian czar, and his people gave (he, him) the nickname "Peter the Great."
7. Peter challenged the Turks with his superior navy and gained a warm-water harbor by defeating (they, them).
8. His mother found Peter a wife, and the marriage was happy for (he, him) and (she, her).
9. In England, he readily learned many new skills about shipbuilding and implemented (they, them) in his own country.
10. The story of Peter the Great inspires all of (we, us) to reach for our goals.

Underline the correct pronoun.

11. (We, Us) Americans should be thankful for the free country in which we live.

12. God has blessed (we, us) citizens of the United States.

13. (We, Us) Christians should do what we can to give back to our country.

14. Many opportunities for service await (we, us) young people.

15. (We, Us) students should learn as much as we can about the government of our country.

Underline the correct pronoun from the choices in parentheses. Identify the case of the pronoun as *subj* (subjective) or *obj* (objective).

_______ 16. (Who, Whom) is the head of government in the United States?

_______ 17. (Who, Whom) makes new laws?

_______ 18. By (who, whom) are the laws enforced?

_______ 19. (Who, Whom) is in charge of all investigations?

_______ 20. By (who, whom) are the laws made and amended?

Review the Skill

Write in the blank an appropriate pronoun to complete the sentence. Use a variety of pronouns; use *you* only once.

_______ 21. Have _?_ ever visited Washington, DC?

_______ 22. My family and _?_ went there on vacation last summer.

_______ 23. While there, _?_ toured the White House.

_______ 24. Fans of the State Dining Room were my sister and _?_ .

_______ 25. _?_ can accommodate one hundred and forty guests for a state dinner.

Write in the blank an appropriate pronoun to complete the sentence. Use a variety of pronouns, but do not use *you* or *it*.

_______ 26. Yesterday, Mrs. Whitfield asked _?_ to go on a field trip with her eighth grade history class.

_______ 27. I will be visiting our state's capital in Lansing, Michigan, with _?_ .

_______ 28. Mrs. Whitfield gave _?_ a list of the names of the students in my group.

_______ 29. She wants _?_ to meet the governor.

_______ 30. Last month the students wrote letters to _?_ .

Write in the blank the correct pronoun to complete the sentence: *we* or *us*.

_______ 31. ? citizens need a leader who will promote righteousness and fair judgment in our country.

_______ 32. A good leader will further the cause of education for ? .

_______ 33. His or her personal character will be a good example to ? .

_______ 34. For our children, ? parents would appreciate adequate health facilities and a healthy environment.

_______ 35. ? people cannot expect all these things from the government.

Write in the blank the correct pronoun to complete the sentence: *who* or *whom*.

_______ 36. ? ruled Spain after the Spanish Civil War until his death in 1975?

_______ 37. After Francisco Franco's death, partial control of the government was given to ? ?

_______ 38. The right to vote was given to ? ?

_______ 39. The people of Spain voted ? into office?

_______ 40. ? are the main government officials?

Use the Skill

Compose a paragraph (5–7 sentences) using both subjective and objective personal pronouns. Do not use *you* or *it*.

- Write a diary entry from the point of view of your favorite literary character.
- Write a postcard home telling about a trip you and a friend are on.

OTHER PRONOUN PROBLEMS

Possessive Pronouns and Contractions

Some possessive pronouns and contractions are homonym pairs. **Homonyms** are words that sound the same (and may or may not have the same spelling) but mean different things. Be careful to spell possessive personal pronouns correctly—without apostrophes.

Your is a possessive pronoun.	The engraving in *your* textbook is of Julius Caesar.
You're is a contraction of *you are*.	*You're* probably aware that Caesar wore a leafy garland.
Its is a possessive pronoun.	*Its* laurel leaves signified military superiority.
It's is a contraction of *it is*.	*It's* a garland worn by Roman rulers.
Whose is a possessive pronoun.	*Whose* crown is kept in the National Museum of Wales at Cardiff?
Who's is a contraction of who is.	The Prince of Wales is the one *who's* wearing a demi-crown.
Their is a possessive pronoun.	The crowns of Henry III and Eleanor of Castile are depicted on *their* tombs in Westminster Abbey.
They're is a contraction of *they are*.	*They're* presently not jeweled, although they appear to have had jewels in the past.
There is an adverb.	You can see many tombs *there*.
Theirs is a possessive pronoun.	Our class studied pictures of the crowns worn by Edward the Confessor and Casimir III. *Theirs* were very ornate.
There's is a contraction of *there is*.	*There's* even a picture of Peter the Great's crown.

Reflexive and Intensive Pronouns

Reflexive pronouns act like a mirror, reflecting the subject. They can function as the direct object, indirect object, or object of a preposition. If the reflexive pronoun were omitted, the sentence would not make sense. In the same way that a mirror cannot reflect something that is not there, a reflexive pronoun cannot be used if the person or thing it refers to is not the subject of the sentence. Refer to Lesson 42 for the list of reflexive pronouns.

Intensive pronouns, on the other hand, do not reflect subjects, they intensify them, suggesting *no one else*. They do not have a formal function in sentences and can be removed without affecting the meaning of the text.

Incorrect: Vivian and *myself* studied the lineage of King David.
Correct: Vivian and *I* studied the lineage of King David.
Correct: I did not study the lineage of King David by *myself*.
Incorrect: Jesus' heritage was interesting to Vivian and *myself*.
Correct: Jesus' heritage was interesting to Vivian and *me*.
Correct: I *myself* was interested in Jesus' heritage.

Never use the nonstandard forms *hisself* or *theirselves*. Instead use *himself* or *themselves*.

Incorrect: Josh found *hisself* a job to pay for a new bike.
Correct: Josh found *himself* a job to pay for a new bike.
Incorrect: His parents *theirselves* had already bought it for him.
Correct: His parents *themselves* had already bought it for him.

Courtesy Order

When you use personal pronouns in pairs that include first-person pronouns, put the one referring to yourself last.

The teacher talked with *Joey and me*.
The teacher talked with *him and me*.
John and I will talk to the teacher.
He and I will talk to the teacher.

Always mention the person you are addressing first.

You and he had the correct answers.
You and they will wait after class for further instructions.
I will be going with *you and her*.

Practice the Skill

Underline the correct word to complete the sentence. If the word is a contraction, write in the blank the words that the contraction represents.

_______ 1. (Whose, Who's) asking (her, me) and (her, me) about the life of President Calvin Coolidge?

_______ 2. Oh, (your, you're) inquiring because (your, you're) younger brother is writing a report about his life.

_______ 3. (I, She) and (I, She) will tell the story to (him, you) and (him, you).

_______ 4. (Its, It's) very interesting.

_______ 5. In 1905, Coolidge married Grace Anna Goodhue. (Their, They're) personalities were very different. She was fun and talkative; he was solemn and silent.

_______ 6. Vice President Coolidge and his family were taking (their, they're) vacation when President Harding died.

_______ 7. Calvin Coolidge was the only president (whose, who's) father, a notary public, administered the oath of office to him.

_______ 8. However, Attorney General Harry M. Daugherty questioned (its, it's) validity because Coolidge's father had authority to swear in only state officials from Vermont.

_______ 9. Coolidge is the president (whose, who's) known for the statement, "I do not choose to run for president in 1928."

_______ 10. Does that answer some of (your, you're) questions?

Write in the blank the correct reflexive or intensive pronoun to complete the sentence.

_______________ 11. Just thirty minutes before the ceremony, Kirsten studied _?_ in the mirror.

_______________ 12. Ted knew _?_ to be emotional in these types of situations.

_______________ 13. Denise _?_ enjoyed the wedding song and violin solo.

_______________ 14. The flower girl and ring bearer taught _?_ how to walk down the aisle properly.

_______________ 15. The wedding cake _?_ was delicious.

_______________ 16. Todd _?_ decorated the wedding car with bells and balloons.

_______________ 17. The wedding party gathered _?_ together for a dinner after the rehearsal.

_______________ 18. The entire day was in _?_ a miracle.

_______________ 19. The bride and groom _?_ did not get any wedding cake on each other.

_______________ 20. The father of the bride thought to _?_ that he had never seen a more beautiful bride.

Review the Skill

Underline any incorrect pronoun and write its correction in the blank. If the sentence contains no pronoun errors, write C in the blank.

________________ 21. Are you on you're way to class?

________________ 22. Yes, its up on the next floor.

________________ 23. Who's class are you going to?

________________ 24. It's the one your mother teaches.

________________ 25. Me and you can walk to class together if you want.

________________ 26. How do you feel about being in your mother's class?

________________ 27. It's fine. No big deal.

________________ 28. Your mom wants to talk to you and Chip.

________________ 29. Their on their way!

________________ 30. Its fun to be a student in the school where your mother teaches.

Underline any incorrect pronoun and write its correction in the blank. If the sentence contains no pronoun errors, write C in the blank.

________________ 31. I myself read a biography on the lives of William and Mary of Orange.

________________ 32. We taught us about their lives.

________________ 33. You yourself stated that they were excellent rulers.

________________ 34. Mary devoted her to religious and charitable projects.

________________ 35. Mary's Catholic father, James II, became king of England in 1685. However, she herself was Protestant.

________________ 36. The Protestant religious and political leaders saved theirselves from problems with Catholic James II by asking Protestant William and Mary to take over the monarchy.

________________ 37. In 1688 William hisself landed in England and permitted James II to flee to France.

________________ 38. In 1689 William and Mary proclaimed them king and queen of England.

____________________ 39. They limited theirselves and their power by adopting what became known as the Bill of Rights.

____________________ 40. The College of William and Mary was founded in 1693 in Williamsburg, Virginia. William and Mary founded it themselves.

BIO POEMS
Writing Traits: Voice, Organization

Listen Up!

Writing poetry may seem daunting. Perhaps you feel like you do not have what it takes. Learning how to write poetry does not have to be a burden when you follow a pattern. You may find that you quite enjoy it! The poem below is a pattern poem called a **bio poem**. Bio poems provide a creative way to write about a favorite character from literature, a historical figure you are studying, or even a friend or family member!

Read the following bio poem about a historical figure. Note the precise language and the organized, logical pattern that the poem follows. Pay attention to the voice of the poem. What does the poem's voice make you think of its subject?

MENTOR TEXT

Ronald.

Heroic, idealistic, intelligent, powerful.

Doting husband to his wife and faithful friend to his country.

Lover of his family, his ranch, and his horses.

Who feels the power of quiet strength, the honorable weight of responsibility, and the enduring spirit of optimism.

Who needs loyal men to walk in front of him, a devoted wife to walk beside him, and a trusting country to stand behind him.

Who fears no pretentious political opponent; nor hollow threat from foreign enemies; nor piercing bullet propelled by a madman.

Who gives comfort to a nation suffering an explosion of grief, gives warning to a contentious Communist president, and gives courage to brave, young troops.

Who would like to see domestic economic strength restored, America's youth strive for higher education, and his beloved country shine as that "city on a hill."

Resident of the Midwestern plains, Hollywood Hills, and Pennsylvania Avenue.

Reagan.

WRITING TOOLBOX

Take Notes!

Summarize the purpose or benefit of writing a pattern poem and the importance of voice in this type of poem.

Bio poems are a type of pattern poem. As short creative biographies, they give details of the subject's personality traits; his relationships; what he loves, feels, needs, and fears; and what his ambitions are.

A bio poem is strictly eleven lines long. Your poem should begin with the first name of your subject and end with his or her last name. Since it is biographical in nature as well as descriptive, consider the voice you want to give to the subject of your poem. As you describe your historical figure or the classmate, friend, or family member you choose, keep Christ-expression in mind.

Line 1	First name
Line 2	Four traits that describe character
Line 3	Relative ("brother," "sister," daughter," etc.) of
Line 4	Lover of (list three things or people)
Line 5	Who feels (three items)
Line 6	Who needs (three items)
Line 7	Who fears (three items)
Line 8	Who gives (three items)
Line 9	Who would like to see (three items)
Line 10	Resident of
Line 11	Last name

Partner Up!

Write a bio poem about a historical figure you have studied or are studying this year or about a character from literature that you both know. Work through the poem line by line, incorporating creative elements and Christ-expression in your collective voice.

Try It Out!

Write a bio poem about someone you know personally. The voice of your poem should be creative and Christ-honoring.

CHAPTER REVIEW

Subjective, Objective, and Possessive Cases

Underline the correct pronouns to complete the sentence.

1. The history of the United States is extremely important to (you and I, you and me).
2. Because the people who settled this country came from many different parts of the world, (they, them) had to overcome many cultural differences.
3. The people and (them, their) descendants had to learn to live together peacefully.
4. Cooperation and patriotism helped the country and (it's, its) people survive hardships.
5. (We, Us) should imitate their attitude of cooperation and patriotism.
6. Early decisions about government, religion, and other things affect (we, us) even today.
7. (You and I, You and me) should be thankful for the sacrifice on the part of our ancestors.
8. (We, Us) have prospered because of the foresight of our Founding Fathers.

We, Us, Who, or Whom

Choose the correct pronoun to complete the sentence. Write in the blank the letter that corresponds to the correct answer.

A we
B us
C who
D whom

_______ 9. _?_ students learned about Roman history in school this year.

_______ 10. _?_ was one of the greatest Roman military leaders?

_______ 11. For _?_ did Julius Caesar make many improvements?

_______ 12. One of his most valuable improvements that affects _?_ today was his new calendar.

_______ 13. By _?_ was Caesar betrayed?

_______ 14. _?_ was considered to be one of the best Roman orators and writers?

_______ 15. _?_ studied Caesar's direct and clear style of writing.

Problem Pronouns

Underline the correct word to complete the sentence.

16. (Your, You're) studying the ancient Greek philosophers in your history class, right?
17. (Their, They're) philosophies are very interesting!
18. (Whose, Who's) philosophy do you find most interesting?
19. (Its, It's) the philosophy that combines knowledge and wisdom.
20. (Theirs, There's) no completely true philosophy outside of the Bible.

Courtesy Order and Reflexive/Intensive Pronouns

Underline the correct pronouns to complete the sentence.

21. The make-up history test was given to (he, him, himself) and (I, me, myself).
22. (She, I, Me) and (she, I, me) had studied ancient history for hours the night before.
23. (He, You, Him) and (he, him, you) have one hour to complete the exam.
24. (He, I, me) and (He, I, me) finished at the same time.
25. Only one point differed between the scores of (he, you, him) and (he, you, him).

Clear Pronoun Reference

Identify each sentence as having correct or incorrect pronoun reference. Write in the blank the letter that corresponds to the correct answer. If you choose *B*, rewrite the sentence correctly in the space provided.

A correct sentence
B incorrect pronoun reference

_______ 26. Diana and Kay studied ancient Greece and Rome. They were full of adventure.

____

_______ 27. Diana asked Kay whether she could explain the Odyssey.

____

_______ 28. Although the Odyssey tells the adventures of Odysseus and his crew, it also portrays the inner struggle between pride and wisdom.

____

_______ 29. Odysseus finally returned, but it was not what he expected.

____

_______ 30. Kay told Diana that she should learn from the victories and failures of Odysseus.

____

CHAPTER 17

CAPITALIZATION AND PUNCTUATION

WHY SHOULD I WORRY ABOUT DETAILS?

In 1962, NASA launched the Mariner I, a rocket whose mission was to fly by Venus and collect data. However, the rocket veered off course minutes later and was destroyed. The problem was a single hyphen that somebody omitted from the computer programming. This small mistake cost approximately $80 million.

Sometimes, being attentive to details can seem like a waste of time. However, the Bible reminds us that attention to details is important. God pays attention to every detail of our lives, including the number of hairs on our heads (Luke 12:7), and Jesus said that not one jot (the smallest Hebrew letter) or tittle (the smallest part of a Hebrew letter) will change from His Word (Matthew 5:18). As you work through this chapter, you will notice that the rules for capitalization and punctuation require you to be very detail oriented. This is good because even the smallest details are important in order to successfully communicate truth to our neighbor. Keep in mind that practicing Christ-expression includes expressing Christ in the smallest details.

PROPER NOUNS

As you learned in Lesson 36, writers capitalize proper nouns and their abbreviations, but they do not capitalize common nouns. The problem comes when they must decide which nouns are common and which are proper. The rules of capitalization in this chapter can help you decide which words to capitalize in your own writing.

People and Places

Names and initials	**W**arren **B**axter **I**nga **M**. **L**indstrom
Titles used with a name • Do not capitalize titles used in place of a person's name.	**P**resident **W**ilson **G**rand **D**uchess **O**lga **D**r. **J**oanne **J**anos **J**oanne **J**anos, **MD** The **s**enator issued a statement today.
Family words used as proper nouns • If a word for a family relationship is modified by an adjective, it is not being used as a proper noun.	Did you remember to send **G**randmother a birthday card? My **g**randmother coached a basketball team when she was young.
Countries Continents	**A**rgentina **S**outh **A**merica
Cities States	**B**ismarck **N**orth **D**akota
Sections of a country or the world • Do not capitalize compass words when they indicate direction.	**U**pper **P**eninsula **M**iddle **E**ast a **n**orthbound flight
Geographic features	**G**rand **C**anyon **G**reat **P**lains *But:* The **m**ountains are beautiful in winter.
Recreational Areas	**S**uperior **N**ational **F**orest **C**entral **P**ark *But:* My cousin played in the **p**ark all afternoon.
Streets and Roads	**C**edar **B**oulevard **P**oinsett **H**ighway *But:* I live on the **s**treet next to the school.
Bodies of Water	**R**ice **C**reek **A**tlantic **O**cean *But:* Dad and I like to fish in that **r**iver.

Planets Stars Satellites Other heavenly bodies • Capitalize the words *earth*, *sun*, and *moon* only when they are listed with another specific heavenly body. • Never capitalize *earth* when it is preceded by *the*.	**M**ercury **A**lpha **C**entauri **I**o **U**rsa **M**ajor The two *Viking* spacecraft launched from **E**arth orbited **M**ars. *But:* The **m**oon and **s**tars are hidden by clouds tonight. What is the **e**arth's circumference?
Names of religions	**C**hristianity **H**induism
All nouns and personal pronouns referring to the one true God • Do not capitalize common nouns or pronouns referring to false gods.	**J**esus taught **H**is disciples. According to Greek mythology, the driver of the sun chariot was the **g**od Helios.
The words *Holy Bible* or *Bible* and the parts of the Bible as well as the names of sacred writings of other religions	**O**ld **T**estament **G**enesis **T**almud
Buildings Structures Monuments	**E**mpire **S**tate **B**uilding **G**olden **G**ate **B**ridge **J**efferson **M**emorial
Aircraft Spacecraft Ships Trains	**S**pirit of **S**t. **L**ouis **V**oyager 2 **A**ndrea **D**oria **O**rient **E**xpress® *But:* We traveled by **p**lane on our vacation this year.
Businesses	**S**ummit **G**ifts **H**obby **L**obby *But:* a **g**ift shop
Brand names of business products	**B**and-**A**id **R**ollerblade® **F**ord® **M**ustang *But:* **i**n-line skates, a **F**ord **c**ar
Government departments Programs Political parties	**C**entral **I**ntelligence **A**gency (**CIA**) **H**ead **S**tart **F**ederalist **P**arty
Schools	**R**iverside **H**igh **S**chool **U**niversity of **V**irginia *But:* a **h**igh **s**chool
Organizations	**R**iverside **L**ions **F**uture **F**armers of **A**merica *But:* the **t**eam, the **c**lub
Members of most organizations	a **R**epublican

Practice the Skill

Underline each capitalization error.

1. Looking into the night sky, we can see the Moon and the stars.
2. The Earth does not orbit the Sun alone; there are seven other planets.
3. Planets that have a size and density similar to the Earth's are known as terrestrial Planets.
4. The terrestrial planets are Mercury, Venus, earth, and Mars.
5. Jovian planets, jupiter, saturn, uranus, and neptune, are larger than earth and have low densities.
6. The reddish planet in the sky is Mars; it has two moons, phobos and deimos.
7. The first planet to be observed by a space probe was venus.
8. In 2006, pluto was no longer considered a planet by scientists.
9. The large size of the Sun is hard to comprehend, but a Star in the constellation orion, betelgeuse, is even five hundred times larger.
10. Our sun is just one Star among an innumerable group of stars called the milky way.

Write in the blank the letter of the choice that follows capitalization rules correctly.

_______ 11. **A** toyota Camry®
B new Testament
C the team of basketball players

_______ 12. **A** the university of Oklahoma®
B NASA
C a College in Massachusetts

_______ 13. **A** the Confederates
B a Soldier
C the book of revelation

_______ 14. **A** Pizza hut®
B Ocean Spray juice®
C Orange Juice

_______ 15. **A** the new Chevrolet® Truck in the garage
B the Washington Monument
C the tallest Building in Washington, DC

_______ 16. **A** traveling on Northwest airlines®
B the space shuttle *Columbia*
C Princeton university®

_______ 17. **A** Aphrodite, the Greek Goddess of love
B the third book of the bible, Leviticus
C Wetterland Music Company

_______ 18. **A** Robson academy
B the republican convention
C the Modern Language Association

_______ 19. **A** the Baseball team in Atlanta
B the Toronto Bluejays®
C the boston Red Sox®

_______ 20. **A** the statue of Liberty
B Brownville Technical school
C a band member

Review the Skill

Underline each capitalization error and write the correction in the blank. If the sentence is correct, write C in the blank.

_______________ 21. Did you know that my uncle Jim lives in colorado?

_______________ 22. Jim d. Bowen lives in the western part of the state near the Colorado River.

_______________ 23. Uncle Jim and aunt Lily have always lived in the West.

_______________ 24. Jim and Lily enjoy the beautiful Mountains in Colorado.

_______________ 25. Their Doctor, Jonathan Carr, MD, lives in an apartment on Crystal Street in the city of Grand Junction.

_______________ 26. The Great Sand Dunes National Monument is one of the most unusual sights in north America.

_______________ 27. Impressive peaks of the Rockies can be found in Rocky mountain National Park.

_______________ 28. Cherry Creek Lake is near Denver, Colorado.

_______________ 29. Many farmers work in the eastern area of Colorado, part of the Great plains.

_______________ 30 My aunt and uncle will take me to visit the Parks in Colorado.

Underline each capitalization error and write the correction in the blank. If the sentence is correct, write C in the blank.

_______________ 31. One of the most nourishing foods that god provides for mankind is milk.

_______________ 32. In the old testament, the richness of Canaan is emphasized when it is described in Exodus 33:3 as "a land flowing with milk and honey."

_______________ 33. Milk has always been a significant source of nutrition, and people in africa and Asia have raised cattle specifically for milk for thousands of years.

_______________ 34. In 1856, Gail Borden developed a procedure for milk condensation, and the company borden still processes milk today.

_______________ 35. Most states process milk according to conditions prescribed by the fda. Milk that meets these conditions is known as grade A milk.

_______________ 36. The students of Brookview High school in Indiana have formed a health club to encourage nutritious eating habits.

_______________ 37. The club, Healthy start, teaches students about nutrition and proper eating habits.

_______________ 38. The club meets in the johnson Building every Tuesday after school.

_______________ 39. The Members of the club are encouraged to drink at least two glasses of milk per day.

_______________ 40. The students of Brookview High in Healthy Start realize how important milk is for the mind and body.

MORE PROPER NOUNS

Cultural and Historical Terms

Nationalities Ethnicities Languages Flags	**M**exican, **P**ortuguese **H**ispanic, **A**sian **S**panish, **F**rench **U**nion **J**ack, **O**ld **G**lory
Months Days • Do not capitalize the names of the seasons.	**J**anuary, **F**ebruary **F**riday, **S**aturday **s**ummer, **w**inter
Holidays	**E**aster, **R**osh **H**ashanah
The abbreviations BC/AD and a.m./p.m. • Notice that BC ("before Christ") is correctly placed after the year and that AD (*anno Domini*, "in the year of the Lord") is correctly placed before the year. • The abbreviations a.m. and p.m. may be either capitalized or not. Whichever you choose, be consistent in your writing.	Julius Caesar first explored England in 55 **BC** William of Normandy conquered England in **AD** 1066. 8:00 **A.M.**, 5:00 **P.M.** 8:00 **a.m.**, 5:00 **p.m.**
Historical events and periods	**B**oston **T**ea **P**arty **R**enaissance **R**oaring **T**wenties
Historical documents	**M**ayflower **C**ompact **T**reaty of **V**ersailles
Special events	**A**utumn **L**eaves **F**estival **N**ew **Y**ork **W**orld's **F**air

Titles

Newspapers and magazines	***C**hicago **T**ribune* ***N**ew **Y**ork **T**imes* ***T**ime* ***R**eader's **D**igest*
Literary compositions	***T**he **P**ilgrim's **P**rogress* "**J**abberwocky" ***H**amlet*

Musical compositions	***The Emperor Concerto*** "**S**ilent **N**ight"
Works of art	Rodin's ***The Thinker*** Monet's ***Water Lilies***
Television and radio programs	***The Flintstones*** ***I Love Lucy***
Specific courses of study	**A**dvanced **A**lgebra **P**hysics 101 *But*: Did you remember to bring your textbook to **h**istory class?

Practice the Skill

Find each capitalization error. Write in the blank the letter of the correction.

_____ 1. During the Middle Ages, New Year's day was celebrated in the month of March.
- **A** ages
- **B** Day
- **C** march

_____ 2. The new year at that time began on March 25, which was a Christian Holiday known as Annunciation Day.
- **A** march
- **B** holiday
- **C** annunciation day

_____ 3. Several holiday customs, including giving gifts to the emperor, were established by the ancient romans.
- **A** Holiday
- **B** Ancient
- **C** Romans

_____ 4. In ad 567 the Church outlawed several Roman customs for many Europeans.
- **A** AD 567
- **B** roman
- **C** Europeans

_____ 5. After 1600, January 1 once again became the first day of the year. In 1752 the date became the official date for New Year's Day for americans.
- **A** january
- **B** Official
- **C** Americans

_______ 6. New Year's Day, a Winter holiday, occurs one week after Christmas.
A new year's day
B winter
C Christmas

_______ 7. A four-day celebration for Chinese People involves colorful dragon costumes and begins in January or February.
A Chinese
B people
C Dragon

_______ 8. Jewish people celebrate New Year's in the Fall on a day they call Rosh Hashanah.
A jewish
B fall
C rosh hashanah

_______ 9. Many Americans observe New Year's eve by staying up until 12:00 a.m. to bring in the new year.
A Eve
B 12:00 A.M.
C Year

_______ 10. Many special celebrations occur on New Year's Day, including the Tournament of roses Parade in California.
A day
B tournament
C Roses

Write in the blank the letter of the choice that is capitalized correctly. (Numbers 11–18 are titles, and numbers 19–20 are course names.)

_______ 11. **A** "What a friend we have in Jesus"
B "What a Friend we Have in Jesus"
C "What a Friend We Have in Jesus"

_______ 12. **A** *A Tale of Two Cities*
B *A tale of two cities*
C *a Tale of Two Cities*

_______ 13. **A** "the necklace"
B "The necklace"
C "The Necklace"

_______ 14. **A** "The Meaning of the look"
B "The Meaning of the Look"
C "The meaning of The Look"

_______ 15. **A** "Weep No More, My Lady"
B "Weep no more, my Lady"
C "Weep no More, my Lady"

_______ 16. **A** the *Chicago tribune*
B the *Chicago Tribune*
C the *chicago tribune*

_______ 17. **A** *American History*
B *american history*
C *American history*

_______ 18. **A** *sixty minutes*
B *Sixty Minutes*
C *Sixty minutes*

_______ 19. **A** world history II
B World History II
C world History II

_______ 20. **A** Introduction to Art
B Introduction to art
C introduction to art

Review the Skill

Underline each capitalization error and write the correction in the blank. If the sentence is correct, write C in the blank.

______________________ 21. Various tribes roamed into what is now Germany around 1000 BC, and some settled just north of the Roman Empire around 100 bc.

______________________ 22. Because several Germanic tribes settled there, including the Franks and Goths, the romans called the land Germania.

______________________ 23. The unification of Germany did not take place until january 18, 1871, when Wilhelm I became the first emperor of the German Empire.

______________________ 24. The reformation in Germany began in 1517 after Martin Luther challenged the teachings of the Roman Catholic Church.

______________________ 25. Beginning in 1934, Hitler ruled Nazi Germany and had millions of European Jews killed. He wanted only those of the aryan race to live in Germany.

______________________ 26. Several Nazi officials were tried for their war crimes in the famous nuremberg trials.

______________________ 27. After defeating Germany in World war II, allied leaders met at the Potsdam Conference and took away much of Germany's land.

______________________ 28. German is the official language of Germany. It is, along with French and Italian, also one of the official languages of Switzerland.

______________________ 29. In the Winter, skiing is a popular sport in the mountains of Germany.

______________________ 30. Many tourists visit the Castles of Germany.

Schloss Marienburg in Niedersachsen

Watzmann National Park, Berchtesgaden

Underline each capitalization error and write the correction in the blank. If the sentence is correct, write *C* in the blank.

_______________ 31. *Reader's digest* is one of the most widely read magazines in the world.

_______________ 32. My favorite Shakespearean play is *macbeth.*

_______________ 33 I really enjoyed calculus 101.

_______________ 34. Handel's *messiah* is performed every year on certain holidays.

_______________ 35. Michelangelo's *Moses* is a famous sculpture.

_______________ 36. One of my favorite poems is "The Road Not Taken" by Robert Frost.

_______________ 37. Norman Rockwell used to supply illustrations for the *Saturday evening post.*

_______________ 38. Every day *Fox and friends*® broadcasts the weather.

_______________ 39. Mr. Rochester is one of the main characters in the novel *Jane Eyre.*

_______________ 40. One very exciting short story is "the last lesson."

PROPER ADJECTIVES AND MORE

First Words and Parts of a Letter

The first word in a sentence	**D**o you like to participate in sports?
The first word in a line of dialogue	Mark said, "**M**y favorite sport is soccer."
Do not capitalize the second part of a divided quotation unless the second part is the beginning of a new sentence.	"**I** enjoy watching football games," said Carlos. "**D**oes that count as participation?" "**M**aybe it does," replied Ethan, "**i**f you mentally make the plays along with the players."
The first word in a line of poetry	**O**h for a closer walk with God, **A** calm and heavenly frame; **A** light to shine upon the road **T**hat leads me to the Lamb!
Only the first word (and any proper nouns or proper adjectives) in each item of a formal outline	I. **H**ounds A. **N**orwegian elkhound B. **D**achshund II. **R**etrievers A. **L**abrador retriever B. **G**olden retriever
The first word and all nouns in the greeting of a letter	**D**ear **M**ina, **D**ear **F**riends,
The first word in the closing of a letter	**S**incerely, **R**espectfully yours,

Proper Adjectives and Single Letters as Words

Proper adjectives	**T**hanksgiving dinner **I**rish linen **J**oe's neighbor
Do not capitalize a word modified by a proper adjective unless the two together form a proper name.	The **B**ritish **I**sles are home to many people who are not **B**ritish **c**itizens.
The personal pronoun I	Josey and **I** were partners in biology class.
The interjection O	Hear our prayer, **O** Lord.
Single letters used as words	Marcus earned a **B** on the physics test. Sara's mom wants her to eat an orange every day for vitamin **C**.

Practice the Skill

Write in the blank the letter of the choice that is capitalized correctly.

_______ 1. **A** Dear mother,
B Dear sir,
C Dear Jenny,

_______ 2. **A** The car is in the garage.
B the car is in the garage.
C the Car is in the garage.

_______ 3. **A** I. Winter Games
A. Cross-country Skiing
B. Tobogganing
B I. Winter games
A. Cross-country skiing
B. Tobogganing
C I. Winter Games
A. cross-country skiing
B. tobogganing

_______ 4. **A** Samuel said, "Denise, it's snowing!"
B Samuel said, "denise, it's snowing!"
C Samuel said, "Denise, It's snowing!"

_______ 5. **A** Sincerely yours,
B Sincerely Yours,
C sincerely yours,

_______ 6. **A** What a friend we have in Jesus,
all our sins and griefs to bear.
B what a friend we have in Jesus,
all our sins and griefs to bear.
C What a friend we have in Jesus,
All our sins and griefs to bear.

_______ 7. **A** "The game is canceled," Said Caleb, "because of the snow."
B "The game is canceled," said Caleb, "Because of the snow."
C "The game is canceled," said Caleb, "because of the snow."

_______ 8. **A** "We are playing volleyball on Thursday," said Alicia.
"would you like to come?"
B "We are playing volleyball on Thursday," said Alicia.
"Would you like to come?"
C "We are playing volleyball on Thursday," Said Alicia.
"Would you like to come?"

_______ 9. **A** Spirit of God, descend upon my heart;
Wean it from earth, through all its pulses move;
B Spirit of God, descend upon my heart;
wean it from earth, through all its pulses move;
C spirit of God, descend upon my heart;
Wean it from earth, through all its pulses move;

_______ 10. **A** Dear Sarah and family,
B Dear Sarah and Family,
C Dear Sarah And Family,

Write in the blank the letter of the choice that is capitalized correctly.

______ 11. **A** American transportation by waterways remains a fascinating part of american history.
B American Transportation by waterways remains a fascinating part of American History.
C American transportation by waterways remains a fascinating part of American history.

______ 12. **A** My classmates and i wonder what it would have been like to travel on an English ship like the *Mayflower*.
B My classmates and I wonder what it would have been like to travel on an English ship like the *Mayflower*.
C My classmates and I wonder what it would have been like to travel on an english ship like the *Mayflower*.

______ 13. **A** I would have enjoyed sailing in one of the fast American clipper ships.
B I would have enjoyed sailing in one of the fast American Clipper ships.
C I would have enjoyed sailing in one of the fast American Clipper Ships.

______ 14. **A** Many American cities are built on Natural harbors.
B Many American Cities are built on natural harbors.
C Many American cities are built on natural harbors.

______ 15. **A** The first steamboat to cross the atlantic Ocean was the American *Savannah*.
B The first steamboat to cross the Atlantic Ocean was the American *Savannah*.
C The first steamboat to cross the Atlantic ocean was the American *Savannah*.

______ 16. **A** The *Servia* was the first passenger ship made completely from steel to cross the Atlantic Ocean.
B The *Servia* was the first Passenger ship made completely from steel to cross the Atlantic Ocean.
C The *Servia* was the first passenger ship made completely from steel to cross the atlantic Ocean.

______ 17. **A** The Chesapeake Bay Bridge-Tunnel in Virginia is 17.6 miles long.
B The Chesapeake bay bridge-tunnel in Virginia is 17.6 miles long.
C The Chesapeake bay Bridge-tunnel in Virginia is 17.6 miles long.

______ 18. **A** Engineers still build Drawbridges to allow ships to pass.
B Engineers still build drawbridges to allow ships to pass.
C Engineers still build Drawbridges to allow Ships to pass.

______ 19. **A** Lighthouses, which help ships navigate along a rocky Shore, are operated by the Coast Guard.
B Lighthouses, which help ships navigate along a Rocky Shore, are operated by the Coast Guard.
C Lighthouses, which help ships navigate along a rocky shore, are operated by the Coast Guard.

______ 20. **A** Boston Light, the country's oldest lighthouse, has been flashing since 1716.
B Boston Light, the Country's Oldest Lighthouse, has been flashing since 1716.
C Boston Light, The Country's Oldest lighthouse, has been flashing since 1716.

Review the Skill

Underline the five capitalization errors.

21.–25. Dear Mom and dad,

I am really enjoying my week at camp. there are seven other campers in my cabin. We're trying to earn points for our team by winning as many games and contests as possible. My counselor, Steve, often asks, "Are you doing your best?"

Last night the speaker said, "joseph was successful because he was faithful in the little things even as a teenager." I've never thought about Joseph as a teenager before. "When he did not understand his difficult situation," the speaker continued, "He had confidence that God was working out everything for good."

Tomorrow we will be hiking and swimming. This week has been full of great activities, but I'm still looking forward to seeing you on Saturday.

Your Son,
Brendon

Underline each capitalization error and write the correction in the blank. If the sentence is correct, write *C* in the blank.

________________ 26. Sheep are valuable for clothing and food. The largest sheep, living in the Altai mountains of Siberia and Mongolia, are about four feet tall.

________________ 27. A notable sheep with a wide spread of horns lives in Asia and is known as the Marco polo sheep.

________________ 28. There are many kinds of North American wild sheep.

________________ 29. Sheep with fine wool are mostly descendants from the Spanish Merino Sheep.

________________ 30. A few sheep are raised for milk, such as the East Friesian Dairy sheep that live in Germany.

________________ 31. Anna earned an a on her poetry test.

________________ 32. "Since then, my God, thou hast
So brave a palace built; o dwell in it,
That it may dwell with thee at least!"
(from "Man" by George Herbert)

________________ 33. She enjoys reading poetry, but i prefer novels and short stories.

________________ 34. Our school uniforms have the letter *l* on them to represent our school mascot, the lion.

________________ 35. Anna and I agree that Frost is one of our favorite American Poets.

END MARKS AND OTHER USES FOR PERIODS

End Marks

Periods

Use a period at the end of a declarative sentence.

I will need a coat this morning.

Use a period at the end of an indirect question.

I asked her whether she wore her coat.

Use a period at the end of an imperative sentence that does not express strong emotion.

Get your coat, please.

Question Marks

Use a question mark at the end of an interrogative sentence.

Has it gotten colder outside since last night?

Exclamation Points

Use an exclamation point at the end of an exclamatory sentence.

Oh, it has started snowing outside!

Use an exclamation point at the end of an imperative sentence that expresses strong emotion.

Close that door now!

Use an exclamation point after an interjection that expresses strong emotion.

Ouch! I shut the door on my foot.

Other Uses for Periods

Initials and Abbreviations • Use a period after most initials or abbreviations.	Mr. H. K. Barker Jr.
Names and Titles • Do not use a period when abbreviating academic degrees or the names of well-known organizations.	USAF (United States Air Force) IBM (International Business Machines) Rosa Santiago, MD
Terms in Addresses • Do not use a period after state or province postal abbreviations.	Rosewood Ave. P.O. Box 50235 MA (Massachusetts) NB (New Brunswick)
Times	9:00 p.m.
Measurements • Do not use a period after abbreviations of metric measurements.	2,000 lb. 50 ft. 52 m 7 kg

Outlines and Lists

Use a period after each number or letter that shows a division of an outline.

I. First main idea
   A. Supporting idea
   B. Supporting idea
      1. Supporting detail
      2. Supporting detail
II. Second main idea

Use a period after each number or letter that precedes an item in a list.

1. walk dog
2. wash car
3. dry dishes

Decimals

Use a period as a decimal point.

$6.34
37.34 °F
25.9%

Practice the Skill

Insert the correct end mark in each of the following sentences.

1. Think about your favorite athletic competition
2. The Olympic Games are very interesting
3. When were the Games first held
4. Remember this important date
5. In 776 BC the first recorded Games were held
6. How did the Olympic Games get its name
7. The early Games were held in Olympia, Greece
8. Wow! The first Olympics had only one event—a footrace
9. In AD 394 the last of the original Olympic Games occurred
10. The tradition was revived in 1896 with an emphasis on both education and athletics

Insert any missing periods or decimal points. Write *C* if the sentence is correct.

_______ 11. The Stadium of Olympia was destroyed in the sixth century but was uncovered by archaeologists in the late 1800s

_______ 12. This discovery caused Baron Pierre de Coubertin to suggest a renewal of the Olympic games, and the IOC (International Olympic Committee) was born.

_______ 13. The Olympic flag represents the continents that participate in the games by five interlocking rings in these colors:

1 black,
2 blue,
3 green,
4 red, and
5 yellow.

_______ 14. St. Louis, Missouri, was the first city in the United States to host the modern Olympic Games.

_______ 15. Two cities in the United States have hosted the Olympics twice: Los Angeles, CA, and Lake Placid, NY

_______ 16. The Olympics have been held at high altitudes, such as at 7,349 ft in Mexico City.

_______ 17. The Games have sometimes ended in tragedy, as the 1972 Olympics in Munich, West Germany, did when terrorists entered the Israeli athletes' compound in the early morning of Sept 5, killing some athletes and taking others hostage.

_______ 18. Some events are judged on a point system. A 10.0 is the highest possible score for both diving and gymnastics.

_______ 19. In 1996 Donovan Bailey of Canada won the shortest footrace, the 100 m run, in less than 10 seconds—984 seconds exactly.

_______ 20. Carlos Lopes of Portugal won the longest footrace, the 26 mi marathon, in just over 2 hrs in 1984.

Review the Skill

Insert the correct end mark in each of the following sentences.

21. The first ice skaters tied animal bones to the bottoms of their shoes
22. I can't imagine skating on bones
23. When were metal blades first used
24. In AD 1250 the first iron blades replaced the polished bones
25. Find out when steel blades were first used
26. Steel skates were introduced in the last half of the nineteenth century
27. Do you like to skate outdoors
28. Watch out for the thin ice
29. Some speed skaters can skate up to thirty-five miles per hour
30. Can you skate that fast

Insert any missing periods or decimal points. Write *C* if the sentence is correct.

_______ 31. The USCF (United States Cycling Federation) establishes rules for road racing.

_______ 32. Mountain bikes, which are built for biking in rugged places, have 26 in wheels.

_______ 33. A popular children's bike, the BMX, is built for racing.

_______ 34. These are three main types of bike racing:
1 track racing,
2 road racing, and
3 motocross racing.

_______ 35. A bicycle introduced in 1870 was called the high-wheeler because its front wheel was 1.5 m high.

_______ 36. The first safety bicycle with equal-sized wheels was produced by J K Starley.

_______ 37. Three men biked 700 mi across Alaska.

_______ 38. They traveled past Denali, which is 20,310 ft high.

_______ 39. They carried less than 20 lbs. to make their load light as they crossed dangerous ice and turbulent rivers.

_______ 40. During their seven-week adventure, they once had to travel for 25 hrs without rest to escape a dangerous storm on the ice.

COMMAS

Commas in a Series

Use a comma to separate three or more items in a series.

Benjamin, David, Matt, and Bryce all passed biology class.
But: Nick and Frank did not pass the test.
Successful students listen to the teacher, read the textbook, and study their notes.

A comma may be used to separate two or more adjectives that modify the same noun. Usually a comma is used if you can reverse the order of the adjectives or replace the comma with the word *and* without changing the meaning.

That tall, thin plant needs direct sunlight.
That thin, tall plant needs direct sunlight.
That tall and thin plant needs direct sunlight.
But: Who broke the new clay flowerpot?

Commas in Compound Sentences

Use a comma to separate the first independent clause from the conjunction in a compound sentence. Do not use a comma before a conjunction that joins the parts of a compound predicate.

Joe likes Mexican dishes, but Mark prefers Greek cuisine.
But: She walked down the street to the doctor's office but rode the bus to the mall.

Commas to Separate

Use a comma to separate some introductory words from the rest of the sentence.

First, I set all the ingredients on the counter.
Finally, the cake was ready after two long hours.

Use a comma or pair of commas to separate a noun of direct address from the rest of the sentence. A noun of direct address names the person being spoken to.

Patricia, will you close the door when you leave?
Will you close the door, Patricia, when you leave?
Will you close the door when you leave, Patricia?

Use a comma to separate a mild interjection from the rest of the sentence.

Oh, Holly forgot her car key.
Take them to her, please.
Yes, I can do that for her.

Use a comma or a pair of commas to separate an interrupting phrase that could be left out of the sentence.

By the way, Renee and Billy are all-star basketball players.
Marcus and Denise, on the other hand, do not like sports at all.

Use a comma to separate an introductory dependent clause from the independent clause in a complex sentence.

Because her mother coaches a volleyball team, Kris learned the game well.

Use a comma to separate a long introductory prepositional phrase from the rest of the sentence; also use a comma to separate two or more introductory prepositional phrases from the rest of the sentence. Do not use a comma if the phrase is immediately followed by a verb.

During the very stormy day, huge puddles formed in the roads.
By the side of the road, a disabled car was waiting for help.
But: On top of the car next to the road was a stray kitten.

Commas with Quotations, Dates, and Addresses; Commas in Letters

Use a comma to separate a direct quotation from the rest of the sentence in a written dialogue.

"Haylee is going to school," said Mom.
"Maybe," she said, "she'll bring that book to you."
Kaylen replied, "Well, it is in my locker."

Use a comma to separate the day from the year in a date. Do not use a comma between only the month and day or month and year.

Jane Austen was born on December 16, 1775.
Ludwig van Beethoven also was born on December 16.
Was he born in December 1775 too?

Use a comma to separate a full date (month, day, and year) from the rest of the sentence.

December 16, 1770, is Beethoven's birthday.

Use a comma to separate the city from a state or a country at the end of a sentence.

Robert Louis Stevenson was born in Edinburgh, Scotland.
He later lived near St. Helena, California.

COMMAS (CONTINUED)

Use a pair of commas to set off a state or country within a sentence.

> My sister moved to Athens, Georgia, after graduating from college.
> Athens, Greece, is an interesting place to visit.
> *But:* The Carson family went to Rome for their vacation.

Do not use a comma to separate the state from the ZIP code in an address.

> Matt Schultz
> 187 Alma Blvd.
> Sterling, WI 24078
> Write to me at this address: Matt Schultz, 187 Alma Blvd., Sterling, WI 24078.

Use a comma after the greeting of a friendly letter and after the closing of all letters.

> Dear Matt,
> Sincerely,

Practice the Skill

Insert any missing commas in the following sentences. Write *C* if the sentence is correct.

_______ 1. Football, basketball, and baseball have fascinated Americans for many years.

_______ 2. Elementary high school college and professional teams play football.

_______ 3. American football teams have eleven players but Canadian teams have twelve.

_______ 4. Strength speed and physical contact are basic elements of the rough tough football game.

_______ 5. Two peach baskets a soccer ball and an indoor gymnasium were the equipment for the first game of basketball.

_______ 6. Basketball was originally played to keep a team in shape and to provide intense well-rounded competition between the football and baseball seasons.

_______ 7. Basketball is a fast exciting and challenging sport between two five-player teams.

_______ 8. One of the most popular American sports is baseball.

_______ 9. Many believe that baseball was invented in America in 1839, but some historians mention the sport in England before that time.

_______ 10. The first catcher's mask was worn in 1875 and the first chest protector was worn in 1885.

Insert any missing commas in the following sentences. Write *C* if the sentence is correct.

_______ 11. As soon as school begins in the fall many Americans look forward to the beginning of football season.

_______ 12. In very early times before the development of modern sports, there existed ball-kicking games similar to football.

_______ 13. One of these games for example was played by the ancient Greeks.

_______ 14. During the first century BC the Romans introduced the game to England.

_______ 15. When football was first played in the United States it was similar to soccer.

_______ 16. In the early days of the development of football in America, teams could have up to twenty-five players.

_______ 17. Finally a convention in 1880 decided the issue.

_______ 18. Walter Camp of Yale persuaded the delegates to establish a standard of eleven players from each team on the field at a time.

_______ 19. Oh did you know that the first professional game was played in 1895?

_______ 20. Although football is a very popular sport a 1991 attempt to begin a spring season failed.

Insert any missing commas. Write *C* if the item is correct.

_______ 21. Imagine an exchange of letters that took place in March 2022 between Joe and his friend Adam, who enjoys professional golf.

_______ 22. Dear Adam

_______ 23. I have recently developed an interest in golf and wondered whether you would send some information on the history of the game to the following address: Joe Vaught 102 Davis St. Summertown TN 38483.

_______ 24. Dear Joe

_______ 25. I myself have loved golf since my first game in June 2015, and I am glad that you have taken an interest in it.

_______ 26. Most people believe that the modern game of golf originated in Edinburgh Scotland.

_______ 27. The city of Edinburgh proclaimed the establishment of an annual golf competition on March 17, 1744.

_______ 28. An article I once read said "The winner of the competition became the official judge for the next game."

_______ 29. On May 14 1754 the town of St. Andrews organized its own competition with established rules similar to those we have today.

_______ 30. Sincerely yours
Adam

Review the Skill

Insert any missing commas in the following sentences. Write *C* if the sentence is correct.

_______ 31. Walking rafting and riding animals are three of the oldest forms of transportation.

_______ 32. Cars were invented later and riding the rapids on a raft became unnecessary.

_______ 33. Rafting was revived and became a recreational sport in the 1960s.

_______ 34. Small adventurous groups travel together in one raft down the river.

_______ 35. Brave rafters enjoy rivers that contain whitewater rapids.

_______ 36. Some rivers have steep waterfalls and some can be very dangerous.

_______ 37. The cold clear water is exhilarating but it can also cause hypothermia.

_______ 38. Several rafting companies rent rafts and offer guided trips down whitewater rivers.

_______ 39. Groups of rafters usually enjoy spending time outdoors together and they also sometimes engage in water battles on the river.

_______ 40. Rafting is a challenging sport and it is a good way to enjoy the beautiful mountain rivers.

Insert any missing commas in the following sentences. Write *C* if the sentence is correct.

_______ 41. Ashley how was volleyball practice?

_______ 42. It was a good practice Mom.

_______ 43. Well why don't you tell me about it?

_______ 44. Before we practiced volleyball Coach Green assigned some warm-ups.

_______ 45. Next, we practiced setting and spiking.

_______ 46. Coach Green in fact wants me to become the setter for the team in a few weeks.

_______ 47. Do you think you're ready Ashley for that responsibility?

_______ 48. I have to practice an extra hour on Friday.

_______ 49. Actually I need to practice on Saturday as well.

_______ 50. Because I like setting and working hard I think I'm really going to enjoy this new position Mom.

Write in the blank the letter of the sentence with correct punctuation.

_______ 51. **A** Jesse Owens was born in Danville, Alabama.
B Jesse Owens was born in Danville Alabama.

_______ 52. **A** He was born in September 1913.
B He was born in September, 1913.

_______ 53. **A** In Ann Arbor, Michigan he broke three track-and-field world records.
B In Ann Arbor, Michigan, he broke three track-and-field world records.

_______ 54. **A** He broke the records on May 25, 1935 at a college competition.
B He broke the records on May 25, 1935, at a college competition.

_______ 55. **A** He qualified for the 1936, summer Olympics.
B He qualified for the 1936 summer Olympics.

_______ 56. **A** In Berlin, Germany, he competed in the Olympic Games.
B In Berlin, Germany he competed in the Olympic Games.

_______ 57. **A** "Owens greatly disappointed Adolf Hitler," my teacher explained "because Owens beat the Germans in several track-and-field events."
B "Owens greatly disappointed Adolf Hitler," my teacher explained, "because Owens beat the Germans in several track-and-field events."

_______ 58. **A** After the Games, Owens said "I've never felt like that before."
B After the Games, Owens said, "I've never felt like that before."

_______ 59. **A** He returned to the United States as a famous man.
B He returned to the United States, as a famous man.

_______ 60. **A** Jesse Owens died on March 31, 1980.
B Jesse Owens died on March 31 1980.

SEMICOLONS AND COLONS

Semicolons

Use a semicolon to separate two independent clauses in a compound sentence with no coordinating conjunction.

Mandy saw her dad at the dentist's office; she met her mom at the library.

Colons

Use a colon to separate the chapter and verse in a Bible reference.

Psalm 118:24

Use a colon to separate the hour from the minutes in an expression of time.

6:15 p.m.

Use a colon after the greeting of a business letter.

Dear Sir:
Dear Dr. Russell:

Use a colon to introduce a list of items at the end of an independent clause.

You will need these ingredients for a cake: flour, sugar, eggs, and butter.

Practice the Skill

Insert any missing semicolons or colons in the following sentences. Write *C* if the sentence is correct.

_______ 1. For many centuries skis were a means of transportation over the snow skiing was not considered a sport.

_______ 2. It was these people who used skis to help them in their travel the Norwegians, the Swedes, and the Lapps.

_______ 3. The first recorded skier in the United States was "Snowshoe" Thompson; he was born and raised in Norway.

_______ 4. Beginning in 1850, Thompson used his skis to deliver the mail he delivered the mail for twenty years between northern California and Carson Valley, Idaho.

_______ 5. Many skiers enjoy the high-speed thrill down the mountain slopes others enjoy the competition.

_______ 6. Three types of skiing provide competition for skiers: downhill skiing, cross-country skiing, and freestyle skiing.

_______ 7. The first ski clubs appeared among Norwegian and Swedish settlers these clubs appeared in Wisconsin and Minnesota over one hundred years ago.

_______ 8. I would like to learn to ski meet me on the northern slopes at 8:30 tomorrow morning.

_______ 9. I will need to take these things warm clothes, a pair of thick gloves, and a good dose of courage.

_______ 10. The beauty of nature that I see while skiing reminds me of my favorite verse: "The heavens declare the glory of God; and the firmament sheweth his handywork." (Psalm 191).

Review the Skill

Insert any missing semicolons or colons in the following sentences. Write *C* if the sentence is correct.

_______ 11. Swimming is one of the world's oldest sports we know that people who lived thousands of years ago were swimmers.

_______ 12. Isaiah speaks of swimming when he writes in Isaiah 2511, "And he shall spread forth his hands in the midst of them, as he that swimmeth spreadeth forth his hands to swim."

_______ 13. In Acts 2742–44, we see from Paul's shipwreck that there were swimmers and non-swimmers in the New Testament.

_______ 14. Because swimming is an enjoyable sport and good exercise, most people like it.

_______ 15. Some people get up before 600 a.m. to enjoy a few laps before the day begins.

_______ 16. Because swimming builds both muscle tone and endurance, a regular swimming workout is one of the best ways to stay in shape.

_______ 17. The following are three common types of swim strokes the crawl, the breaststroke, and the butterfly.

_______ 18. Swimming was a common activity in England by the mid-1800s today's modern pools keep swimming popular.

_______ 19. Several people have swum the English Channel it is twenty-one miles wide at its narrowest point.

_______ 20. In 1940 John Sigmund swam 292 miles down the Mississippi River he swam for almost ninety hours.

QUOTATION MARKS, UNDERLINING, AND ITALICS

Quotation Marks

Use quotation marks to show words taken from another source.

William Shakespeare wrote the words "A rose by any other name would smell as sweet."

Use quotation marks to show the words of the speakers in a dialogue. Do not use quotation marks with indirect quotations.

Quotation: "May I borrow your book?" Sam asked.
Indirect quotation: Sam asked to borrow the book.

Sometimes the quotation tag (such as *"he said"*) comes in the middle of the quoted sentence. In that case commas surround the quotation tag, and both halves of the divided quotation are enclosed in quotation marks.

"I need to borrow your book," Sam said, "because I lost my copy."

Other Punctuation with Quotation Marks

Use a comma to separate the quotation from the rest of the sentence.

Luci said, "Let's go to Hamburger Haven. I want a milkshake."
"I would like a cheeseburger," said Noah.

Always place periods and commas before the quotation marks.

Luigi remarked, "I prefer hot dogs with slaw."
Yuri considered the choices. "I will eat almost anything," he decided.

Place question marks and exclamation points either before or after the quotation marks, depending upon the meaning of the sentence. If the entire sentence is a question or an exclamation, place the question mark or exclamation point after the quotation marks.

Did Luci mention a flavor when she said, "I want a milkshake"?
Only Yuri would say, "I will eat almost anything"!

If only the quotation is a question or an exclamation, place the question mark or exclamation point before the quotation marks. No period or comma follows a question mark or exclamation point.

Yuri asked, "Are you hungry?"
Noah replied, "Yes, I am starved!"

Always place semicolons and colons outside the quotation marks.

Washington Irving is remembered for stories such as "The Legend of Sleepy Hollow"; several of his stories were collected in *The Sketch Book* in 1820.
These are the main characters in Irving's "The Legend of Sleepy Hollow": Ichabod Crane, Katrina Van Tassel, Brom Van Brunt, and the mysterious Galloping Hessian.

Use quotation marks around these kinds of titles:

Short stories	"Rip Van Winkle"
Chapters	"Discoveries"
Poems	"Opportunity"
Essays	"The Art of Seeing Things"
Periodical articles	"Doing Things Right!"
Songs	"Beneath the Cross of Jesus"
Television and radio episodes	"To Walk on the Bright Side"

Underlining for Italics

Underline or italicize words and letters being discussed. Use underlining in handwritten papers. Italic print, the equivalent, is used in printed books or papers.

> Did you know that the word <u>music</u> used to be spelled with a <u>k</u> at the end?
> Did you know that the word *music* used to be spelled with a *k* at the end?

Underline or italicize the names of large vehicles.

Ships	*Titanic*
Planes	*Spirit of St. Louis*
Trains	*Orient Express*®
Spacecraft	*Columbia*

Underline or italicize the titles of long works.

Books	*The Cay*
Magazines	*National Geographic*®
Newspapers	the *Portland Oregonian* (The word *the* is not part of a newspaper's title.)
Musical compositions	Brahms's *A German Requiem*
Television and radio series	*Masterpiece Theatre*®
Epic poems	*Beowulf*
Plays	*Oklahoma!*

Underline or italicize the names of works of art.

Paintings	*The Ascension*
Sculptures	*Moses*

Practice the Skill

Insert any missing quotation marks. Write *C* if the sentence is correct.

_______ 1. Mrs. Helbert asked the class, Did you enjoy our unit on sports?

_______ 2. Susan responded, I have learned about many different kind of sports.

_______ 3. I wanted to learn more about skiing, she said, since Dad enjoys it so much.

_______ 4. Well, said Mrs. Helbert, what about the rest of you?

_______ 5. Harrison said that he enjoyed the lesson about the Olympic Games.

_______ 6. John, what do you think? asked Mrs. Helbert.

_______ 7. I really liked all the history that we learned about different sports, especially baseball, said John.

_______ 8. Brad added that he liked reading about football.

_______ 9. I'm glad all of you have enjoyed something about the sports unit, said Mrs. Helbert.

_______ 10. Now just study it well for the test tomorrow, she added as the bell rang to dismiss the class.

Underline any words that should be italicized. Write *C* if the sentence is correct.

_______ 11. The word sports could bring many different images to mind.

_______ 12. One might think about reading the Soccer Journal.

_______ 13. Another might picture himself watching a game on Monday Night Football®.

_______ 14. Some probably read the sports page in USA Today® to get a general overview of everything going on in the world of sports.

_______ 15. Others may prefer to read a book, such as the Official Encyclopedia of Baseball, for detailed information about one sport.

_______ 16. Some people would like to learn about the US yacht America, the first vessel to win the America's Cup.

_______ 17. Young people may enjoy reading about Micky Mantle, a famous player for the New York Yankees.

_______ 18. Christians would appreciate the information about sports in Billy Sunday, a play about the preacher who started out as a baseball player.

_______ 19. A band director might even associate sports with John Philip Sousa's Washington Post March or another march that is played at halftime of a sporting event.

_______ 20. Sports provide interest and education no matter what we think of when we hear the word mentioned.

Review the Skill

Write in the blank the letter of the sentence that uses quotation marks correctly.

_______ 21. **A** "Swimming is fun, said Todd, I especially like to dive."
B "Swimming is fun," said Todd. "I especially like to dive."

_______ 22. **A** "Swimming is good exercise too," said Sarah.
B "Swimming is good exercise too, said Sarah."

_______ 23. **A** Sarah says that she swims one hour three times each week.
B Sarah says "that she swims one hour three times each week."

_______ 24. **A** "I don't think I could ever swim as well as Sarah," said Rebecca, "because she's been swimming a long time."
B "I don't think I could ever swim as well as Sarah", said Rebecca, "because she's been swimming a long time."

_______ 25. **A** Sarah answered, "Oh, don't worry about that; with practice, you'll be a great swimmer!"
B Sarah answered, "Oh, don't worry about that; with practice, you'll be a great swimmer"!

_______ 26. **A** A discussion of the health benefits of swimming appears in the article Swimming for Exercise.
B A discussion of the health benefits of swimming appears in the article "Swimming for Exercise."

_______ 27. **A** The article says, "Swimming provides an excellent workout for both the upper and lower body."
B The article says, "Swimming provides an excellent workout for both the upper and lower body".

_______ 28. **A** Have you read the section that says, "Swimming builds endurance?"
B Have you read the section that says, "Swimming builds endurance"?

_______ 29. **A** Many people ask, "What if I cannot swim well?".
B Many people ask, "What if I cannot swim well?"

_______ 30. **A** The article states, "It may be profitable for some to consider taking lessons"; others may need only to practice.
B The article states, "It may be profitable for some to consider taking lessons;" others may need only to practice.

Insert any missing quotation marks. Underline any words that should be italicized. Write C if the sentence is correct.

_______ 31. A Midsummer Night's Dream is one of Shakespeare's most popular plays.

_______ 32. Have you read The Early Years yet? It is the first chapter in our textbook.

_______ 33. Nathaniel Hawthorne wrote a short story called Young Goodman Brown about the life of a Puritan man.

_______ 34. "Holy Sonnet 10," a poem showing the ultimate weakness of death, was written by John Donne.

_______ 35. In 1819 the SS Savannah became the first steam engine to cross the Atlantic Ocean.

_______ 36. The Gingham Dog and the Calico Cat is a humorous poem by Eugene Field.

_______ 37. The beautiful Canon in D is Pachelbel's most famous musical work.

_______ 38. Benjamin West created many beautiful paintings including The Ascension.

_______ 39. Amazing Grace is a well-known hymn.

_______ 40. If you like stories about adventure, danger, and heroes, you should read the epic poem Beowulf.

APOSTROPHES AND HYPHENS

Apostrophes

Use an apostrophe to show an omission of letters or numbers.

Did you know that *o'clock* is a contraction for the phrase *of the clock*?
Many people name the stock market crash of '29 as one cause of the Great Depression.

Use an apostrophe to form the plurals of letters, signs, and words.

How many *b*'s are in the word *bubble*?
Do not use *&*'s to replace *and*'s in formal writing.

Do not use an apostrophe to form the plural of numbers.

Queen Victoria ruled Great Britain for most of the 1800s.

Use an apostrophe to form the possessive of nouns.

- To form the singular possessive, add *'s* to the singular form of the noun.

cat—cat's	The cat's collar is new.
puppy—puppy's	The puppy's leash is tangled.
James—James's	James's pets are playful animals.

- Traditionally, only an apostrophe is added to the proper names of Jesus and Moses.

Jesus—Jesus'	Call upon Jesus' name.
Moses—Moses'	Miriam was Moses' sister.

- If the plural ends with an *s*, add only an apostrophe to make it possessive.

boys—boys'	Who is those boys' mother?

- If a plural does not end with an *s*, add *'s* to make it possessive.

men—men's	The ties are in the men's department.

Hyphens

Use a hyphen between the words of multiword numbers up to ninety-nine.

Eleven of the twenty-six students have younger siblings.

Use a hyphen between the two parts of a fraction that is written out.

Only one-half of the students have older siblings.

Use a hyphen to show the omission of a connecting word.

The play will be presented October 12-15.

Use a hyphen to divide words at the end of a line. Divide words only between syllables; never divide a one-syllable word.

- Leave at least two letters and a hyphen on the first line.

  Incorrect: We have a new puppy. Are pets allowed in your a-
  partment building?

  Correct: We have a new puppy. Are pets allowed in your apart-
  ment building?

- Put at least three letters on the next line.

  Incorrect: A soldier must never behave in a coward-
  ly way.

  Correct: A soldier must never behave in a cow-
  ardly way.

- Leave the hyphen on the first line; do not carry it to the second line.

  Incorrect: Although chemistry is interesting, I prefer geol
  -ogy and botany.

  Correct: Although chemistry is interesting, I prefer geol-
  ogy and botany.

Practice the Skill

Insert any missing apostrophes in the following sentences. Write C if the sentence is correct.

______ 1. *Skydiving* does have a *y* but no *z*s or any of the other letters needed to spell *crazy*, which is what some consider the sport to be.

______ 2. Skydiving began in the 1930s, when air shows were popular.

______ 3. World War II increased skydivers prestige by making practical use of their parachuting skills.

______ 4. After the end of the war, skydivers chose to continue the activity for sport.

______ 5. The first American sport-parachuting center opened in Massachusetts in 59.

______ 6. Judges at parachuting competitions rate a divers body position in the air, his work with other divers, and his landing.

______ 7. By the early 1970s, several divers had mastered the landing and could touch down directly on a target.

_______ 8. A diver in free fall (before he has opened his parachute) shouldnt do turns or loops unless he has had much diving experience.

_______ 9. In group competitions, several divers can join hands or pass a baton when theyre correctly controlling their speed and rate of descent.

_______ 10. A skydivers equipment includes two parachutes on a harness, boots, helmet, goggles, and gloves.

Insert any missing hyphens in the following sentences.

11. Rugby is a popular sport in Great Britain, New Zealand, France, Aus
tralia, and South Africa.
12. It might be described as one third soccer, one third American football, and one third something entirely its own.
13. Athletes had been using their feet in ball games since the Middle Ages, but twenty three years into the nineteenth century, something new came along.
14. Tradition at England's Rugby School says that William Ellis, a foot
ball player, apparently got tired of kicking the ball. He picked it up and ran with it instead.
15. The game that eventually resulted uses a ball that is 24 25.5 inches in circumference and 11 11.5 inches in length, making it bigger than an American football.
16. A rugby field is bigger than an American football field, which is about one half the size of a rugby playing area.
17. Both rugby and football have goal areas, but the rugby goal is usually twenty five yards long, while football's end zone is only ten.
18. Rugby players can score 2 5 points, depending on whether they have made a try (similar to a touchdown) or a kick of some sort.
19. The person carrying the ball may pass it off, but only sideways or back
wards, since none of his teammates are allowed to be in front of him.
20. If the player carrying the ball is tackled, he drops it so that another team
mate can try to retrieve it.

Review the Skill

Insert any missing apostrophes in the following sentences. Write C if the sentence is correct.

_______21. Bowling is one of many peoples favorite sports.

_______22. Bowlers roll a heavy ball down a wooden lane and try to knock down pins in groups of ten.

_______23. In the United States, bowling was popular in the early 1900s, but professional bowling did not begin until the ’50s.

_______24. If a bowler doesnt knock down all the pins during his first try, he is allowed to bowl again.

_______25. Knocking over all the pins on the first try is called a strike.

_______26. Hitting all of the pins by the end of the bowlers second try is called a spare.

_______27. Making three strikes in a row is a difficult feat; it’s called a turkey.

_______28. A bowler wears special shoes because bowling shoes soft soles will not scratch the floor.

_______29. Bowlings popularity is largely due to the fact that the sport is quite easy to learn.

_______30. A perfect score of three hundred isnt easy to achieve; a bowler must bowl twelve strikes in a row.

Insert any missing hyphens in the following sentences. Write *C* if the sentence is correct.

_______ 31. A popular sport around the world is horseman ship, which involves training and riding horses.

_______ 32. The attractive and handsome Clydesdale is much taller than the average man, while the Shetland pony's height is usually under forty six inches.

_______ 33. Young horses tend to be more spirited; therefore, it is wise for a beginner to start on a trained horse that is about fourteen years old.

_______ 34. Jumping competitions are usually short events, but horses and their riders also compete in cross-country events that can be over ten and one half miles long.

_______ 35. The movement of a horse is called its gait. A fast gait is called the canter, in which the horse moves about 10 17 mph.

If a word can be divided at the end of a line, rewrite the word in the blank with a hyphen at each place the word could be divided. If the word cannot be divided with a hyphen, write *C* in the blank.

_______________ 36. saddle

_______________ 37. thoroughbred

_______________ 38. pony

_______________ 39. competition

_______________ 40. bridle

PARENTHESES, BRACKETS, DASHES, AND ELLIPSES

Parentheses

Use parentheses to enclose words, phrases, or clauses that give additional information. Keep your meaning clear by limiting the number of parenthetical expressions you use.

Charles Lindberg (1902–74) was a pioneer in aviation.
The president of the club (Cooper Smith) was presented with an award.
One of the most popular pets is the house cat (*felis catus*).

Punctuation marks usually go outside the parentheses. However, when an entire sentence is enclosed in parentheses, a question mark or an exclamation point goes before the final parenthesis.

"Let every soul be subject unto the higher powers" (Romans 13:1).
Terry, I hear that our meeting (can you come?) will be on March 16.

Brackets

Use brackets to enclose words inserted into a quotation for clarification.

Original Quote: "Early Roman society consisted of two social classes. They differed greatly from each other in the social and political privileges of their members."

Quote with Insertions: "They [Roman social classes] differed greatly from each other in the social and political privileges of their members."

If you want to quote a passage that contains an error, you have two choices. One option is to replace the error with your own correction enclosed in brackets.

Original: "One common literary device found in poetry is onomonopea."
Correction: "One common literary device found in poetry is [onomatopoeia].

You may also copy the quote exactly and indicate that the error is original rather than a misquotation. Add the Latin word *sic* ("thus") enclosed by brackets immediately after the error to indicate that you have reproduced the original faithfully.

"One common literary device found in poetry is onomonopea [*sic*]."

Dashes

Use a pair of dashes to set off an interrupting phrase or clause.

Abraham Lincoln—many historians believe he was our best president—led the United States through the Civil War.

Use dashes to indicate faltering speech, an abrupt breaking off of a sentence, or an abrupt change in thought.

Faltering Speech: "I—uh—don't know the answer to that question."
Abrupt Break in a Sentence: The doctor came in and announced, "Your reports show—"
Abrupt Change in Thought: The teams playing in the Superbowl are—do you even like football?

Ellipses

Use ellipses to show when you are omitting words within a quoted passage. Remember that your omission should not distort the meaning of the original.

Original Text: "The First Punic War was fought over control of the island of Sicily. The Romans feared the Carthaginians would become too strong on the island. A powerful rival force could control the waters between Sicily and Italy and thus hinder Roman trade in the Mediterranean. Sicily could also become a base for a Carthaginian attack on southern Italy. The only way Rome could stop Carthage was to break its naval supremacy."
Text with Ellipsis: "The First Punic War was fought over control of the island of Sicily. The Romans feared the Carthaginians would become too strong on the island. . . . The only way Rome could stop Carthage was to break its naval supremacy."

Use ellipses to indicate hesitant pauses in speech or show that a sentence has just slowly trailed off before completion.

"I think I remember who was president during World War I. It was . . . Woodrow Wilson!"
"Wasn't Bryan going to. . . ."

Practice the Skill

Insert any missing parentheses, brackets, dashes, or ellipses in the following sentences.

1. "Gimnastics *sic* is a sport based on acrobatic exercise; each performance is called a routine."
2. In the early 1800s, Friedrich Jahn a German schoolteacher built the first modern gymnastic equipment.
3. Although, gymnastics in various forms has always been a part of the modern Olympic Games did you watch the last Olympics?
4. Gymnastics helps to develop important physical qualities in an athlete balance, flexibility, and strength.
5. Male gymnasts can compete in six events: the floor exercise, the pommel horse a side horse, the rings, the vault, the parallel bars, and the horizontal bar.
6. Female gymnasts compete in just four events: the vault, the uneven bars, the balance beam only four inches wide, and the floor exercise.
7. Those who take part in all the events are called all-around gymnasts; others those in only one or two events are called specialists.
8. Both men and women perform vaults, but
9. Both also participate in the floor exercise a routine performed on a square mat.
10. The men's floor exercise 50–70 seconds has a shorter time limit than the women's floor exercise 70–90 seconds.

Review the Skill

Insert any missing parentheses, brackets, dashes, or ellipses in the following sentences. Write *C* if the sentence is correct.

_______ 11. An inventor from Belgium in the late eighteenth century Joseph Merlin made the first roller skate.

_______ 12. Before the 1970s—a great decade by the way—roller skate wheels were sometimes made from wood.

_______ 13. J. L. Plimpton significantly improved the roller skate when he designed a process cramping that allowed the wheels to continue moving along curves.

_______ 14. Skates that connect to one's own shoes are called clamp-on skates.

_______ 15. Most people roller skate for recreation. However, many skate in one of the two basic types of competitions artistic skating and speed skating.

_______ 16. Indoor speed skaters compete on an oval track 100 meters 328 feet in length.

_______ 17. Specialized skates speed skates are built with wheels that allow the skates to move faster than regular skates.

_______ 18. There was once this one skater who

_______ 19. Another type of skate the in-line skate has wheels in a straight line in the middle of the skate.

_______ 20. Many people exercise outdoors using in-line skates also known by the brand name Rollerblades®.

Use the Skill

Write about an interesting conversation you have had with someone. Use each punctuation mark introduced in this lesson at least one time.

BUSINESS LETTERS

Writing Trait: Voice

Listen Up!

Have you ever participated in any type of business, such as being interviewed for a job, working for somebody, or selling something? If you have, how did you talk to the people you were doing business with? Chances are, you probably talked more formally than you do to your friends or siblings. You probably said, "Please," "Thank you," or "Yes, Sir" more often than you normally do.

Just as conducting business requires you to speak more formally with your employer or customer, writing a business letter requires you to use a formal tone. You want the reader to take you seriously, and your letter's voice should therefore show signs that you are serious. Look at the mentor text below and note the writer's voice. What does his tone tell you as a reader?

Heading

1345 Wade Avenue
Williamsport, OH 45739 — **Return Address**
April 9, 2021 — **Date**

Opening

Dr. Howard Fields, Director
Christian Camp for Teens
West Lake Road
Winston, OH 45608 — **Inside Address**

Dear Dr. Fields: — **Salutation**

Body

I am an eighth grader in Williamsport Christian High School. Yesterday we had an assembly called "What to Do This Summer."

Your camp was mentioned as a good place for teens to vacation during the summer. I think I would like to come.

Would you please send me some information on the dates and prices of your camps? Thank you very much.

Closing

Sincerely yours, — **Complimentary Closing**

Tom Weathers

Tom Weathers — **Writer's Identification**

Take Notes!

Read the following information and outline the necessary parts of a business letter.

In the near future, you may be required to write a business letter. Some business letters young people commonly write are cover letters to go along with a résumé for a job or college application. Since the person reading your business letter is a potential employer, an admissions counselor, or some other important person, it is key that you learn to use this type of letter to give the reader a favorable impression.

The tone of a business letter should be polite and concise. However, you also want to communicate that you are friendly and sincere. Carefully reread the business letter in the mentor text box. Does the letter have a polite and appropriately serious tone? Does it make a request clearly? Do you think the person who received the letter would be favorably impressed by the tone of the writer?

Notice the different parts of the business letter. The heading includes the writer's address and the date. The opening includes the address of the person receiving the letter and the salutation or greeting. The body is the main part of the letter—the message. The closing is the complimentary closing and the writer's name and signature.

Notice also how the letter is punctuated and set up on the page. To appear as professional as possible, a business letter should always be typed, but if typing is impossible for some reason, the letter must be neatly written. Whether typed or handwritten, the spacing and form are the same. All lines begin at the left margin. The paragraphs of the body are single-spaced, but there is a double space between paragraphs, between heading and body, and between body and closing. The writer has both signed his name and typed it below his signature.

Partner Up!

Write a formal letter to your partner. Pretend he works for a business and you have a question for him. Have your partner read it and reply to your question.

Try It Out!

Research a current problem that is facing the country and write a business letter to your state or congressional representative. Explain why your concern is such a significant problem and suggest potential laws that can fix this problem.

CHAPTER REVIEW

People and Places

Underline the capitalization errors in the following paragraph.

1.–10. My parents, robert and wendy bodine, are missionaries in Brazil. Since my family is originally from Michigan's upper peninsula, we were unprepared for the hot, humid weather. Since I have lived here in south America, I have hiked in parts of the Andes mountains and rafted down the Amazon river. One of my favorite places to visit is the snow-capped Aconcagua. It is the highest mountain in the Western Hemisphere. The Moon seems especially bright out in the country where we live. In fact, sometimes my family enjoys camping out under the stars. However, we often visit brasília, Brazil's capital, when we want to vacation in the city.

Cultural and Historical Terms

Identify the word that is an example of a capitalization error. Write in the blank the letter that corresponds to the correct answer.

_______ 11. Venezuela declared its independence from Spain on july 15, 1811.
- **A** Independence
- **B** July
- **C** no error

_______ 12. The official language of Venezuela is spanish.
- **A** venezuela
- **B** Spanish
- **C** no error

_______ 13. Christopher Columbus landed in Venezuela in ad 1498.
- **A** Columbus
- **B** Venezuela
- **C** AD

_______ 14. The Venezuelan people are a mixture of Caucasian, African, and American indian.
- **A** caucasian
- **B** african
- **C** Indian

_______ 15. The name *Venezuela* is Spanish for little venice.
- **A** Name
- **B** spanish
- **C** Little Venice

Angel Falls, Venezuela

Titles, First Words, Parts of Letters

Identify the word that is an example of a capitalization error. Write in the blank the letter that corresponds to the correct answer.

_______ 16. Recently, I read a short article about Chile in *newsmax*.
- **A** Article
- **B** chile
- **C** *Newsmax*

_______ 17. The article categorized facts about the Chilean people in the following way:

I. People
  A. Language
  B. Ancestry
  C. population
II. Way of life
  A. Rural life
  B. Urban life

- **A** language
- **B** Population
- **C** rural

_______ 18. one of the most beautiful sections of the country is Chile's southern landscape.
- **A** One
- **B** Country
- **C** Southern

_______ 19. I wrote a letter to missionaries in Chile. "Dear friends" was my greeting to them.
- **A** Missionaries
- **B** dear
- **C** Friends

_______ 20. I asked my mother, "do you think I could go on a missionary trip to Chile?"
- **A** Mother
- **B** Do
- **C** Missionary

Proper Adjectives and Single Letters as Words

Find the capitalization error in each sentence and write the word correctly in the blank. If there is no capitalization error, write C in the blank.

_______________ 21. One of my favorite types of food is brazilian food.

_______________ 22. Did you know that the sculpture of Antonio Lisboa ranks among the earliest examples of Brazil's colonial art?

_______________ 23. Before its independence, Brazil was one of portugal's colonies.

_______________ 24. I studied hard and received an a on my geography test on Brazil.

_______________ 25. Brazil's history interests me; someday i would like to visit.

End Marks, Periods, and Commas

Insert missing end marks, periods, and commas in each sentence where needed.

26. Idaho has majestic mountains rushing rapids peaceful lakes and steep canyons
27. Boise which is the capital of Idaho is located in the southwestern section
28. Although potatoes are the most profitable crop in Idaho beef and dairy cattle are another source of income
29. Landon Fister Jr gets up at 5:00 am to watch the beautiful sunrise over the Sawtooth Mountains in Idaho
30. My brother lives at 506 Forest Ave Sandpoint ID 83865

Semicolons, Colons, and Quotation Marks

Identify the punctuation marks that are missing. Identify quotation marks that should be removed. Write the letter that corresponds to the correct answer.

A semicolon
B colon
C quotation marks
D remove quotation marks

_______ 31. "Here's a list of study facts for the test": agricultural resources, mineral resources, and other resources.

_______ 32. Prospectors discovered gold during the 1860s thousands of miners rushed to Idaho to make their fortunes.

_______ 33. Did you know that the state's leading mineral products include the following silver, phosphate rock, and gold?

_______ 34. My teacher told us "that she wanted us to know everything in our notes and our reading."

_______ 35. I think this is your highest grade, my teacher told me.

Quotation Marks, Italics, Apostrophes, and Hyphens

Underline the word in parentheses that is written correctly.

36. The name (Idaho, *Idaho*) became official after the region split from the Oregon territory.
37. Idaho's state song is ("Here We Have Idaho", *Here We Have Idaho*).
38. The (elk's, elks') head on the state flag represents wildlife.
39. Around (three-fifths, three fifths) of Idaho's people live in urban areas.
40. Scientists near Idaho Falls built a model reactor for the first nuclear submarine, the (*Nautilus*, "Nautilus").
41. In the early (1900s, 1900's), engineers completed a canal on the Columbia River.
42. All of Idaho's (forty four, forty-four) counties contain valuable mineral deposits.
43. Because of the huge mountains, Idaho is a (skier's, skiers) paradise.
44. The first newspaper in Idaho was the (Golden Age, *Golden Age*).
45. "Did you know that your great-grandfather sold (newspapers"?, newspapers?") my mother asked.

All Punctuation Marks

Add correct punctuation marks to the following sentences.

46. Many tourists vacation in Idaho because of the skiing camping and whitewater rafting my favorite activity
47. Water is said to be Idahos most valuable resource it is apparent that Idaho has no water shortage
48. Here is a list of Idahos biggest newspapers Idaho Statesman Post-Register Tribune Times News and Idaho State Journal
49. Mom do you think we could visit Idaho I asked
50. Idaho is absolutely beautiful

Shoshone Falls, Idaho

POETRY
INFORMATIVE
NARRATIVE
PERSUASIVE

CHAPTER 18

MULTIGENRE PROJECT

HOW CAN I USE KNOWLEDGE WISELY?

God has given us the Bible not only for personal study and memorization but also for living wisely in this world. The more practiced we become at applying it daily, the more our writing will reflect Christ-expression—expressing our love for God and God's truth to others.

INTRODUCING THE MULTIGENRE PROJECT

Creating the Multigenre Project

Your toolbox is now filled with tools to select from for accomplishing your writing and speaking goals. To demonstrate your skilled use of these tools, you will create a multigenre project, a group assignment that allows you to mix these skills with a good dose of collaboration, choice, and imagination.

A multigenre project differs from a typical researched report. Both require a unifying topic, research, organization, and citations, but notice the contrasts:

Typical Report
- Individual assignment
- Single prose piece
- Standard prose composition
- Single voice
- Single format

Multigenre Project
- Small group assignment
- Multiple genre pieces
- Original, creative writing
- Multiple voices
- Multiple formats

Putting It All Together

Your multigenre project will include an introduction, a timeline, a biographical essay, four genre pieces, a works-cited page, a final reflection, and a visual presentation. The following mentor texts will model these written components based on the life of Chick-fil-A's founder, Truett Cathy.

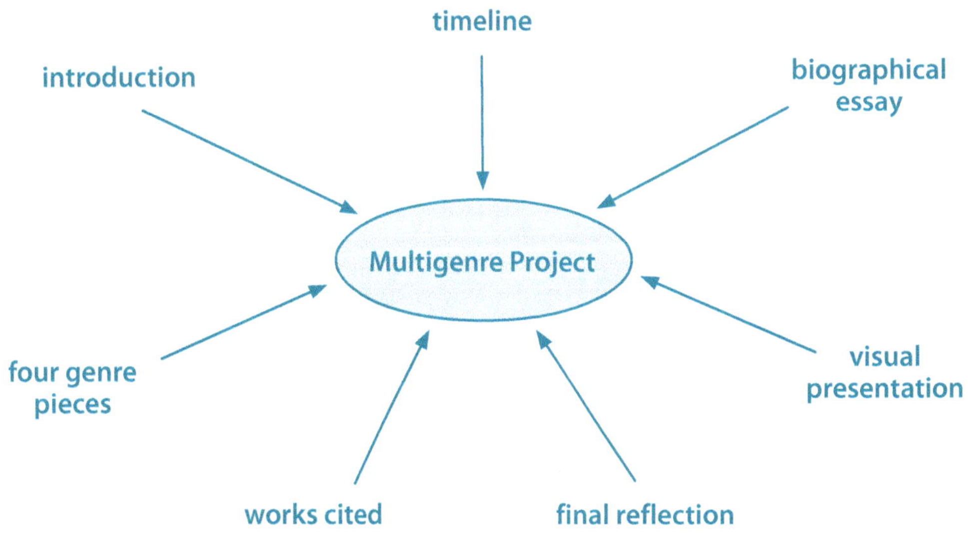

Have you waited in line at Chick-fil-A before?

Sometimes the line in our neighborhood Chick-fil-A is almost out to the street! Why is Chick-fil-A so popular? What has made it so successful? We selected Chick-fil-A's founder, S. Truett Cathy, for our project so we could find out what led him to start his restaurant chain, what initiatives he was involved in, and what the key to his success was.

Select a famous person to research and write about.

MENTOR TEXT: A TIMELINE

Important Moments in S. Truett Cathy's Life

1921
born
March 14

1946
opened the Dwarf Grill

1948
married Jeannette McNeil

1949
two brothers died

1967
opened the first Chick-fil-A

Create a timeline of important events in the life of the person you have chosen.

began advertising using cows

1995

initiated the phrase,

"my pleasure"

2001

died
September 8

2014

2008

received the President's Call to Service Award

1984

founded the WinShape Foundation

Write a biographical essay about the person, making sure to incorporate each of the events on the timeline.

S. Truett Cathy

A Man Who Found Pleasure in Service

Not many restaurant chains enjoy as positive a reputation as Chick-fil-A. Clean restaurants, fresh food, funny cows who cannot spell, a closed-on-Sunday policy, and kind employees who say it is their pleasure to serve are a few of the qualities that set Chick-fil-A apart and make its customers feel valued. This unique atmosphere did not develop by accident, but rather was carefully designed by its founder, S. Truett Cathy. Cathy's life can be best described as a life that was lived to serve others.

S. Truett Cathy was born on March 14, 1921 (Pallardy). His childhood was marked by poverty, especially since he lived through the Great Depression. Cathy began his life of service at a very young age. He started his first business selling sodas at the age of eight (*Eat Mor Chickin* 20). At age fourteen, Cathy helped his family by working as a newspaper delivery boy. He determined to provide the best service to his customers by treating them as if they were the most important people in the world, and this practice made Cathy become one of the most successful paper boys in town (*Eat Mor Chickin* 23–28).

In 1946, Cathy and his brother Ben started their first restaurant, the Dwarf Grill, later renamed the Dwarf House (Parker). They created unique policies that influenced what Chick-fil-A would become today. One of these policies was to go to great lengths to show customers how much they are cared for. Cathy would even send a customer's family free food if the customer was in the hospital or passed away ("Humble Beginnings"). Chick-fil-A continues this practice of giving away food with their "Be Our Guest" cards, which give customers a free menu item rather than a discount (*How Did You Do*

It 43). Cathy also served God and his employees by closing on Sundays in order to honor the Lord and ensure that all employees received a day of rest. Today, Chick-fil-A is so committed to being closed on Sundays that one of their restaurants in the Mercedes-Benz Stadium remained closed while the stadium was hosting the Super Bowl in 2019 (Taylor).

Although the Dwarf Grill was successful due to the brothers' hard work and excellent customer service, Cathy's life was not without hardships. Perhaps the greatest hardship Cathy faced during this time was the loss of his two brothers, Ben and Horace, in a plane crash in 1949 (*Eat Mor Chickin* 54–55). Cathy writes, "The loss hit me particularly hard on Monday morning, when I saw where Ben made out the report sheet on Saturday afternoon in good health. I realized again that he would never be back, and my tears flowed" (*Eat Mor Chikin* 55). Despite these losses, Cathy continued to grow his business and serve others.

During the 1960s, Cathy invented the recipe for his famous chicken sandwich. He opened his first Chick-fil-A restaurant in a mall because it was easier and cost less than building a separate restaurant. His business was so successful that in 1986, he began building free-standing Chick-fil-As. His business gained even more popularity in 1995 when he put up a billboard featuring cows that wrote "Eat mor chickin" ("Who We Are").

Although this success made him a wealthy man, Cathy saw his wealth as an opportunity to give to and serve others. He was famous for saying, "I'd like to be remembered as one who kept my priorities in order" ("A Life Centered on Family"). Cathy prioritized people over things by starting a scholarship program for employees, launching the WinShape Foundation to help disadvantaged children, and personally mentoring and fostering dozens of young people. His generosity has had a great impact on thousands of people.

Although Cathy died in 2014, his legacy of service lives on. Thousands of young people continue to benefit from the charity programs he founded, and millions of people continue to experience excellent customer service whenever they dine at Chick-fil-A. Cathy's life of service is an inspiration to all who know his story.

MENTOR TEXT: FOUR GENRE PIECES

1967

opened the first Chick-fil-A

Informative: Radio Interview

Interviewer: Hello, and welcome to WOWW Radio, your number one radio station for the Atlanta area. We are here today with a local entrepreneur and philanthropist who is making quite a name for himself. Truett Cathy was born in Georgia and lived in poverty during childhood, but he has gained success over the past several decades in the restaurant business. Truett still owns his first restaurant, now renamed the Dwarf House, and I'm telling you, if you haven't been there, you need to go. I went last week and had the best breakfast ever. More recently, Cathy has gotten into the chicken sandwich business by starting a franchise called Chick-fil-A. He is here now to talk about it. Mr. Cathy, thank you for joining us.

Cathy: Thanks for having me.

Interviewer: So what made you decide to get into the chicken sandwich business?

Cathy: Well, when I was a youngin', I would watch my mama cook chicken for the folks in our boarding house. She would season the chicken the night before and cook it with the lid on. Her chicken was always so good that after I started my restaurant, I got to thinking that folks might like a good chicken sandwich instead of always eating a burger. I spent several years coming up with a good recipe and would give samples to my customers and ask how they liked it. After a while, they said, "Truett, this is good. Don't change it."

Interviewer: Well Truett, I have tried your sandwich, and I for one am glad you didn't change it. Tell me about why you decided to start a restaurant in the mall. Before you came along, nobody really did that.

Cathy: When the Greenbriar Shopping Center opened in Atlanta, I noticed that there weren't really any places to eat. My sister suggested I open a restaurant in the shopping center and sell my chicken sandwich. It was much cheaper to open in the mall, and we had lots of folks walking by who were hungry from all that shopping. At first, the owners were worried that we would make the mall smell and that people would leave chicken bones everywhere. I just showed them how we would ventilate the place so the smell would go outside, and since our chicken is boneless, they didn't need to worry about trash.

Interviewer: And the rest is history. One of the things people really like about your restaurant is the excellent customer service. People feel like your employees care about them. How did you train people to do that?

Cathy: I always treated people with respect at the Dwarf Grill. It's just the Christian thing to do. I am very careful to only hire people who care about people as much as I do. I want to do more than just sell chicken. I want to honor the Lord and show my customers the love of Jesus. I tell my employees that when a customer says "thank you," don't just grunt or nod. You say, "My pleasure." If you work at Chick-fil-A, we want you to find pleasure in serving people. That's what we're all about.

Interviewer: You referred to your Christian faith. I know your faith has led you to closing on Sundays, but mall owners are wanting you to be open so they can make more money. Do you think you will ever open on Sundays?

Cathy: As long as I have a say, we will never open on Sunday. First of all, it honors the Lord when we close. Second, I care for my employees just as much as my customers. Everybody needs a day to rest and spend time with family. Closing on Sundays makes sure everybody can do that.

Interviewer: Well folks, there you have it. If you haven't been to the Dwarf House or Chick-fil-A, you need to go. Mr. Cathy, thank you so much for being with us today.

Cathy: My pleasure.

Write one selection for each of the genres you have practiced in this course: informative, narrative, and argumentative. A fourth genre, poetry, has been added to challenge your creative skills.

MENTOR TEXT: FOUR GENRE PIECES

1995

began advertising using cows

Narrative: Diary

August 12, 1996

Dear Diary,

After selling chicken for thirty years, who knew that our mascot would be a cow? It all happened about a year ago when we wanted to start advertising more, but commercials were just too expensive. We hired the Richards Group to help us figure out a way to advertise, and they suggested we use billboards. Well, that started out okay. Our first billboard had a rubber chicken that said, "If it's not Chick-fil-A, it's a joke." People seemed to like that, so our next billboard had two cows painting the message, "Eat mor chikin." All of a sudden, everybody started talking about us and how funny they thought the cows were. This past summer there were even some teenagers in Chattanooga who stole one of our cows, and it got national attention. We had *CNN* and so many newspapers report on the "cow-napping." This has really been helping our business. I definitely think we should keep the cows.

2001

initiated the phrase, "my pleasure"

Poetry: Acrostic Poem

Cathy's vision
Hearts for service
Investing in others
Closed on Sundays
Knowing my priorities
Food and smiles
Immaculate restaurants
Loving like Christ
Always my pleasure

Argumentative/Persuasive: Letter to the President

318 Chestnut St.

Jonesboro, GA 30236

April 2008

President George W. Bush

1600 Pennsylvania Ave. NW

Washington, DC 20500

Dear President Bush:

I would like to nominate S. Truett Cathy for the President's Call to Service Award. As someone who has had the privilege of knowing Cathy personally, I would like to explain why he is so deserving of such a distinguished honor.

Unlike many billionaires who merely donate money to charitable causes, Cathy has spent his life personally investing in others. He has taught Sunday School for over fifty years at my church, First Baptist Church, in Jonesboro, GA. Not only was I one of his students when I was young, but my son is now also in his class. Both of us have been greatly influenced by his care and interest in our lives.

Truett Cathy has touched the lives of the young people in our church, along with helping many young people all over the nation. In 1984 he started WinShape, which aims to help young people from difficult backgrounds succeed in life, and he has personally fostered hundreds of children throughout his life.

Truett Cathy deserves to be nationally recognized. It is people like Truett Cathy who make our nation great.

Sincerely,
John Smith

2008

received the President's Call to Service Award

MENTOR TEXT: WORKS CITED

Cathy, S. Truett. *Eat Mor Chikin: Inspire More People.* Looking Glass Books, 2002.

---. *How Did You Do It, Truett?* Looking Glass Books, 2007.

Pallardy, Richard. "S(amuel) Truett Cathy." *Britannica.* 4 Sept. 2020. www.britannica.com/biography/S-Truett-Cathy. Accessed 9 Sept. 2020.

Parker, Dick. "A Life Centered on Family." *The Chicken Wire*, 11 Aug. 2016. thechickenwire.chick-fil-a.com/inside-chick-fil-a/a-life-centered-on-family. Accessed 27 Feb. 2020.

---. "Humble Beginnings." *The Chicken Wire*, 11 Nov. 2016. thechickenwire.chick-fil-a.com/inside-chick-fil-a/humble-beginnings-how-truett-cathys-love-for-customers-grew-from-a-coke-and-smile. Accessed 27 Feb. 2020.

Taylor, Kate. "There's a Chick-fil-A in Atlanta's Mercedes-Benz Stadium—but the chain is refusing to open it on Super Bowl Sunday." *Business Insider*, 22 Jan. 2019. www.businessinsider.com/chick-fil-a-closed-on-super-bowl-sunday-2019-1. Accessed 9 Feb. 2020.

"Who We Are." *The Chicken Wire.* www.chick-fil-a.com/about/who-we-are. Accessed 11 Sept. 2020.

MENTOR TEXT: FINAL REFLECTION

Writing a project collaboratively using multiple genres was a different experience.

It was helpful to have the support of team members in decision-making and writing skill. It was helpful to choose a famous person to research. Selecting genre types forced me as the writer to think about genre characteristics and look at topics in different ways.

I learned that I can take leadership when necessary which is a good thing, but I need to be a better team player. In a future collaborative project, I need to learn to give and take, remembering that my teammates have good ideas too.

I learned that Cathy was a leader with strong character. He persevered in difficult times and took the initiative to try new and creative things. He prioritized God in his personal life and in his business. I believe the success of his business stems from his desire to put the Lord first despite outside pressures to conform. Cathy is a great role model for me. I desire to stand up and do what pleases God now and in every future endeavor.

Assume a Role

To produce a successful product, teamwork is vital. Your final project is no exception. Teamwork is different when you think about it as a way of Christ-expression. Christ-expressing teamwork means every choice you make together is for the glory of God. When you present your final project, you are putting yourselves not only in the place of your audience but also in the place of your teammates. With every word and action, consider how you would want to be treated. Jesus addressed this important principle in Luke 6:31, "And as ye would that men should do to you, do ye also to them likewise." Presenting an exceptional project will be a result of deliberate teamwork.

To set your team up for success, you will need to divide the work up equally. Teammates need to help others on the team when necessary. The project is everyone's responsibility. Use the Keys for Collaboration to guide the team.

Keys for Collaboration

- Come prepared to participate by bringing appropriate materials.
- Communicate ideas clearly.
- Contribute appropriate ideas; stay on topic.
- Listen respectfully and attentively.
- Be open to others' ideas.

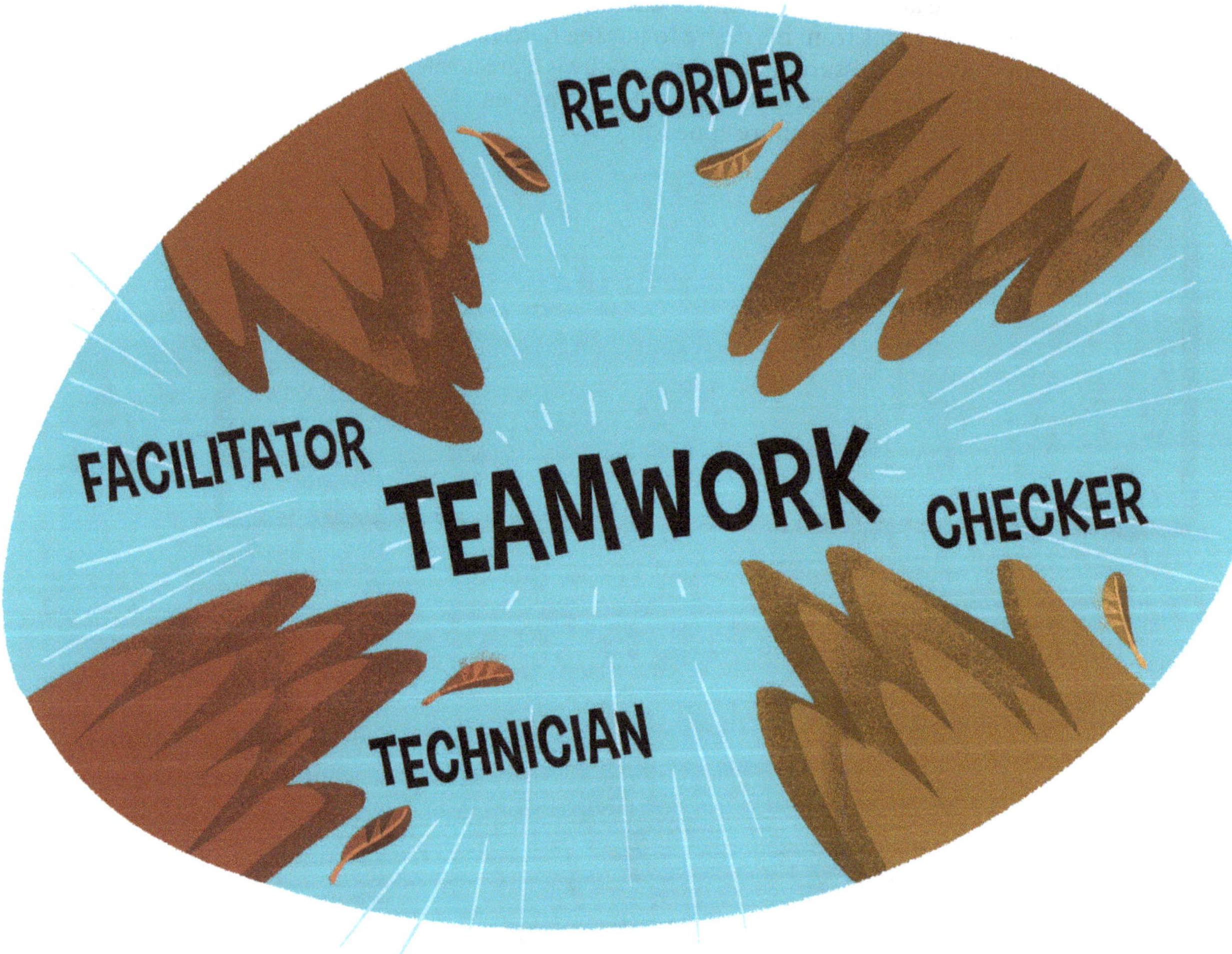

Develop a Plan

Using the model in Chapter 6, develop a research plan for gathering information.

Broad Topic

Your project purpose or goal is to research the life of a past or current famous person, find intriguing information about that person, and present that biographical information in an engaging way.

Narrowed Topic

Brainstorm a list of important people you and your team would like to know more about. The person you choose for this project should, most importantly, be interesting to you and your team members. The selection should also pique the curiosity of your audience. Who will your audience be? Your classmates? Students in other grades? Your parents?

Do some preliminary research to see what information is available. Are there existing biographies or autobiographies that provide overviews of the person's life? Are there primary sources available? Are there other credible sources that provide additional insight? Keep in mind that current personalities may not have much written about them yet.

Research Question

The main question to answer is *What are the defining life moments or events in the person's life?*

Related Questions

When determining related questions, begin by asking *What do we already know?* and *What do we want to know?*

Plan the Project Components

Use the mentor texts in Lessons 162–63 to help plan the following project components.

The Introduction

In preparation for an introductory paragraph, consider the following questions:

- Why did you choose this person?
- Why is this person important?
- What did you already know about this person?
- What do you want to learn about this person?

The Timeline

From the preliminary research, brainstorm a chronological list of the most important events and accomplishments in the chosen person's life. Narrow the list to the events that had the greatest impact on the person's life. For instance, in the timeline for Truett Cathy's life, the death of his brothers was significant, and its effect on Cathy and his future was powerful and well documented.

The Biographical Essay

Using the model in Chapter 1, create an outline. Decide the order in which the timeline events will be incorporated. They do not necessarily need to be in chronological order but can be in categories, such as events which influenced the person's character, events which influenced others, and events which influenced the person's reputation. This essay should be foundational to all the project content.

Four Genre Pieces

Write a different genre piece for four of the most influential events from the timeline. Make sure you have a thorough understanding of the event and its significance in that person's life. Ask such questions as *What led up to it?* and *What happened as a result?* The genre pieces can make reference to other biographical facts, but most importantly, they should elevate specific events in the person's life. When selecting a genre for each event, ask *What do I want to be able to express?* and *Which genre most effectively expresses what I want to communicate?* Consider different genres to determine which one works best.

Notice how the different genre forms correspond with specific events in Cathy's timeline.

Choosing different genres for each event will require looking at the event from a different angle and perhaps a different viewpoint. For instance, a memoir is a reflective firsthand account. It needs to be written in first person as though the selected person had written it. The content should include not just facts but also creative expressions of the person's thoughts and feelings.

Do a little research on each genre's distinguishing characteristics and different forms, and create a format template for each genre. For instance, a play script has specific page margins and specified placements for setting descriptions, act and scene headings, and stage directions. Using this genre form would require communicating the facts and significance of the event mainly in dialogue.

In the S. Truett Cathy project, the radio interview corresponds with the timeline event "opened the Dwarf Grill." It is a form of the informative genre because it mainly relates factual details. The acrostic poem corresponds with the timeline event "opened the first Chick-fil-A." It capsulizes the philosophy on which Truett built his restaurant chain. The diary corresponds with the timeline event "began advertising using cows." It is a form of the narrative genre because it relates an account chronologically. The letter to the President corresponds with the timeline event "received the President's Call to Service Award." It is a form of the argumentative/persuasive genre because it attempts to persuade an audience.

The Works Cited

Create a Works-Cited page that includes all the sources used in the project.

Final Reflection

The purpose for writing a final reflection paragraph is to express your thoughts about what you learned about the person and the process.

- What did I learn from the multigenre project?
- What was the most enjoyable part of the process?
- What was the most difficult part of the process? How did I handle it?
- What did I learn about myself?
- What, if anything, would I do differently next time?
- What did I learn about this person?
- What surprises, if any, did I find out about this person?
- What overall impression of the person did I come away with?
- What can I learn from this person that I can apply in my life?

Digital Presentation

Prepare to present your report using your choice of digital format. Remember to include each part of the project in your presentation and add a catchy title to engage your audience.

Colors, Visuals, and Sound

Using colors, visuals, and sounds in your presentation will help to engage the audience while clarifying and illustrating the content you are talking about. However, these visual and audio aids can be detrimental to your presentation if they distract and overwhelm the audience. It is important to incorporate visual and audio aids effectively and appropriately.

Visual Aids

charts
photos
graphs
brochures
comic strips
maps
cartoons
book covers
collages
animations

Audio Aids

sound effects
audio clips
music
media clips

DRAFTING

The Introduction

Begin the report with a paragraph introducing the person the team has chosen. Tell why that person was chosen and what the team wanted to find out about that person.

The Timeline

Create a timeline that includes the important events in your chosen person's life.

The Biographical Essay

Follow the steps for "Drafting Your Plan" in Lessons 57–59. Refer to the Revising Checklist in Lessons 60–61 to make sure you are incorporating the characteristics of an informative essay. Remember to include information about each event on the timeline.

Four Genre Pieces

Although each genre piece will be in a different form than was used in the respective writing chapters, each should retain certain genre characteristics. Incorporate the following components when composing the genre pieces.

Informative Genre

- factual (examples, quotations, anecdotes)
- straightforward, precise
- logical, organized
- leaves out personal opinion

Narrative Genre

- themes, story elements, action, dialogue
- details, vivid verbs, descriptions that appeal to the senses
- beginning, middle, and end; logical progression of events
- realistic portrayal of characters, engaging, appropriately paced

Argumentative/Persuasive Genre

- advertising techniques, facts and statistics
- logical reasoning, quotes from authorities, examples, specific words
- clear and logical order
- appropriate language for audience

Poetry

- big ideas compressed into relatively small space
- images created, varied sounds and rhythms
- end rhyme or free verse
- feelings expressed, read with expression, rhythmic pacing

The Works Cited

Create a Works-Cited page for the project.

Final Reflection

Write a paragraph addressing the following questions:

- What did I learn from the multigenre project?
- What was the most enjoyable part of the process?
- What was the most difficult part of the process? How did I handle it?
- What did I learn about myself?
- What, if anything, would I do differently next time?
- What did I learn about this person?
- What surprises, if any, did I find out about my famous person?
- What overall impression of the person did I come away with?
- What can I learn from this person that I can apply in my life?

Self and Peer Revising

Carefully revise the components of the project, using the following Revising Checklist. Revise the individual genre pieces based on the five traits of revising checklists found in Chapters 7, 11, and 15. Ask a peer to do the same. Remember to follow the peer review guidelines in Lesson 6.

	Revising Checklist
Important Person Selection	❑ Creates curiosity and interest ❑ Credible sources available
Introduction	❑ Grabs reader's attention ❑ Introduces the person ❑ Explains why the person was chosen ❑ Explains what information was researched
Timeline	❑ Lists significant events and accomplishments chronologically ❑ Cites accurate dates
Biographical Essay	❑ Meets Revising Checklist specifications (Lessons 60–61)
Genre Pieces	❑ Includes four different genre forms ❑ Elevates designated specific events ❑ Uses genre-appropriate format ❑ Uses other genre-form-specific characteristics
Works Cited	❑ Records all sources referenced ❑ Uses correct MLA format
Reflection	❑ Addresses the following questions: ❑ What did I learn from the multigenre process? ❑ What was the most enjoyable part of the process? ❑ What was the most difficult part of the process? How did I handle it? ❑ What did I learn about myself? ❑ What, if anything, would I do differently next time? ❑ What did I learn about this person? ❑ What surprises, if any, did I find out about this person? ❑ What overall impression of this person did I come away with? ❑ What can I learn from this person that I can apply in my life?
Presentation	❑ Begins with catchy title ❑ Includes all components in accurate order ❑ Incorporates effective and appropriate visual and audio aids

As you know, the process of writing is not complete until the finishing touch is added—carefully rereading the work for correct conventions, the sixth writing trait. Since this team project has multiple components prepared by different team members, the process will take more time and be more complex but will definitely be worth the effort.

Proofreader's Checklist

- ☐ The project follows the teacher's formatting guidelines and correct MLA format.
- ☐ There are no spelling errors.
- ☐ There are no grammar errors.
- ☐ There are no errors in capitalization or punctuation.

Digital Presentation

Now that you have completed your project, it's time to publish your project by giving a collaborative presentation with your team. Before checking out the following pointers, however, remember that your ultimate goal is Christ-expressing teamwork—treating one another as you desire to be treated.

Assigning Roles

Outline the components of the presentation and assign team members to present each one. An introduction and a conclusion are especially important. The introduction needs a speaker who can effectively grab the audience's attention, and the conclusion needs a speaker who can clearly bring the report to an end by summarizing the team's key ideas and findings. As much as possible, all members should have an equal amount of speaking time.

Unifying the Content

The goal for the oral presentation is to tie all the visual parts together into a unified portrait of the team's chosen person. You do not need to share or display each part in its entirety. Collaboratively plan the specific amount of content each person will share. Remember, your audience has not done all the work your team has done; they may or may not know anything about this person. They are depending on you to unite all the pieces, leaving them with an unforgettable picture. Use your team's imagination and creativity.

Here are some ideas the team can use for unifying the presentation:

- Explain in your own words what you are displaying; you do not have to nor should you read every word.
- Give some narration between parts to connect them, such as an introduction to the event or how the event relates to the previous or next event.
- Introduce the next speaker and what he or she will discuss.
- Transition between genre pieces by giving an explanation for why that particular form was used.
- Transition between genre pieces with pictures that show developments in the person's life (such as changes in location, age, jobs, etc.).

Use the digital presentation tips from Lessons 63–65 to ensure that the final digital presentation displays the content in the most visually engaging way.

Rehearsing the Presentation

Rehearsing your presentation is essential to help your team work together and transition between speakers smoothly. It helps to relieve nerves and build confidence. Rehearsing ensures that all content has been covered and allows for constructive feedback and group changes. Each member must not only understand his assigned content, but also the overall content and its order. Think about these questions:

- Am I prepared to present my information knowledgeably?
- Do I know my teammates' information enough to help them if I need to?
- Have I encouraged my teammates, helping to build their confidence for their own part in the presentation?
- Have I worked with my teammates to make the content engaging?

As you practice, remember to follow the tips from Lessons 63–65 to help you prepare for a successful presentation.

Giving the Presentation

You should now have the tools for smoothly and confidently sharing your hard work. Keep the following questions in mind as you present your part of the project:

- Am I remembering my integrity as a speaker—taking the presentation seriously and communicating the truth skillfully?
- Am I respecting my team members—listening appreciatively to my teammates' presentations?
- Am I taking ownership of the presentation—remembering it is not *mine* but *ours*?

Conducting a Question-and-Answer Session

Follow up the presentation by interacting with the audience in a question-and-answer session. Make sure to follow the recommendations given in Lessons 63–65.

Here are some suggestions you might follow:

- Give your classmates slips of paper to submit questions on. The presenting group can determine which group member will answer the question.
- Provide topics for which questions will be accepted. These can even be given prior to the presentation. Suggested topics could include questions about the events on the timeline, the individual genre pieces, and the team's overall impression of the person.
- The presenters can ask open-ended questions to encourage audience participation, such as, What do you consider the person's most important contribution? Was there anything you found surprising about this person? What is your overall impression of this person?

Reflecting on the Process

After the presentation, there is still more for you to learn. Reflecting on the whole process can be the most educational part of your team project. To reflect on the process well, you need to identify what worked and what did not work. Together as a team, write answers to the following questions:

- Did we work as a team or as a group of individuals?
- Did we listen to our teammates' ideas or did we disregard them?
- Did we inspire each other or did we discourage each other?
- Did this project allow me to demonstrate the skills I've learned throughout the year?
- Did this project improve my writing skills?

HANDBOOK

SPELLING SKILLS

Spelling Hints

Spell by syllables.

Dividing a word into its individual syllables will help you to spell it correctly. Think about prefixes, suffixes, and other word parts as you are spelling words by syllables.

mis + spell	misspell
dis + courage	discourage
thankful + ly	thankfully

Use a dictionary.

Use your dictionary to look up words when you are unsure of the correct spelling. Though you may be unsure of a word's spelling, you probably know enough of the word to find it in the dictionary.

Keep a list of words that are problems for you.

When you realize that you have misspelled a particular word, add the word to your list.

Look for possible groupings among your problem words.

If you notice that your list of problem words includes several similar words, try to find a rule for that group. For example, if you have a problem with *ie* and *ei*, study that rule and write those words correctly.

Study your list of problem words systematically.

Begin by writing a word several times, concentrating on its appearance and its sound. Repeat this procedure on three or four different days within the next week. Then ask someone to quiz you on that word. If you can write the word correctly without hesitation, transfer it to your "learned" list. If a problem remains, keep working on the word.

Spelling Singular Present-Tense Verbs and Plural Nouns

If the word ends in *ch*, *sh*, *s*, *x*, or *z*, add *-es*.

bunch	bunches	marsh	marshes
mass	masses	ax	axes
buzz	buzzes		

If the word ends in a consonant followed by *y*, change final *y* to *i* and add *-es*.

try	tries
lily	lilies
folly	follies

If the word ends in a vowel followed by *y*, add *-s*.

buy	buys
pray	prays
chimney	chimneys

If the word ends in *f* or *fe*, consult your dictionary. For most, add *-s*; for others, change the *f* to *v* and add *-es*.

chief	chiefs	fife	fifes
elf	elves	life	lives

If the word ends in *o*, consult your dictionary. For most, add *-es*; for others add *-s*.

go	goes	potato	potatoes
trio	trios	portfolio	portfolios

Add *-s* to most other words.

bug	bugs	plate	plates
jar	jars	board	boards

Some nouns have irregular plural forms. Consult your dictionary for nouns with irregular plurals.

alumnus	alumni
goose	geese
deer	deer

Spelling with *ie* or *ei*

When the sound is "long *e*," put *i* before *e* except after *c*.

i before *e*	except after *c*
believe	ceiling
yield	perceive
grief	receipt

Exceptions: caffeine, either, leisure, neither, protein, seize, sheik, weird

When the sound is "long *a*," put *e* before *i*.

vein beige sleigh

Adding Suffixes

Doubling a final consonant

If a one-syllable word ends with a single consonant preceded by a single vowel, double the final consonant before adding a suffix.

hop	hopped
run	running
spin	spinner

If a multisyllable word with its main accent on the final syllable ends with a single consonant preceded by a single vowel, double the final consonant before adding a suffix.

begin	beginning
admit	admitted
confer	conferring

If a word ends with a single consonant preceded by two vowels, do not double the final consonant before adding a suffix.

droop	drooping
pair	paired
fool	foolish

Changing final *y* to *i*

If a word ends with a consonant and *y*, change the final *y* to *i* before adding a suffix.

fry	fried
cleanly	cleanliness
mercy	merciful

However, if the suffix itself begins with *i*, do not change final *y* to *i*.

fry	frying
apply	applying
fortify	fortifying

Dropping final silent *e*

Drop the final silent *e* that is preceded by a consonant before adding a suffix beginning with a vowel.

live	living
achieve	achievable
tune	tuning

Exceptions: noticeable, courageous

Keep the final silent *e* before adding a suffix beginning with a consonant.

live	lively
achieve	achievement
tune	tuneful

Exceptions: truly, argument, judgment

Troublesome Words

Homonyms and other commonly confused words

accept/except

Accept is a verb that means "to receive"; it is never a preposition. *Except* is a preposition that means "not including."

I guess I must *accept* someone else's help.
Every tent *except* mine had been raised.

Calvary/cavalry

Calvary is the hill outside Jerusalem where Jesus was crucified. *Cavalry* refers to "a military force which serves on horseback."

One of my favorite hymns recounts Jesus' painful journey to *Calvary*.
Tennyson's poem "The Charge of the Light Brigade" is about a famous *cavalry* battle.

fewer/less

Fewer is used with plural count nouns, such as *fewer* coins. *Less* is used with non-count nouns, such as *less* water.

Margo had *fewer* papers to take home than William.
William had *less* time for soccer practice because of his additional homework.

hear/here

Hear is a verb meaning "to receive sound by the ear." *Here* is an adverb meaning "at or in this place."

From our apartment we can *hear* the bubbling brook.
Wait *here* while I get my fishing rod.

led (v)/lead (n)

Led is the past tense of the verb *lead*, meaning "to guide or conduct by going before." The noun *lead* is a type of metal.

Joe *led* the way down the steep path.
Current EPA regulations require that paint cannot include *lead*.

loose/lose

The adjective *loose* means "unfastened." The verb *lose* means "to misplace or not to win."

Her *loose* shoelace caused a problem during the race.
Did you *lose* your jacket?

passed/past

Passed is the past tense of the verb *pass*, meaning "moved ahead." *Past* can be used as an adjective that means "gone by in time" or as a noun that means "before the present."

We *passed* several restaurants before we selected one.
Past vacations have required us to eat at various restaurants.

peace/piece

Peace means "harmony in relationships." A *piece* is a part of a whole.

The two countries signed a treaty and were finally at *peace*.
Now both nations have a *piece* of the disputed territory.

plane/plain

The noun *plane* can refer to an airplane or a flat surface. The adjective *plain* usually means "ordinary" or "obvious."

Dora's uncle flies a *plane* in an airshow.
The wings of his aircraft are long *planes* designed to lift the craft off the ground as air passes around them.
He usually wears a *plain* blue uniform when he flies.
Although he would not brag, the *plain* facts about his flying record show him to be a careful pilot.

quiet/quite

Quiet is an adjective meaning "silent." *Quite* is an adverb meaning "completely" or "really."

Jack stayed *quiet* for the whole sermon.
The grandparents were *quite* impressed by his maturity.

than/then

Than is a conjunction used to introduce the second part of a comparison. *Then* means "at that time" or "next in order."

David is a better writer *than* I.
He rises early in the morning and likes to write *then*.
First, he wrote a short story; *then* he wrote a poem.

to/too/two

The preposition *to* means "toward." *Too* is an adverb meaning "in addition to," "excessively," or "very." *Two* is a number word often used as an adjective.

We ran *to* the stop sign.
Mary ran *too*.
We don't run *too* fast.
We run at least *two* miles every morning.

wear/where

Wear is a verb that means "to have on" or "to damage." *Where* is an adverb indicating place or position.

Did you *wear* your new shoes?
Be careful not to *wear* them out.
Where are your old ones?

Other Usage Problems

ain't

Ain't is a nonstandard contraction for *am not*. Replace *ain't* with *is not*, *am not*, *are not*, *isn't*, or *aren't*.

Incorrect: We *ain't* late for the meeting.
Correct: We *aren't* late for the meeting.

alot/a lot

Alot is not a word; it is a misspelling of *a lot.*

Incorrect: Rorie has *alot* of time on his hands now that he's broken his leg.
Correct: Rorie has *a lot* of time on his hands now that he's broken his leg.

alright/all right

Alright is not a word; it is a misspelling of *all right.*

Incorrect: His leg is broken, but his arm is *alright.*
Correct: His leg is broken, but his arm is *all right.*

between/among

Between is a preposition generally used to compare just two items or people. *Among* is a preposition used to compare three or more items or people.

The peach was divided *between* the two sisters.
Gardening tasks were divided *among* the garden club members.

bring/take

Bring implies movement toward the speaker or listener, whereas *take* refers to movement away from the speaker or listener.

Please *bring* your books to class with you.
When you are finished cleaning, *take* the garbage to the curb.

how come/why

How come is an informal expression for *why* and does not belong in academic writing. *Why* is an adverb meaning "for what purpose, reason, or cause."

Informal: *How come* we're wearing our blue jerseys for the game?
Standard: *Why* the hummingbird can fly is one of the great scientific mysteries.

learn/teach

The verb *learn* means "to get knowledge by study or experience." *Teach* means "to give knowledge or skill to another person or an animal."

We *learn* by listening.
Darla is *teaching* her pupils to paint.

STUDY SKILLS

Developing an Interest

Most of us have several areas of interest. Imagine you did not know anyone who enjoys the same things as you. You would not have anyone to talk and share ideas with. God has gifted each of us with a unique curiosity about specific areas. Sometimes we may not think that we like a subject at first. Then the teacher does a class demonstration or states a fact that we find particularly exciting, and we start to learn more about that subject. Most of us have had the experience of not liking something initially and then learning to like it after additional time and experience with it. Interests can be developed and information can be learned by using several methods.

1. Take an active interest in your classes. Participate in class discussions and activities.
2. Concentrate on the teacher or the reading. When you find yourself wandering mentally, immediately bring yourself back to conscious concentration on the teacher and what is taking place in the classroom.
3. Write down (or mark) important points. If the teacher or textbook emphasizes a point, highlight it or write it down.
4. Practice guessing. What will the teacher or book say next?
5. Connect the information that you are learning. How does what you are learning now connect to what you learned yesterday or even to what you learned in another class?
6. Ask (or write down) questions, especially about information that you do not understand. Try to find the answers in your textbook. If you do not find them, request to see the teacher at a convenient time.

Using the Parts of a Book

When you understand the parts of a book, you can find the information in it more quickly. Not all books contain the same parts, nor are the parts arranged in the same order in all books.

Every book, though, begins with a **title page**, which gives the title of the book, the name of the author or editor, the name of the publisher, and the place of publication. On the back of this page is the **copyright page**, which lists, among other things, the year that the book was copyrighted. *Copyright* means that the author or publisher has the legal right to that book; no one else can reprint any part of it without permission.

A **table of contents** gives the chapter or unit divisions with page numbers in numerical order. A **list of illustrations** is similar to a table of contents; it lists where the pictures are in the text.

Some books also include **acknowledgments**, the names of people the author or editor wants to thank, and an **introduction** or **preface**, which states the purpose of the book.

The largest part of every book is the **text**. In both fiction and nonfiction books, the text is usually divided into units, sections, or chapters.

Many nonfiction books also contain additional sections of information that are placed after the text. One of these is the **bibliography**; it lists either the books that the author used in writing the text or the titles of some additional books about the same subject.

Extra helps, such as charts, diagrams, long lists, and notes of explanation, are included in the **appendix**. One kind of appendix is a **glossary**, which gives the definitions of special vocabulary used in the text. Textbooks may have glossaries and other appendices.

An **index** is an alphabetical listing of key words and phrases with all the page numbers where they appear in the text. Sometimes the index also lists the page numbers of the illustrations.

You may notice that fiction books usually have only a title page, a copyright page, a table of contents, and a text. This is because the main purpose of fictional writing is usually to entertain, not to inform.

Reading Textbooks

Whenever you receive a new textbook, look at the pictures and read the captions. Stop to read interesting parts that catch your interest as you leaf through the book for the first time. Look over the table of contents. The table of contents will tell you two important things: the major topics in the textbook and the logical organization that the author uses to discuss those topics.

Organization is very important to textbook authors. Look again at the table of contents to see how the author has logically organized the chapters and units of the textbook. The sequence in which the author has chosen to give the information also has significance. He may have started from the simplest to the most difficult concept, or he may have decided to state the information in chronological order. Look to see whether you can determine from the table of contents how the book has been organized.

Turn to the text and look at a chapter in the book. Chapters are organized in a particular way as well. The chapter may have bold headings that introduce main topics and smaller bold headings to introduce smaller parts of the main subject. Each heading tells you which part of the topic will be discussed. The rest of the information in most textbooks is in regular paragraph form. When the teacher assigns reading, read each paragraph, looking for the one topic in that paragraph. If you have trouble understanding the information, write the topic sentence in your notebook. Then look into the paragraph for details that you can list under the topic sentence. By reading the chapter this way, you are also making study notes that will help you to study more efficiently for the test. Read the information under the pictures and study the pictures and illustrations as well. These are ways that help you to understand better the information that the author has placed in the chapter.

Helpful Tips

The purpose of studying is to learn information. Sometimes intelligence has nothing to do with good grades. Usually the students who make the best grades are the ones who have learned the best methods for studying. The following ideas will help you to prepare better for study time.

Be prepared for each class period.

- Come to class with your textbook.
- Bring paper, a pen, and a notebook.
- Bring any assignment that is due for the day.
- Be in class on time.

Take time every day to prepare for each class.

- Write down all homework assignments in an assignment booklet.
- Have a definite place to keep papers and returned assignments.
- Take home every book that is needed for that day's assignments.
- Have a definite place at home where you always study.
- Keep all needed materials in that place at all times.
- Study in a quiet place, not near a television or while talking to a friend on the telephone.

Put these study skills to practice and organize your study time. When you sincerely and consistently do your homework and prepare for tests, the Lord will help you conquer many difficulties.

Scheduling Your Study Time

First, establish a priority schedule. Although you probably keep a busy schedule, you generally have time to do what must be done. To create priorities means that you decide what is the most important and do that first. Then decide what is next and so forth. Establish a monthly and a weekly calendar for yourself. Place in it all the activities in which you are involved, such as church, sports practice, family obligations, and after-school jobs. Then schedule in study time for each evening.

Second, a detailed homework schedule is a must. Place all assignments and test dates in an assignment book or calendar daily. If you have no assignment for a particular class for that day, write *none* in the assignment booklet so that you will know that you did not simply forget to write down the assignment.

When a teacher assigns a long-term project, write the assignment down on the day that it is due as well as on several days well before the due date. Schedule time to work on one part of the assignment each week and continue to work until the project is completed by or before the due date.

Third, have a plan for your daily study schedule. This plan must include the *when*, *where*, and *how* of the study time.

When: You have choices. Your choices are to study right after school or between dinner and bedtime. Be consistent once your study schedule has been established and you will not have to stay up late or rise early on a regular basis in order to complete assignments.

Where: Establish one place to study. Choose a well-lit and comfortable place. If you are very tired on a particular day, ask your mom or another family member to check in on you occasionally in case you fall asleep. By choosing one study place, you condition your mind to study when you are in that place.

How: Which subject do you study first and for how long? Look at your assignment book. Decide which subject is your hardest or which of that day's assignments will require the most time. You probably will discover that working from hardest to easiest is the better plan. Then if you complete all the assignments and have any additional time to do so, return to the hardest for a brief review session.

Once you have determined the order of your study, decide approximately how long the homework for each class usually takes. Of course, on some evenings the times will vary. You should always set aside some time to review. These review sessions will save study time later by allowing the information to become firmly rooted in your long-term memory.

Study and Memory Techniques

After you complete your daily reading and written homework assignments, you will need to study for your tests and quizzes. Here are some techniques to improve your memory.

1. Determine to remember. In other words, pay attention as you study. Do not be mentally lazy.
2. Ask yourself questions about your notes and answer them aloud. Write down questions regarding material that is unclear to you; then ask the teacher those questions when you return to class.
3. Use flash cards, whether paper or electronic, to quiz yourself.
4. Create your own written quizzes as you study. Put the quiz away for a day or two and then try to answer the questions. Those that you cannot answer correctly are the ones that need extra study time.
5. Ask a friend or family member to quiz you occasionally.
6. Cluster information that you are learning. When you are given much information at one time to study, such as for a final exam, try to organize the material into related groups or clusters. Learn the information by category groups: the industrial products from New England, the industrial products from the Middle Atlantic states, the industrial products from the Southwest, and so forth.
7. Use different memory devices to help you remember. Create rhymes, acronyms, acrostics, or other word games during your study times to help you remember detailed information. An acronym is a word in which each letter stands for another word. An acrostic is a word in which each letter stands for a word or phrase. Here is an example of an acronym:

   To remember the names of the Great Lakes (Superior, Huron, Michigan, Erie, Ontario), rearrange the first letters (S, H, M, E, O) into a single word: HOMES.

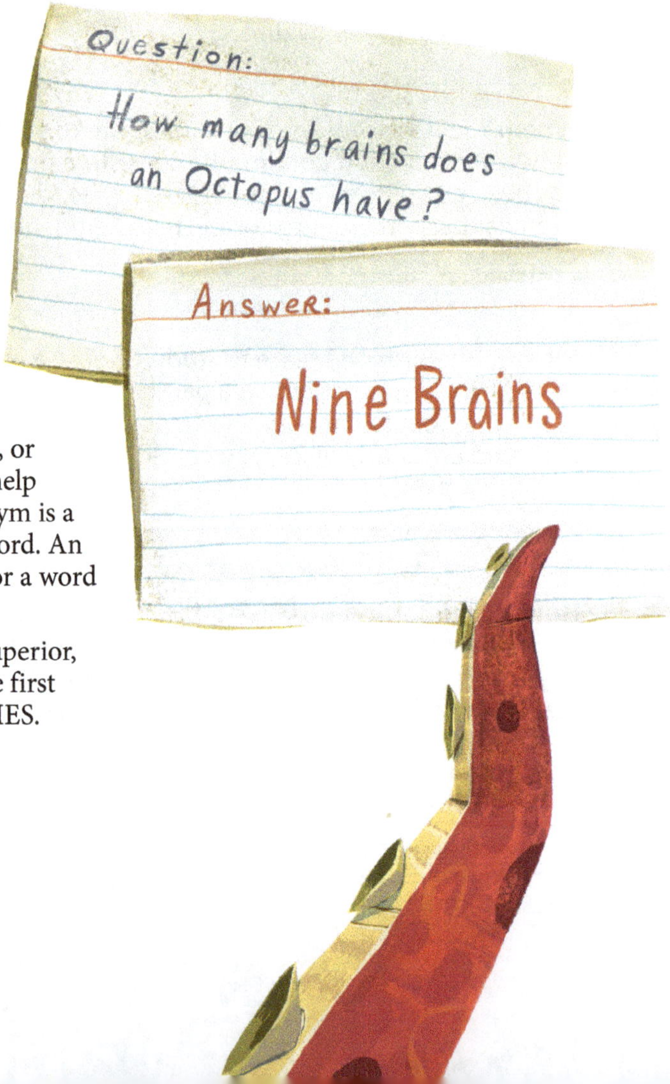

Improving Your Reading Comprehension

Schoolwork requires much reading. You probably do not understand the meaning of every word that you read, and you do not always have time to look up every unfamiliar word. How can you discover the meanings of these words while you continue to read your assignments?

Context Clues

One method is defining a word from context clues. You often can discover enough clues from other words in a sentence to give you at least an understanding of an unfamiliar word's meaning in the sentence. Look around the italicized word below to understand by context what the word *disheveled* means.

> His clothes were *disheveled* because he had slept in them for days.

Disheveled means to be in disarray or disorder.

Definitions

Sometimes the writer may write the definition of an unfamiliar word into the sentence. Keep reading because the definition may be included in the sentence.

> Debbi was quite the *flibbertigibbet*; she is known for being a chatterer.

Restatements

If the text does not give a definition of the word, look for a restatement. Extra information may be included after the word that may explain it.

> The *foofaraw* surrounding the arrival of the spelling bee champion—the parades, banners, flowers, crowds, and earsplitting applause—made one think that the queen had arrived.

What does *foofaraw* mean? The sentence mentions five things that happened as the winner of the spelling bee arrived. You probably guessed that *foofaraw* means "a fuss over a trifling matter."

Examples

Sometimes the meaning of a word may be revealed by examples. The examples used may give enough information to enable you to guess the meaning of the unknown word.

> The most-anticipated *soiree* of the year is the junior-senior banquet.

What does *soiree* mean? The sentence above gives an example of what is looked forward to. From this example, you can determine that *soiree* means "a party or reception." A dictionary then would further inform you that a *soiree* is an evening party or reception.

Word Parts

All words come from a root word; in fact, some root words are words themselves. Many words also have prefixes and suffixes. Sometimes knowing the meanings of the parts of a word will give you enough clues to determine the meaning of the complete word.

Prefixes

A **prefix** is added to the beginning of a word.

Prefix	Meaning	Example
circum-	around, about	circumnavigate
intro-	in, inward	introspection
re-	again, backwards	reversible
sub-	under	submarine

Suffixes

A **suffix** is added to the end of the word.

Suffix	Meaning	Example
-ion	action, process	exception
-ate	act upon in a particular manner	accelerate

Roots

A **root** is the main part of the word or one of the main parts of the word. Many roots can stand alone as words without any prefixes attached.

Root	Meaning	Example
act	do	react
bene	well, good	benevolent
fact	make, do	benefactor
spect	look at, watch	inspection
vert	verse, turn	introvert

Taking Tests

Studying and doing homework is part of learning, but it is also part of an organized plan to help you do well on tests and quizzes. You have no doubt learned that waiting to prepare an assignment until the night before it is due is not a good way to earn good grades for a class. The more often you review material and the longer the period of time, the more information your memory will retain.

How to Take Classroom Tests

1. Before you begin, look over the test to see how many and what types of questions there are.
2. Read all directions carefully.
3. Work through the entire test in one of two ways:
    - Start at the beginning of the test and keep going. Answer those questions about which you are confident and those about which you are 50 to 75 percent certain of the answers. In some way mark those questions that you do not know or need to spend more time thinking about. Come back to them later.
    - Start at the most difficult section of the test and do it first. Be careful, however, not to spend too much time on that one section. Again, mark questions with which you are having problems and come back to them later.
4. Try to answer all questions, even if you must guess at some.
5. Think carefully and be selective about what you write. It is better to write a little about what you do know than to write a lot about what you do not know.
6. Write neatly. Correct answers will not count if the teacher cannot read what you have written.

How to Answer Objective Test Questions

Multiple Choice

1. Read each question carefully. Formulate an answer before you look at the choices.
2. Read all the choices carefully. Eliminate those that you know are wrong.
3. Pay attention to qualifiers, such as *always*, *never*, *all*, *must*, *seldom*, *generally*, *probably*, or *usually*. These words will change the meaning of the question.
4. Choose the best answer from the choices that are left.

Example: __C__ Which of the following animals is not a marsupial?

A kangaroo
B wombat
C giraffe
D opossum

Matching

1. Read each question carefully. Formulate an answer before you look at the choices.
2. Match the questions and answers that you know are correct.
3. From the choices remaining, choose the best answer for each question.

Example: **A** William Bradford
B Anne Bradstreet
C Cotton Mather
D Jonathan Edwards

__*D*__ 1. "Sinners in the Hands of an Angry God"

__*B*__ 2. "To My Dear and Loving Husband"

__*A*__ 3. *Of Plymouth Plantation*

__*C*__ 4. *An Essay for the Recording of Illustrious Providences*

True/False

1. Read each item carefully. If any word in the item is false, the entire item is false.
2. Look for words like *always* or *never*; these words often signal a false item.

Example:

__*false*__ A word ending in *-ing* always functions as a predicate.

Short Answer

1. Accurately and completely answer the questions that you know.
2. If you do not know the answer, make the best guess you can. You may receive partial credit for your answer.

Example:

__*Esther*__ What Bible queen saved her people from destruction?

How to Take Standardized Tests

Periodically you will be required to take standardized tests. You will have a better chance of doing well if you are familiar with the types of questions usually included on standardized tests.

Reading Comprehension

The reading comprehension section tests your ability to analyze a written passage. The questions may ask about the main ideas, details, or meaning of the passage. You may have to evaluate information or draw conclusions. The following strategies will help you on this part of the test:

1. Look at the questions briefly.
2. Read the paragraph and answer the questions you definitely know.
3. Read the other questions carefully as time allows, eliminating answers that you know are incorrect.
4. Choose the most logical answer from those remaining.

Example: The Young Voters Group canvassed the entire area, passing out leaflets for their candidate. Many had the opportunity to enlist the help of others in distributing yard signs and getting community members registered to vote. The group's political effort was a success.

___B___ In this paragraph the word *canvassed* means
A to cover an area with fabric
B to solicit voters
C to construct a tent
D to obstruct justice

The paragraph has no information leading the reader to think that *to cover an area with fabric*, *to construct a tent*, or *to obstruct justice* would be the correct choice. *To solicit voters* is clearly the intended answer.

Vocabulary

Standardized tests also contain a vocabulary section that tests your knowledge of common English words. This section may include two types of questions. One type gives a sentence (or part of a sentence) with a word in bold print. You must then choose the word that best matches the meaning of the word in bold print. Context clues (such as the word *retreated* in the example sentence) will help you choose your answer.

Example: ___B___ The forlorn lady retreated to her **chamber** to consider the king's advice.
A castle
B room
C thoughts
D court

Another type of question may list several sentences, each including the same underlined word. You must choose the sentence in which the word has the same meaning as in the original sentence.

Example: ___D___ The senator was accused of being part of the right wing.
A The ball player had to wing the ball to home plate.
B The injured bird could not use its left wing at all.
C One wing of the house contained five bedrooms.
D One wing of the state's house of representatives proposed a bill.

In the original sentence, *wing* means "either of two groups with opposing views." *Wing* in the first choice means "to throw." In the second choice, *wing* means "a movable organ for flying." In the third choice, *wing* means "a structure attached to a building." *Wing* in the fourth choice means "either of two groups with opposing views."

Grammar, Usage, and Mechanics

Standardized tests often combine questions about grammar, usage, and mechanics in one section. Other tests include several separate sections of questions. Depending on the test, the questions may appear in different formats. For example, the test may show a sentence with several words underlined and labeled, requiring you to choose the word that contains the error. If the sentence is correct, you choose the "no error" option.

Example: ___C___ Ginger, the cat, runs through bushs regularly. No error

A B C D

The correct choice is *C* because the correct spelling should be *bushes.*

Another type of question may show you a sentence with part of the sentence underlined. You must choose one of the possible replacements for the underlined part. If the underlined part is correct, choose the answer that indicates that no change is necessary.

Example: ___A___ One of the packages have lost its bow.

A has lost its
B has lost their
C have lost their
D correct as is

Choice *A* is correct because the verb *has* agrees with the singular subject *One*, and the pronoun *its* agrees with the singular antecedent *One.*

Other standardized tests have separate sections for mechanics (capitalization and punctuation). The question may divide one sentence into several parts. Each part is listed separately. You choose the part that contains an error. If the sentence is correct, choose the answer that indicates that no change is necessary.

Example: ___B___ **A** Hattie ran to the window
B and looked outside;
C but she saw nothing.
D no mistakes

Choice B contains an error. A semicolon usually joins independent clauses without a coordinating conjunction. A comma is the proper punctuation to separate two independent clauses joined by a conjunction.

INDEX

A

B

C

L

M

N

O

P

Q

R

S

PHOTO CREDITS

Key: (t) top; (c) center; (b) bottom; (l) left; (r) right; (bg) background; (i) inset

Chapter 1

3bg Dragon Tiger/iStock/Getty Images Plus/Getty Images; **11** Jim Richardson/National Geographic Image Collection/Alamy Stock Photo; **12** Zacarias Pereira da Mata/Shutterstock.com; **18** Aleksei Popov/Alamy Stock Photo; **21** Bruce Wilson/Shutterstock.com

Chapter 2

38 Hitesh Sawlani/Moment Open/Getty Images; **39** Tim Graham/Alamy Stock Photo; **46** GlobalP /iStock/Getty Images Plus/Getty Images; **47** Sylvain Sonnet/The Image Bank/Getty Images; **51** CaronB /iStock/Getty Images Plus/Getty Images; **52** Lawrencetfay/iStock/Getty Images Plus/Getty Images; **56** juanmces/iStock/Getty Images Plus/Getty Images; **57** Album/Alamy Stock Photo; **61** Rosemary Calvert /Stone/Getty Images; **62** DekiArt/E+/Getty Images; **63** Through the Lens/Moment/Getty Images

Chapter 3

66 netris/iStock/Getty Images Plus/Getty Images; **70** © 2010 JupiterImages Corporation; **72–73** Olesksii Hlembotskyi/iStock/Getty Images Plus/Getty Images; **78** alexsl/iStock/Getty Images Plus/Getty Images; **79** Dmitrii Melnidov/Alamy Stock Photo; **80–81** Spiderplay/E+/Getty Images; **82**t FALKENSTEIN-FOTO/Alamy Stock Photo; **82**b Paul Thompson/FPG /Stringer/Hulton Royals Collection/Getty Images; **83** Suze777/iStock/Getty Images Plus/Getty Images; **85** sjhaytov/iStock/Getty Images Plus/Getty Images; **86** Jacek_Sopotnicki/iStock/Getty Images Plus/Getty Images; **88** MENAHEM KAHANA/Staff/AFP/Getty Images; **89**, **105** UniversalImagesGroup/Getty Images; **92** Ghislain & Marie David deLossy/Culturea/Getty Images; **103** Map Resources; **104** edmetz/iStock/Getty Images Plus/Getty Images; **107**r Bettmann/Getty Images; **107**l f11photo/Shutterstock.com

Chapter 4

112 Bruce Bennett/Getty Image News/Getty Images; **116**l _ultraforma_/iStock/Getty Images Plus/Getty Images; **116**r Peter Unger/Stone/Getty Images; **117**tl PaulPaladin/Alamy Stock Photo; **117**tr alexnikit1981 /iStock/Getty Images Plus/Getty Images; **117**b donatas1205/Shutterstock.com; **120** "Buffalo Bill Cody by Sarony, c1880"/Sarony/Wikimedia Commons /Public Domain; **126** Luis Castaneda Inc/Photodisc /Getty Images

Chapter 5

130–31 Jeremy Woodhouse/Photodisc/Getty Images; **132**l "German troops parade through Warsaw, Poland, 09-1939 - NARA - 559369"/National Archives /Wikimedia Commons/Public Domain; **132**r © Tallandier/Bridgeman Images; **133** INTERFOTO /Alamy Stock Photo; **142** "Victory-garden" by Morley/Wikimedia Commons/Public Domain; **143** Universal History Archive/Universal Images Group /Getty Images; **149** © Ark Encounter; **150–51** devdogg/iStock/Getty Images Plus/Getty Images

Chapter 6

163 *The Great and Only Barnum: The Tremendous, Stupendous Life of Showman P. T. Barnum*, by Candace Fleming, illus. by Ray Fenwick, Schwartz & Wade Books, 2009

Chapter 7

184t bluejayphoto/iStock/Getty Images Plus/Getty Images; **184**b World History Archive/Alamy Stock Photo; **185** malerapaso/iStockphoto/Getty Images Plus/Getty Images; **187** Nancy C. Ross/iStock /Getty Images Plus/Getty Images

Chapter 8

199 subjug/iStock/Getty Images Plus/Getty Images; **201** Deborah Feingold/Corbis Premium Historical /Getty Images; **204** RonOrmanJr/iStock/Getty ImagesPlus/Getty Images; **206**t "20170420 Beinecke Rare Book Library Interior Yale University New Haven Connecticut" by Michael Kastelic/Wikimedia Commons/CC BY SA 4.0; **206**b Enzo Figueres /Moment Mobile/Getty Images; **211** princessdlaf /iStock/Getty Images Plus/Getty Images; **215** Pat Greenhouse/Boston Globe via Getty Images

Chapter 9

229i Damon Tighe/500px Plus/Getty Images; **229**bg bogdan ionescu/Shutterstock.com; **230** Lester Ryan Alcid/EyeEm/Getty Images

Chapter 10

253 Oleksandr_Delyk/Shutterstock.com; **254–55** Rixipix/iStock/Getty Images Plus/Getty Images; **259** "The Yacht 'America' Winning the International Race, Fitz Hugh Lane 1851"/Wikimedia Commons/Public Domain; **270** Lifestyle pictures/Alamy Stock Photo

Chapter 12

294t ALBERTO GUERRERO/iStock/Getty Images Plus/Getty Images; **294**b slowmotiongli/iStock/Getty Images Plus/Getty Images; **295** "Euspinolia militaris," hormiga panda-Flickr-Pato Novos/by Pato Novoa /Wikimedia Commons/CC BY 2.0; **295**i "Hormiga panda" by Chris Lukhaup/Wikimedia Commons/CC BY SA 4.0; **296**t Dgwildlife/iStock/Getty Images Plus /Getty Images; **296**b Fuse/Corbis/Getty Images; **297** Mike Warburton Photography/Moment/Getty Images; **305** Predrag Vuckovic/E+/Getty Images; **306** Mark Seridan-Johnson/Shutterstock.com; **307** Hakan Hjort/Johner RF/Getty Images; **308** stanley45/iStock /Getty Images Plus/Getty Images; **309** Jozef Polc /500px/500Px Plus/Getty Images; **311**t kolesnikovserg /iStock/Getty Images Plus/Getty Images; **311**b Joseph Kostansek/iStock/Getty Images Plus/Getty Images; **312**t feedough/iStock/Getty Images Plus/Getty Images; **312**b ChubarovY/iStock/Getty Images Plus/Getty Images; **313** eAlisa/iStock/Getty Images Plus/Getty Images; **317**tl, **317**br Universal History Archive /Universal Images Group/Getty Images; **320** Pacific Press/LightRocket/Getty Images; **321** Lloyd Cluff /Corbis Documentary/Getty Images

Chapter 13

325 syolacan/E+/Getty Images; **326** Peter Adams/The Image Bank Unreleased/Getty Images; **328** AFP Contributer/AFP/Getty Images; **329**t florintt/E+ /Getty Images; **329**b julichka/E+/Getty Images; **330** canadastock/Shutterstock.com; **331** OLIVER LANG /DDP/Getty Images; **333** Howard Kingsnorth/Stone /Getty Images; **334**t Pictorial Press Ltd/Alamy Stock Photo; **334**b Historical Images Archive/Alamy Stock Photo; **335** BJU Photo Services; **345** Everett Historical Collection/Shutterstock.com; **345**bg 2windspa/E+ /Getty Images; **346** Historic Collection/Alamy Stock Photo; **349** "Charles Wesley"/Wikimedia Commons /Public Domain; **350**t Rudy Sulgan/The Image Bank /Getty Images; **350**b Jupiter Images/PHOTOS.com /Getty Images Plus/Getty Images; **351** tupungato /iStock/Getty Images Plus/Getty Images; **354** Rosemary Calvert/Stone/Getty Images; **355** scisettialfio/iStock/Getty ImagesPlus/Getty Images

Chapter 14

359 grandriver/iStock/Getty Images Plus/Getty Images; **360** Lisa Noble/Moment Mobile ED/Getty Images; **361** ROMAOSLO/E+/Getty Images; **362–63** SUNGJIN AHN PHOTOGRAPHY/Moment /Getty Images; **364** Kevin Schafer/The Image Bank /Getty Images; **367** Alexander Spatari/Moment/Getty Images; **368** mtcurado/ iStock/Getty Images Plus /Getty Images; **369** NI QIN/E+/Getty Images; **370**tr DGLImages/iStock/Getty Images Plus/Getty Images; **370**tl kaczor58/Shutterstock.com; **370**br Sarah Casillas/DigitalVision/Getty Images; **373**bl VladimirKoval/Shutterstock.com; **373**br kolesnikovserg/iStock/Getty Images Plus/Getty Images; **374**tl d anutaratanya/iStock/Getty Images Plus/Getty Images; **374**tr Nipitphon Na Chiangmai /EyeEm/Getty Images; **375**t Donaldson Collection /Contributor/Michael Ochs Archives/Getty Images; **375**b Pictorial Press Ltd/Alamy Stock Photo; **376**t Eric D ricochet69/Alamy Stock Photo; **376**bg kukiatB /iStock/Getty Images Plus/Getty Images; **380**t Keith Homan/Shutterstock.com; **380**b Tetra Images-Jamie Grill/Brand X Pictures/Getty Images

Chapter 15

390, **394** The Advertising Council, Inc. and the National Highway Traffic Safety Administration

Chapter 16

403 Theodore Trimmer/Shutterstock.com; **405** Hal Cook/BJU Photo Services; **413** moodboard/Brand X Pictures/Getty Images; **414** Photo by Mike Kline (notkalvin)/Moment/Getty Images; **416**l, **416**r Print Collector/Hulton Archive/Getty Images; **418**l World History Archive/Alamy Stock Photo; **418**r Bettmann /Bettmann/Getty Images; **419** George Shelley/The Image Bank/Getty Images; **424** fstop123/E+/Getty Images; **426** MidoSemsem/Shutterstock.com

Chapter 17

432 bjdlzx/E+/Getty Images; **434** SeanXu/iStock /Getty Images Plus/Getty Images; **435** Mega Pixel /Shutterstock.com; **440** Floortje/iStock/Getty Images Plus/Getty Images; **441**l ROMAOSLO/iStock/Getty Images Plus/Getty Images; **441**r DieterMeyrl/E+ /Getty Images; **442** japatino/Moment/Getty Images; **444** Linnea Rheborg/Getty Images Sport/Getty Images; **447** John Carnemolia/AustralianPictureLibrary /Corbis Documentary/Getty Images; **450** Leonard Zhukovsky/Shutterstock.com; **451** lazyllama /Shutterstock.com; **453** Robert Niedring/Alloy/Getty

Images; **457** Grindstone Media Group/Shutterstock.com; **458** The Print Collector/Alamy Stock Photo; **459** David Madison/Stone/Getty Images; **460**t supparsorn/iStock/Getty Images Plus/Getty Images; **460**b Getty Images/Getty Images Sport/Getty Images; **474**bl Africa Studio/Shutterstock.com; **474**r dial-a-view/E+/Getty Images; **475** Zocha_K/E+/Getty Images; **478** technotr/iStock/Getty Images Plus/Getty Images; **479** Africa Studio/Shutterstock.com; **482** FabioFilzi/E+/Getty Images; **484** Anna Gorin /Moment/Getty Images; **485** powerofforever/iStock /Getty Images Plus/Getty Images

Chapter 18

489tr, **496**t, **496**b ZUMA Press, Inc./Alamy Stock Photo; **489**cl Roman Tiraspolsky/iStock Editorial /Getty Images Plus/Getty Images; **489**b Allen Creative/Steve Allen/Alamy Stock Photo; **490**, **492**b Franck Fotos/Alamy Stock Photo; **491**t Stars and Stripes/Alamy Stock Photo; **491**bl Imgorthand/E+ /Getty Images; **491**br Abaca Press/Alamy Stock Photo; **492**t Ken Hawkins/Alamy Stock Photo; **493**t pamela_d_mcadams/iStock/Getty Images Plus/Getty Images; **493**b Stanley Leary/Alamy Stock Photo; **497** JIM WATSON/AFP via Getty Images

ACKNOWLEDGMENTS

Chapter 1

Text excerpt from article "What Is Cyberbullying" dated May 30, 2019. stopbullying.gov.

Chapter 2

Text excerpt from *Gunner's Run* by Rick Barry. Copyright © 2007 BJU Press. All rights reserved.

Text excerpt from *The Great Fire* by Jim Murphy (New York: Scholastic, Copyright © 1995), 100.
- Quoting from Joseph Medill, *Chicago Tribune*, ca. 1871.

Text excerpt from *A Pioneer Sampler* by Barbara Greenwood (New York: Houghton Mifflin Harcourt, 1994), 84.

Chapter 3

Text excerpt from *Regina Silsby's Secret War* by Thomas J. Brodeur. Copyright © 2004 BJU Press. All rights reserved.

Text excerpts from *This Land Is Our Land* by Linda Barrett Osborne (New York: Abrams Books for Young Readers, 2016), 73.
- Quoting from a radio address by Ambassador Myron Taylor delivered November 1939.
- Quoting from an interview with Elise Radell in *American Mosaic: The Immigrant Experience in the Words of Those Who Lived It* by Joan Morrison and Charlotte F. Zabusky, eds. (Pittsburgh, PA: University of Pittsburgh Press, 1980), 138.

Text excerpts from *Across Five Aprils* by Irene Hunt (New York: Berkley Books, 1964), 7.

Chapter 4

Text excerpts from *The Trumpeter of Krakow* by Eric P. Kelly (New York: Macmillan, 1966), 1–2.

Chapter 5

Text excerpt from Inaugural Address, John F. Kennedy, Delivered January 20, 1961, https://www.presidency.ucsb.edu/node/234470

Text excerpts from "Critter Corner: The Icelandic Horse - Small But Mighty" by Pat Betteley, *Faces*, November 2018, Copyright © by Carus Publishing Company. Reproduced with permission.

Chapter 6

Text excerpt from "Benjamin Franklin: American Author, Scientist, and Statesman" by Gordon S. Wood, Theodore Hornberger, et al., from *Encyclopaedia Britannica* online, Copyright © 2020.

Chapter 8

Text excerpt from *Dust of the Earth* by Donnalynn Hess. Copyright © 1994 BJU Press. Used by permission of the author. All rights reserved.

Text excerpt from "The Adventure of the Blue Carbuncle" by Sir Arthur Conan Doyle in *Jewel Cases*. Copyright © 2002 BJU Press. All rights reserved.

Text excerpt from *Anne of Green Gables* by L. M. Montgomery (London: L. C. Page, 1908), 27–28.

Chapter 9

Text excerpts from *The Story of Doctor Dolittle* by Hugh Lofting (New York: Frederick A. Stokes, 1920), 108–109, 120.

Chapter 10

Text excerpt from *The Story of My Life* by Helen Keller (New York: Grosset and Dunlap, 1905), 119.

"Almost Identical Answers" from *1002 Humorous Illustrations for Public Speaking* by Michael E. Hodgin, Copyright © 2004 by Michael E. Hodgin. Used by permission of Zondervan. www.zondervan.com.

Text excerpts from "Ida Lewis: Heroine of Lime Rock Lighthouse" by Timothy Tocher, *Cricket*, April 2019, Copyright © by Carus Publishing Company. Reproduced with permission.

Chapter 11

Text excerpt from *COME GO WITH ME: OLD-TIMER STORIES FROM THE SOUTHERN MOUNTAINS*, Copyright © 1994 by Roy Edwin Thomas. Reprinted by permission of Farrar, Straus and Giroux Books for Young Readers. All Rights Reserved.

Chapter 12

Text excerpt from "A Dreadful Masterpiece" article dated December 30, 1940, taken from *Ernie's War: The Best of Ernie Pyle's World War II Dispatches*, ed. David Nichols (New York: Random House, 1986), 43–44. Permission to reprint the excerpt kindly granted by the Scripps-Howard Foundation.

Text excerpt from *The Great and Only Barnum: The Tremendous, Stupendous Life of Showman P. T. Barnum* by Candace Fleming, (New York: Schwartz & Wade, 2009), 2.

Text excerpts from *This Land Is Our Land* by Linda Barrett Osborne (New York: Abrams Books for Young Readers, 2016), 85–86.
- Quoting from Joseph Kim, "Hope brought me to America: A North Korean defector tells his inspiring story" by Max Fisher, dated June 21, 2013, washingtonpost.com (accessed by Linda Barrett Osborne, June 27th, 2014).
- Quoting from Ha Young Kwen, who is quoting from an interview with Joseph Kim, "Interview with a North Korean refugee," *LA Youth* newspaper, dated November - December 2010, archived online at layouth.com. (accessed by Linda Barrett Osborne, June 27th, 2014).

Chapter 13

Text excerpts from *The Wind in the Willows* by Kenneth Grahame (New York: Grosset & Dunlap, 1913), 85–86.

Text excerpts from *The Wonderful Wizard of Oz* by L. Frank Baum (Chicago: Geo M. Hill, 1900), 35–36; 36-37.

Chapter 14

Text excerpts from *A Journey to the Center of the Earth* by Jules Verne (New York: Penguin, 1968), 89–91.

Chapter 16

Text excerpts from *A Journey to the Center of the Earth* by Jules Verne (New York: Penguin, 1968), 89–91.